T0385768

THE QUEST
to SAVE *the*
OLD TESTAMENT

*Mathematics, Hieroglyphics, and Providence in
Enlightenment England*

THE QUEST
to **SAVE** *the*
OLD TESTAMENT

*Mathematics, Hieroglyphics, and Providence in
Enlightenment England*

DAVID NEY

STUDIES IN HISTORICAL AND SYSTEMATIC THEOLOGY

The Quest to Save the Old Testament: Mathematics, Hieroglyphics, and Providence in Englightenment England
Studies in Historical and Systematic Theology

Lexham Academic, an imprint of Lexham Press
1313 Commercial St., Bellingham, WA 98225
LexhamPress.com

The image on page 114 is "The Christian Covenant in Hieroglyphics" by Hubert-François Gravelot. c. 1730s. Public domain.

Print ISBN 9781683596264
Digital ISBN 9781683596271
Library of Congress Control Number 2022933803

Lexham Editorial: Todd Hains, Elizabeth Vince, Allie Boman, Mandi Newell, Abigail Stocker
Cover Design: Brittany Schrock
Typesetting: Mandi Newell

對斑鳩

CONTENTS

FOREWORD

—

In St. Paul's letter to the churches in Galatia, we witness a fascinating and, to us moderns, counterintuitive phenomenon. Portraying the Galatians' dire crisis of standing on the precipice of apostasy, Paul "reads" the Galatian Christians as the post-exodus generation of Israelites wandering in the wilderness on their way to Canaan.

The Lord of Israel had said to Moses in Deuteronomy that the people of Israel, freshly delivered from their slavery in Egypt, "have been quick to turn from the way that I commanded them" (9:12 NRSV; the Septuagint's word for "quick" is ταχύ). Borrowing this language, Paul writes to his Galatians converts, who have lately been "set ... free from the present evil age" (1:4): "I am astonished that you are so quickly [ταχέως] deserting the one who called you in the grace of Christ and are turning to a different gospel" (1:6). What underlies Paul's rhetorical move here?

Pastor and New Testament scholar Todd Wilson has argued that Paul here performs "a recapitulation and transmutation of [the story of Israel] in the life of his churches."[1] But it might be even more accurate to say that he "scripts" his churches into the scriptural narrative of God's elect people.[2] Either way, Paul's creative engagement with the text of Scripture demonstrates that, for him, the Old Testament is no past prologue; it is an active divine agent that allows Paul to understand the true stakes of the crisis in Galatia.

This way of reading the Old Testament is unfamiliar to most modern biblical scholars. Or, if it is familiar, it remains deeply unconvincing. The importance of David Ney's study of the "Hutchinsonian" tradition of reading the Old Testament is that it shows, historically, why Paul's mode of biblical

---

1. Todd A. Wilson, "Wilderness Apostasy and Paul's Portrayal of the Crisis in Galatians," *New Testament Studies* 50 (2004): 550–71, here 571.

2. Wilson, "Wilderness Apostasy," 553.

exegesis became so unappealing to modern readers and that it demonstrates, theologically, why it can and ought to be revived.

There are now many advocates for Christian "figural" reading of the Old Testament, but none that I am aware of showcase the historical attention, theological acumen, and hermeneutical incisiveness of this one. It should be read not only by historians but also, and hopefully especially, by those who wish to contribute to the ongoing work of reading our world in light of the story God is writing in and with the text of Scripture.

Wesley Hill
Holland, Michigan
The Third Sunday in Easter 2022

INTRODUCTION

—

In 2017 Brent A. Strawn published a book with the provocative title *The Old Testament Is Dying*. This turn of phrase broadcasts the author's uncomfortable conclusion that "for many contemporary Christians, at least in North America, the Old Testament has ceased to function in healthy ways in their lives as sacred, authoritative, canonical literature." These individuals, Strawn continues, "do not regard the Old Testament in the same way (or as highly) as the New Testament, do not understand the Old Testament, would prefer to do without the Old Testament, and for all practical purposes do exactly that by means of their neglect and ignorance of it, whether in private devotion or public worship both."[1] The steady stream of proposals for a newly invigorated and authentically Christian reclamation of the Old Testament indicates that Strawn is not alone in his assessment.[2] The problem for Strawn and the rest is not that isolated figures such as Andy Stanley vocally dismiss the Old Testament. Such dismissals are indicative of this more ominous problem: a church which has functionally embraced a New Testament Christianity.

The conviction that the Old Testament struggles to function as Scripture for Christians in the modern West has a long history. At the end of the nineteenth century, A. F. Kirkpatrick (1849–1940) complained that the Old Testament had "become a discredited, and therefore disused book," and he therefore set out to refute the popular opinion that "the Old Testament

---

1. Brent A. Strawn, *The Old Testament Is Dying: A Diagnosis and Recommended Treatment* (Grand Rapids: Baker Academic, 2017), 4–5.

2. Other post-World War II proposals to revive the authority of the Old Testament include John Bright, *The Authority of the Old Testament* (London: SCM, 1967); Brevard Childs, *Introduction to the Old Testament as Scripture* (Philadelphia: Fortress, 1979); Christopher Seitz, *Word Without End: The Old Testament as Abiding Theological Witness* (Waco, TX: Baylor University Press, 2004); Iain Provan, *Seriously Dangerous Religion: What the Old Testament Really Says and Why It Matters* (Waco, TX: Baylor University Press, 2014); Ellen F. Davis, *Opening Israel's Scriptures* (Oxford: Oxford University Press, 2019); Don C. Collett, *Figural Reading and the Old Testament: Theology and Practice* (Grand Rapids: Baker Academic, 2020).

is of no particular moment, all that we need being the New Testament."[3] Kirkpatrick was not the first to publicly decry the death of the Old Testament. That honor should probably be given to the idiosyncratic natural philosopher John Hutchinson (1674–1737). In his 1724 work *Moses's Principia*, Hutchinson argued that the death of the Old Testament should be placed squarely on the shoulders of the author of the *Principia Mathematica* and his disciples. According to Hutchinson, the Old Testament had fallen into disrepute because while people were praising Isaac Newton (1643–1727) as the font of wisdom, they should have been looking to Moses. That Christians have decried the degradation of the Old Testament since the dawn of modernity is extremely important to note, as it confirms that the status of the Old Testament is bound to culturally specific perspectives upon the text. Old Testament degradation is the product of the particular cultural context known today as "modernity." This much is uncontroversial. What is less obvious is the nature of the tie that binds them. This study will follow Hutchinson's lead and test, as a hypothesis, his intriguing claim that Old Testament degradation was the result of the rise of Newtonian science.

Historians have found it all too easy to dismiss Hutchinson and his followers—known then and now as Hutchinsonians—as Counter-Enlightenment buffoons.[4] It is curious that they have been treated this way given that they were, in the words of David Katz, "absolutely central to English and Scottish theology in the eighteenth and early nineteenth century."[5] But eigh-

---

3. A. F. Kirkpatrick, "The Old Testament in the Christian Church," *The Old and New Testament Student* 13, no. 1 (1891): 8.

4. Upon reading an early Hutchinsonian sermon, Arthur Bedford (1668–1745) remarked, "I agreed with all the learned World, that there was nothing in it, which was worth an answer." At the beginning of the nineteenth century, S. T. Coleridge (1772–1834) dismissed "the Cabbala of the Hutchinsonian School as the dotage of a few weak-minded individuals," and at the end of the century, Leslie Stephen (1832–1904) echoed Coleridge's sentiment. In 1974, Vivian Green dismissed Hutchinsonianism as "a somewhat freakish movement" that had "only a small following at Oxford." Recent assessments have been less curt but equally dismissive in their appraisals. Arthur Bedford, *Observations on a Sermon Preach'd before the Corporation of Bristol* (London: 1736), 1; Samuel Taylor Coleridge, *Aids to Reflection and the Confessions of an Inquiring Spirit*, ed. James Mursh (London: G. Bell, 1901), 314; Leslie Stephen, *History of English Thought in the Eighteenth Century* (London: Smith, Elder, & Co., 1876), 1.390; V. H. H. Green, "Religion in the Colleges, 1715–1800," in *The Eighteenth Century*, ed. L. S. Sutherland and L. G. Mitchell, vol. 5 of *A History of the University of Oxford* (Oxford: Oxford University Press, 1986), 456; Scott Mandelbrote, "Eighteenth-Century Reactions to Newton's Anti-Trinitarianism," in *Newton and Newtonianism: New Studies*, ed. James E. Force and Sarah Hutton (Dordrecht: Kluwer Academic, 2004), 110.

5. David S. Katz, "Moses's Principia: Hutchinsonianism and Newton's Critics," in *The Books of Nature and Scripture: Recent Essays on Natural Philosophy, Theology, and Biblical Criticism in the*

teenth-century historiography has long been fertile ground for what Herman Butterfield famously called "Whig History." Butterfield complained against the "Whiggishness" of his fellow British historians, which compelled them to interpret sequences of events as causal lines of progressive development and therefore led them to only engage particulars that could be easily conformed to this pattern.[6] "Nowhere," laments Katz, "is [the] tendency towards 'Whig History' more apparent than in the almost complete neglect suffered by the Hutchinsonians."[7]

The time has come for a reassessment of their work. In the first place, recent scholarship confirms that Hutchinson was acute in his assessment that the Old Testament had been decisively compromised. At the beginning of the eighteenth century, the status of the Old Testament was at an all-time low in England, and it is Hutchinson and his disciples, more than anyone else, who speak into this issue of critical concern. Hutchinson is more than just another voice that can be added to the chorus of contemporary Old Testament advocates. When he wrote in defense of the Old Testament, he wrote as one who had experienced the important cultural and intellectual shifts which took place in the years 1680–1715—years which have long held interest to

---

Netherlands of Spinoza's Time and the British Isles of Newton's Time, ed. James E. Force and Richard H. Popkin (Dordrecht: Kluwer Academic, 1994), 201–12.

6. Herbert Butterfield, *The Whig Interpretation of History* (London: G. Bell and Sons, 1931), 12, 24–25. Since Butterfield's intervention, the term has been widely and pejoratively applied to histories that view the past as an inevitable and progressive march toward enlightenment, particularly in constitutional history, the history of science, and the history of philosophy. In 2005 Womersley applied Butterfield's critique to the study of Renaissance historiography when he argued that "the establishment of the 'chief topic' of the history of historiography as 'the development of the historical-mindedness peculiar to our culture' " has "resulted in a serious misrepresentation" of the subject (David Womersley, "Against the Teleology of Technique," *Huntington Library Quarterly: Studies in English and American History and Literature* 68 [2005]: 95). Womersley here quotes vol. 3 of George Huppert, "The Renaissance Background of Historicism," *History and Theory* 5 (1966): 48. Despite these and other pleas, many historians continue to assume that the Bible "became" a historical document in the seventeenth century. See, for example, Matt Goldish, *Judaism in the Theology of Sir Isaac Newton* (Dordrecht: Kluwer Academic, 1998), 27; John Sandys-Wunsch, *A History of Modern Biblical Interpretation* (Collegeville, MN: Liturgical Press, 2005), 22, 127.

7. David S. Katz, "The Occult Bible: Hebraic Millenarianism in Eighteenth-Century England," in *The Millenarianism and Messianism in Early Modern European Culture, Vol. 3: The Millenarian Turn; Millenarian Contexts of Science, Politics and Everyday Anglo-American Life in the Seventeenth and Eighteenth Centuries*, ed. James E. Force and Richard H. Popkin (Dordrecht: Kluwer Academic, 2001), 123. In 1968 Carroll complained that many intellectual histories don't even mention Hutchinsonianism (X. William Carroll, "Hutchinsonisme: Une vue de la nature comme théophanie au cours du dis-huitième siècle" [PhD diss., Université de Strasbourg, 1968], 1).

historians as crucial for the construction of modernity as the dawn of the Enlightenment.

A reassessment of Hutchinson and his followers must extend beyond the simple acknowledgement that they identified the modern problem of Old Testament degradation. Their explanatory claims must be taken seriously. When they are, it becomes possible to appreciate why they were regarded by many serious and devout scholars as not only credible but compelling. We can begin, on this score, with Hutchinson's foundational observation that his contemporaries were looking to Newton rather than Moses for natural-philosophical wisdom. This claim was plausible because many Christians had, in recent memory, looked to Moses as the philosopher who had hidden esoteric knowledge (known as *prisca theologia* or *prisca sapientia*) in his text. And while this practice was in full retreat by the time Hutchinson entered the fray, many Christians continued to take for granted that the Bible spoke truthfully about the natural world, and they were thus intuitively disposed to attentively consider Hutchinson's proposal. According to Hutchinson, Christians must turn to the Bible because the knowledge they seek is not the brute facts which the modern empirical method affords. What they seek, rather, is providential knowledge, knowledge of God's workings in the world.

The great irony of Hutchinson's project to rehabilitate the Old Testament is that it was encumbered by the same problem that led the Newtonians to denigrate it in the first place. Hutchinson shares with them a philosophy of history which makes his appeal to natural philosophy necessary.[8] The great success of Newtonian natural philosophy inclined Hutchinson to follow Newton and Newton's protégé, Samuel Clarke (1675–1729), by celebrating the providential order of nature in contradistinction to history, with the result that history loses its providential weight. I am calling this view "devolutionary history." Newton, Clarke, and Hutchinson strive to bind the Old Testament to the providential order of creation, but they find that, as a text, it is subject to devolution and therefore does more to obscure this order than reveal it. They are inclined to believe that a successful defense of the

---

8. Philosophies of history seek to understand "the study of the past and the past itself" through "the application of philosophical conceptions and analysis" (Gordon Graham, "Philosophy of History," in *Concise Routledge Encyclopaedia of Philosophy*, ed. Edward Craig and Edward Craig [New York: Routledge, 2013], 356). Throughout the course of this book I will emphasize the way in which philosophies of history order the past through conceptual analysis.

Old Testament will commend it as ahistorical. Yet the extent to which they manage to do so is also the extent to which they fail in their defense of the Old Testament as Scripture, for the extent to which the Old Testament is able to engage historical existence is the extent to which it has the potential to serve as a guide to human life and conduct.

While Newton, Clarke, and Hutchinson argued in ways that inadvertently subvert the scriptural status of the Old Testament, Hutchinson's followers provided an alternative that renders the Old Testament doctrinally and morally authoritative. Of the Hutchinsonians, I will focus on George Watson (1723–1773), George Horne (1730–1792), and William Jones of Nayland (1726–1800).[9] Watson, Horne, and Jones adapt Hutchinson's approach to the Old Testament to endue Old Testament figures with doctrinal and moral significance.[10] This figural view generates a figural, rather than devolutionary, interpretation of history. For Watson and Horne—and especially for Jones—the particulars of human history are given providential signification as they are reinterpreted as scriptural figures. Scripture is accordingly treated as indispensable for the discernment of the workings of providence in history and the proper human response to them.

Over the past thirty years the study of the history of biblical interpretation has gained momentum as scholars have come to acknowledge the central place of the Bible in the formation of Western civilization and consciousness.[11] It has become evident that the history of biblical interpretation can be employed as a weapon to undermine determinate readings of Scripture.[12] For some postmodern critics, the history of interpretation proves that because

---

9. The William Jones studied in this work is commonly referred to as "William Jones of Nayland" to distinguish him from the great eighteenth-century Orientalist Sir William Jones.

10. Figural approaches to Scripture trace the theological import of particular people, places, and objects as they are picked up and developed by other canonical authors. The most important contemporary theological account of figural reading is Ephraim Radner, *Time and the Word: Figural Reading of the Christian Scriptures* (Grand Rapids: Eerdmans, 2016). For an introduction to figural reading in the Anglican tradition, see Ephraim Radner and David Ney, eds., *All Thy Lights Combine: Figural Reading in the Anglican Tradition* (Bellingham, WA: Lexham Press, 2021).

11. See, for example, Willis Glover, *The Biblical Origins of Modern Secular Culture: An Essay in the Interpretation of Western Thought* (Macon, GA: Mercer University Press, 1984); Henning Graf Reventlow, *The Authority of the Bible and the Rise of the Modern World* (Philadelphia: Fortress, 1985).

12. See Stephen Fowl, *Engaging Christian Scripture: A Model for Theological Interpretation* (Eugene, OR: Wipf and Stock, 2008). Fowl argues against both "determinate" and "anti-determinate" readings and in favor of "underdetermined" ones (*Engaging Christian Scripture*, 10).

Scripture can be taken to mean anything, it obviously means nothing at all.[13] Inasmuch as this book highlights ways that conflicting views concerning history and providence altered perceptions of the Old Testament, it might be marshalled to this end. Nevertheless, Hutchinsonian scriptural interpretation confirms that the hermeneutical circle becomes a hermeneutical spiral because the text pressures the reader's perception of God and the world. It was engagement with Scripture—and, particularly, with the Old Testament—that led the Hutchinsonians to reject Newtonian devolutionary history. Hutchinsonian engagement with Scripture, therefore, calls to attention the importance of the Old Testament in forging and upholding the Christian conviction that history is a work of God.

THE RISE OF DEVOLUTIONARY HISTORY

"One day, the French people, almost to a man, were thinking like Bossuet. The day after, they were thinking like Voltaire."[14] This at least is what Paul Hazard argued in his classic interpretation of the Enlightenment, *The European Mind: The Critical Years, 1680–1715*. Hazard painted the transition from pre-modernity to modernity in the starkest imaginable terms. For Hazard, the coming of secular modernity was a Night of the Long Knives, a revolution that happened overnight as the explosive forces of rationalism and empiricism took Europe by storm. But historians have come to see that the intellectual and cultural shifts that created what we now call modernity were drawn out over several centuries. And there were many conservative Catholics like Bossuet in France and in the rest of Europe after the arrival of Enlightenment deists like Voltaire, just as there continue to be some of them today.

When it comes to the particular case of England, work by J. C. D. Clark and his students has confirmed that the death of the *ancien régime* must be delayed until at least the middle of the nineteenth century. Clark sees his

---

13. Morgan and Barton, for example, describe the problem of historical interpretation as follows: "Texts, like dead men and women, have no rights, no aims, no interests. They can be used in whatever way readers or interpreters choose" (Robert Morgan and John Barton, *Biblical Interpretation* [Oxford: Oxford University Press, 1988], 7). The attendant assumption that the history of biblical interpretation is largely the history of the abuse of the Bible continues to be affirmed. See, for example, Janice Capel Anderson and Stephen D. Moore, "Introduction: The Lives of Mark," in *Mark & Method: New Approaches in Biblical Studies*, ed. Janice Capel Anderson and Stephen D. Moore (Minneapolis: Fortress, 1993), 14.

14. Paul Hazard, *La Crise de la conscience européenne* (Paris: Boivin, 1935); *The European Mind: The Critical Years, 1680–1715*, trans. J. Lewis May (New Haven: Yale University Press, 1953), xv.

own work as "postponing the loss of the 'world we have lost.'" Yet there can be no doubt that something crucial did take place in Europe at the turn of the eighteenth century, as Hazard boisterously proclaimed. Thus, even for Clark, while this turn did not welcome modernity, it established a new society which "combined monarchy *and* liberty, religion *and* science, trade *and* landed wealth with a minimum distinction between 'modernity' and pre-modernity,' and so saw no conflict between 'traditional' and 'modern' society."[15] For intellectual and cultural historians, the challenge continues to be to precisely articulate the nature of the shift. While in Hazard's day constructing modernity was a straightforward task, requiring only that the historian give an account of how Bossuet gave way to Voltaire, it is now evident that the shifts that were taking place at the cusp of modernity were not merely brought about by a small group of radicals, but rather were generated by multiple groups within society responding not merely to perceived changes but to the responses that these changes generated in their friends as well as their enemies. Modernity, in this case, becomes the creation, not of a privileged few (whether they be labelled heroes or villains), but of all members of a modernizing society. This is an unavoidable conclusion, writ-large, given that society is by definition something that belongs to all of its members.

As historians extended their gaze from the radicals to other members of eighteenth-century society, they quickly realized that while the eighteenth century was subject to a particular though initially marginal Enlightenment project which agitated to upend the establishment, competing groups had their own Enlightenment projects, just as each nation had particular interests which were unique to its particular intellectual and cultural drift. This does not mean that the contributions of Voltaire and other *philosophes* were unimportant. But it does mean that Voltaire's orthodox opponents were equally involved in the task of cultural construction. This observation applies to the Bible itself. The Enlightenment did not, as Whig historians suppose, do away with the Bible.[16]

---

15. J. C. D. Clark, *English Society, 1660–1832: Religion, Ideology and Politics during the Ancien Régime*, 2nd ed. (Cambridge: Cambridge University Press, 2000), 16.

16. What the Enlightenment did do, however, was create a Bible that was uniquely its own—an "Enlightenment Bible," to borrow a phrase from Sheehan. While even radicals who rejected biblical authority played a part in constructing this Bible, pride of place must be given to those who created it and transmitted it to posterity. See Jonathan Sheehan, *The Enlightenment Bible: Translation, Scholarship, Culture* (Princeton: Princeton University Press, 2005).

The Bible was not the hapless victim of the enlightened mind. It was, rather, a driving force behind intellectual and cultural shift. Even Spinoza, who in Jonathan Israel's energetic presentation is given singular importance as the fountainhead of the radical Enlightenment and the harbinger of modernity, forged his most controversial ideas as a philological critic of the Bible.[17] The subversive positions that members of Israel's radical Enlightenment took with respect to pressing issues of political, cultural, religious, and philosophical concern were, more often than not, stated as opinions about proper biblical interpretation. Similarly, the rejoinders to these claims by members of what Israel calls the mainstream moderate Enlightenment were equally scripturally articulated. Members of a third group, which has been called the counter- or conservative Enlightenment—those who self-consciously saw themselves as defenders of the conservative majority and resisted change—were often as alarmed by the mainstream moderates as they were by the radicals. As we would expect, conservative scholars were careful to cover their tracks by consistently appealing to the Bible. But such appeals do not, *prima facie*, give any indication about "party" membership given the ubiquity of scriptural discourse. Nor were conservatives immune from the forces which altered Christian engagement with the biblical text. As Dmitri Levitin observes, the controversies that raged over the text and meaning of the Bible can no longer be credibly reduced to "a battle between philosophical rationalists and the 'undiscriminating bigots of orthodoxy.'"[18] Members of all three "enlightenments" were trying to interpret the Bible with integrity within an emerging cultural context. All were responding to intellectual and cultural foment, and scriptural discourse was the forum in which their specific responses were articulated. In all three cases, the Bible was not merely the recipient of change. It was, at every turn, engagement with the biblical text which broke new ground as the instigator of cultural transformation.

---

17. Jonathan Israel has articulated his vision of the Enlightenment centered on Spinoza across several volumes and thousands of pages. See, in particular, *Radical Enlightenment: Philosophy and the Making of Modernity, 1650–1750* (Oxford: Oxford University Press, 2001).

18. Dmitri Levitin, "From Sacred History to the History of Religion: Paganism, Judaism, and Christianity in European Historiography from Reformation to 'Enlightenment,' " *The Historical Journal* 55, no. 4 (2012): 1160.

The prevailing view of the Enlightenment Bible—which Hazard helped to popularize—is that it was given over to history at the dawn of the Enlightenment by Spinoza and Richard Simon and that, once historicized, it could no longer bear the enormous weight of Christian doctrine and piety.[19] According to this genealogy, "'real' history had replaced Christian 'ideology'" by the mid-eighteenth century.[20] The burgeoning work that is now being done on the history of scholarship, however, maintains that the Bible was thoroughly historicized by the end of the sixteenth century. It is probably better to refer to this development not as historicization but as antiquarianization. Christians had always known that the Bible was a historical document. What was new in the Renaissance was the burgeoning interest in exploring the Bible as a monument of antiquity and in relation to other monuments of antiquity. The Huguenot scholar Joseph Scaliger (1549-1609) and his pupil Hugo Grotius (1583-1645) were instrumental in this shift.[21] Scaliger's *De emendation temporum* (1583) and *Thesaurus temporum* (1606) entrenched the "methodological principle that Old Testament history could only be understood within a contextual scaffolding constructed from pagan narratives."[22] Scaliger's researches, which exposed "historical puzzles, contradictions, and even downright mistakes in the biblical narrative," also confirmed that, like other ancient texts, the Bible had a history and was therefore itself subject to history.[23]

Scholars are only now beginning to appreciate the depth and sophistication of the historical research of the Renaissance, which was part of an established historiographical tradition which can credibly be traced all the way back to Eusebius of Caesarea (260/265-339/340).[24] Renaissance historiography

---

19. See Hazard, *The European Mind*, chapter 3.

20. Levitin, "From Sacred History," 1120.

21. For an appraisal of Scaliger's influence on later scholars, see Anthony Grafton, *Joseph Scaliger* (Oxford: Clarendon Press, 1983), 1:134-60 and G. J. Toomer, *John Selden: A Life in Scholarship* (Oxford: Clarendon Press, 2009), 1:213. For a summary of Scaliger's work on ancient chronology, see Grafton, "Joseph Scaliger and Historical Chronology: The Rise and Fall of a Discipline," *History and Theory* 14, no. 2 (1975): 156-85.

22. Levitin, "From Sacred History," 1124.

23. Levitin, "From Sacred History," 1124.

24. According to the great historian Momigliano, Eusebius's *Ecclesiastical History* must be regarded as "one of the most authoritative prototypes ever created by ancient thought" (Arnaldo Momigliano, *The Classical Foundations of Modern Historiography* [Berkeley: University of California Press, 1990], 141).

was not directed only toward elevating and duplicating the best of Greek and Latin learning, but Hebrew antiquity as well. Burnett speaks of the "explosive growth of Hebrew studies within schools and universities during the late sixteenth and seventeenth centuries," and Manuel observes that by 1694 Carlo Giuseppe Imbonati (d. 1697) could survey the Hebraic scholarship of the last two centuries and list some 1,300 Christian authors, many of whom had composed large numbers of works.[25] The Renaissance revival of Hebraic learning, Manuel continues, was "not comparable to the revival of Greek and Roman, yet it was an intellectual movement of no mean proportions."[26]

The impressive Hebraic scholarship of the Renaissance does more than simply refute the established thesis of the historicization of the Bible. It exposes as simplistic the notion that a historicized text and the Christian faith cannot abide. In the middle ages, the theft of relics was frowned upon as the contravention of the eighth commandment. Yet this disapproval was eclipsed by the even stronger sense that the theft of relics was to be admired as the expression of a sublime piety. In the Renaissance, ancient manuscripts were considered sacred vessels of enormous worth—such worth that even pious scholars were not above stealing folios or "forgetting" to return borrowed manuscripts. Antiquarian research, like all fields of study, brought material temptations and potential intellectual and religious pitfalls. Yet there can be no doubt that the antiquarianization of the Bible, and the Old Testament in particular, coexisted with Christian piety throughout the Renaissance.[27] In England, the antiquarianization of the Old Testament became a problem for its status as Christian Scripture at the dawn of modernity when the providential import of history was called into question with the birth of Newtonian physico-mathematics.

25. Frank Manuel, *The Broken Staff: Judaism through Christian Eyes* (Cambridge: Harvard University Press, 1992), 66. It was, as Manuel observes, a "magnificent age of scholarship" driven by scholars for whom "the production of a hundred volumes in a lifetime was considered a feat but not impossible" (*The Broken Staff*, 67).

26. Manuel, *The Broken Staff*, 66–67.

27. See Debora Shuger, *The Renaissance Bible: Scholarship, Sacrifice, and Subjectivity* (Waco, TX: Baylor University Press, 2010).

NEWTON AND NEWTONIANISM

The terms "Newtonian" and "Newtonianism" can be used, narrowly, to refer to Newton and his work, or extended to his disciples and their work. They also carry conceptual weight. "Newtonian" and "Newtonianism" can denote a particular brand of experimental philosophy which, based upon the enormous success of Newton's *Principia Mathematica*, proposed that mathematical rigor was the supreme goal of all empirical research. Newton didn't create this brand of empiricism, but it grew to a feverish pitch in the wake of his exploits as scholars sought to duplicate his work in fields as diverse as ethics and medicine. "Newtonian" and "Newtonianism" can also denote the natural-philosophical apparatus that accompanied Newton's mathematical renderings, his "system" which described not merely the workings of the physical universe but also God's active involvement within it as *pantokrator*, the Lord God of Dominion. The term "Newtonianism" correspondingly denotes a Christian apologetic built upon the argument from design which, accordingly, was doctrinally monotheistic and minimalistic.

There were deists, such as Matthew Tindal (1657–1733) in England and Voltaire in France, who regarded themselves as Newton's true heirs. But Newton and his immediate associates were not deists. As "mainstream" opponents of Enlightenment radicalism, they resisted those who dared to denigrate revealed religion at every turn. The primary strategy of the Newtonians along these lines was to argue that revealed religion was consistent with natural religion. Yet their work often seemed to indicate that by this they had in mind the New Testament alone. The Newtonians, like their radical opponents, took for granted that history had a devolutionary shape and that the Old Testament, as subject to history, was the product of devolution. They hoped to salvage the New Testament by excising it from history. Jesus, for them, was the heavenly messenger who taught the principles of natural religion, principles transcribed in the New Testament. Newtonians didn't often reject the Old Testament outright. Like Marcion of Sinope, they reserved a restricted place for it within their religious vision. This being said, as they celebrated the glories of the New Testament, they inadvertently denigrated the Old Testament. It is appropriate to speak of the Newtonian Old Testament as a sacrificial lamb given over to the vicissitudes of history for the greater good, preserving the true religion of Christ and his apostles.

As a historian of idolatry, Newton's goal was to document the decline and fall of the natural-philosophical and monotheistic *ur-religion* which God had imparted to Adam, which had been revived first by Noah and then by Christ, and which he believed he had been appointed to reintroduce.[28] Newton acknowledged that Moses had acquired his religious knowledge from the Egyptians and that his religion was accordingly impure. But he equally insisted that Moses had inherited an unbroken tradition of *prisca theologia* which could be traced back to the Creator God himself. Newton's difficulty is that he could not avoid the conclusion that this knowledge had been obscured by the Old Testament text. When Newton looked to history, he was embarrassed by an Old Testament text which appeared hopelessly entangled within a confused web of contradictory testimonies. This inclined him to believe that human history is toxic to divine truth. According to this devolutionary philosophy of history, propositions that have their origin in human testimony, and therefore in history, are inherently less certain than propositions derived directly from nature. Newton's treatment of the Old Testament suggests that the view that is supposed to be the climactic achievement of the "Enlightenment project," Lessing's famous dictum that "accidental truths of history can never become the proof of necessary truths of reason," was already operative in early eighteenth-century England.[29]

Newton felt the heavy burden of devolutionary history upon his textual labors: he recognized that his Old Testament was in danger of disappearing beneath the mire of historical contradiction. His solution was to turn to that which he knew, from experience, could provide certain knowledge: numbers. Newton hoped to demonstrate, by means of chronological science, that the Old Testament was the earliest and therefore most distinguished testimony of the religion of nature. The Old Testament text itself may have been given over to obfuscation, but the numbers Newton extracted from it

---

28. Dmitri Levitin, "John Spencer's 'De Legibus Hebraeorum' 1683–85 and 'Enlightened' Sacred History: A New Interpretation," *Journal of the Warburg and Courtauld Institutes* 76 (2013): 81.

29. Gotthold Ephraim Lessing, "The Proof of the Spirit and of Power," in *Lessing's Theological Writings*, ed. and trans. Henry Chadwick (Stanford, CA: Stanford University Press, 1956), 53. For Lessing, historical knowledge is made impossible by the "ugly, broad ditch" that separates humans from their history ("The Proof," 55). Taubes summarizes Lessing's basic question as follows: "How does rational Christianity, which is devoid of history, relate to the historical development of Christianity?" (Jacob Taubes, *Occidental Eschatology* [Stanford, CA: Stanford University Press, 2009], 131). See also Gordon E. Michalson, *Lessing's "Ugly Ditch": A Study of Theology and History* (University Park: Pennsylvania State University Press, 1985).

stood high above the fray. Numbers had lifted his celestial mechanics out of the morass of contradictory theories, and numbers would likewise elevate the Old Testament to its rightful place of distinction. Yet Newton's solution birthed another problem. He had given his disciples a text which they could approve of as arithmetically true—and devotionally irrelevant. Newton's numbers looked down from on high but said nothing. In Newton's configuration, the Old Testament is no longer valuable on its own terms and on account of its contents. It is instrumentalized as a tool that can be used apologetically to defend the revelation of the New Testament.

When Newton's hand-picked successor as the prestigious Lucasian Chair of Mathematics, William Whiston (1667–1752), gave the Boyle lectures in 1707, they had largely been used to demonstrate how Newtonian natural philosophy could shelter revealed religion from the onslaught of skeptics.[30] Whiston took another approach: he applied Newton's interest in scriptural prophecy to apologetic use. Whiston begins by boasting that he will successfully defend Christianity by applying the Newtonian experimental method to the Bible. All that this requires, according to Whiston, is to line up Old Testament texts and their New Testament fulfillments.[31] When Whiston was pressed to demonstrate a precise "mathematical" correspondence in a bruising pamphlet exchange with deist Anthony Collins, however, he was horrified to discover that no such correspondence existed. He therefore postulated that the present Hebrew copies are different from the genuine Hebrew and Greek originals, which were extant in the days of Christ. The culprits, according to Whiston, were second-century Jews who "altered and corrupted their Hebrew and Greek copies of the Old Testament" to obscure what had been an irrefutable demonstration of Christ's messiahship.[32]

---

30. John Dahm, "Science and Apologetics in the Early Boyle Lectures," *Church History* 39, no. 2 (1970): 175–76.

31. William Whiston, *The Accomplishment of Scripture Prophecy: Eight Sermons Preached at Boyle's Lecture in 1707* (Cambridge: 1708), 13–15.

32. William Whiston, *An Essay Towards Restoring the True Text of the Old Testament: And for Vindicating the Citations Made Thence in the New Testament* (London: 1722), 220. William Whiston, *Memoirs of the Life and Writings of Mr. William Whiston* (London: 1749), 308. On the wider debate concerning prophetic fulfillment, in which Collins and Whiston played leading roles, see David Ney, "Reconciling the Old and New Testaments in the Eighteenth-Century Debate over Prophecy," in *Change and Transformation: Essays in Anglican History*, ed. Thomas Power (Eugene, OR: Pickwick, 2013), 85–112.

In *An Essay Towards Restoring the True Text of the Old Testament: And for Vindicating the Citations made thence in the New Testament* (1722), Whiston called upon textual scholars to undertake a great search for uncorrupt ancient manuscripts to restore the Old Testament text to its original purity.[33] Although Whiston wanted to uphold the Old Testament, his theory compels him to argue that the Old Testament text he had inherited is corrupt and useless. He might equally have concluded that exact correspondence had been obscured because his New Testament had been tampered with, but he simply took for granted that the Old Testament was a product of historical devolution and that his job, as a Christian apologist, was to defend the New Testament at all costs. Whiston's apologetic signals a shift in the status of the Old Testament from Christian revelation to Christian revelation's handmaid.

Although Whiston broadcasts the corruption of the Old Testament, he was—like the deists—dismissed by most Christians as fanatical. It is only with Newton's protégé Samuel Clarke that we witness the flowering of modern New Testament Christianity. In contrast to Newton himself, Clarke was prepared to leave Moses out in the cold on account of his subjection to historical devolution. Clarke rejected Newton's project of propping up the Old Testament with numbers. This rejection, however, must not be interpreted as a disinterest in mathematics. Far from it! Clarke, always the true disciple, sought to honor his master by extending the profile of Newtonian mathematical philosophy. In Clarke's hands, the term "mathematical" makes the transition from the language of numbers to the vernacular. Clarke believed that while Israelite religion is historically contingent, natural religion, the true religion which Christ reintroduced, is grounded in the immutable mathematical truths of nature. Clarke's dismissal of the Old Testament as the product of historical devolution confirms that while Hutchinson may have been off base in his defense of Old Testament scriptural authority, he was right to identify that the Old Testament was dying and that this death was tied to the rise of Newtonianism.

Newton and Clarke do not bear the weight of the shift to a New Testament Christianity alone. Their work, and the rationalizing tendency in matters of religion which it promotes, must be set within a larger cultural and

---

33. Whiston, *An Essay*, 333.

intellectual context.[34] The importance of the Newtonians within the spec-
ter of cultural shift, as it applies to the Old Testament, is that they demand
that its degradation be understood in relation to the rise of empirical science
as it pertains to the question of providence. The historicization of the Old
Testament may well have been a precondition for Old Testament degradation.
But the degradation of the Old Testament cannot be understood apart from
the Newtonian conviction that history is devolutionary.

HUTCHINSON AND HUTCHINSONIANISM

John Hutchinson's career as a natural philosopher began when he was
hired as a research assistant to one of the leading lights of the Royal Society,
the esteemed Newtonian natural philosopher John Woodward (1665–1728).
Hutchinson, however, grew tired of his lowly position. He began to enter-
tain ambitions of establishing himself as a reputable natural philosopher in
his own right, but membership in the Royal Society under Newton's presidency proved beyond reach. A vicious falling out with Woodward propelled
Hutchinson to set his face against the Newtonian establishment, and he
soon became Newton's noisiest opponent. Hutchinson vehemently rejected

---

34. The decline of the Old Testament at the dawn of modernity has received much scholarly
attention. Reedy argues that the scholarship and piety of early eighteenth-century English
Christians was molded by an emerging emphasis upon the clear and distinct presentation of
Jesus in the New Testament and that this led to the degradation of the Old Testament (Gerard
Reedy, *The Bible and Reason: Anglicans and Scripture in Late Seventeenth-Century England*
[Philadelphia: University of Pennsylvania Press, 1985], 113–17). According to Hill, the failure of
the Old Testament to provide consensus in the religious tumult of mid-seventeenth-century
England, and the attendant conviction that over-reliance upon the Old Testament ("Judaizing")
was the source of this tumult, inclined defenders of the new establishment to rely almost exclusively on the New Testament in their attempt to forge an ecumenical vision of Christianity
(Christopher Hill, *The English Bible and the Seventeenth-Century Revolution* [London: Allen Lane,
1993], 436). Sutcliffe highlights the decline of Christian Hebraism and the attendant conviction
that the Old Testament was central to the overarching shape of global history (Adam Sutcliffe,
Judaism and Enlightenment [Cambridge: Cambridge University Press, 2003], 32–41). Stroumsa
maintains that the seventeenth-century antiquarianization of the Old Testament that accompanied the rise of the newly conceived category of "religion" led to the Old Testament being
placed on the same level as other antique and religious documents (Guy Stroumsa, *A New Science:
The Discovery of Religion in the Age of Reason* [Cambridge, MA: Harvard University Press, 2010],
78–103). Reventlow argues that the ultimate rejection of the authority of the Old Testament
in eighteenth-century England followed logically from the humanistic and spiritualistic ten-
dencies that had been gaining momentum since the beginning of the Renaissance (Reventlow,
The Authority of the Bible, 411–12). Lucci suggests that early eighteenth-century scholars who
dismissed the Old Testament did so in order to sever moral religion from the historical realm
(Diego Lucci, *Scripture and Deism: The Biblical Criticism of the Eighteenth-Century British Deists*
[Bern: Lang, 2008], 187–209).

Newton's theory of universal gravitation. He understood quite rightly that it was deployed by Newtonians to render heterodox theological conclusions. But most of all he worried that, thanks to Newton's towering influence, mathematical learning had eclipsed scriptural learning. He saw that those who had looked to Scripture to guide them were instead chasing after Newton's approval—much as he had once done!

Hutchinson's answer on all three accounts was his *Moses's Principia*, an Old Testament commentary which doubled as a natural-philosophical treatise. In *Moses's Principia*, Hutchinson scoffs at the idea that an "occult" force called gravitation, which Newton had hypostatized, could be responsible for both celestial and terrestrial motion. Hutchinson insisted that matter is inert, and only God can move it. His demonstration of this postulate depended upon his creative appropriation of a well-established stream of natural philosophy, which Newton knew well, known as "corpuscularianism." According to Hutchinson, God deploys "agents," fine particles (corpuscles) which take the form of fire, light, and air, in order to affect all the celestial and terrestrial movements of the universe. For Hutchinson, this philosophy is both Trinitarian and scriptural because the Scriptures declare that fire, light, and air are emblems of the Father, the Son, and the Holy Spirit. Hutchinson's elegant theory thus claimed to overcome not merely Newton's natural-philosophical speculations, but his antitrinitarianism and scriptural degradation as well.

The rise of Hutchinsonianism is best understood with reference to the Bangorian Controversy, which was arguably the most electric dispute in eighteenth-century England. The controversy erupted in 1717 when Clarke's disciple Benjamin Hoadly (1676–1761) preached his famously inflammatory sermon "The Nature of the Kingdom of Christ" before King George I.[35] Hoadly claimed that Jesus's words "My kingdom is not of this world" (John 18:36) confirm that there is no scriptural warrant for any form of church government. Defenders of the establishment were by then accustomed to dealing with the aggravating invective of deists who were clamoring for change from the margins of literary society. What was so alarming about Hoadly's sermon was

---

35. The exposition of Clarke's principles by his disciple Hoadly created "the most bitter domestic ideological conflict of the century," the Bangorian Controversy (Clark, *English Society*, 352).

that he was, as a minister of the Church of England in the favor of the king, subverting the Christian establishment from within. Hutchinson might have noted that Hoadly's spiritualist ecclesiology seemed to presuppose the same devolutionary philosophy of history that had destabilized the Old Testament. But Hutchinson responded to the controversy as a natural philosopher, and he was thus predisposed to seek out the natural-philosophical foundations of Hoadly's subversive message.

Hutchinson earnestly believed that Newton's occult philosophy was threatening to capsize the Christian establishment. Yet he failed to grasp just how pervasive Newton's influence was, and he could not see that he was, in many respects, a Newtonian. When Hutchinson is interpreted in Newtonian context, it becomes difficult to embrace the facile characterization of Hutchinson as a predominantly anti-Newtonian and therefore Counter-Enlightenment figure. Specifically, once Hutchinson's Old Testament apologetic is properly acknowledged to be at the center of his project, a very different picture comes to light: a Hutchinson that looks rather like Newton himself. Hutchinson the Newtonian took for granted that God's agency in creation was evident in his workings within the natural world rather than in human history. As a Newtonian, Hutchinson believed that he could save the Old Testament from history by binding it to the evidently providential order of nature.

Hutchinson boasted that he was, like Newton, a mathematician of the first order, but Hutchinson's literary remains give no indication of mathematical proficiency. To Hutchinson's credit, however, he seems to have intuitively recognized that demonstrating the accuracy of Old Testament chronology was not going to have the desired effect of restoring the scriptural status of the text. Christians needed to have their confidence restored that the Old Testament was necessary for the fulfillment of the Christian vocation. The challenge for him, as for Newton, was finding a way to render Scripture words—which were evidently the product of history and were accordingly subject to historical devolution—revelatory along these lines. While Newton rescued the text from history by translating words into numbers, Hutchinson's solution was to transmogrify words into hieroglyphs. In Hutchinson's Old Testament commentaries, Hebrew words are recast as ancient word-pictures which conceal the natural-philosophical truth spoken by God to Adam and transmitted to Moses. Recasting Hebrew words as hieroglyphs is Hutchinson's way of proving that the Old Testament is not the product of history.

Hutchinson drew upon several strands of esoteric philosophy, including not only hieroglyphics but also hermeticism, alchemy, and kabbalah.[36] The most important of these, for Hutchinson, was emblematicism, an important stream within the book culture of the Renaissance which juxtaposed images and texts to generate moral lessons. Hieroglyphics, hermeticism, alchemy, kabbalah, and emblematicism all took for granted that *prisca theologia* could be uncovered by exploring the mysteries of the natural world, and they all took for granted that the study of ancient texts was crucial to this task. As natural philosophers working at the cusp of modernity refined their empirical method, however, many came to dismiss the textual natural-philosophical learning of the Renaissance. This rejection is forcefully expressed in Royal Society ornithologist John Ray's *The Ornithology of Francis Willughby* (1678). Ray boasts that he has stripped away the antiquated ornithological tradition of Isodore's *Etymologies*, which sought after "*Homonymous* and *Synonumous* words, or the divers names of Birds, *Hieroglyphics, Emblems, Morals, Fables, Presages* or ought else appertaining to *Divinity, Ethics, Grammar*, or any sort of Humane Learning," instead of focusing upon the physical specimens themselves.[37]

On the surface, Ray's statement is a straightforward proposal regarding scientific method. But the traditions he repudiates were interested in far more than just facts about the natural world. They were means of discerning the imprint of the divine hand upon creation, and they presupposed that such discernment required textual mediation. It is easy, retrospectively, to criticize Hutchinson for his failure to appreciate the importance of Newtonian physico-mathematics. Yet he was reacting not merely to Newton's scientific method but to his providential vision. Hutchinson rejected the Newtonian conceit that numbers had the ability to unveil the providential meaning of

---

36. For an introduction to these and other related esoteric traditions, see Wouter J. Hanegraaff, *Dictionary of Gnosis & Western Esotericism* (Leiden: Brill, 2006).

37. John Ray and Francis Willughby, preface to *The Ornithology of Francis Willughby* (London: 1678). Harrison maintains that Ray's work signals a turn away from Renaissance natural philosophy to empirical study, and that this corresponds to a turn away from the allegorical to the literal study of the Bible (Peter Harrison, *The Bible, Protestantism, and the Rise of Natural Science* [Cambridge: Cambridge University Press, 1998], 2).

the universe. As an emblematicist, he insisted that this ability belonged to words—though not just any words. For Hutchinson, it belonged uniquely to the runes of the Hebrew language which conceal the truths of primordial religion. Hutchinson was convinced that select Hebrew hieroglyphs could be set beside natural-philosophical objects to illuminate not merely their scientific but, most importantly, their providential import. A common devolutionary view of history propels Newton to look to mathematics and Hutchinson to look to Hebrew.

Although early Hutchinsonians were intent to defend Hutchinson's hieroglyphic renderings of select Hebrew words, later Hutchinsonians applied Hutchinson's hermeneutic to all Scripture words. This shift was at once a rejection of Hutchinson's devolutionary view of history. For while Hutchinson had wanted to affirm the ability of words to illuminate the providential order, he was driven to transmogrify Hebrew words into hieroglyphs because of his skepticism concerning human language as historically embedded. Later Hutchinsonians were happy to acknowledge that Scripture words, as human words, were historical and that this did not compromise their status as emblems of divine light. And because they received every word of Scripture as potentially emblematic, they upheld as providential far more than merely the objects of the natural world: they upheld the Church of England, the English commonwealth, and countless other elements of human society as providentially ordered. The first three figures in this study—Newton (Chapter One), Clarke (Chapter Two), and Hutchinson (Chapter Three)—all struggled to affirm the Old Testament as Scripture in light of their commitment to a devolutionary philosophy of history. The next three figures—Watson (Chapter Four), Horne (Chapter Five), and Jones (Chapter Six)—rejected the Newtonian devolutionary philosophy of history and were able, in its place, to reclaim a providential view of history.

Watson's interpretation of the Old Testament grants it a central place in the providential interpretation of historical particulars. There is, however, some ambiguity in his work as to whether Scripture is the foundation of providential order or the subsequent testimony to it. Horne takes up this second approach. Horne sees Scripture, along with the natural world and the church, as the three primary, ultimately independent, witnesses to the providential order established by God in the act of creation. For Jones, on the other hand, the providential witness of every natural and historical object is only established when that object is reinterpreted emblematically by means of Scripture words. From the point of view of traditional Christian theology, the strength of Jones's approach is that it is better suited than that of Horne to protect against the danger that besets the Newtonian vision of providence—the danger of restricting God's providential order to favorite objects or categories of objects. With Watson and Horne, and especially with Jones, we witness the flowering of a figural and tropological Hutchinsonian scriptural hermeneutic. It is figural not merely because it traces the development of scriptural figures across the Old and New Testament: it is figural because it trains readers to interpret the world in figural and therefore providential terms. Likewise, it is tropological because it does not merely ask readers to interpret biblical texts as morally binding: it is tropological because it recast everyday realities as part of an overarching providential order.[38]

Interpretations of Hutchinsonianism have tended to locate the high point of the movement in 1750s Oxford.[39] In actual fact, Hutchinsonian influence was greatest at the turn of the nineteenth century. The Hutchinsonians have long last been rightfully acknowledged as the most important High-Church precursors of the nineteenth-century Oxford movement.[40] The growing prominence of the Hutchinsonians in the second half of the eighteenth century, both as establishmentarians and as scriptural apologists, goes against the "Whiggish" assumption that the history of Christianity in eighteenth-century England is the story of steady and inevitable decline. This being said, the

---

38. Tropology is the figurative interpretation of Scripture in order to render moral guidance. Since tropological readings interpret everyday realities as part of an overarching moral order, they can play an important role in extending the domain of providence over the realm of human experience. Apologists who refuse to interpret the Old Testament tropologically struggle to defend the Old Testament as necessary for providential discernment. For a historical introduction to the tropological interpretation of Scripture, see Henri de Lubac, *Medieval Exegesis: The Four Senses of Scripture*, vol. 2, trans. E. M. Macierowski (Grand Rapids: Eerdmans, 2000), 127–78.

39. See, for example, C. D. A. Leighton, "'Knowledge of Divine Things': A Study of Hutchinsonianism," History of European Ideas 26(2000): 168.

40. Peter Nockles's *The Oxford Movement in Context: Anglican High Churchmanship, 1760–1857* (Cambridge: Cambridge University Press, 1994) played an important role in bringing Hutchinsonianism into scholarly view. Nockles emphasizes the importance of Hutchinsonianism in the consolidation of a High-Church movement prior to the advent of Tractarianism (*The Oxford*, 13, 16, 23, 45–47, 54–58, 65, 194, 270).

story of Hutchinsonianism is equally not the story of the triumphant reassertion of scriptural authority. It is an account of Christians who struggled to uphold the Old Testament as an equal partner in the Christian canon in a church which was increasingly inclined to believe that the New Testament alone was to be celebrated as Christian Scripture.

The Hutchinsonian defense of the Old Testament is a forceful affirmation that the "necessary truths of reason" must not be the interpretive foundation of the "incidental truths of history." The Hutchinsonians are to be regarded as the great opponents to Enlightenment rationalism because they insist that the order of the world cannot be divined by means of rational deductions from first principles.[41] To follow the quest to save the Old Testament, however, is not simply to rehearse the well-trodden debates between eighteenth-century empiricists and rationalists concerning the grounds of human knowledge. The Hutchinsonians were not motivated simply to acquire knowledge but to acquire a *providential* knowledge of both history and nature. The Hutchinsonians insist that providential discernment is possible. But they equally hold that humans must be mindful of their creaturely limitations. Humans must begin the process of providential discernment not with abstract speculations concerning the world, but with the concrete objects that comprise human experience as historically embedded. These objects, the Hutchinsonians insist, must be interpreted in light of God's Word, since God alone knows the true identity of the things he has made. The Hutchinsonians were not the only eighteenth-century Christians who affirmed the empirical grounds of providential knowledge, nor were they the only ones to insist that this knowledge must be made subject to Scripture. What distinguished them is that their pursuit of providential discernment made the words of the Old Testament central to Christian life as it inevitably must be lived, within the divinely authored temporal order we call history.

---

41. "At its simplest," says Darwall-Smith, "Hutchinsonianism was a reaction to rationalism, which, it was feared, had dethroned divine revelation in favour of human reason" (Robin Darwall-Smith, *A History of University College, Oxford* [Oxford: Oxford University Press, 2008], 271). The Hutchinsonians strongly affirmed the empirical grounds of knowledge. For a discussion of Hutchinsonian sensualist epistemology, see Chapter Four.

1
—

A CATALOGUE OF NUMBERS: ISAAC NEWTON'S OLD TESTAMENT

Throughout his life, Isaac Newton exerted an enormous amount of energy on the interpretation of the Old Testament. His primary object was to defend the Old Testament by demonstrating, by means of astronomical and mathematical science, that the Old Testament is the authentic record of the oldest civilization of the world. Newton, however, wasn't simply motivated by the Renaissance conviction that "older is better." He believed that the only way to save the Old Testament was to bind it to the primitive ideal. By locating the Old Testament at the beginning of recorded time, Newton hoped to protect it from the devolutionary force of history. What is more, he hoped to demonstrate that the truths deposited in the Old Testament at the beginning of time were, like the truths of natural philosophy, grounded in the nature of things and thus shielded from devolutionary history. Newton's work on the Old Testament is the forum within which he sought to reconcile his conviction that God's providence is supremely evident in the mathematical workings of nature with a traditional Christian affirmation of scriptural authority.

Since the dispersal and retrieval of Newton's "non-scientific" manuscripts in the Sotheby sale of the Portsmouth Collection in 1936, scholars have come to see that biblical studies occupied a central place in Newton's thought.[1] As

---

1. The manuscripts contain thousands of folios containing perhaps 1.2 million words. The fascinating story of the dispersal of Newton's "non-scientific" manuscripts has become something of "a founding myth" for the new Newtonian studies (Allison Coudert, "Forgotten Ways of Knowing: The Kabbalah, Language, and Science in the Seventeenth Century," in *The Shapes of Knowledge from the Renaissance to the Enlightenment*, ed. D. R. Kelley and R. H. Popkin [Dordrecht: Kluwer Academic, 1991], 96). See Sarah Dry, *The Newton Papers: The Strange and True Odyssey of Isaac Newton's Manuscripts* (Oxford: Oxford University Press, 2014).

the manuscripts began to reveal their secrets in the post-war era, scholars quickly came to realize that the portrait of Newton they had inherited was hagiography, the fruit of Whig historiography and positivism.[2] And the new portrait that progressively emerged looked very little like the old one.[3]

Scholars of the new Newtonian studies insist that Newton was not a two-headed monster: sometimes modern, sometimes ancient; sometimes "scientific," sometimes "pre-scientific." They maintain that Newton's belief that the Lord God of Israel is rendered *pantokrator* on account of his dominion over all things brings cohesion to Newton's various pursuits, whether "scientific," historical, or alchemical.[4] As Dobbs puts it, Newton was not just "interested in finding laws of nature; his was a religious quest" rooted in the "conviction that God acted in the world."[5] In 1993 Markley remarked that Dobbs's

---

2. Positivism is a system that holds that every rationally justified assertion can be scientifically justified or is capable of mathematical proof. See Michael Proudfoot and A. R. Lacey, *The Routledge Dictionary of Philosophy*, 4th ed. (New York: Routledge, 2010), 311–14.

3. Margaret Jacob recalls a lecture Westfall gave in the 1970s about Newton's early alchemy as follows: "There were audible gasps, and under a barrage of hostile questioning Westfall retorted in exasperation 'I did not write these manuscripts,' or words to that effect. Very few in the audience wanted Newton to be a practicing alchemist, as well as a serious religious thinker" (Margaret Jacob, introduction to *Newton and Newtonianism: New Studies*, ed. James E. Force and Sarah Hutton [Dordrecht: Kluwer Academic, 2004], x).

4. For the importance of the divine name *pantokrator* in Newton's thought, see James E. Force, "Providence and Newton's *Pantokrator*: Natural Law, Miracles, and Newtonian Science," in *Newton and Newtonianism: New Studies*, ed. James E. Force and Sarah Hutton (Dordrecht: Kluwer Academic, 2004), 65–92. In Popkin's words, the goal of the new Newtonian studies is to demonstrate that "one does not have to construct a Newton who had an internal switch by which he could turn off the scientific Newton and turn on the religious Newton, and vice versa" (Richard H. Popkin, introduction to *Newton and Religion: Context, Nature, and Influence*, ed. James E. Force and Richard H. Popkin [Dordrecht: Kluwer Academic, 1999], xvi–ii). For a summary of the agenda of the new Newtonian studies, see Margaret J. Osler, "The New Newtonian Scholarship and the Fate of the Scientific Revolution," in *Newton and Newtonianism: New Studies*, ed. James E. Force and Sarah Hutton (Dordrecht: Kluwer Academic, 2004), 1–13. In order to emphasize the consistency of Newton's thought, some scholars have found it helpful to appeal to the methodological parallels in his theological and "scientific" writings. See Maurizio Mamiani, "Newton on Prophecy and the Apocalypse," in *The Cambridge Companion to Newton*, ed. I. Bernard Cohen and George Smith (Cambridge: Cambridge University Press, 2002), 387–408. Although some have disputed Mamiani's claim that Newton's scientific method was forged as an application of his biblical hermeneutic to empirical study, Mamiani's conclusion that Newton's hermeneutical method has much in common with his experimental method is widely acknowledged. Newton's opinion that Scripture and nature are to be interpreted with the same method can be traced to Isaac Barrow, according to Reedy (Gerard Reedy, *The Bible and Reason: Anglicans and Scripture in Late Seventeenth-Century England* [Philadelphia: University of Pennsylvania Press, 1985], 56).

5. B. J. T. Dobbs, *The Janus Faces of Genius: The Role of Alchemy in Newton's Thought* (Cambridge: Cambridge University Press, 1991), 12.

groundbreaking work on Newton's alchemy may have put "the final nail in the coffin of positivist readings of Newton by ... demonstrating that Newton's theocentric interpretation of nature was profoundly antimechanistic."[6] In 2004 Jacob remarked that "by the 1980s everyone who studied Newton had come somewhat belatedly to recognize the importance of his theology."[7] This turns out to have been an exaggeration, for in 2003 Faur was able to tell the story of a Jewish Newton who rejected Christianity.[8] In 2007 Feingold scoffed at the notion that Newton sat "long hours at his desk, missing dinners and ignoring visitors, just because the power of belief in divinity drove him on."[9] And in 2012 Buchwald and Feingold suggested that Newton only turned to the Bible because he was emotionally vulnerable.[10] For scholars of the new Newtonian studies, the real conundrum is not Newton, but his interpreters.

The positivist reading of Newton poses a genuine problem for the new Newtonian studies not merely because of its persistence but because it is the traditional reading. Its genealogy can be traced back to Henry Pemberton (1694-1771), the editor of the third edition of Newton's *Principia*.[11] As Jacob puts it, "The old positivist Newton is a dead duck, but the larger shift, one that made his alchemy an embarrassment and that mechanized the Western understanding of nature, still needs explaining."[12] Positivist readings of Newton are only possible because of ideological shifts taking place during Newton's lifetime—shifts he ironically helped to create.[13] Unlike positivists, Newton believed that the entire realm of human experience—a realm that includes everything from the findings of his optical experiments to the relics of ancient civilization—can render certain knowledge because it is subject to

---

6. Robert Markley, *Fallen Languages: Crises of Representation in Newtonian England, 1660-1740* (Ithaca, NY: Cornell University Press, 1993), 132.

7. Jacob, "Introduction," x.

8. José Faur, "Newton, Maimonidean," *Review of Rabbinic Judaism* 6 (2003): 215-49.

9. Mordecai Feingold, "Honor Thy Newton," *Early Science and Medicine* 12 (2007): 228.

10. Jed Buchwald and Mordecai Feingold, *Newton and the Origin of Civilization* (Princeton: Princeton University Press, 2012), 129.

11. Markley, *Fallen*, 189-96.

12. Jacob, "Introduction," xi.

13. Newtonian scholars are accordingly compelled to produce not merely readings of Newton with internal coherence, but readings that account for Newton's relationship to his culture and his relationship to Newtonianism. This, unfortunately, has not been the strength of the new Newtonian scholarship, which tends to emphasize Newton's radical distinctiveness.

God's providential governance. Newton's difficulty is that he equally insisted that the entire realm of experience is subject to devolution. He therefore attempted to ground experiential knowledge in that which is not subject to corruption: mathematics. Newton's privileging of mathematics as the ahistorical grounds upon which truth is established opened the door to positivistic readings of his work. It was also a decisive element in the erosion of Old Testament authority in eighteenth-century England. Christians struggled to find reasons to hold on to the Old Testament once they concluded that it was not—as Newton maintained—a wellspring of mathematical certainties.

ISAAC NEWTON, PHILOLOGIST

In his will, England's preeminent natural philosopher Robert Boyle (1628–1691) made provisions for the foundation of an annual lectureship "for proving the Christian Religion, against notorious Infidels, viz. Atheists, Theists, Pagans, Jews, and Mahometans."[14] The first Boyle lecturer was the brilliant young classical scholar Richard Bentley (1662–1742).[15] In his lectures, Bentley opted to engage Newtonian science, rather than classical studies, as the basis of his apologetic.[16] As he argued that the facts and observations of science demonstrate the existence of a rational Creator, Bentley drew upon many

---

14. Robert Boyle, *The Works of the Honourable Robert Boyle*, 6 vols. (London: 1772), 1:clxvii; John Dahm, "Science and Apologetics in the Early Boyle Lectures," *Church History* 39, no. 2 (1970): 172–86. Jacob finds that the Newtonian use of the Boyle lectureship for the defense of the Christian religion played an important role in the solidification of Hanoverian legitimacy. See Margaret Jacob, *The Newtonians and the English Revolution, 1689–1720* (Ithaca, NY: Cornell University Press, 1976).

15. Bentley finally received his due in Kristine Haugen, *Richard Bentley: Poetry and Enlightenment* (Cambridge, MA: Harvard University Press, 2011). Haugen's useful discussion of Bentley's Boyle Lectures is contained on pages 101–5. Bentley's lectures reached their sixth edition in 1735 and were reprinted as late as 1815. They were also translated into Latin, German, French, and Dutch (Dahm, "Science," 175n17).

16. Although Bentley is known to historians of philosophy and science as the first public proponent of Newtonian natural theology, Bentley's engagement with Newtonian natural philosophy was at the periphery of his own scholarly career as a biblical scholar and literary critic. De Quehen insists that "his command of Latin, Greek, and biblical studies was prodigious" and that his "grasp of critical principles … has confirmed him as 'the greatest scholar that England or perhaps Europe ever bred' " (Hugh de Quehen, "Bentley, Richard [1662–1742]," *Oxford Dictionary of National Biography*, Oxford University Press, accessed January 22, 2014, http://www.oxforddnb.com.myaccess.library.utoronto.ca/view/article/2169). Levine is slightly more modest in his assessment of Bentley, but he has no doubt that Bentley was "the greatest philologist of the age" (Joseph Levine, *The Battle of the Books: History and Literature in the Augustan Age* [Ithaca, NY: Cornell University Press, 1991], 41).

themes that Boyle had rehearsed in his own work. Bentley's unique contribution to the emerging paradigm of naturalistic apologetics known as
"physico-theology" was his appeal to the Newtonian theory of universal
gravitation to combat the "atheistical" notion that motion and matter can
account for all natural phenomena. According to Bentley, gravitation is
the "energy and impression" of God in creation which demonstrates God's
continued providential oversight.[17]

Bentley corresponded with Newton about his epoch-making *Principia
Mathematica* before delivering the lectures.[18] In the course of their correspondence, Newton told Bentley, "When I wrote my treatise about our
Systeme I had an eye upon such Principles as might work with considering
men for the beleife of a Deity & nothing can rejoyce me more then to find it
usefull for that purpose."[19] This conviction is consistent with his statement
in Newton's appendix to the second edition of the *Principia*, known as the
"General Scholium," that to discourse of God "from the appearances of things,
does certainly belong to Natural Philosophy."[20] Newton was supremely confident his mathematical principles of natural philosophy were demonstrably

---

17. Bentley's appeal to Newton's *Principia* has become, in Haugen's words, "The most famous
element" of his Boyle Lectures, and deservedly so. Bentley's appeal set the precedent for the Boyle
Lectures of the following decades and remains a decisive moment in the history of Christian
apologetics. Its influence on modern apologetic enterprises such as creation science is palpable.
Creation scientists take for granted Bentley's conviction that divine providence is most clearly
seen not in the realm of human history but in nature. They also take for granted that scientific
experimentation can discern the imprint of God's hand on his creation. In Bentley's own words,
universal gravitation confirms that "an immaterial living Mind doth inform and actuate the
dead Matter, and support the Frame of the World" (Richard Bentley, *Eight Sermons Preach'd at
the Honourable Robert Boyle's Lecture* [Cambridge: 1724], 278).

18. Isaac Newton, *The Mathematical Principles of Natural Philosophy*, trans. Andrew Motte
(London: 1729), 2:392.

19. Isaac Newton, "Original letter from Isaac Newton to Richard Bentley, 10 December 1692,"
189.R.4.47, ff. 7–8, 4r., Trinity College Library, Cambridge, UK. In this letter, Newton proceeds
to explain to Bentley how the system of the world requires the existence of a divine power not
merely for its constitution but also for its preservation (see Newton, "Letter [...] to Richard
Bentley," 189.R.4.47, ff. 7–8, 8r.). I have retained the original spellings in my quotations of all the
scholars I quote in this study.

20. Newton, *The Mathematical*, 388. For an overview of the theological vision underlying
Newton's *Principia*, see Stephen Snobelen, "'God of Gods, and Lord of Lords': The Theology of
Isaac Newton's General Scholium to the Principia," *Osiris*, 2nd Series 16 (2001): 169–208.

certain and that they therefore provided a sure demonstration of God's providential dominion.[21]

Newton's immense non-scientific labors—alchemical, theological, and chronological—were similarly directed toward the goal of bringing "mathematical" certainty to the subject matter at hand to extend his proof of divine providence to all areas of the human experience. The primary difficulty Newton encountered was that the knowledge these disciplines provide is historically contingent, mediated by fallen and flawed human interpreters of divine order. Newton took for granted that biblical data is subject to corruption. This corruption is the primary obstacle he seeks to overcome to establish a "mathematical" scriptural apologetic.

To appreciate the nature of historically contingent knowledge in Newton's thought, it is necessary to locate him within the preeminent controversy of his day: the "battle of the books."[22] Although the battle of the books has come to be interpreted as a confrontation between "Ancients" and "Moderns" over the merits of the new empirical sciences, Joseph Levine has definitively established that this was but "one-half of the argument."[23] Equally important was the rearguard action concerning the merits of late-renaissance philology. This half of the debate was instigated by Bentley's philological demonstration that the beloved *Epistles of Phalaris* were forgeries.[24] It is entirely appropriate to speak of Bentley as a Newtonian when it comes to natural philosophy, but it is equally appropriate to speak of Newton as a "Bentleyan"

21. Following Descartes, Newton's work attempts to achieve what Brown calls "the regularization of providence." It is easy to see how Newton struggled to account for the providential character of history given this emphasis on regularity! See Stuart Brown, "The Regularization of Providence in Post-Cartesian Philosophy," in *Religion, Reason and Nature in Early Modern Europe*, ed. Robert Crocker (Dordrecht: Kluwer Academic, 2001), 1–16.

22. The conflict took place on both sides of the English Channel. In France it was known as "La querelle des Anciens et des Modernes," and in England it took the corresponding title of "The quarrel of the Ancients and Moderns." The conflict is sometimes referred to as the "battle of the books" thanks to Swift's polemical rendering of the controversy. See Jonathan Swift, *A Tale of a Tub* (London: 1704).

23. Joseph Levine, "Ancients and Moderns Reconsidered," *Eighteenth-Century Studies* 15, no. 1 (1981): 78.

24. "Philology" is the term Renaissance scholars used to refer to the technical study of classical texts by means of highly specialized linguistic and historical critical tools. See Levine, *The Battle*, 41–46.

when it comes to literary criticism.[25] Like Bentley, Newton wholeheartedly embraced the philological criticism, and like Bentley, he recognized that the philological method must be applied consistently to every object that comes under scholarly scrutiny.[26] When Newton wrote about the Bible, he treated it as a historical artifact and recognized that, as a historical artifact, it is not immune to philological deconstruction.[27]

What frightened the Ancients about the philological method is that it moved the locus of authority away from the text to the history behind the text. For Bentley, the cherished texts of the classical canon are but "individual and variable pieces written in specific and differing circumstances and in need of historical explication."[28] Bentley gives the impression, however, that the real authority lies not with history itself but with the philologist who holds the key to unlocking this history. His point is simple: his opponents can level every possible tool in their arsenal against him, but they cannot

---

25. James Force tackles the question of Newton's relationship to the debate between the Ancients and Moderns in his article "Newton, the 'Ancients' and the 'Moderns,'" in *Newton and Religion: Context, Nature, and Influence*, ed. James E. Force and Richard H. Popkin (Dordrecht: Kluwer Academic, 1999), 237–57. Force's basic argument is that Newton's love of ancient wisdom renders him an Ancient. This conclusion is misguided on two accounts. First, as Levine convincingly demonstrates, both the Ancients and the Moderns held ancient wisdom in high regard. The Moderns held that the best they could hope for was to equal the prodigious learning of the Ancients (*The Battle*, 34–35). Second, Force ignores "fully-half of the argument," the argument concerning the merits of philological scholarship. Newton's wholehearted embrace of philological scholarship places him firmly in the Moderns' camp.

26. The work of Popkin, Iliffe, Mandelbrote, and Snobelen confirms that Newton must be counted among the philologists (Richard H. Popkin, "Newton as a Bible Scholar," in *Essays on the Context, Nature, and Influence of Isaac Newton's Theology*, ed. James E. Force and Richard H. Popkin [Dordrecht: Kluwer Academic, 1990], 114). Popkin goes so far as to say that the picture of the biblical text Newton presents is essentially the same as the notorious iconoclasts of the day, Baruch Spinoza and Richard Simon. Like Spinoza and Simon, he rejects the sole Mosaic authorship of the Pentateuch and believes that textual criticism can uncover the redactional layers of the various books of the Bible. Like Simon, Popkin also insists that the existence of multiple authors does not detract from the divine status of the biblical books ("Newton as a Bible Scholar," 105). Popkin observes that Newton's *Chronology of Ancient Kingdoms Amended* "is a most interesting effort to employ newly discovered scientific findings to evaluate the historical status of the Bible" ("Newton as a Bible Scholar," 111).

27. Newton admits that the Old and New Testaments, as historical artifacts, are not immune to the corrupting force of history, and he holds that his divinely appointed task, as a philologist, is to cleanse them from historical accretions. The clearest example of this approach is Newton's unpublished work "Two Notable Corruptions of Scripture," New College MS 361 (4), New College Library, Oxford. In this work Newton uses textual criticism to prove that Nicene Trinitarian doctrine is not found in the New Testament.

28. Levine, *The Battle*, 75.

change what he, the expert, clearly sees—namely, that the language of the *Epistles* is not, as it claims, sixth-century BC Sicilian Greek. This is precisely Newton's repeated argument in his dispute with Robert Hooke (1635–1703) and Anthony Lucas (1633–1693) over the status of his optical experiments. The empirical approach to verification promoted by Boyle and adopted by the Royal Society held that "an historically specific event such as an experiment or 'trial' could become more credible by being witnessed many times and in many different places by a large group of reliable people."[29] Newton, however, insisted that "what's done before many witnesses is seldome without some further concern then that for truth: but what passes between friends in private usually deserves ye name of consultation rather than contest."[30] Newton affirms the importance of the crucial instance, which he believes shoulders the burden of proving the certainty of the experiment in question.[31] In answer to Lucas's criticisms, he asserts that the truthfulness of his own optical experiments depends upon his ability, as an expert witness, to accurately measure and relate, with mathematical rigor, his own observations.[32]

Newton carries this same emphasis on his authority as an expert interpreter to his philological scholarship. He rejects the notion that priests hold the keys to Scripture, and he seems to believe that God gives the right to interpret Scripture to an "elect remnant of true believers" of which he is a member.[33] As a true believer that has resisted the tide of religious corruption, Newton thinks he has the ability not merely to "give" the biblical text over

---

29. Rob Iliffe, "Those 'Whose Business It is To Cavill': Newton's Anti-Catholicism," in *Newton and Religion: Context, Nature, and Influence*, ed. James E. Force and Richard H. Popkin (Dordrecht: Kluwer Academic, 1999), 112.

30. Isaac Newton, *Correspondence*, ed. H. W. Turnbull (Cambridge: Cambridge University Press, 1959), 1:416. Newton's opinion on this matter is consistent with his supreme confidence in himself and his refusal to trust other interpreters.

31. For a detailed discussion of the relationship between Newton's experimental method and that of the Baconians, see Dana Jalobeanu, "Constructing Natural Historical Facts: Baconian Natural History in Newton's First Paper on Light and Colors," in *Newton and Empiricism*, ed. Zvi Biener and Eric Schliesser (Oxford: Oxford University Press, 2014), 39–65.

32. Iliffe, "Those," 113–15.

33. Scott Mandelbrote, "Isaac Newton and Thomas Burnet: Biblical Criticism and the Crisis of Late Seventeenth-Century England," in *The Books of Nature and Scripture*, ed. James E. Force and Richard H. Popkin (Dordrecht: Kluwer Academic, 1994), 162. Since Newton conceives of *prisca theologia* in both religious and natural-philosophical terms, he understands the "remnant" in corresponding terms. Members of the remnant cling to true Noachide religious and natural-philosophical principles (Force, "Newton," 244).

to history, but to rescue it from history as well. The way to rescue the text, Newton believes, is to bind it to a primitive ideal.

NEWTON'S PRIMITIVISM

When Newton looked to the future, he anticipated both purgation by fire and scientific and religious renovation.[34] Although Newton, like other Moderns, was confident in the ultimate progress of knowledge, he insisted, like other Moderns, that such progress is merely the retrieval of that which has been lost to history.[35] His primitivistic impulse leads him to speak longingly about what might be described as three "golden ages"—that of Adam, that of Noah, and that of Jesus Christ. Newton's confidence that he might even stand "on ye shoulders of giants" stands in tension with his deeply held conviction that human corruption grows over time.[36]

Newton's natural philosophy is part of the Renaissance tradition known as "pious philosophy," which seeks to reconcile biblical knowledge (whether Adamic or Mosaic) and contemporary natural philosophy and metaphysics.[37] For Newton, Adam is the paragon of religious and philosophical knowledge, and all true human knowledge can be traced back to him. Noah and Jesus, like Moses and the prophets, are but reformers; the religion of Noah and the religion of Jesus are but revivals of Adam's primordial religion, which was based upon a simple creed: love of God and love of neighbor.

Newton spends much more time reflecting upon the Noachide instantiation of primordial religion than he does reflecting upon the Adamic, perhaps because all pre-Noachide monuments have been lost to history.[38] Nowhere

---

34. Allison Coudert, "Newton and the Rosicrucian Enlightenment," in *Newton and Religion: Context, Nature, and Influence,* ed. James E. Force and Richard H. Popkin (Dordrecht: Kluwer Academic, 1999), 41.

35. Newton's belief that the best modern discoveries are but rediscoveries of *prisca theologia* calls into question, as Force demonstrates, the characterization of Newton as endorsing a progressivist philosophy of history (Force, "Newton," 254).

36. Isaac Newton, "A Letter to Robert Hooke, 5 February 1676," in *Correspondence of Isaac Newton,* ed. H. W. Turnbull (Cambridge: Cambridge University Press, 1959), 1:416.

37. See Ann Blair, "Mosaic Physics and the Search for a Pious Natural Philosophy in the Late Renaissance," *Isis* 91 (2000): 32–58.

38. The idea that the seven principles of Noachide religion are the foundation of natural religion was important in creating the category of "religion" and in the development of modern religious studies (Guy Stroumsa, *A New Science: The Discovery of Religion in the Age of Reason* [Cambridge: Harvard University Press, 2010], 46–49).

is Newton's supreme confidence in his philological scholarship as evident
as in his reconstruction of Noachide religion, which Newton calls the religion of the Prytanea.[39] Newton has no doubt that at the time of Noah, "There
was one Pyræum in every city placed in the principal part of the city. And
in the Prytaneum was the Court where the Council or Senate of the city
met." The Prytaneum was also the location for the "performance of holy rites"
by "the chief Magistrates of the City & the King," which consisted of "hon-
ours & sacrifices" offered to the one true God.[40] Newton's reconstruction of
Noachide religion is highly idealized, a utopic vision of unsullied harmony
between God, nature, and humankind. As centers of both religious and natural-philosophical learning, the Prytaneum were founded upon Copernican
principles. The temple edifices themselves, with their hieroglyphic representations, were microcosms of the heliocentric universe, and the sacrifices
at the center of vestal worship were celebrations of the heliocentric divine
order of creation.[41]

For Newton, the only golden age that has ever approached that of Noah
is that of the apostolic church. One of Newton's favorite terms for the apostolic church is a term he extracts from the oracles of St. John's Apocalypse,
"the host of heaven." Like the Noachides before them, the host of heaven
adhered to a simple creed and moral code and refused to be dogmatic about

---

39. In a context in which scholars were eager to refute or champion Spencer's claim that
Moses was dependent upon Egypt, Newton presents a third way: Egyptian and Hebrew religion
are both based upon Noachide religion, though they are both corruptions of it (Rob Iliffe, *Priest
of Nature: The Religious Worlds of Isaac Newton* [Oxford: Oxford University Press, 2017], 198).

40. Isaac Newton, Draft chapters of a treatise on the origin of religion and its corruption,
Yahuda MS 41, fols. 1r and 3r, Yahuda Newton Manuscripts, National Library of Israel, Hebrew
University of Jerusalem, Jerusalem, Israel.

41. Newton is captivated by the simplicity of the heliocentric theory, and this love for simplicity extends both to doctrinal and ethical matters. It comes as no surprise, therefore, that
Newton holds that the only conviction that was binding upon the Noachides was belief in the
one true God, and their only ethical requirements were the love of God and the love of man.
The seven Noachide precepts listed in the Babylonian Talmud are developed by Newton in his
personal copy of the 1717 edition of *Opticks*. They are: (1) to have one supreme Lord; (2) to not
profane his name; (3) to abstain from blood or homicide; (4) to avoid fornication and (5) theft;
(6) to be merciful to beasts; and (7) to set up magistrates (Gary Trompf, "On Newtonian History,"
in *The Uses of Antiquity: The Scientific Revolution and the Classical Tradition*, ed. Stephen Gaukroger
[Dordrecht: Kluwer Academic, 1991], 218). Newton returned to these principles in his *Irenicum* in
1718, and Conduit believed they were Newton's personal creed. This fundamental importance of
love of God and love of man in Noachide religion convinced Newton that it was, as Trompf puts
it, "the ancient basis for the principal part of the religion of Christians" ("On Newtonian," 219).

metaphysical conclusions, particularly when it came to differing conclusions about the nature of Christ, whom Newton refers to as "the prince of the host."[42] Newton's study of early Ebionite and Nazarene texts led him to conclude that, although the Jewish Christians tended to see Jesus in primarily human terms and the Gentile Christians tended to see him as divine, they did not let this difference of opinion compromise their unity.[43]

Given that the Christian religion did not impose doctrinal particulars on the Noachide foundation of natural religion, it is worth asking whether it added anything new. Newton's answer is that Christianity's contribution is the revelation that Jesus of Nazareth is the Messiah. The religion of Noah and the religion of Christ are the two principal pillars of Newton's historical scheme and his normative vision. Given that the flood erased pre-Noachide history, Noachide religion stands at the dawn of religious history as the foundation of natural religion. The importance of the Christian religion, likewise, lies in its foundational character, this time with respect to revealed religion. Newton regards Noachide religion as the foundation of natural religion and Christianity as the foundation of revealed religion.[44]

The greatest difficulty that Newton has is that he is unable to reconcile his affirmation that true religion, as natural religion, is everywhere the same, and his historicization of religion, which entails particularity of expression. "Religion," says Newton, "is partly fundamental & immutable partly circumstantial & mutable."[45] Ultimately Newton's affirmation of historical

42. Matt Goldish, "Newton's 'Of the Church,'" in *Newton and Religion: Context, Nature, and Influence*, ed. James E. Force and Richard H. Popkin (Dordrecht: Kluwer Academic, 1999), 111.

43. Newton calls the basic doctrinal tenets that all believers were expected to uphold "milk for babes," and the optional further theological discourse and study to be undertaken only by scholars "meat for men of full age." The apostolic church managed to successfully uphold the distinction between "milk and meat" by insisting that believers never compromise their unity on account of the more complicated theological issues—centrally, the nature of the divinity of Christ. See Goldish, *Judaism*, 130. This appraisal of the pristine church is the basis of Newton's curious defense of the Church of England. Newton holds that the Church of England has managed to uphold the pristine distinction between milk and meat, for it does not regard the heretical Trinitarian creeds it embraces as fundamentals (Keynes MS 3, 51, King's College, Cambridge, UK). See also Goldish, *Judaism*, 135–36; and "Newton's," 152–54.

44. This primitivism, however, is also what destabilizes the importance of the Christian revelation. If earlier is always better, then the religion of Christ is inferior to Noachide religion, and even Noachide religion falls short of the Adamic ideal.

45. "The first was the Religion of Adam, Enoch, Noah, Abraham Moses Christ & all the saints & consists of two parts our duty towards God & our duty towards man or piety & righteousness,

particularity gives way to his drive to universalize religious truth. In particular, his insistence that the pristine church was basically indifferent to christological doctrine severely restricts his ability to affirm the newness of Christian revelation. In 1694 Newton wrote to David Gregory (1659–1708), telling him that,

> Religion is the same at all times, but the religion which they received pure from Noah and the first men, they debased with their own inventions ... Moses began a reformation but retained the indifferent elements of the Egyptians. Christ reformed the religion of Moses.[46]

Newton's primitivism leads him to relativize all historical instantiations of true religion as revivals of an ahistorical core, the true theology or *prisca theologia*. Newton calls this true religion either "natural religion" or "Noachide religion." He therefore concludes that "all the reformations of religion, of Noah, Abraham, Moses, the Jewish prophets and Jesus, are restorations of the oldest religion in the world," that of the venerable Noah.[47] As a "priest of nature," Newton saw himself in direct continuity with Noah, and he believed that his mathematical demonstration of the heliocentric order of the universe was proof of the veracity of Noachide natural religion.

NEWTON'S DEVOLUTIONARY
PHILOSOPHY OF HISTORY

Although Newton is happy to discuss primitive religious norms, such discussions constitute a tiny fraction of his theological and historical output. For Newton, the primary task of the historian is not to elucidate ideals but to narrate their postlapsarian corruption. Newton's work on ancient history outlines the devolution of Noachide religion, and his work on church history recounts the devolution of Christianity. As Robert Markley puts it, "Newton's

---

piety which I will here call Godliness & Humanity" (Isaac Newton, A short Schem of true religion, Keynes MS 7, 1r, King's College, Cambridge, UK).

46. Newton, *Correspondence*, 3:338. Despite the apparent necessity of prophets to revive true religion, Newton seems to think that true religion is accessible to all humans, even apart from revelation. "There is," says Newton, "but one law for all nations the law of righteousness & charity dictated to the Christians by Christ to the Iews by Moses & to all mankind by the light of reason & by this law all men are to be judged at the last day" (Newton, A short Schem, 2r).

47. Trompf, "On Newtonian," in *The Uses of Antiquity*, ed. Stephen Gaukroger (Dordrecht: Kluwer Academic, 1991), 217.

fascination with the origins, corruption, and cyclical renovations of a pristine monotheism locates his sprawling, if fragmentary, historical project in the context of the dominant genre of seventeenth-century historiography—universal history."[48] Following other universal historians, Newton finds in the idea of *prisca theologia* the overarching concept he needs to fit all the historical data he encounters into this conceptual scheme.

Like many of his contemporaries, Newton regards this devolution of *prisca theologia* as simultaneously doctrinal and natural-philosophical.[49] The family of manuscripts which focuses most explicitly on natural-philosophical devolution is "Theologiae Gentilis Origines Philosophicae."[50] Kenneth Knoespel describes the manuscripts in primitivist terms as "devoted to showing how ancient religious practice could reveal physical truths about the universe."[51] This primitivism is explicitly articulated in the first chapter of the manuscript, which explains how the theology of ancient gentiles was philosophical in nature, including knowledge of astronomy and physics. The rest of the work is a demonstration of this claim through what Knoespel calls "serious discussion of natural phenomena ... modulated through mythological narrative."[52] Like Copernicus, Galileo, Kepler, and their followers, Newton

---

48. Markley points out that for Milton, universal histories are efforts "to justify the ways of God to humankind by finding evidence of providential order in the millennia-long cycles of moral depravity, political disorder, economic hardship, and ecological devastation that constitute postlapsarian history" (Robert Markley, "Newton, Corruption, and the Tradition of Universal History," in *Newton and Religion: Context, Nature, and Influence*, ed. James E. Force and Richard H. Popkin [Dordrecht: Kluwer Academic, 1999], 122). Markley observes that "The political, moral, ecological, and economic corruption of their own times encourages writers in the 1600s to read history as an ongoing fall from a golden age of prosperity and virtue, and, consequently, to see their own tasks as the recovery of universal patterns of meaning in an otherwise meaningless world" ("Newton," 123). The goal of seventeenth-century universal historians was to find providential order among the rubble of past civilizations. See Nicholas Wickenden, *G. J. Vossius and the Humanist Concept of History* (Assen, Netherlands: Van Gorcum, 1993), 136.

49. Piyo Rattansi and J. E. McGuire's article "Newton and the 'Pipes of Pan' " (*Notes and Records of the Royal Society* 21 [1966]: 108–43) played a crucial role in this development.

50. Isaac Newton, Rough draft portions of and notes for "Theologiæ Gentilis Origines Philosophicæ" and "The Original of Monarchies," Yahuda MS 16, National Library of Israel, Jerusalem; Three bundles of notes for a work on the ancients' physico-theology, Yahuda MS 17, National Library of Israel, Jerusalem, Israel.

51. Kenneth Knoespel, "Interpretive Strategies in Newton's *Theologiae Gentilis Origines Philosophicae*," in *Newton and Religion: Context, Nature, and Influence*, ed. James E. Force and Richard H. Popkin (Dordrecht: Kluwer Academic, 1999), 180.

52. Knoespel, "Interpretive Strategies," 186.

"understood the progress of astronomy as being also a reversion towards propositions comprehended intuitively by the Ancients."[53]

"Theologiae Gentilis Origines Philosophicae" is equally an account of the gradual concealment and eventual disappearance of the true doctrine of God. In it, Newton reflects upon linguistic problems associated with human nomenclature—what Bacon called "idols of the marketplace." The work is a historical account of how, after Babel, the names of biblical individuals were obscured by inaccuracies of translation—inaccuracies that inevitably led to the individuals' veneration as gods. Newton uses the process of gradual linguistic obfuscation to give a euhemeristic account of the emergence of pagan polytheism: the names of the first humans were eventually transferred to the stars; these stars were then attributed with animated spirits; and finally they were venerated as gods.

Newton also tells the story of the gradual corruption of *prisca theologia* through inaccurate representation in another important unpublished treatise, "The Original of Religions." In this work Newton outlines his theory of religious devolution as follows:

> Now the corruption of this religion I take to have been after this manner. ffirst the frame of the heavens consisting of Sun Moon & Stars being represented in the Prytanæa as the real temple of the Deity men were led by degrees to pay a veneration to these sensible objects & began at length to worship them as the visible seats of divinity. And because the sacred fire was a type of the Sun & all the elements are parts of that universe which is the temple of God they soon began to have these also in veneration. For tis agreed that Idolatry began in the worship of the heavenly bodies & elements.[54]

Newton here follows Renaissance tradition by laying much of the blame for the devolution of primal religion at the feet of the Egyptians. "The Original

---

53. Paolo Casini, "Newton: The Classical Scholia," History of Science 22, no. 1 (1984), 10. Newton believed that the Noachides were in possession of his knowledge of universal gravitation, and in the 1680s he resolved to write a great treatise in which all his mathematical conquests would harmoniously coexist with the mathematics of the ancients (Massimo Galuzzi, "Newton's Attempt to Construct a Unitary View of Mathematics," *Historia Mathematica* 37 [2010]: 548).

54. Newton, Draft chapters of a treatise, 8r.

of Religions" is thus a historical account of how idolatry spread from Egypt to Greece, and then into Italy and the West.[55]

The devolution of primal religion is schematized in Newton's interpretation of the Old Testament. A case in point is his exposition of 2 Kings 17, which describes the Assyrian exile of the people of Israel.[56] Newton begins his exposition with a transcription of the verses from the Authorized Version:

> They followed vanity & became vain & went after ye heathen that were round about them, concerning whom ye Lord had said that they should not do like them. And they left all ye commandements of ye Lord their God, & made them molten images even two Calves, & made a grove & worshipped all ye host of Heaven & served Baal.[57]

Newton insists that the idolatries of Israel can be attributed to the corruption of the ten tribes during the Assyrian captivity. As he reflects upon this corruption, however, he concludes that Israelite religion had been idolatrous from the very beginning. Newton boldly pushes Israel's fall into idolatry past the reign of Jeroboam and into the depths of primordial history to uphold his opinion that the origin of ancient idolatry must be located in the days of Noah. Newton concludes his exposition with the following observation: "Israel during all her abominations from first to last scarce ever forsook the true God absolutely but only corrupted his worship by mingling their own inventions with it as too many of our neighbouring christians dayly do."[58] For Newton, the ubiquity of idolatry binds people from all ages together in a common predicament. This enables him to affirm that human history is, in fact, "universal."

---

55. Newton, Draft chapters of a treatise, 10v.

56. This exposition, which is contained in three manuscripts, totals roughly 10,000 words. Isaac Newton, Exposition of 2 Kings 17:15-16, Yahuda MS 21, National Library of Israel, Jerusalem, Israel; Exposition of 2 Kings 17:15-16, MS 130, Harry Ransom Humanities Research Center, University of Texas, Austin, Texas; Part of an exposition of 2 Kings 17:15-17, Babson MS 437, The Babson College Grace K. Babson Collection of the Works of Sir Isaac Newton, Huntington Library, San Marino, California. The material has not, to my knowledge, yet been treated in a published work.

57. Newton, Exposition, Yahuda MS 21, 1r.

58. Newton, Exposition, Babson MS 437, 2. Newton's emphasis upon the ubiquity of idolatry both before and after Christ mutes his supersessionism.

Newton's voluminous reflections upon ecclesiastical history echo his reflections on ancient history. In these ecclesiastical reflections, the religion of Christ stands in for the religion of Noah as the primal religion whose doctrines are infallibly true. The primary actor in the drama, however, is not Christ, but the church, and the role the church plays is precisely the role that Israel and the nations play in ancient history. For Newton, the history of the church is the story of the gradual corruption of a primitive ideal. The episode that garners the most attention from Newton is the Arian controversies of the fourth century. In Westfall's words, "The conviction began to possess him that a massive fraud, which began in the fourth and fifth centuries, had perverted the legacy of the early church. Central to the fraud were the Scriptures, which Newton began to believe had been corrupted to support trinitarianism."[59] Athanasius plays the role of principal antagonist in this drama, but he is by no means alone. Athanasius stands at the head of a vast horde of idolaters—gnostic Jews, false converts from heathenism, overzealous monks, Trinitarian metaphysicians, power-mongering bishops, and superstitious Catholics.[60] The role of each of these groups within Newton's scheme is the same—to the point that they can be regarded as interchangeable parts. With each group, the primitive simplicity of the gospel is obscured and ultimately replaced by something that is "really no gospel at all" (Gal 1:7 NIV).

Newton believes that unsavory men who "may deservedly be called the synagogue of Satan" infiltrated the apostolic church from its inception. In Newton's mind,

a dayly flow of such converts into the Churches it could not be but that in a few years the hypocrites would be more then double or triple to

---

59. Robert Westfall, *Never at Rest: A Biography of Isaac Newton* (Cambridge: Cambridge University Press, 1983), 313.

60. For Newton, the "corrupters of religion, ancient and modern, were legion; the contemporary papists and their antecedents, the pagan idolaters; the English sectarian enthusiasts—the new prophets—and their equivalents, the hallucinating monks of early Christianity; the Pharisaical Jews who rejected Christ; contemporary deists and atheists like Hobbes and their ancient counterparts the theological Epicureans, for whom all was chance; and finally, the philosophers who mixed up metaphysics and religion, particularly the modern rationalist system-makers Descartes and Leibniz, and their predecessors the gnostics, Cabbalists, and Platonists. These were the enemies of Newton's God" (Frank Manuel, *The Religion of Isaac Newton* [Oxford: Clarendon Press, 1974], 21). In "Of the faith which was once delivered to the saints," Newton claims that "system-building was pre-eminently responsible for the perversion of the only truly revealed religion, primitive Christianity" (Manuel, *The Religion*, 22).

the sincere not to say more then ten or twenty times their number. Now by this influx of fals converts the mystery of iniquity grew in these respects.[61]

The Trinitarian controversies, like the Assyrian exile, provoked a greater descent into idolatry, but like the exile, they cannot be seen as that which destroyed a primitive perfection that had endured for centuries preceding them. Judaism and Christianity were both poisoned at their inception. This suggests that the problem of decay is inherent in historicity.[62] For Newton, primitive religion is an ideal that allows him, as an enlightened philologist, to sift through the vicissitudes of history to distinguish the "fundamental & immutable" from the "circumstantial & mutable." The power of history's corrupting glare, however, is such that the immutable immediately gives way to the mutable, and the fundamental to the circumstantial.

Although Newton holds that the corrosive effect of history upon truth is almost immediately felt, he does not believe that history is void of providential oversight. Newton refuses to play the part of a primitivist who hurdles over the vicissitudes of history to reflect upon an Edenic prehistory. He gazes intently over the wreckage of human history to discern faint outlines of patterns and concepts, and he digs beneath the rubble in search of hidden gems of pristine knowledge. Newton chooses to do the work of the historian because he believes that "only through a circumstantial account of the degradation of the Church in a series of stages and its doctrinal deviation from the primitive creed could Christianity be stripped of its spurious accretions."[63] He mines the monuments of history because he believes they are the divinely appointed means of providing humans access to *prisca theologia*. His great obstacle, however, is that the monuments of history do not merely tell the story of historical devolution; they are themselves subject to it.

---

61. Isaac Newton, Fragment on the history of apostasy, Yahuda MS 18, 1v, National Library of Israel, Jerusalem, Israel.

62. The claim that Newton invariably reads history through a devolutionary lens is something that Manuel, the first great interpreter of Newton's unpublished manuscripts, saw well. Manuel observed that "most of Newton's theological writings are devoted to exposing falsifiers of New Testament texts, prevaricators in Church Councils, corrupters of primitive natural religion, metaphysical befuddlers of the true relations between God and man" (*The Religion*, 65).

63. Manuel, *The Religion*, 68.

THE PROBLEM OF HUMAN TESTIMONY

The monuments of history are inherently problematic for Newton firstly on account of their origination as instantiated human testimony. As a philologist, Newton refuses to take human testimony at face value and subjects it mercilessly to critical scholarship. This intense conviction that human testimony must be subjected to criticism is helpfully understood in relation to Newton's work as Warden of the Mint (1696–1727), which entrusted him with the enormous responsibility of protecting the British market from currency debasement. Newton was just settling into this new job when he ran up against one of the criminal masterminds of the day, William Chaloner (d. 1699). Newton was forced to sift through a complex web of conflicting testimonies to bring Chaloner to justice, and the experience taught him he could trust nothing that came from human lips.[64] As warden, Newton put his philological skills to practical use, and he quickly became an expert at discerning the difference between counterfeit and genuine coins. His work as warden enabled him to pursue, as a public vocation, the craft which privately consumed him in his philological studies: exposing the frauds of history.[65]

Shortly after his death, a portion of Newton's work on the Old Testament was made available to the public through John Conduitt's (1688–1737) publication of Newton's *Chronology of Ancient Kingdoms Amended* (1728).[66] Newton's work on ancient chronology was the most well-known aspect of his "non-scientific" output, largely due to the publication of this work. Both the published work and Newton's numerous unpublished drafts and notes, which were the product of more than thirty years of study and have become available for public consumption, confirm that his primary aim is to establish the chronological priority and therefore divine origin of Israelite civilization.[67] When

64. Buchwald and Feingold speculate that this experience intensified Newton's skepticism concerning the trustworthiness of all human words, including words from the past. "Newton grew astonishingly free in treating words from the past. He implicitly justified his occasionally extraordinary manipulations ... by framing many statements as 'poetical fictions,' words that could not be trusted" (Buchwald and Feingold, *Newton*, 238).

65. Iliffe, *Priest of Nature*, 15.

66. Isaac Newton, *The Chronology of Ancient Kingdoms Amended*, ed. John Conduitt (London: 1728).

67. Draft sections of *The Chronology of Ancient Kingdoms Amended* are contained in the following manuscripts: Draft passages on chronology and biblical history, Yahuda MS 25, National Library of Israel, Jerusalem, Israel; Draft chapters of *The Chronology of Ancient Kingdoms Amended*, Yahuda MS 26; Seven drafts of Newton's defence of *The Chronology of Ancient Kingdoms Amended*,

Newton surveys ancient pagan chronologies, he finds nothing but question-able logic and inaccurate tabulation: "The Greek Antiquities are full of poet-ical fictions"; "how uncertain their Chronology is, & how doubtful"; "And as for the chronology of the Latines, that is still more uncertain."[68] Concerning the Assyrians, their preeminent historian Ctesias "feigned a long series of kings of Assyria whose names are not Assyrian nor have any affinity with the Assyrian names in scripture."[69] And as for the Egyptians, their priests "had so magnified their antiquities before Herodotus, as to tell him that from Menes to Mæris ... there were 330 kings whose reigns took up as many ages, that is eleven thousand years, & had filled up the interval with feigned kings who had done nothing."[70]

The problem of the inherent unreliability of ancient testimony is exac-erbated for Newton by his refusal to rely on modern interpreters to help him sift through the wreckage of antiquity—presumably because they are equally subject to the corrupting forces that trouble human testimony. Seventeenth-century chronologists made their living by proposing novel schemes of world history. They were, however, careful to locate their work within the parameters set by Joseph Scaliger (1540-1609) or James Ussher (1581-1656).[71] Newton flatly dismisses these parameters. He moves the date of the flood back 577 years, cuts off about four centuries from Greek history, and short-ens Egyptian history by 600 years, sometimes shifting forward established

---

Yahuda MS 27; Drafts of the "Short Chronicle" and "Original of Monarchies," MS 361 (1), New College Library, Oxford, UK. Newton describes his object as follows: "I have drawn up the fol-lowing Chronological table, so as to make Chronology suit with the Course of Nature, with Astronomy, with Sacred History, with *Herodotus* the Father of History, and with itself" (*The Chronology*, 8).

68. Newton, Drafts of the "Short Chronicle," 8r.

69. Newton, Drafts of the "Short Chronicle," 31r.

70. Newton, Drafts of the "Short Chronicle," 31r.

71. For a brief introduction to Renaissance biblical chronology that highlights Scaliger's importance, see Anthony Grafton, "Dating History: The Renaissance & the Reformation of Chronology," *Daedalus* 132, no. 2 (2003): 74-85. Grafton published a much-needed biography of Scaliger: *Joseph Scaliger: A Study in the History of Classical Scholarship*, 2 vols. (Oxford: Clarendon, 1983). Ussher's chronology was to become commonly accepted in England through its inclu-sion in the front matter of the 1701 edition of the Authorized Version of the Bible. See Martin Gorst, *Measuring Eternity: The Search for the Beginning of Time* (New York: Broadway Books, 2002), chapter 2. For the story of how Ussher's chronology came to be discredited in the nineteenth century, see Ronald L. Numbers, "'The Most Important Biblical Discovery of Our Time': William Henry Green and the Demise of Ussher's Chronology," *Church History* 69, no. 2 (2000): 257-76.

dates no less than 1,800 years.[72] He is thus "the first since Scaliger to propose a new system of technical chronology"; and, like Scaliger, he "boasted openly of having been the first to reveal the true epoch of the Olympiad."[73]

Following Ussher, Newton sought to defend the chronology of the Masoretic Text over and against those offered by the Septuagint, and more generally, by the numerous unreliable accounts of pagan antiquity.[74] Newton's radical revisionism is an attempt to give Israel pride of place among ancient kingdoms. He fudges the date of the fall of Troy to establish the priority of Solomonic glory.[75] He celebrates Israel's political institutions as models for English constitutional government.[76] And he seeks to establish, over and against John Spencer and other renegade advocates of Egyptian priority, that the genealogy of *prisca theologia* passes from Jews to Phoenicia and Egypt, and only then on to Europe.[77]

Robert Markley sees Newton's chronological scheme as an effort to move beyond "the conceptual dead end of relying on the Bible to secure both the meaningfulness of the history and the coherence of the natural world."[78] Buchwald and Feingold conclude that he "followed Scaliger and Selden in considering pagan sources to have near parity with Scripture."[79] Buchwald and Feingold therefore propose that Newton's work "contributed to the eventual rejection of the hold of Scripture over chronology."[80] Newton establishes a hierarchy of authority, pitting sources against one another in an attempt to secure a sure foundation.[81] If Newton plays fast and loose with the words

---

72. David S. Katz, *God's Last Words: Reading the English Bible from the Reformation to Fundamentalism* (New Haven: Yale University Press, 2004), 101; A. T. Fomenko, *Empirco-Statistical Analysis of Narrative Material and Its Application to Historical Dating*, trans. O. Efimov (Dordrecht: Kluwer Academic, 1994), 97.

73. Buchwald and Feingold, *Newton*, 425.

74. Newton treated the gods as ancient but fully historic kings. As Lincoln puts it, he rationalized their stories and altered the years given in their stories in the hopes of recovering "history from myth" (Bruce Lincoln, "Isaac Newton and Oriental Jones on Myth, Ancient History, and the Relative Prestige of Peoples," *History of Religions* 42 [2002]: 4).

75. Trompf, "On Newtonian," 229–30.

76. Trompf, "On Newtonian," 226.

77. Trompf, "On Newtonian," 220.

78. Markley, "Newton," 134.

79. Buchwald and Feingold, *Newton*, 433.

80. Buchwald and Feingold, *Newton*, 435.

81. As an expert interpreter, "Newton thereby reserved to himself the right to determine not just which historical sources were credible, but which parts of even these credible sources

of Scripture—an accusation leveled against him even in his own day—he justifies his own deviations as necessary sins that establish the priority of Hebrew Scripture and Israelite civilization.[82] Although Newton fights passionately to defend Hebrew Scripture, the supreme confidence he places in his own words, and the lack of confidence he places in Scripture words, may well have the effect of compromising scriptural authority, as Markley, Buchwald, and Feingold maintain.

SAVING LANGUAGE FROM HISTORY

Although Newton believed that human testimony was given over to corruption, he did not despair the ability of human language to convey truth. Throughout his life he engaged a number of different strategies to protect human testimony from the forces that threaten to overwhelm it. When he interprets texts, Newton is keenly aware that the codified script and syntax he reads must be carefully deciphered to uncover the kernel of truth hidden beneath the husk. For this reason he proposes rules for textual interpretation. Newton's rules, found at the beginning of an untitled treatise on Revelation, seek to "flatten out" language by eliminating all historical accretions, as well as all metaphorical and poetic elements.[83] This quest for linguistic perspicuity also provoked Newton to create a scheme for reformed spelling, as well as various alternative symbols and phonetic transcriptions that he hoped would contribute to the reformation of the English language.[84] Newton's zeal

---

were nevertheless untrustworthy and to be discarded" (Buchwald and Feingold, *Newton*, 221).

82. Buchwald and Feingold claim that "fidelity to evidence often prompted Newton to depart from the Word of Scripture—or at least from common perception of what Biblical phrasing meant. He followed Scaliger and Selden in considering pagan sources to have near parity with Scripture when the history of gentile nations is recounted and, consequently, he felt free to supplement the spare biblical narrative with details drawn from myth or his imagination." One example Buchwald and Feingold give in this respect is Newton's insistence that the first world empire was in Egypt rather than Mesopotamia (Buchwald and Feingold, *Newton*, 433).

83. Newton articulates sixteen rules for the interpretation of prophetic language in Isaac Newton, Untitled Treatise on Revelation, Yahuda MS 1.1, National Library of Israel, Jerusalem, Israel, 12r. Kochavi crystallizes these sixteen rules into four points: (1) the entire prophetic text must be treated as one homogenous structure; (2) the entire text must be decoded in minute detail; (3) the interpretation of prophetic revelation must be simple; and (4) the interpreter must interpret the text with the aid of historic events (Matania Kochavi, "One Prophet Interprets Another: Sir Isaac Newton and Daniel," in *Newton and Religion: Context, Nature, and Influence*, ed. James E. Force and Richard H. Popkin [Dordrecht: Kluwer Academic, 1999], 109).

84. Ralph Elliott, "Isaac Newton as Phonetician," *The Modern Language Review* 49, no. 1 (1954): 7.

to overcome linguistic deficiencies is also evident in his attempt to create a universal language.[85] Like many other universal language progenitors, Newton made Aristotelian taxonomy the foundation of his system because he hoped to create a language founded on the natures of things themselves.[86] The common thread that underlies these various pursuits is that they are all attempts to save language from history. Newton's desire to save language from history is also what accounts for his clear preference for ancient learning. Because he believed that ancient learning is closer to the primal source of all truth, Newton readily embraced the well-established conviction that correspondence between language and nature is to be found not among the moderns but among the ancients.

Although Newton devalues vernaculars as subject to the corruption of history, he retains the hope that esoteric knowledge can be extracted from ancient languages. Like many of his contemporaries, Newton is convinced that ancient philosophy was divided between the sacred and the mundane, and he believed that *prisca theologia* was esoteric, a secret system of ancient scholar-priests who preserved and transmitted Adamic knowledge through types and enigmas.[87] Newton echoes Gerardus Vossius (1577–1649), Samuel Bochart (1599–1667), and John Marsham (1602–1685) in portraying these scholar-priests in the Platonic mode of philosopher-kings appointed to protect *prisca theologia* from the barbaric masses. Following Vossius, Bochart, and

---

85. Mathematician and philosopher John Wilkins, one of the founders of the Royal Society, remarked that "there is scarce any subject that hath been more thoroughly scanned and debated amongst Learned men, than the *Original of Languages* and *Letters*" (John Wilkins, *An Essay Toward a Real Character, and a Philosophical Language* [London: 1668], 2). The introduction to Wilkins's essay provides a helpful summary of the state of the question at that time. Scholars were so intent on finding or recreating the "original of languages" because of their belief that the form of history was one of decline. Newton's interest in "the original of languages" must be placed alongside his interest in "the original of religions" and "the original of monarchies" as but one component of his quest to overcome historical devolution.

86. M. M. Slaughter, *Universal Language and Scientific Taxonomy in the Seventeenth Century* (Cambridge: Cambridge University Press, 1982), 154. Curiously, Newton suddenly stopped this classification after 2,400 entries. Elliott insists that Newton's subsequent correspondence with Wilkins demonstrates that he did not immediately lose interest in his scheme, but there can be no doubt that Newton eventually decided there were more promising approaches to the problem of linguistic decrepitude.

87. Knoespel, "Interpretive Strategies," 188.

Marsham, Newton also insists that these philosopher-kings intentionally concealed their insights within obscure myths and hieroglyphs.[88]

The distinction between the sacred and the profane is an important element of Newton's thought. For Newton, every historical artifact that retains residual *prisca theologia* of the philosopher-kings is to be regarded as sacred. Everything else is profane. Newton applies the distinction to both ancient pagan texts and to the Bible. In other words, ancient pagan texts and the Bible both contain the sacred and the profane. Newton's prodigious engagement with the Bible suggests that he regards much of the Bible as a desolate wasteland and that only select parts can be mined for the precious ore of sacred wisdom. If the notes Newton scribbled in the margins of his own Bible are any indication as to his belief in the location of this wisdom, it could be argued that Newton believes that *only* Daniel and Revelation are to be regarded as sacred.[89]

Newton's treatment of Scripture as an unequal witness is also confirmed by his belief that the Hebrew language is endued with the residual secrets of the philosopher-kings.[90] Newton's fascination with Hebrew, however, is muted by his passion for what he calls "prophetic language." For Newton, prophetic language, rather than Hebrew, stands in for the lost language of Adam, the *prima lingua* which is able to achieve exact correspondence between words and things. Newton regards as prophetic any word or phrase that conceals yet preserves truth from history: "John did not write in one language, Daniel in another, Isaiah in a third & the rest in other peculiar to themselves; but they all wrote in one & the same mystical language."[91] The books of Daniel and Revelation are of special interest to Newton presumably because they are the books which have best preserved this prophetic witness.

---

88. David Haycock, "'The Long-lost Truth': Sir Isaac Newton and the Newtonian Pursuit of Ancient Knowledge," *Studies in History and Philosophy of Science* 23 (2004): 612–13.

89. Newton owned more than thirty Bibles. John Harrison concludes that the Bible which Newton reserved for personal use contains "numerous notes and biblical reference by Newton throughout and esp. at Daniel and Revelation" (*The Library of Isaac Newton* [Cambridge: Cambridge University Press, 1978], 101).

90. Scholars question Newton's proficiency in Hebrew; Goldish, for instance, supports John Hutchinson's claim that Newton lacked proficiency in Hebrew (Goldish, *Judaism*, 55).

91. Isaac Newton, Two incomplete treatises on prophecy, Keynes MS 5, 1r, King's College, Cambridge, UK. Newton says that this language was known to the "sons of the Prophets as the Hieroglyphic language of the Egyptians."

Prophetic language therefore transcends and is arguably indifferent to the identity of the "host" language. Hebrew, Greek, and presumably Aramaic characters are all potentially "prophetic." In each case, the kernel of esoteric knowledge can be extracted from the signifier, the husk, and then the husk is discarded. As Newton interprets the Bible, he removes the husk to unveil the kernel by converting a dizzying array of prophetic images into a series of dates.

Newton is ultimately unsatisfied with a biblical hermeneutic that simply translates esoteric wisdom into the contemporary idiom. He is consistent in his historicism. The Bible is no different than pagan texts, for they are all given over to history and thereby to devolution. But for Newton, the problem isn't just that all texts are suspect because they are subject to the manipulations and mistakes of human authors and transcribers. The problem with textual evidence, Newton maintains, is more fundamental still: for Newton, "language ... must distort by virtue of its nature from the very moment of utterance."[92] Newton longed to render truth in a form that is not subject to the vicissitudes of history, and this quest leads him away from the vernacular, away from universal language, and away even from prophetic language to mathematics.

SAVING THE OLD TESTAMENT
THROUGH MATHEMATICS

Ralph Elliott speculates that Newton may have ultimately left his universal language unfinished "because of the pressure of other concerns, especially the mathematical studies to which he devoted himself at Cambridge."[93] Elliott rightly wishes to affirm the continued importance of linguistic studies to Newton, but he is unable to overcome the dualism inherent in positivist readings of Newton since he draws a stark line between Newton's mathematical interests and his linguistic work. Robert Markley overcomes this bifurcation in his seminal work *Fallen Languages*. Like Elliott, Markley suggests Newton's output betrays a gradual movement away from linguistic to mathematical studies. Markley, however, insists that Newton sees mathematics itself as a

---

92. Buchwald and Feingold, *Newton*, 283.

93. Ralph Elliott, "Isaac Newton's 'Of an Universall Language,' " *The Modern Language Review* 52, no. 1 (1957): 6.

language.[94] According to Markley, Newton turns to mathematical language to grant him the certainty that human language is impotent to provide. Peter Harrison puts it like this:

> The identification of mathematics as a language of nature was the final stage in the imposition of the new ordering principles to which physical objects were subject. It represents, on the one hand, the last stage in the evacuation of meaning from the natural world, and on the other the triumph of mathematical physics.

For Newton, "mathematical relations seemed intrinsic to nature."[95] He therefore stabilizes the historical record by translating human language into mathematical truth, and he does this by mathematizing *prisca theologia*.[96]

Newton's Old Testament interpretation can equally be seen as part of his quest to extract kernels of mathematical truth concealed beneath the husk of human testimony. A case in point is Newton's mathematical study of Solomon's temple. Following Italian interpreter Juan Baptista Villalpando (1552–1608), Newton argues that Solomon's temple and Ezekiel's temple are one and the same, and he labors to reconcile their scriptural accounts by rationalizing discrepancies as textual corruptions.[97] Given that Newton believes that Ezekiel presents the most mathematically accurate description of the

---

94. Markley's analysis is consistent with traditional interpretations inasmuch as it admits that Newton held that mathematical knowledge was superior to historical knowledge, but it challenges them by insisting that the division between mathematical and historical cannot be neatly mapped onto Newton's "scientific" and theological works. Since Markley's analysis affirms that mathematical knowledge is the goal of both Newton's "scientific" and theological studies, it gives preference to Newton the "scientist," but because it makes the problem of devolutionary history the grounds upon which both areas of his work are established, it grounds Newton's "scientific" work in deeper theological concerns.

95. Peter Harrison, *The Bible, Protestantism, and the Rise of Natural Science* (Cambridge: Cambridge University Press, 1998), 262.

96. Although Newton consistently claims to revere classical learning, his distrust of historical testimony translates into a consistent reluctance to acknowledge his debt to other authors. As Casini puts it, Newton's writings are "sparing of historical recollections or references; whether because of a precise methodological choice, or because of a reluctance to make known thoughts not expressed in a clear mathematical form" (Casini, "Newton," 1).

97. Tessa Morrison, *Isaac Newton's Temple of Solomon and His Reconstruction of Sacred Architecture* (Basel: Springer Basel, 2011), 39–40. Newton believes Ezekiel's description of the temple is the most accurate description of Solomon's temple found in Scripture, but he admits that it is not free from corruption (Morrison, *Isaac Newton's Temple*, 74).

temple, he fudges the numbers given in 2 Kings. Newton also recognizes, however, that Ezekiel's rendering of the temple is obscure and incomplete, and he therefore rationalizes and supplements even Ezekiel's measurements to make them mathematically rigorous.[98]

Newton's interest in Old Testament measurements is twofold. First, they are relatively resistant to the corruptions that normally afflict human language. Second, Newton believes the temple is a microcosm of the universe. Since the structure of the universe is mathematical, the revelation of its structure must also be given in mathematical form. Newton's decipherment of the complex web of conflicting numbers demonstrates the accordance of the scriptural testimony with the structure of the universe and thereby establishes scriptural authority upon the surest foundation of all: nature. Manuel complains that Newton

> had precious little interest in historical character or motivation. To know a quantity and an exact date was one of the ultimate goals of his realistic history. In the end his passion for factual detail shriveled the past to a chronological table and a list of place names. His history was sparse; specific as a businessman's ledger, it allowed for no adornments, no excess. It had the precisianism of the Puritan and his moral absolutism; existence was stripped to a bony framework. The world had been full of deceivers—the lying chronologists, ancient and modern, and the fraudulent Athanasian Church Fathers. In separating the true from the false in myth, in the Gospel, in Greek and Roman historians, Newton was performing God's work."[99]

Newton's fixation upon numbers is hardly surprising given that the translation of linguistic data into mathematical syntax is fundamental to

---

98. Newton's most prolonged engagement with the problem of the measurements of the temple is MS Babson 0434, which also includes what Morrison calls "a meticulous study of the cubit to further understand the dimensions of the temple." Newton's discussion here is reminiscent of Bentley's work on the fledgling discipline of Numiscences (Morrison, *Isaac Newton's Temple*, 62). See also Isaac Newton, "Dissertation upon the Sacred Cubit of the Jews and the Cubits of the Several Nations," in John Greaves, *Miscellaneous Works of Mr. John Greaves* (London: 1737), 405–33; drafts concerning Solomon's temple and the sacred cubit, Yahuda MS 2.4, National Library of Israel, Jerusalem, Israel; Of the temple & synagogues of the Jews, Yahuda MS 26.3, National Library of Israel, Jerusalem, Israel.

99. Frank Manuel, *Isaac Newton: Historian* (Cambridge: Cambridge University Press, 1963), 10.

chronological science.[100] This being said, Newton went well beyond the necessary structure of the discipline. Like many of his Renaissance forebears, he wanted numbers that were demonstrably grounded in the nature of things. Like them, he therefore sought to ground his mathematical conclusions in natural-philosophical structures.[101] Christopher Wren (1632–1723) observed that "theology admits her debt to astronomy," through chronology.[102] Bernard Fontenelle (1657–1757) observed that

> The principal Point of Sir Isaac Newton's System of Chronology, as it appears by this Extract, is, by following some faint Traces of the ancient Greek Astronomy, to find out the Position of the Equinoctial Colour, with regard, to the fixed Stars, in the Time of Chiron the Centaur.[103]

Fontenelle's observation is crystallized in Newton's bold declaration that "the surest arguments for determining times past are those taken from Astronomy."[104]

Newton's Old Testament apologetic is dominated by his appeal to the mathematical structures of nature. Buchwald and Feingold observe that Newton holds that "the best kinds of ancient words were ones that could be turned into numbers," but he also holds that the best numbers are those that were never subject to linguistic forms because they were derived from

---

100. The difficulty that Renaissance chronologers had is that there was no established method to determine which numbers were to be selected from the heap of ancient sources—sources that often contradicted not merely each other, but themselves. For a study of the relationship between biblical chronology and mathematics in the Renaissance, see Nicolas Popper, "'Abraham, Planter of Mathematics': Histories of Mathematics and Astrology in Early Modern Europe," *The Journal of the History of Ideas* 67, no. 1 (2006): 87–106.

101. See Anthony Grafton, "Some Uses of Eclipses in Early Modern Chronology," *The Journal of the History of Ideas* 64, no. 2 (2003): 213–29.

102. Quoted in Buchwald and Feingold, *Newton*, 118. Throughout his work, Newton distinguished mathematical demonstration and plausible conjecture. For example, once Newton established "when the Egyptians had embarked on astronomical observations, Newton felt secure in explaining why such interest arose among them" (Buchwald and Feingold, *Newton*, 429). Isaac Newton, Papers relating to chronology and "Theologiæ Gentilis Origines Philosophicæ," New College MS 361 (3), fols. 63, 129.

103. Quoted in Rob Iliffe, *Early Biographies of Isaac Newton, 1660–1865* (London: Pickering & Chatto, 2006), 23.

104. Newton, Papers relating, 166r.

nature itself.[105] On the one hand, Newton can be interpreted as a rationalist, as he holds that mathematical certainties are truly independent of human experience. On the other hand, he is an empiricist inasmuch as the mathematical structures he seeks to discern are found in nature and are immune from historical devolution. Newton believes his biblical chronology is certain because his computations are astronomically grounded.[106]

MATHEMATICS AND CORRUPTION

Newton appeals to mathematics in his work on the Old Testament because he believes mathematical truths stand outside of history, the realm of human corruption. His Old Testament apologetic therefore depends upon his ability to make that which is subject to history (the Old Testament) the purveyor of that which is not (mathematical truth). Newton turns to mathematics to provide him with the certainty that human language fails to provide because he believes the severity of the human ailment is such that it corrupts all historically contingent knowledge.[107] For Newton, mathematical structures of nature provide demonstrable certainty because they were divinely instituted prior to Adam's fall and are therefore not subject to it.

Harrison's *The Fall of Man and the Foundations of Modern Science* examines a number of important early empiricists, including Bacon, Boyle, Glanville, Hooke, and Locke, who rejected Calvinist dogma but upheld an Augustinian doctrine of original sin. Given Newton's location within the Royal Society, he

---

105. Buchwald and Feingold, *Newton*, 244. Buchwald and Feingold describe Newton's hierarchy of certainty as follows. He regards the "securely produced number," numbers taken from his experiments, with utmost confidence. Next are numbers "whose reliability was uncertain." These include astronomical observations extracted from ancient testimony. And, finally, the least reliable numbers are those taken from "purely textual remarks" (Buchwald and Feingold, *Newton*, 283). Newton's desire to ground numerical data in astronomical data suggests that he did not entirely let go of the Aristotelian view that the stars are inherently stable since they stand above and beyond the world of human flux.

106. Manuel finds that the use of mathematics and empirical data allows Newton to draw together diverse strands of knowledge into a single tradition of *prisca theologia*: "by using new mathematical notations and an experimental method he combined the knowledge of the priest-scientists of the earliest nations, of Israel's prophets, of the Greek mathematicians, and of the medieval alchemists" (Manuel, *The Religion*, 23).

107. The only place I have found where Newton discusses the doctrine of original sin is the fragment "Of the temple & synagogues of the Jews." Newton's view may be idiosyncratic, but he takes very seriously the Augustinian notion that sin is passed on from generation to generation (Newton, *Of the temple*, 4r).

would appear to be a likely candidate for such a view. This, however, is an option Harrison emphatically rejects. According to Harrison, Newton is a rationalist, not an empiricist. This conclusion enables Harrison to present Newton as a scholar who, unlike Bacon and the empiricists, wasn't much troubled by the epistemological effects of the fall.[108]

Admittedly, Newton's epistemology has far more in common with that of René Descartes than it does with probabilists like Blaise Pascal, despite the fact that Newton wrote his *Principia Mathematica* to subvert Descartes's *Principia Philosophiae*. Newton's new laws of motion are clearly meant to replace Descartes's laws of nature.[109] Newton's chief complaint is that Descartes's analysis is qualitative rather than quantitative and therefore lacks specificity of reference.[110] Newton sees mathematical knowledge as knowledge that can be assigned to particular objects through a quantitative analysis that maps spatial possibilities onto nature because he believes nature is a geometrically organized whole.[111] In Newton's mind, Descartes is guilty of providing vain "hypotheses" because he fails to substantiate his mathematical claims by demonstrating their accord with nature.[112] In the

108. Harrison highlights that Newton's quest to mathematize knowledge was consistent with Descartes's rationalist project because it sought to overcome the probabilistic certainties of empirical knowledge (Peter Harrison, *The Fall of Man and the Foundations of Science* [Cambridge: Cambridge University Press, 2007], 237).

109. Stephen Gaukroger, *The Collapse of Mechanism and the Rise of Sensibility* (Oxford: Clarendon Press, 2010), 55, 67. Despite this opposition, Oakley finds clear continuity between Descartes and Newton's conceptions of natural law (Francis Oakley, "Christian Theology and the Newtonian Science: The Rise of the Concept of the Laws of Nature," in *Creation: The Impact of an Idea*, ed. Daniel O'Connor and Francis Oakley [New York: Scribner, 1969], 449–52).

110. In Dear's estimation, Newton was right to criticize Descartes, for although his explanation has "the force of mathematical demonstration," it "entirely ignores quantities." For Dear, Descartes's appeal to mathematics is merely a "convenient cultural association that lends an air of authority to an argument" (Peter Dear, *Discipline and Experience: The Mathematical Way in the Scientific Revolution* [Chicago: University of Chicago Press, 1995], 212).

111. Galuzzi, "Newton's," 539. Burtt describes Newton's project as the unification of "the mathematical and experimental methods" (Edwin Burtt, *The Metaphysical Foundations of Modern Science* [London: Routledge, 1924], 216).

112. Iliffe, *Priest of Nature*, 84. Although Newton's project can be described in Cartesian terms as an attempt to lay a mathematical foundation of knowledge, this must not be allowed to obscure an even deeper association: Newton's association with Galileo Galilei and Johannes Kepler. Galileo and Kepler, like Descartes, seek to "mathematize" knowledge. Their complaint with the scholasticism of the day is not that it lacks an empirical component but that it does not have the tools to render empirical knowledge mathematical. They believe, in other words, that the way to "mathematize" knowledge is to "mathematize" nature, and Newton's work should be interpreted along these lines (Buchwald and Feingold, *Newton*, 10).

preface to the first edition of the *Principia*, he boasts that in setting forth the "mathematical principles" of natural philosophy, he will succeed where others have failed,[113] and his compatriots quickly came to believe that he had fulfilled his promise.[114] John Craig's (1663–1731) ode to Newton is entirely characteristic: "Astronomy remain'd still in the dark till the immortal Newton gave us his Philosophical Principles of Natural Philosophy. Now we know by mathematical Demonstrations that the Sun is the center of our System."[115] The view that Newton had made disobedient nature subject to mathematics established mechanics as the foundation of all physical sciences, and by the end of the century it was possible to endorse "Newtonianism" as the mathematical demonstration that the universe is self-regulating.[116]

In his important study on the role of mathematics in the scientific revolution, Peter Dear concludes that Newton believed "physico-mathematics" or "mixed mathematics" is "applicable to all areas of natural philosophy, insofar as all parts of physics implicated considerations of quantity."[117] Dear maintains that Newton's method demonstrates a movement away from "making experience" to "making experience to establish physico-mathematical

---

113. Newton, *The Mathematical*, 382.

114. Slaughter finds that Newton's *Principia* "put an end to the debate between the empirics and the atomists and completed the rejection of Aristotle. Newton's work demonstrated that (scientific) knowledge is gained not through empiricism alone, but through empirical observation in combination with mathematics. Newton formulated the hypothetico-deductive method where demonstration is achieved through mathematical physics ... With Newton's system, the end of science is redefined, not as the discovery of the nature of things but the prediction of their behavior regardless of whether their natures are known or not. With the rejection of the Aristotelian paradigm of science, classification could no longer be seen as means of explaining and representing the nature of nature. Taxonomy was supplanted by mathematics as the method and the language of science" (Slaughter, *Universal*, 194).

115. John Craig, A letter to an unidentified recipient, 7 April 1727, Keynes MS 132, King's College, Cambridge, UK.

116. John Gascoigne, "Ideas of Nature: Natural Philosophy," in *Eighteenth-Century Science*, ed. Roy Porter, vol. 4 of *The Cambridge History of Science* (Cambridge: Cambridge University Press, 2003), 284, 294. In Snobelen's words, "The belief that Newton invented a 'clockwork universe' that was initially created by God and then left to tick away on its own" became "firmly entrenched in the popular imagination" (Stephen Snobelen, "The Theology of Isaac Newton's *Principia Mathematica*: A Preliminary Survey," *Neue Zeitschrift für Systematische Theologie und Religionsphilosophie* 52, no. 4 [2010]: 378). Nevertheless, for Newton, "a continued miracle is needed to prevent the sun and fixed stars from rushing together through gravity" (Gascoigne, "Ideas," 228). See also Edward Davis, "Newton's Rejection of the 'Newtonian World View': The Role of Divine Will in Newton's Natural Philosophy," *Fides et Historia* 22, no. 2 (1990): 6–20.

117. Dear, *Discipline*, 223. Dear argues that this view can be placed squarely at the feet of Newton's mentor, Isaac Barrow.

justifications."[118] It must equally be said, however, that quantity is inherently important to Baconians.[119] Newton's emphasis upon mathematical demonstration should therefore not be taken to exclude him from among Harrison's Augustinian empiricists.

For Harrison, one of the hallmarks of this tradition is a deep skepticism concerning the reliability of the senses. Harrison identifies Bacon's *desidiratum* for improved instruments such as microscopes and telescopes as grounded in the conviction that artificial assistance for the senses is necessary in the postlapsarian world.[120] Newton must be located in this tradition since he followed Bacon both in questioning the reliability of the senses and in dedicating himself to the creation of improved instrumentation.[121] This being said, Newton's own position intensifies that of Bacon and his professed disciples. Take Hooke, for example: for Hooke, a good telescope is necessary because the human eye is limited in its observational powers. But for Newton, the human eye is not merely limited but also flawed.[122] Newton goes well beyond previous attempts to assist the eye through improved instrumentation in his famed optical experiments by manipulating the eye *itself* to investigate how this alters sensory data.[123] Newton was the first to recognize that colors that appear identical may in fact only be sensibly so. Indeed, it was just this conviction which enabled Newton to initiate a second natural-philosophical revolution, this time in the realm of optical science. For Newton, the eye is irreparably deceptive and must somehow be overcome to judge the physical characteristics of light.[124]

---

118. Dear argues that this represents a movement away from "relying on patterns of gentlemanly conduct for its integrity" to relying upon "associated academic status or established disciplinary practices" (*Discipline*, 248).

119. In 1660 John Wilkins described the business of the Royal Society as "physico-Mathematical-Experimentall Learning" (quoted in Dear, *Discipline*, 2).

120. Harrison, *The Fall*, 175.

121. Newton was, after all, inducted into the Royal Society on account of his improved telescope.

122. The Newtonian revolution in optics can therefore be attributed to this intensification of the tradition. Then again, Bacon himself observed, "In the first place, the impressions of the sense itself are faulty, for the sense both fails and deceives us" (Francis Bacon, *Novum Organum: Or True Directions Concerning the Interpretation of Nature* [London: 1620], lxx).

123. Buchwald and Feingold, *Newton*, 36.

124. Buchwald and Feingold, *Newton*, 87–89.

That Newton's own empirical approach is an intensification of Baconian skepticism is also clearly seen in Newton's approach to measurement. Newton performed his experiments repeatedly, tabulated the results, and then calculated the mean of his tabulations. Buchwald and Feingold describe the function of the mean in Newtonian computation as "the weapon with which he slew the inevitable dragons of sensual error."[125] But Newton's empirical method can be interpreted as an acknowledgement that sensual error can *never* be overcome. Whereas Boyle, Hooke, and other members of the Royal Society kept refining their measurement techniques in the hope of acquiring a single measurement that achieved perfect accuracy, Newton recognized that the best he could hope for was approximation.[126]

Harrison rightly observes that the importance of experiments ultimately becomes somewhat muted in Newton's method. As Snobelen puts it, Newton boasts that he has "proved everything by geometry and only made use of experiments to make them intelligible and convince the vulgar."[127] Harrison interprets this conviction as Newton's rejection of empiricism. If Newton ultimately steps outside of the empiricist tradition, however, it is not because he minimizes the powers of original sin but because he intensifies the Baconian position by conceding that postlapsarian sensual limitations can never be overcome. Newton maintains that in a fallen world, senses are rendered inherently "weak, unreliable, and inadequate to probe the hidden structure of phenomena."[128] Newton's confidence in mathematical demonstration must ultimately be attributed to the fact that he believes mathematical structures exist outside of human history and are therefore not subject to corruption.[129]

125. Buchwald and Feingold, *Newton*, 93.

126. Scholars continue to debate the methodology of Newton's *Principia*. I. Bernard Cohen introduced the influential notion of the "Newtonian style" in his 1980 work *The Newtonian Revolution*. According to Cohen, Newton proceeds by using a series of "mental constructs," approximations that allow him to compare his model with objects of nature (I. Bernard Cohen, *The Newtonian Revolution* [Cambridge: Cambridge University Press, 1980], 52–156). Steffen Ducheyne challenges Cohen's view, arguing that Newton pursued a hypothetical-deductive method in "Mathematical Models in Newton's Principia: A New View of the 'Newtonian Style,'" *International Studies in the Philosophy of Science* 19, no. 1 (2005): 1–19.

127. Stephen Snobelen, "On Reading Isaac Newton's *Principia* in the 18th Century," *Endeavour* 22, no. 4 (1998): 163.

128. Buchwald and Feingold, *Newton*, 89.

129. Newton's view clearly echoes Bacon and Locke. In *Novum Organum*, Bacon remarked that the "faulty meaning of words cast their rays ... on the mind itself." In his *Essay Concerning Human Understanding*, Locke suggested that "the very nature of words makes it almost unavoidable for

The founding fathers of the empirical method placed a strong emphasis on divine inspiration and personal experience because they understood
that their experiments were located within the contingent realm of experience.[130] This circumspect acknowledgement is the basis of their emphasis
on the precariousness of postlapsarian experimentation. It equally serves
to explain, however, why Newton believed "he had proved everything by
geometry and only made use of experiments to make them intelligible and
convince the vulgar." As Dear puts it, Newton believed that "a knowledge
of past events was not true knowledge; a knowledge of the current state of
affairs was itself mere history."[131] Experiments could not possibly serve as
the foundation of his natural-philosophical system since human experience
is always subject to corruption. What Newton needed, and what he believed
he found in mathematics, was an epistemological foundation that was not
subject to the vicissitudes that marked the experiential realm. Newton, as we
have seen, regards the touch of fallen humanity as inherently corrupt and
corrupting. But if human sin plays such a decisive role in Newton's linguistic and historical studies, how could it play no part in his "scientific" work?
Harrison's interpretation can fall back into traditional positivistic renderings
of Newtonian psychology. Medusa rears her ugly head once again: Newton
the rationalist ignores the problem of human sin in his "scientific" work but
is secretly consumed by it in his private theological musings.

Newton's consistent appeal to mathematics in his diverse scholarly pursuits confirms that he was deeply troubled by epistemological problems

---

many of them to be doubtful and uncertain in their significations" (quoted in Buchwald and
Feingold, Newton, 243). Buchwald and Feingold observe that Newton's hierarchical ordering
of the trustworthiness of human testimonies is closely related to a hierarchical ordering of
different types of testimony. At one end of the spectrum is "the securely produced number";
next in line is the number "whose reliability was uncertain," and least reliable is "the purely
textual remarks" that he finds in the sources he reads. This astute observation is open to mis-
interpretation. For Newton, the devolution from certainty to uncertainty takes the form of the
movement away from the mathematical to the linguistic (Buchwald and Feingold, Newton, 243).
This does not mean, however, that some numbers are inherently inferior to others. All numbers are inherently stable, but the stability of some numbers has been obscured by the extent
of their engagement with human history, which is why Newton believes in the superiority of
astronomical data. Astronomical data are to be preferred because they are derived from the
mathematical structures of nature rather than from history.

130. Harrison points out that many Renaissance scholars treated the terms "experimental"
and "experiential" synonymously (The Fall, 132).

131. Dear, Discipline, 11.

associated with human sin. Newton hoped to overcome these problems by converting human experience into mathematical syntax.[132] Whether alone in the laboratory or pouring over ancient manuscripts,

> Newton strove to convert fallible human information into quantified knowledge based on reliable numerical data. For Newton, numbers were what counted: words were slippery, as suspect as the stories dreamt up by the counterfeiters he persecuted at the Mint.[133]

Nevertheless, the point isn't just that Newton turns to mathematics to resolve his epistemological quandaries in both natural philosophy and theology. The point is that Newton is driven by the same question in both domains: how can human experience be rendered as the bearer of divine truth? As Markley puts it, Newton's "fragmentary universal history becomes the analog of his scientific efforts to uncover the means to reclaim humankind from corruption."[134]

CONCLUSION

Newton believed that the natural world and human history are both governed by the hand of divine providence. His remarkable success in demonstrating God's governance of the natural world through his mathematization of natural law can be described as "mathematizing providence." He anticipated that a similar demonstration in the realm of human history could be achieved through a similar process of mathematization. This accounts for the strategies of providential discernment outlined in this chapter: Newton's concerted efforts to translate biblical idiom into chronological data, his intense interest in the measurements of the temple, and his mathematical interpretation of *prisca theologia*. It must be emphasized, however, that Newton's devolutionary philosophy of history was not merely what provoked these efforts. It provided a conceptual framework that enabled them to be presented as mechanisms of

---

132. Greenham notes that while Newton might have conceptually distinguished what we now call sciences and arts, he approached texts the way he approached natural-philosophical objects. With great confidence in his own rational powers, he thought he could solve the riddles of both nature and history (Paul Greenham, "Clarifying Divine Discourse in Early Modern Science: Divinity, Physico-Theology, and Divine Metaphysics in Isaac Newton's Chemistry," *The Seventeenth Century* 32, no. 2 [2017]: 252).

133. Patricia Fara, "Isaac Newton and the Left Eye of History," *Metascience* 22 (2013): 324.

134. Markley, "Newton," 135.

providential discernment. For example, Newton's mathematical demonstration that Israel is the first civilization carries no providential import until it is located within Newton's larger devolutionary scheme.

Iliffe remarks that when Newton died in March 1727, "there was feverish activity to record, describe, explain and praise Newton's life and works."[135] Newton was heralded as

> The greatest of Philosophers, and the Glory of the British Nation. Who by the Strength and Compass of his Genius, the vast Extent of his Capacities, and the Depth of his Judgement, together with the indefatigable Diligence and Application, has given greater Light to Philosophy, than all the Industry of former Ages.

Newton's reputation rested entirely on the success of his "scientific" endeavors. *Mist's Weekly Journal* boasted that Newton,

> By his subtil Speculations, and uncommon Penetration in the Principles into the Principles of Things, has discovered to the World, and established upon the undeniable evidence of Demonstration, what was once look'd upon as dark and inexplicable, and beyond the Limits of human Knowledge. Who by the most accurate Reasonings and Deductions has traced out the abstrusest Causes, solved the most difficult Phaenomena, and laid down such incomparable Rules and Propositions as may hereafter be the Foundation of new Improvements and Discoveries.[136]

The elevation of Newton to the status of immortal genius contributed to the elevation of empirical science as that which alone could grant infallible certainty.

Conduitt's controversial decision to publish Newton's *Chronology of Ancient Kingdoms Amended* the year after his death, however, made things difficult for Newton's disciples and eulogizers.[137] There was considerable public interest in

---

135. Iliffe, *Early*, xii.

136. A letter reacting to Newton's death from *Mist's Weekly Journal*, Keynes MS 129.13, King's College, Cambridge, UK.

137. Newton had aimed to establish the same certainty in his historical studies that he had established in his "scientific" studies. One of the reasons he did not publish his historical studies was his fear of controversy. But the fact that Newton seemed to be continually revising

the manuscript, but when it was published the reviews were mixed.[138] Some of Newton's allies defended and even praised the work. Many others, such as Newton's erstwhile confidant Whiston, vigorously attacked it.[139] One of the central issues in the ensuing controversy was whether the historical disciplines could, in fact, be successfully mathematized.[140]

Buchwald and Feingold conclude that although "Newton's greatest legacy was the conviction that, in principle, every natural phenomenon can be described by a mathematical law ... he failed in his attempt to extend mathematical dominion over human civilization." The question many scholars found themselves asking in the wake of this disappointment was, "If even Newton was wrong, what could be hoped by those who laboured after him?"[141] This perceived failure of Newton's chronological system contributed to the separation of sciences from humanities which proved fertile soil for the development of positivism.[142] In the 1690s John Locke had already recognized

---

his historical studies also suggests he withheld publication because he was never fully satisfied with them.

138. Buchwald and Feingold, *Newton*, 331.

139. Buchwald and Feingold, *Newton*, 352. Whiston summarily dismissed *The Chronology* as Newton's own curious invention, based partly on "historical Authors; but partly, upon the Poetick Stories of Mythologists laid together by himself; and partly, nay principally, upon fond Notions, Vehement Inclinations, and Hypotheses of his own." Unlike Newton's natural-philosophical work, his chronology is "an Imaginary or Romantick Scheme ... built upon no manner of real foundation whatsoever" (William Whiston, *A Collection of Authentick Records Belonging to the Old and New Testaments* [London: 1728], 962–64; quoted in James E. Force, *William Whiston: Honest Newtonian* [New York: Oxford University Press, 1995], 141). Although interest in historical chronology was already on the wane at the time of publication, Katz calls Newton's work "a minor bombshell" (Katz, *God's Last*, 101). It is probably taking things too far to speak, as Buchwald and Feingold do, of a "war on Newton" in England. If there was a war on Newton, it was surely in France. Newton's chronology was diametrically opposed to those of two of France's brightest lights, René-Joseph Tournemine and Étienne Souciet, and they led the charge against it (Buchwald and Feingold, *Newton*, 317).

140. Jean Hardouin, for instance, "disapproved altogether of geometers and mathematicians invading the precincts of history" (Buchwald and Feingold, *Newton*, 379). In the long run, however, the *philosophes* came to agree with Newton that history could be made "scientific" by means of making it subject to rational inquiry (Peter Gay, *The Enlightenment: An Interpretation; The Science of Freedom* [New York: W. W. Norton & Company, 1969], 378). Many eighteenth-century historians, such as Edward Gibbon, believed that mathematics could play an important role in this rationalization. See F. P. Lock, *The Rhetoric of Numbers in Gibbon's History* (Newark, NJ: University of Delaware Press, 2012).

141. Quoted in Fara, "Newton," 327.

142. Newton's work was part of a larger trend, which is helpfully understood through the study of the semantic shift of the term "*historia.*" In the Renaissance, "*historia*" was an umbrella term that included both natural history and classical history. By the middle of the eighteenth

that "Newton had achieved a level of demonstrative rigor that was probably inimitable in spheres outside natural philosophy."[143] Newton had quietly doubted this possibility as well.[144] But in an optical paper published in the 1682 *Philosophical Transactions*, Newton had speculated that optics could be made "mathematical" and thus provide as much certainty as any other field.[145] And having delivered this promise with flair in his *Opticks*, he boasted in his concluding queries that he expected that natural philosophy "in all its Parts" would be perfected by the successful implementation of his mathematical method and that this method would enlarge "the Bounds of moral Philosophy."[146]

As we shall see in the next chapter, Newton's disciples were captivated by this promissory note. One thing, however, that they were quite unwilling to do was to follow Newton in his quest to transcribe the Old Testament into mathematical syntax. Newton had, in his failure, confirmed that they should direct their attention elsewhere, to texts and subjects which might be potentially mathematized. Newton defended the Old Testament as a text which could help to unveil the providential order of history, but his appeal to mathematical natural-philosophical structures as the basis of providential order ultimately made his appeal to the Old Testament implausible and unnecessary. Newton bequeathed to his disciples his positivistic assumption that authentic knowledge is, if not quantitative, then at least mathematical in the sense of being subject to rational demonstration and consistent with natural philosophy.

If the golden standard of knowledge is physico-mathematics, then classical texts—notably, the Old Testament—will inevitably be regarded as deficient. But the problem with Newton's Old Testament isn't just that it can never measure up. The problem is that Newton's attempt to promote the Old Testament as a catalog of numbers created a text which struggles to edify the

---

century, however, natural history was taken to be part of physics rather than history (Brian Ogilvie, "Natural History, Ethics, and Physico-theology," in *Historia: Empiricism and Erudition in Early Modern Europe*, ed. Gianna Pomata and Nancy Siraisi [Cambridge, MA: MIT Press, 2005], 98).

143. Rob Iliffe, "Philosophy of Science," in *Eighteenth-Century Science*, ed. Roy Porter, vol. 4 of *The Cambridge History of Science* (Cambridge: Cambridge University Press, 2003), 284.

144. Iliffe, *Priest of Nature*, 236.

145. Iliffe, *Priest of Nature*, 126–27.

146. Isaac Newton, *Opticks: Or, a Treatise of the Reflections, Refractions, Inflections and Colours of Light*, 2nd ed. (London: 1718), 381.

reader. If the natural philosopher was bound to be disappointed by Newton's performance, the devout Christian was even more so. Newton's Old Testament offered those seeking to live their lives in conformity with God's governance very little in the way of assistance. The full extent of this failure becomes crystal clear in the work of Samuel Clarke, Newton's closest disciple.

2

—

LEFT FOR DEAD: SAMUEL CLARKE'S OLD TESTAMENT

In 1990 Peter Harrison remarked that "for all of the deists, and for many rationalistic divines as well, the fundamental theological question of the age of reason was how revealed religion was related to natural religion."[1] Recent work on natural theology in the early Enlightenment has confirmed that interest in the relationship between natural and revealed religion was not confined to progressive thinkers. In 2009 Wayne Hudson argued that by the 1730s, the crucial issue for British Christians in general was "whether Christianity was to be understood as a universal law of nature or as a historically positive religion."[2] For leading Anglican divine and philosopher Dr. Samuel Clarke, the answer is clear: Christianity—and, specifically, the reformed Church of England—is the nearest approximation to natural religion that can anywhere be found.

Clarke celebrated this perceived conformity to natural religion because he believed that the principles of natural religion, like mathematical laws of nature, are certain, demonstrable, and immutable. This led him to devalue outward expressions of human religion as the mere husk that conceals the kernel of true religion, principles of natural religion grounded in these universal laws. When Clarke applied this framework to his reading of biblical and ecclesiastical history, he concluded that the religious observances of

---

1. Peter Harrison, *"Religion" and the Religions in the English Enlightenment* (Cambridge: Cambridge University Press, 1990), 164.

2. Wayne Hudson, *Enlightenment and Modernity: The English Deists and Reform* (London: Pickering & Chatto, 2009), 45.

Old Testament Judaism and Roman Catholicism hindered Jews and Catholics from following the true light of nature.[3]

As a mathematician, Newton sifted through human testimony to extract quantitative data, but for Clarke the logician, the term "mathematical" became synonymous with "consistent with reason" or "consistent with natural law."[4] For Clarke, therefore, mathematics became an evaluative tool for all human testimony, even testimony devoid of quantitative data. Doctrines and texts that fail the test of mathematical certainty are rejected as products of human idolatry that are devoid of providential import. The two great failures in this respect are Trinitarian doctrine and Old Testament religion. Having rejected Newton's attempt to mathematize the Old Testament, Clarke creates a dispensational scheme which passes from the establishment of natural religion to its Israelite devolution, to the establishment of revealed religion to its Trinitarian devolution. Within this scheme, the New Testament is celebrated as the revelation of the immutable principles of natural religion, which is monotheistic rather than Trinitarian, but the Old Testament, encumbered as it is by human religious accretions, is given over to devolutionary history, and its status as Christian Scripture is therefore called into question.

ENGLISH SPIRITUALISM AND THE STATUS OF THE OLD TESTAMENT

The status of the Old Testament in England was severely compromised at the beginning of the eighteenth century, and Clarke should be placed at the center of this development. Christopher Hill's *The English Bible and the Seventeenth-Century Revolution* highlights the central role that the Old Testament played in the mid-seventeenth-century ferment, and his analysis suggests that it was the status of the Old Testament, rather than the Bible as a whole, that was diminished by this complicity.[5] For the divines of the

---

3. In the hands of Picart and Bernard, this approach was famously applied to the religious observances of the known religions of the world. See Lynn Hunt, Margaret Jacob, and Wijnand Mijnhardt, *The Book that Changed Europe: Picart & Bernard's Religious Ceremonies of the World* (Cambridge, MA: Belknap, 2010).

4. Clarke's appeal, like that of Descartes, is largely devoid of quantitative analysis, and in this Newton's criticism applies equally to him.

5. Hill argues that the "breaking of the absolute authority of the Bible in all spheres is one of the many triumphs of the human spirit" (Christopher Hill, *The English Bible and the Seventeenth-Century Revolution* [London: Allen Lane, 1993], 436). Hill's analysis, like so many

Restoration settlement, the New Testament was seen to offer an amenable alternative to the theocratic vision of the Old Testament, for it taught, as Hill points out, that Christ's kingdom is not of this world.[6] It was, therefore, a spiritualist vision of Christianity that decidedly favors the New Testament that became entrenched in the Williamite and Hanoverian establishments.[7]

Hill is not the first to draw attention to the growing preference that the English had for the spiritual gospel of the New Testament. His work complements Henning Graf Reventlow's magisterial *The Authority of the Bible and the Rise of the Modern World*, which traces the development of humanistic and spiritualistic impulses in England from the sixteenth to the eighteenth century. In Reventlow's work, these impulses lead to the outright rejection

---

other "Whig" interpretations of early modern thought, overemphasizes the extent of the deist challenge to biblical authority and cannot be sustained in light of the dominant role that the Bible played in practically all aspects of eighteenth-century English life. Hill does make several important observations, however, that confirm that while biblical authority may not have been destroyed by the tumult of mid-century, it was certainly altered by it. One of the most important changes was an increasing refusal to concretize the experience of Old Testament Israel. The English would, of course, affirm their identity as God's chosen people well into the twentieth century. This vision, however, came to be cast in increasingly abstract and spiritualistic terms as the quest to establish theocratic forms receded into the past with the solidification of the Restoration settlement. As visions of theocratic rule gave way to pragmatic compromise, militant millenarianism gave way to pietistic millenarianism. With the hopes of a Congregationalist establishment thwarted, John Bunyan was forced to concede, as he gazed longingly out of his prison window, that the city of God was a celestial city.

6. Hill finds that it was easy for warring parties to appeal to the Old Testament because of its extensive historical record, but he argues that in Restoration England, the spiritualistic vision of the New Testament came to be seen as an amenable substitute. Hill finds, however, that the New Testament was ultimately left behind as well: "Because the Bible could be all things to all men, a book for all seasons, it ultimately lost its usefulness as a guide to political action" (Hill, *The English*, 415). Nevertheless, the preference that eighteenth-century Christians came to have for the New Testament was more than just a turn toward pietism. As Josiah Woodward's *An Account of the Rise and Progress of the Religious Societies in the City of London* (London: 1744) demonstrates, early eighteenth-century London was swept up in the quest to uncover and reinstitute the historic form of apostolic Christianity.

7. The spiritualism referred to here is an interpretation of Christianity that emphasizes personal piety and heavenly salvation rather than bodily religion as expressed in sacramental worship, institutional expression, or societal reform. The spiritualistic vision that characterized the Latitudinarian establishment is starkly presented in Benjamin Hoadly's notorious sermon *The Nature of the Kingdom or Church of Christ: A Sermon Preach'd before the King at the Royal Chapel at St. James's, on Sunday March 31, 1717* (London: 1717). The term "Latitude-men" first appeared in the anonymous tract *A Brief Account of the New Sect of Latitude-men* (Cambridge: 1662). The term was initially applied to the Cambridge Platonists but came to refer to clerics such as Burnet, Stillingfleet, and Tillotson who took charge of the Church of England under William and Mary. Spurr calls the usefulness of the term into question given its referential imprecision (John Spurr, "'Latitudinarianism' and the Restoration Church," *The Historical Journal* 31 [1988]: 61–82).

of the Old Testament by key representatives of what he calls the "late stage" of deism (ca. 1730–1745), Thomas Chubb (1679–1747) and Thomas Morgan (d. 1743).[8] In Reventlow's account, Morgan is the true hero—or villain—and the latter's magnum opus, *The Moral Philosopher* (1737), is the apogee of a tradition. Reventlow argues that Morgan's work

> Represents a landmark in English intellectual history because it denotes the definitive end of the Old Testament in this role. Though large and imaginative books appeared, to defend it against Morgan ... the days when it had normative validity for the contemporary forms of church and state had gone for ever.[9]

For Reventlow, Morgan's outright rejection of the Old Testament builds upon the tradition of ethical rationalism that instrumentalizes knowledge of God as the means to moral virtue, and the direct source of this tradition in Morgan's thought is Clarke.[10]

Reventlow rightly insists that the deist polemic is an important marker in shifting cultural perspectives on biblical authority. But like Hill, he overemphasizes the importance of deism. Reventlow's implicit justification for this emphasis is his belief that, as harbingers of the Enlightenment, the deists were the prophets of modernity. Specifically, he appeals to the now-deconstructed assumption that there was "a heyday of popular deism."[11] Reventlow's conclusion that the deist repudiation of the Old Testament signals an

---

8. Reventlow points out that the Old Testament is excluded from being a legitimate part of the Christian Bible in Chubb's posthumous writings, and he observes that Chubb's approach corresponds to earlier Puritan perspectives in which the Old Testament is seen to promote a Jewish religion antithetical to Christianity: it depicts a violent God, and one that reveals laws and doctrines that contradict common sense. Reventlow wonders whether Chubb's dismissal of the Old Testament can be traced to Morgan's influence (Henning Graf Reventlow, *The Authority of the Bible and the Rise of the Modern World* [Philadelphia: Fortress, 1985], 395).

9. Reventlow, *The Authority*, 395.

10. For Morgan, as for the early deists, the *telos* of both natural and revealed religion is the formation of virtuous men, and this is the basis of his conviction that natural and revealed religion are equivalent. Reventlow points out that Morgan is following Tindal exactly when he defends the New Testament as the best rendering of the religion of nature (Reventlow, *The Authority*, 397).

11. Reventlow, *The Authority*, 355. As Barnett puts it, to view "eighteenth-century Europe through the prism of the deistic *philosophes* is simply to accept uncritically the world as the *philosophes* claimed they saw it" (S. J. Barnett, *The Enlightenment and Religion: The Myths of Modernity* [Manchester: Manchester University Press, 2003], 16). Barnett observes that although historians traditionally assumed that anyone who emphasized natural religion was a deist, there were so

important intellectual and cultural shift at the cusp of modernity is unas-
sailable. The problem is that his genealogy asks those at the margins of intellectual opinion to bear the weight of cultural shift. It is, after all, a little odd
that it falls to Morgan (Reventlow calls him but "little known") to usher in
not merely the modern dismissal of the Old Testament, but modernity itself.
Morgan simply isn't able to carry this load. His work cannot serve as proof
that the days when the Old Testament "had normative validity for contemporary forms of church and state had gone forever." Like most deists, Morgan
was a dissenter and a social outcast, and his polemic was as much directed
toward the fact that the priests held the keys of Scripture as it was an argument against scriptural authority.[12]

Morgan's outright rejection of the Old Testament is important. But it is
important as a beacon that draws our attention to the crisis in the function
of the Old Testament that was taking hold in church and society. Truth be
told, Morgan's polemic is rather unremarkable. From the middle of the seventeenth through to the beginning of the nineteenth century, there were
numerous dissenting voices that challenged the scriptural consensus that
undergirded English religious and political life. Although the most able
polemicists were skillful at brewing up controversy, the majority either
went unnoticed or were roundly defeated. As J. C. D. Clark points out, "the
response of orthodox churchmen was more widespread, more scholarly, and
polemically more effective."[13]

---

few deists that the Anglican clergy often seemed confused about who they were arguing against
(*The Enlightenment*, 19).

12. Morgan was a Presbyterian minister but was expelled from the ministry early on for
his unorthodox views (Peter Harrison, "Thomas Morgan," in *The Oxford Dictionary of National
Biography*, accessed June 30, 2015, http://www.oxforddnb.com.myaccess.library.utoronto.ca/
view/article/19239?docPos=6). In his aggrandizement of Morgan's importance, Reventlow even
goes so far as to suggest that "the scorn which Morgan poured on the theory of the typological
relationship between Old and New Testaments still presented by orthodox theologians can be
evaluated in the history of ideas only as rearguard action. Typology as a hermeneutical method
was already in full retreat" (*The Authority*, 398). The heyday of the use of Old Testament typology as a defense for New Testament revelation was still in the future at the time of Morgan's
work. See David Ney, "Reconciling the Old and New Testaments in the Eighteenth-Century
Debate over Prophecy," in *Change and Transformation: Essays in Anglican History*, ed. Thomas P.
Power (Eugene, OR: Pickwick, 2013), 110–12. For accounts of English deism that highlight the
relationship between deism and dissent, see J. A. I. Champion, *The Pillars of Priestcraft Shaken:
The Church of England and Its Enemies, 1660–1730* (Cambridge: Cambridge University Press, 2014);
Harrison, "Religion," 61–98.

13. J. C. D. Clark, *English Society, 1688–1832: Ideology, Social Structure, and Political Practice*
(Cambridge: Cambridge University Press, 1985), 360.

The point is not so much that Morgan was without influence—indeed his works were devoured by the French *philosophes*—but that tracing his influence is unnecessary because his position was already operative in Clarke's work.[14] Morgan was a devoted follower of Clarke, and his work is significant as a sort of exposé:[15] Clarke stopped short of Morgan's bold declaration that the Old Testament is a useless historical artifact, but the pieces of the puzzle Morgan puts together to construct this argument are all present in Clarke's work.[16]

CLARKE'S IMPORTANCE

A chance encounter with William Whiston in a Norwich coffee house in 1697 was one of the decisive events in Clarke's life.[17] Their conversation concerned the new Newtonian philosophy, and Whiston, the only student

---

14. John Hutchinson decried the downfall of the Old Testament a full thirteen years before Morgan published *The Moral Philosopher*.

15. Reventlow, *The Authority*, 397.

16. These include the disparaging of historical data as subject to corruption, the historicization and dismissal of Mosaic law, and the emphasis on the spiritual and immutable principles of natural religion. It must be added, however, that while Morgan, like Clarke, should be located within the Reformed tradition of Old Testament interpretation, Morgan departs from this tradition through his rejection of not only judicial and ceremonial law but moral law as well (Thomas Morgan published *The Moral Philosopher, in a dialogue between Philalethes a Christian Deist, and Theophanes a Christian Jew* [London: 1737], 400). I will argue that this important difference is minimized by the fact that Clarke degrades the Old Testament to the extent that the moral law contained therein is of questionable value.

17. Clarke went to Gonville and Caius College at the age of sixteen and was assigned to a tutor by the name of Ellis (James Ferguson, *An Eighteenth Century Heretic: Dr. Samuel Clarke* [Kineton, UK: Roundwood, 1976], 7). Ellis gave Clarke his first great project, the task of translating Jacques Rohault's treatise on Cartesian philosophy into Latin. Clarke later expanded the work to the extent that the extensive notes he added to the text in order to refute Descartes played a central role in the early dissemination of Newtonian philosophy. At Cambridge, Clarke studied classics, philosophy, mathematics, and divinity. His proficiency in such a wide array of subjects was unremarkable and indeed was considered essential for anyone with serious scholarly aspirations. But his ability to remain "up to date" with the latest insights in these diverse fields throughout his life stood out even in his own day (Ferguson, *An Eighteenth*, 4). Clarke's protégé Ashley Arthur Sykes boasted that at college, Clarke "excell'd in natural Philosophy, in *Mathematicks*, in *Divinity*, in *Critique* [classical studies], as if he had made but one of them his sole study. Indeed, whatever Science, or whatever branch of Knowledge he applied himself to, he was so great a master of, that had another excell'd in any one of those extensive parts of Literature, in the same degree as he excell'd in every one of them, he would on that sole account of deserved the reputation of a great man" (Ashley Arthur Sykes, "The Elogium of the Late Truly Learned, Reverend and Pious Samuel Clarke," in *Historical Memoirs of the Life and Writings of Dr. Samuel Clarke*, 3rd ed. [London: 1748], 1). As a mature scholar, Clarke made lasting contributions to all four fields; in philosophy: *A Demonstration of the Being and Attributes of God: More Particularly in Answer to Hobbs, Spinoza, and Their Followers* (London: 1705), *A Discourse Concerning the Unchangeable*

known to have attended Newton's early lectures and actually understood them, was astounded at Clarke's profound appropriation of the Newtonian system.[18] Perceiving that Clarke was no ordinary undergraduate, Whiston introduced him to his patron, John Moore, bishop of Norwich (1646–1714). Within a year Clarke was ordained to the priesthood and established as Moore's personal chaplain.[19] In 1706 Moore, eager to find Clarke opportunities equal to his considerable talents, gave him the living of St. Benet Paul's Wharf, the Welsh church of London, and also had Clarke appointed as chaplain in ordinary to Queen Anne (1665–1714).[20] In 1709 Clarke was appointed to St. James Westminster (Picadilly) upon Moore's recommendation, a post Clarke retained for the rest of his life.[21] Among Clarke's parishioners were geologist John Woodward (whom we will encounter in chapter 3) and Newton himself. St. James was no ordinary living. It was, in the words of Clarke's twentieth-century biographer James Ferguson, "one of the most important in London and probably the most fashionable."[22]

As rector of St. James, Clarke was strategically positioned at the center of English ecclesiastical, intellectual, and political life. The living of St. James was highly coveted as the ideal stepping-stone to ecclesiastical preferment.[23]

Obligations of Natural Religion, and the Truth and Certainty of the Christian Revelation (London: 1706), *A Collection of Papers, which Passed Between the Late Learned Mr. Leibnitz and Dr. Clarke* (London: 1717); in the mathematical sciences: a Latin translation of the *Opticks* (Isaac Newton, *Optice: Sive de Reflexionibus, Refractionibus, Inflexionibus & Coloribus Lucis Libri Tres*, ed. Samuel Clarke [London: 1706]); in divinity, several collections of sermons and *The Scripture-Doctrine of the Trinity* (London: 1712); and in classics: a translation of Caesar's *Commentaries* (*C. Julii Caesaris quae extant*, ed. Samuel Clarke [London: 1712]) and the first twelve books of the *Iliad* (*Homeri Illias Graece et Latine* ed. Samuel Clarke, [London: 1729–1732]).

18. Ferguson, *An Eighteenth*, 8; Michael Buckley, *The Origins of Modern Atheism* (New Haven: Yale University Press, 1987), 168.

19. Buckley, *The Origins*, 169.

20. Ferguson, *An Eighteenth*, 35.

21. Ferguson, *An Eighteenth*, 40.

22. See also Gerald Cragg, *Reason and Authority in the Eighteenth Century* (Cambridge: Cambridge University Press, 1964), 34. Cragg calls St. James's Westminster "one of the leading pulpits in England." At the heart of Picadilly, an upscale new subdivision just to the north of Westminster Palace, St. James was the parish of many of the most influential members of the court. The prestige of association with St. James was such that pews had to be purchased, and Clarke had a vestry of twenty-five of London's most notable citizens, including Newton himself, to help with the maintenance of parish life (Ferguson, *An Eighteenth*, 200). Newton also served as governor of the smaller King Street Chapel in Clarke's parish (Ferguson, *An Eighteenth*, 216).

23. The three rectors that preceded Clarke were all elevated to the bishop's bench—two of them to Canterbury. St. James's was consecrated in 1685 and Thomas Tenison, the first rector,

Indeed, even after the publication of his notorious antitrinitarian *The Scripture-Doctrine of the Trinity* (1712) and his trial before Convocation in 1714, Clarke was offered preferment and was reportedly even considered for Canterbury.[24] As late as 1727 Clarke was offered the see of Bangor, and Queen Caroline (1683-1737) sent Prime Minister Walpole (1676-1745) himself to convince Clarke to accept the post.[25] 1727 was also the year in which Newton's lucrative post of Master of the Mint was reserved for Clarke when it was evident that the author of the *Principia* was dying. Clarke, however, submitted to Whiston and Thomas Emlyn's (1663-1741) pleas that he decline the post. He seems to have concluded that his priestly vocation required him to teach the faith of the apostolic church to his parishioners with singular dedication.[26]

Clarke had no mean influence as priest and preacher. The popularity of his sermons in the first half of the eighteenth century was second only to those of Archbishop John Tillotson (1630-1694).[27] Bishop Benjamin Hoadly revered them as classics, claiming that they "must last as long as any language remains to convey them to future times." Samuel Johnson thought they were the best sermons in the land.[28] In addition to his sermons, Clarke's reputation rests on his two sets of Boyle Lectures, which went through twelve editions in the eighteenth century.[29] To many of his contemporaries, the

---

was elevated to the see of Lincoln and then Canterbury; his successor, William Wake, went to Lincoln and Canterbury; Thomas Trimnell was consecrated to Norwich and then Winchester (Ferguson, *An Eighteenth*, 198).

24. Ferguson has no doubt that Clarke would have been elevated to the see of Canterbury had he not espoused heretical views (James Ferguson, *The Philosophy of Dr. Samuel Clarke and Its Critics* [New York: Vantage Press, 1974], 9). Voltaire tells the story that when the queen wished to confer the see of Canterbury on Clarke, bishop "Gibson informed her that Clarke was the wisest and most honest man in her kingdom, but that he lacked one qualification for the position: he was not a Christian!" (Buckley, *The Origins*, 172; Voltaire, "Lettre VII," in *Oeuvres complètes de Voltaire* [Paris: 1879], 22:100-102).

25. Although Clarke ultimately refused, the discussions were said to have extended well into the night. Clarke insisted that he would not accept preferment that required him to sign the Thirty-Nine Articles (Ferguson, *An Eighteenth*, 209).

26. Ferguson, *An Eighteenth*, 158; Maurice Wiles, *Archetypal Heresy: Arianism through the Centuries* (Oxford: Clarendon Press, 1996), 126.

27. A collection of 173 Clarke sermons went through eight editions from 1730 to 1751.

28. William Seward, "Samuel Clarke," in *Anecdotes of Some Distinguished Persons, Chiefly of the Present and Two Preceding Centuries* (London: 1796), 2:335. Seward also claims that Johnson held that Clarke was "the most complete literary character that England ever produced." See also Cragg, *Reason*, 34.

29. Clarke's *Demonstration* was published separately in 1705 and 1706, and his *Discourse* in 1706 and 1708. They were published together in 1711, 1716, 1719, 1725, 1728, 1732, 1738, 1749, 1766,

lectures presented a "final and convincing" refutation of deism.[30] Even deist Matthew Tindal confessed, "I own, the Doctor got immortal Honour by that Discourse; how 'tis admir'd, the seventh Edition shews."[31] Bishop William Warburton (1698–1779) quoted with approval Voltaire's verdict that Clarke was "a reasoning engine."[32]

Clarke also received considerable recognition as a philologist. His Latin translation of Newton's *Opticks* was considered a masterpiece and was decisive in the dissemination of Newtonianism on the continent.[33] An accurate assessment of Clarke's influence must also acknowledge Clarke's importance in the dissemination of antitrinitarianism.[34] His *Scripture-Doctrine* is without question the most important antitrinitarian text ever written in the English

---

and 1767. Hoadly chose not to include Clarke's Boyle Lectures in his edition of Clarke's collected works, perhaps because they were so widely available.

30. Ferguson, *The Philosophy*, 9. Clarke's influence was felt across the Atlantic, but in the nineteenth century, American theology and philosophy intentionally distanced itself from the great Newtonian thinker. See Brooks Holifield, *Theology in America: Christian Thought from the Age of the Puritans to the Civil War* (New Haven: Yale University Press, 2003), 180.

31. As a philosopher, Clarke ranked second in popular opinion only to Locke (Ferguson, *An Eighteenth*, 40–41). For his doctoral defense, he defended the propositions that "No Article of the Christian Faith delivered in the Holy Scripture, is disagreeable to Right Reason" and "Without the Liberty of Humane Actions there can be no Religion" (Benjamin Hoadly, preface to *The Works of Samuel Clarke*, ed. Benjamin Hoadly [London: 1738], 1:vi). It was a performance long remembered as a virtuoso display of the decaying art of formal academic disputation. In the late 1770s the Reverend Henry Yarborough recounted how "he never was so delighted in his life with any academical exercise of that kind" (J. J., "Anecdotes Relative to the Great Dr. Samuel Clarke," *The Gentleman's Magazine: And Historical Chronicle* 53 [1783]: 228).

32. Voltaire praised Clarke as "*le plus clair, le plus méthodique & le plus fort, de tous ceux qui ont parlé de l'être suprême*" and calls Clarke, "*une vraie machine à raisonnements*" (Voltaire, "Platon," in *Oeuvres complètes de Voltaire* [Paris: 1879], 20:229).

33. Bentley, often considered the greatest textual scholar England ever produced, refers to Clarke's philological skill in the highest terms. Bentley went out of his way to secure for Clarke a manuscript of Caesar's commentaries from King's Library (Ferguson, *An Eighteenth*, 21).

34. Clarke's Trinitarian theology is best described as subordinationist. He insists that while the Son can perhaps be called "God" on account of his proximity to the Father, it is probably best not to do so, since he is not God in the same sense that the Father is God. The Son's divinity is derivative from and dependent upon the divinity of the Father. Following Newton, Clarke was intent on preserving the providential dominion of God the Father, and he worried that Nicene Trinitarian doctrine compromised this authority. Sarum observed that "The *Necessary Existence* of *One* only GOD, and the Impossibility of the Existence of More Than One [Clarke] justly esteem'd as the Foundation of All" (Benjamin Sarum, preface to *Sermons on the Following Subjects* [...] *By Samuel Clarke, D. D.* [London: 1743], 1:xxxvii; *The Works*, 1:x). Clarke's quest for the simple and primitive Trinitarian doctrine led him to reject the Nicene definition, and in particular, the notion that God is three persons (*hypostases*) in one being (*ousia*). For further discussion concerning Clarke's views see note 100 below.

language. It had an immediate impact on England's religious landscape and played a decisive role in winning over prominent intellectuals Daniel Whitby (1637–1726), Ashley Arthur Sykes (1684–1756), John Jackson (1686–1763), and probably Hoadly to the antitrinitarian cause. Clarke was also reputed to have won over no less a figure than Queen Caroline herself.[35] For churchmen fearful that the assault on Trinitarian doctrine was about to bring both church and state to ruin, Whiston was seen, in Cragg's words, as "an irritant rather than a menace." Clarke, on the other hand, "was a personal and intellectual force of the first magnitude."[36]

In our day, Clarke's towering influence on intellectual life in the first half of the eighteenth century has been all but forgotten; his sermons lie fallow in the pages of dusty volumes, and the decisive influence of his antitrinitarianism is noted only by historians of Unitarianism. As for his classical scholarship, it is largely unknown even to scholars familiar with Clarke's work. If Clarke is recognized today, it is as a philosopher—specifically as a Newtonian philosopher. And yet, even in this capacity he is often regarded as little more than Newton's minion, undoubtedly because his correspondence with Gottfried Wilhelm Leibniz on Newton's behalf remains his only work that continues to be widely read.[37] Yet as Mills Daniel remarks, "Clarke was at the heart of key scientific, ethical, philosophical theological, and even

---

35. Ferguson, *An Eighteenth*, 220; Domenico Bertoloni Meli, "Caroline, Leibniz, and Clarke," *Journal of the History of Ideas* 66 (1999): 473. Clarke also produced what Duffy calls "the first and most influential" antitrinitarian book of common prayer (Eamon Duffy, "Review of 'An Eighteenth Century Heretic: Dr. Samuel Clarke' by J. P. Ferguson," *The Journal of Ecclesiastical History* 31, no. 3 [1980]: 369). Clarke's liturgy was published anonymously as *The Book of Common Prayer Reformed According to the Plan of the Late Dr. Samuel Clarke* (London: 1774). The British museum has a copy of Clarke's prayerbook; every Trinitarian passage has a violent slash of the pen (William Placher, *The Domestication of Transcendence: How Modern Thinking about God Went Wrong* [Louisville: Westminster John Knox, 1996], 178).

36. Cragg, *Reason*, 34.

37. See Ezio Vailati, *Leibniz & Clarke: A Study of Their Correspondence* (New York: Oxford University Press, 1997); H. G. Alexander, ed., *The Leibniz-Clarke Correspondence* (Manchester: Manchester University Press, 1998); Samuel Clarke and Gotthold Wilhelm Leibniz, *Correspondence*, ed., Roger Ariew (Indianapolis: Hackett, 2000); Edward J. Khamara, *Space, Time, and Theology in the Leibniz-Newton Controversy* (Frankfurt: Ontos, 2006). Wiles hails Clarke as moving "far ahead of Newton and Whiston in philosophical aspects of theology" (*Archetypal*, 110). The conspicuous contemporary neglect of Clarke is startling, but the tide may finally be beginning to turn with the publication of Emily Thomas, *Absolute Time: Rifts in Early Modern British Metaphysics* (Oxford University Press, 2018), and Dafydd Mills Daniel, *Ethical Rationalism and Secularisation in the British Enlightenment: Conscience in the Age of Reason* (Cham, Switzerland: Springer, 2020).

political debates in Britain."[38] That Clarke had, in his own day, a powerful influence upon the theological and philosophical landscape of England is important to my argument. First, his prominence and popularity ensured that his perspective on the Old Testament was widely disseminated. Second, because he operated at the center of English society rather than at the margins, like Morgan, his approach must be taken seriously as operative in the mainstream.

CLARKE ON NATURAL AND REVEALED RELIGION

Shortly after the publication of Newton's *Principia* in 1687, British intellectuals began to attempt to "mathematize" their respective disciplines. Following Newton, scholars sought to achieve mathematical certainty by establishing their work on the foundation of mechanical and quantifiable natural laws. In 1701 George Cheyne (1671/72–1743) published *A New Theory of Continu'd Fevers*, which explained fevers mechanically by arguing for a reductionist chemistry founded on Newtonian physics. Cheyne claimed to have been inspired by the need for a "Principia Medicinae Theoreticae Mathematicae," the way forward having already been shown "by that stupendiously Great Man, Mr. *Newton*," who has provided "the only key, whereby the secrets of Nature are unlock'd."[39] In 1702 Richard Mead (1673–1754) followed suit by publishing *A Mechanical Account of Fevers*. "It may be hoped in a short time," said Mead, "that mathematical learning will be the distinguishing mark of a physician from a quack."[40] Alexander Pitcairne (1652–1713) proposed a mechanical account of the lungs, John Freind (1675–1728) gave a mechanical account of menstruation, and James Keill (1673–1719) proposed a mechanical interpretation of animal secretions.[41] These endeavors were at the cutting edge of what quickly became a European-wide phenomenon: the quest to mathematize all natural processes.[42]

---

38. Mills Daniel, *Ethical Rationalism*, 26.

39. George Cheyne, *A New Theory of Acute and Slow Continu'd Fevers*, 2nd ed. (London: 1702), 27, 24. See also John Henry, introduction to *Newtonianism in Eighteenth-Century Britain* (Asheville, NC: Thoemmes Continuum, 2004), xvii.

40. Richard Mead, "Preface," in *The Medical Works of Richard Mead, M. D.* (London: 1762), x.

41. Arnold Thackray, *Atoms and Powers: An Essay on Newtonian Matter-Theory and the Development of Chemistry* (Cambridge, MA: Harvard University Press, 1970), 70.

42. Thackray, *Atoms*, 83. Newton paved the way for this development when he claimed, in his letter to Oldenberg, that "the science of colours was mathematical, and as certain as any

Natural philosophers weren't the only ones who hoped to make use of mathematics to bring credibility to their work. Theologians and ethicists were equally inspired by the physico-mathematics of Newton's *Principia*. In 1799 John Craig published *Theologiae Christianae Principia Mathematica*, which proved the certainty of biblical events using Newton's method of fluxions. Clarke, Shaftesbury, Maclaurin, Hutcheson, and Bentham all eagerly took up the research proposal of the *Opticks* and hoped to extend Newtonian mathematical certainty to moral philosophy.[43] Far from England, in Italy, the great philologist Vico sought to establish "principles of humanity" akin to Newton's "principles of nature," and Beccaria—who was elated when friends nicknamed him "little Newton"—endeavored to revolutionize the political and especially penal systems of Europe's nations on the basis of Newtonian universal gravitation. "We are all disciples of Newton now," said Voltaire at the end of his life. "We thank him for having alone found and demonstrated the true system of the world, of having alone taught mankind to see the light."[44]

The theistic implications of Newtonianism were widely though not universally considered and were robustly pursued by those who knew Newton's personal apologetic ambitions. Newton's disciple, mathematician Colin Maclaurin (1698–1746), held that the certainty of mathematics was "the surest bulwark against the skeptics."[45] The most famous attempts to mathematize providence were undoubtedly the Boyle Lectures—particularly those of Bentley, Whiston, Clarke, and William Derham (1657–1735). Bentley, Whiston, Clarke, and Derham effectively appealed to the popular opinion that the conclusions of Newtonian physico-mathematics were deductively certain, and

other part of Optics" (Samuel Horsley, ed., *Isaaci Newtoni Opera Quae Estant Omnia* [London: 1782], 4:342). For the influence of Newton's experimental and mathematical method on eighteenth-century science, see Rob Iliffe, "Philosophy of Science," in *Eighteenth-Century Science*, ed. Roy Porter, vol. 4, *The Cambridge History of Science* (Cambridge: Cambridge University Press, 2003), 272–75.

43. Henry, *Newtonianism*, xxv. Maclaurin is largely known for his defense of Newton's method of fluxions. Newton's method of fluxions is his differential calculus. Because Newton didn't publish his method of fluxions, he became embroiled with Leibniz in the famous priority dispute. See Alfred Rupert Hall, *Philosophers at War: The Quarrel Between Newton and Leibniz* (Cambridge: Cambridge University Press, 1980).

44. Voltaire, "Lettre de Voltaire à L'académie Française," in *Oeuvres complètes de Voltaire* (Paris: Firmin Didot, 1870), 2:243.

45. Colin Maclaurin, "Letters," MS 206, University of Aberdeen, Aberdeen, UK.

they all attempted to bind the Christian religion to physico-mathematics to render it immune to criticism.

The task Clarke sets for himself in his first set of Boyle Lectures, *A Demonstration of the Being and Attributes of God*, is to lay the foundation of natural religion, and in his second set, *A Discourse Concerning the Unchangeable Obligations of Natural Religion*, he endeavors to establish the truths of revealed religion upon this foundation. Clarke argues in his *Discourse* that the doctrines and moral duties presented in Scripture demand adherence because they are, at the same time, the "unchangeable obligations of natural religion."[46] According to Clarke, natural religion outlines the essential elements of revealed religion in the form of a "superstructure" within which are placed Christian doctrines.[47] At bottom, natural and revealed religion are one and the same, differing only in terms of precision of articulation.

Clarke claims that "*Mathematical* Reasonings may be applied to *Physical* and *Metaphysical* Subjects."[48] By this he means that the entailment relations of deductive logic secure a certainty in metaphysical subjects that approaches or equals that of physical subjects that rely explicitly upon mathematical deductions.[49] As a Newtonian, Clarke believes that to be mathematical is to be certain, and he boasts throughout both sets of lectures of having secured

---

46. For Clarke, natural and revealed religion occupy the same epistemological space. Clarke believes that natural and revealed religion can be integrated into a comprehensive metaphysics. This corresponds to what Barbour calls the "systematic synthesis" of science and religion (Ian G. Barbour, "Ways of Relating Science and Theology," in *Physics, Philosophy, and Theology: A Common Quest for Understanding*, ed. Robert J. Russell, William R. Stoeger, S. J., and George V. Coyne, S. J. [Vatican City State: Vatican Observatory, 1995], 42–43).

47. Samuel Clarke, preface to *A Discourse Concerning the Unchangeable Obligations of Natural Religion* (London: 1706). Clarke acknowledges that mathematical certainty is difficult to achieve when dealing with moral subjects, but he nevertheless insists that he will manage to get as close to this divine standard as possible (*Discourse*, 17). Clarke claims to distinguish between mathematical and moral considerations, but this distinction clearly breaks down in practice since all true moral principles are bound to the laws of nature and are therefore "mathematical" (*Discourse*, 80). Men are obligated, by means of natural reason, to discern moral obligations in the same way that they can be expected to perceive the truthfulness of the most obvious mathematical propositions (*Discourse*, 203).

48. Samuel Clarke, *A Collection of Papers, Which Passed Between the Late Learned Mr. Leibnitz, and Dr. Clarke* (London: 1717), 73; Benjamin Hoadly, ed., *The Works of Samuel Clarke* (London: 1738), 4:606.

49. Samuel Clarke, preface to *A Demonstration of the Being and Attributes of God: More Particularly in Answer to Hobbs, Spinoza, and their Followers* (London: 1705). For a clear example of this mathematical method, see Clarke's defense of the infinity of God in *A Demonstration*, 70–74.

his conclusions on account of a mathematical method.[50] In his first set of lectures, Clarke employs his mathematical method to establish "a chain of twelve propositions" which secures "the existence, the omnipresence, the omnipotence, the omniscience, and the infinite wisdom and beneficence of the Creator as plainly as Euclid demonstrates the equality of the angles at the base of an isosceles triangle."[51] These truths concerning the being and attributes of God, which Clarke proves in his first set of lectures, are reintroduced as laws of nature in his second set. For Clarke, natural religion is the set of moral duties derived from these laws of nature. Clarke was well-versed in Aristotelian logic, and he insists, according to syllogistic reasoning, that the duties of natural religion presented in his *Discourse* are as certain as the attributes of God he has established in his *Demonstrations*.[52]

Clarke claims that the moral maxims of his *Discourse* are derived from the divine attributes he has established in his *Demonstrations*. But he begins his *Discourse* by praising "the clearness, immutability, and universality of the laws of nature," and it turns out that it is natural law rather than the being and attributes of God that guarantee the certainty of his moral maxims. The divine attributes in his *Demonstrations* and moral obligations in his *Discourse* are derived from a common source: natural law. As natural laws, moral laws follow from what Clarke calls the "fitnesses" of things.[53] Fitnesses are eternal

---

50. In Clarke's *Discourse* he boasts, for example, that his previous work, *Demonstrations*, achieves a "*demonstrative* force of reasoning, and even *Mathematical* certainty" (*Discourse*, 17).

51. Leslie Stephen, *History of English Thought in the Eighteenth Century* (New York: G. P. Putnam's Sons, 1881), 1:121.

52. Clarke's Boyle Lectures play a leading role in Buckley's landmark work *At the Origins of Modern Atheism* because they present a form of Christian theology that is philosophically attractive but devoid of Christian particularity. Buckley highlights the way Clarke's natural theology imitates Newtonian mathematics. Buckley says that Clarke "is not the first to take Newton's natural philosophy and construct a systematic natural theology, but he is probably the best" (*The Origins*, 173).

53. Stoic influences can be readily discerned in Clarke's appeal to the course of nature. Stoic ethical ideals were intended to shape human life "in accordance with necessities that govern the world into which we are all born" (Genevieve Lloyd, *Providence Lost* [Cambridge, MA: Harvard University Press, 2008], 130). Like Newton, Clarke firmly believes that his conclusions are merely the retrieval of truths known to the ancients (*A Demonstration*, 47). Clarke's devolutionary view of history can be clearly perceived in his low opinion of contemporary philosophical authorities (Newton excepted). He has a clear preference for ancient philosophy in general and Plato in particular (*A Demonstration*, 66–67; *Discourse*, 77, 89–90, 98–99, 109, 115, 192, 198–99, 208–9, 213, 216, 221–22, 228, 238, 243–44, 246–47, 255, 274, 293, 299). Clarke acknowledges but minimizes Plato's endorsement of polytheistic worship (*Discourse*, 221–22). Clarke also praises Plato for identifying that divine revelation is a necessary supplement to the light of natural reason (*Discourse*, 243).

and unchangeable relations between given situations and moral obligations, "which have not their origin from arbitrary and positive institutions, but are of eternal necessity in their own nature."[54] Thus the practice of natural religion is the cognitive identification of given relations and the will to act in conformity with them. Clarke describes these relations as both natural and moral laws. For Clarke, the duties of natural religion are obligations imposed upon humans by nature itself.[55] Moral truths such as the golden rule

> Are so notoriously plain and self-evident, that nothing but the extremist ... Stupidity of Mind ... can possibly make any man entertain the least Doubt concerning them. For a Man endued with *Reason*, to deny the Truth of these Things; is the very same Thing ... as if a man that understands *Geometry* ... should ... perversely contend that the *Whole* is not equal to all its *Parts*.[56]

Stephens observes that for Clarke, "The law of nature thus becomes a code of absolutely true and unalterable propositions, strictly analogous to those of pure mathematics."[57] Clarke grabs hold of mathematics to preserve objective moral truth. But in the process, he may well be guilty of assimilating ethics to mathematics.

Ferguson complains that Clarke tends to hypostatize abstractions.[58] This complaint echoes that of Clarke's great antagonist, Daniel Waterland (1683–1740), who maintained that by seeking to establish unalterable rules for moral action, Clarke sets up "some co-eval and extrinsic principle to which God is

---

Clarke includes far more references to Plato and other ancient philosophers in his *Discourse* than his *Demonstrations*. This suggests that Clarke ultimately finds himself in need of an authority to supplement the testimony of nature in his construction of the moral principles.

54. Ferguson, *The Philosophy*, 174.

55. Clarke, *A Discourse*, 3. For a more in-depth treatment of Clarke's ethics, see James Le Rossignol, *The Ethical Philosophy of Samuel Clarke* (Leipzig: 1892).

56. Clarke, *A Discourse*, 31–32.

57. Stephen, *History*, 124. Like Clarke, Locke believes that mathematics is the paragon of certainty, and he speculates that mathematics can help ethical theory become a science that produces authentic knowledge (John Locke, *An Essay Concerning Human Understanding* [London: 1706], 491). Buckley observes that Clarke's method follows from "appearances" to God, and in this Clarke duplicates Newton's method of analysis-synthesis (Buckley, *The Origins*, 90).

58. Ferguson, *The Philosophy*, 211. Many in Clarke's day worried that he was promoting reason over revelation and the individual over the institutional (Daniel, *Ethical Rationalism*, 27).

joined and which he is obliged to follow."[59] John Gill (1675–1742), Waterland's ally, took this argument one step further. "One would be tempted to think," Gill argued, "if all this is true, that this same nature and fitness of things is Deity, and rather deserves the name of God."[60]

In Clarke's day, his insistence that moral laws are given in their established relations with natural laws was praised as much as it was derided. Tindal, for instance, celebrated Clarke's prioritization of natural laws as a sure demonstration that natural and revealed religion are equivalent. Tindal observed that Clarke makes the "law of nature" so perfect "as to take in everything that God requires of Mankind."[61] Tindal therefore argues that, according to Clarke's scheme, true Christianity is "as old as creation" because it is the moral system that urges Christians to conform behavioral patterns to the established order of the natural world.[62] Tindal believed that Clarke successfully established the principles of natural religion upon mathematically demonstrable laws of nature, and he concluded that, in so doing, Clarke demonstrates that revelation is superfluous.[63]

---

59. A refutation of Clarke's moral theory of "fitnesses" can be found in Waterland's "Supplement to the Nature of the Christian Sacraments Considered," in *The Works of Rev. Daniel Waterland* (Oxford: Clarendon, 1823), 5:499–549. See Ferguson, *The Philosophy*, 197.

60. John Gill, *The Moral Nature and Fitness of Things Considered* (London: 1738), 5. One of Clarke's most vocal opponents was William Carroll. In his *Remarks upon Mr. Clarke's Sermons, Preached at St. Paul's against Hobbs, Spinoza, and other Atheists* (London: 1705), Carroll claims that he will demonstrate, first, that "Mr. C. by the Sceptical Hypothesis he imploys, Absolutely cuts off all Possible Means of Knowing the Nature, or of Proving the Existence of the One Only True God, against *Hobbs, Spinoza*, or any other *Atheists* whatever." Second, he claims that he will show that "in Reference to God, or Spirits, he reduces *Humane Understanding*, to the most incurable State of *Scepticism*." Interestingly, Carroll claims, like Clarke, to make use of a mathematical method. He boasts that he will prove these first two points "geometrically." Finally, Carroll proposes to demonstrate that Clarke's "Sermons do rather *Establish* than *Destroy*, do rather *Confirm* than *Confute Spinoza's* Hypothesis."

61. Matthew Tindal, *Christianity as Old as the Creation* (London: 1730), 319.

62. Tindal argues as follows: if there were "from the beginning but one true Religion, which all Men might know was their duty to embrace; and if this is true, I can't well conceive how this character can consist with *Christianity*; without allowing it, at the same time, to be *as old as the Creation*" (*Christianity*, 7–8).

63. Tindal, *Christianity*, 335. Tindal knows that Clarke desperately wants to affirm the necessity of revealed religion. His point, however, is that this stubborn conservatism is inconsistent with Clarke's premises. Tindal finds that, for Clarke, revealed religion cannot possibly add anything to natural religion: "external Revelation can't alter the Nature of Things, and make that to be fit, which is in itself unfit; or make that necessary, which is in itself unnecessary; it can only be a Transcript of the Religion of Nature" (*Christianity*, 334).

Tindal's astute analysis highlights Clarke's dilemma. If revelation is found to be equivalent to natural religion, then revelation is unnecessary. But if revelation contradicts natural religion, then revelation is false. Because natural law functions as an independent standard of adjudication, Clarke is forced to alternate between demeaning natural religion to emphasize the necessity of revelation and praising natural religion to affirm the rationality of revelation.[64] On one hand, he insists "Reason itself, without Any Revelation, was abundantly sufficient to lead men from the wonderful operations of unintelligent and lifeless Matter, to the Knowledge of an Intelligent, Living, and Al-wise Cause,"[65] but on the other, he says that "The Light of nature, and Right Reason, was altogether insufficient to restore true Piety."[66] To be fair to Clarke, however, it must be acknowledged that his position is not without nuance. Clarke does have some means to affirm the necessity of revelation—means afforded him by his Newtonian account of historical devolution.

NATURAL RELIGION, REVEALED RELIGION, AND SCRIPTURE

Like Newton and other "moderns," Clarke celebrates advances in natural philosophy but insists that progress is not possible in matters of religion. "Matters of speculation grow and improve over time," says Clarke, "But Matters of Revelation and divine Testimony are on the contrary complete at first; and the Christian Religion was most perfect at the Beginning."[67] Clarke learned from Newton that the historian's task is to document religious devolution. Clarke's historical narrative takes the form of a dispensational scheme in which natural religion devolves into Israelite religion, and then is revived

---

64. Ferguson finds that "the doctor's scheme is an inconsistent one: at first he adequately demonstrates that the law of nature is all-sufficient, perfect and clear; then all these admissions are retracted" (*An Eighteenth*, 236).

65. Samuel Clarke, *One Hundred and Seventy Three Sermons on Several Subjects and Occasions* (Dublin, 1734), 1:14; *The Works*, 1:14.

66. Samuel Clarke, *A Discourse Concerning the Being and Attributes of God*, 3rd ed. (London: 1711), 228; Tindal, *Christianity*, 376. The difficulties Clarke encounters as he tries to insist upon the correspondence of revealed religion with natural religion, while nevertheless insisting that revealed religion is necessary, can also be seen in Locke's *The Reasonableness of Christianity: As Delivered in the Scriptures*, ed. John Higgins-Biddle (Oxford: Clarendon, 1999).

67. Clarke, *The Scripture-Doctrine*, viii; *The Works*, 4:iii.

through the revelation of Christ, only to be overcome, once again, by Roman Catholic idolatry.

For Clarke, natural religion is the religious component of natural law. As such, it was enshrined in nature before the dawn of history, and its precepts remain unalterable since they are grounded in nature rather than history. Clarke celebrates natural religion as the pristine religion of the first humans, those living in "the state of nature," and he regards this state of nature as the dispensation that extends from Adam to Moses.[68] Clarke describes this dispensation as the condition in which "God made himself known to men by the arguments of reason."[69] Clarke insists that those living in the state of nature had true knowledge of God and that this knowledge was salvific. He also affirms that this knowledge was deficient in order to justify the necessity of further revelation. Indeed, the sufficiency of natural religion turns out to be an entirely hypothetical sufficiency, for the state of nature was actually far from idyllic.

Clarke, in true Latitudinarian fashion, insists that the doctrine of original sin is a monstrous human innovation because it minimizes human moral responsibility and power.[70] The doctrine of the fall, however, continues to play a central role in Clarke's thought as the foundation of his philosophy of

---

68. Clarke's affirmation that the religion of those living in the state of nature was salvific is important to his theodicy. Clarke affirms this sufficiency in opposition to the favorite deist assertion that the claim that revelation is necessary for salvation negates the justice of God. According to Clarke, "They who obeyed the word of God, according to the manner in which it was Then respectively revealed to them, were each of them entitled to the Benefit of the whole salvation; and, notwithstanding their different degrees of Knowledge, are all of them finally to be gathered together into One in Christ; so that He, to whom much is revealed, shall have nothing over; and He, to whom was revealed but little, shall have no lack; when, at the consummation of all things, they shall all meet in one great and general Assembly of the first-born which are written in Heaven; Patriarchs, Prophets, and Apostles; and whosoever have in all Ages, after the pattern of these great Examples, obeyed the Commandment of God as made known to them, whether by the Light of Nature, or by the Law of Moses, or by the Gospel of Christ" (One Hundred, 1:455; The Works, 2:431–32).

69. Clarke appeals to what is surely the favorite verse of eighteenth-century natural theologians, Romans 1:20, to justify this claim (Clarke, One Hundred, 1:485; The Works, 1:461). Although many of Clarke's contemporaries were eagerly reflecting theologically upon the peoples of newly discovered worlds, Clarke is cautious to avoid speculations concerning "primitives," and he confines his reflections upon the state of nature to his dispensational scheme.

70. The defense of human freedom is an important part of Clarke's philosophy. See Clarke, A Demonstration, 178–81; J. H. Gay, "Matter and Freedom in the Thought of Samuel Clarke," Journal of the History of Ideas 24 (1963): 85–105; W. R. Rowe, "Clarke and Leibniz on Divine Perfection and Freedom," Enlightenment and Dissent 16 (1997): 60–82.

history, just as it did for Newton. Following Newton, Clarke says that human history is the story of the gradual encroachment of idolatry upon natural religion. In Clarke's estimation, human idolatry is "the *principal* of all the *Works of the Devil*, and the most immediate and direct opposition to God."[71] Clarke privileges Romans 1:20 as the starting point of his philosophy of history because it shows how humans

> Changed the Truth of God into a Lye, worshipping and serving the Creature instead of the Creator, who is Blessed for ever; Idolatry quickly spread itself into Many Branches; And as Some worshipped the Host of Heaven, the Sun and Moon, and Stars, because of their beauty and Usefulness; so Others, carried away with flattery towards their Kings and Governors, deified and worshipped, and their Deaths, those who in their life-time, for exercising lordship over them, had been stiled Benefactors.[72]

The immediate impact of idolatry upon natural religion was such that Clarke ultimately concedes that only Adam and Eve lived in a pristine state of nature: in this uncorrupted state, right reason was sufficient for the practice of true religion, but after the fall, "there was plainly wanting *a Divine Revelation*, to recover Mankind out of their universally degenerate Estate, into a State suitable to the Excellency of their Nature."[73]

Within Clarke's dispensational scheme, the great historic divide is the divide which separates the history of the Jews from the history of the church,

---

71. John Clarke, ed., *An Exposition of the Church-Catechism by Samuel Clarke* (London: 1729), 24; *The Works*, 3:645.

72. Clarke, *One Hundred*, 1:14; *The Works*, 1:14.

73. Clarke, *Discourse*, 10. Clarke's account of the growth of idolatry is almost identical to that of Newton. Clarke conceives of this process as having taken place in three stages. First, men set up in opposition to God "some imagination of their own, if not as a formal Object of Worship, yet at least as that to which Alone they ascribe all those great Effects, which are indeed the bountiful Gifts of God to Mankind" (*One Hundred*, 1:13; *The Works*, 1:13). Next, they began to worship these objects as false gods, "not indeed totally in exclusion of, but in conjunction with the Worship of the One True God of the Universe" (*One Hundred*, 1:14; *The Works*, 1:14). This initial polytheism obscured the continual worship of God and led to the idolatrous worship of God through "representing him under visible and corporeal images" (*One Hundred*, 1:15; *The Works*, 1:15). Finally, idolatrous worship led to the rejection of God as men began to seek after "other mediators rather than Christ the only true mediator" (*One Hundred*, 1:16; *The Works*, 1:16). For Clarke, the growing force of idolatry in human history is such that it has the potential to overwhelm all religious institutions.

and the religion of the Old Testament from that of the New. In this config-uration, the Old Testament becomes a testament to natural religion, just as the New Testament becomes a tribute to revealed religion. The equivalence of natural religion and revealed religion in Clarke's scheme provides him with the opportunity he needs to affirm the equivalence of the Testaments. The true test of scriptural authority, for Clarke, though, is his treatment of scriptural texts as texts which are able to procure virtue.

For Clarke, the purpose of true religion is to make men more virtuous.[74] He insists that the design of Christ's religion "is to amend and reform the Manners of Men,"[75] and he defends Christianity as the religion best suited to this task. To justify this claim, Clarke has only one perfect standard to appeal to, the only religion that was both instituted by God and free from human corruption: natural religion. He therefore insists that

> The whole *intent* and *office*, the whole *end* and *design*, both of the *Light of Nature*, and of the *Gospel of Christ*; is to teach men to *judge* and *distin-guish* rightly, concerning this great and essential Difference of Things; to show them the *Importance* of acting wisely in this matter; and to warn them of the *Consequences* of whichsoever part they take.[76]

The Christian religion, like natural religion, is a moral system that produces authentic divine worship by promoting good deeds.

Clarke, however, insists that while the end and design of the natural reli-gion and revealed religion are equivalent, they are not equally successful in the accomplishment of the task. Both teach that "that denying Ungodliness and worldly Lusts, we should live soberly, righteously, and godly in this pres-ent world,"[77] but revealed religion brings something new. With the Christian revelation comes "the glorious Appearance of * the Great GOD, and [of] our Saviour *Jesus Christ*."[78] The message of Christ is a "most clear and full discov-ery of the Will of God; *Teaching us*, in a more exact and perfect manner than

74. Ferguson, *An Eighteenth*, 12.
75. Clarke, *One Hundred*, 2:412; *The Works*, 2:203.
76. Clarke, *One Hundred*, 2:50; *The Works*, 2:49.
77. Clarke, *One Hundred*, 2:369; *The Works*, 2:172.
78. Clarke, *The Scripture-Doctrine*, 38; *The Works*, 4:19.

ever."[79] For Clarke, the comparative perspicuity of the revelation of Christ both informs men of their duty and equips them to successfully undertake it.

Throughout his life, Clarke was an ardent defender of New Testament religion. Clarke frequently appeals to the clarity of the moral law as revealed in the obligations of the gospel of Christ.[80] Clarke's first published work, *Three Practical Essays* (1699), is an attempt to present the original simplicity of Christian worship, baptism, confirmation, and Eucharist. Clarke's premise is that the theological and practical disagreements that had long obscured the performance of Christian rites could be set straight by a clear exposition of Christ's ordinances.[81] His second work, *A Paraphrase of the Four Evangelists* (1702), follows a similar line of reasoning. Clarke's impetus for the project was simple: biblical paraphrase brings to light the inherent rationality of the text, and thereby disarms all human resistance to the commands of God.[82]

Throughout his life, Clarke was consistent in his celebration of the clarity of the New Testament. Clarke appears to hold, however, that the paraphrase of New Testament texts is required because, as human documents, they obscure the religion of nature. Clarke suggests that the parts of the New Testament are not equally clear. For Clarke, the clearest part of all is "the Sermons of our Saviour himself in the Gospels," which "are so plain and intelligible, that hardly any well-disposed person *can* misunderstand them."[83] Among the sermons Clarke finds the Sermon on the Mount is supreme because it contains a succinct summary of "the moral and eternal Law of God, explaining the Duty and Obedience we owe to God, and the Love and Charity we must perform to men."[84] And since, for Clarke, all that God requires of humans is to apply divine commands according to the doctrine

79. Clarke, *One Hundred*, 2:277; *The Works*, 2:76.

80. Newman applied the deistic notion that natural religion contains Christian truth in embryonic form to Christianity itself. For Newman, Christian doctrine is fully present in embryonic form in the writings of the apostles but requires the magisterium to bring it to full articulation. See John Henry Newman, "An Unpublished Paper by Cardinal Newman on the Development of Doctrine," *The Journal of Theological Studies* 9, no. 2 (1958): 324–35.

81. Like Whiston and many of his contemporaries, Clarke believes he can extract the apostolic order for church life from the documents of the New Testament (Ferguson, *An Eighteenth*, 10).

82. Paraphrase is a curious genre, as it relies upon the contradictory assumptions that the scriptural text is sufficiently perspicuous to enable paraphrase and sufficiently obscure to require it.

83. Clarke, *One Hundred*, 1:340; *The Works*, 1:322.

84. Clarke, *One Hundred*, 2:519; *The Works*, 2:308.

of "fitnesses," it is tempting to ask why God bothered to give his people more than this sermon. Clarke wanted to defend the entire Bible as authoritative, and he was particularly concerned to prove that the New Testament is the pure revelation of Christ. The logic of his position, however, implies that only a tiny fraction of the New Testament should actually be regarded as such.

Clarke celebrates the Sermon on the Mount as the distillation of the revelation of Christ because he finds it relatively easy to defend the idea that the words it contains are consistent with natural religion and mathematical reason. But as soon as Christ's words are uttered, they become implicated in human history and are given over to devolution. Clarke is able to affirm that Christian revelation is consistent with natural religion and natural law only by extracting it from history. In his own day, Clarke was widely praised as having reconciled Christian revelation with natural religion. The price he paid for this accomplishment, however, was enormous. He was compelled to recast the New Testament as the pure spiritual doctrine of Christ. Having done so, equivalence with this spiritual doctrine became a cypher which could be used to discern the relative authority of biblical texts, most notably those of the Old Testament.

CHURCH HISTORY: THE DEVOLUTION
OF REVEALED RELIGION

For Clarke, the human propensity to idolatry entails that when humans receive the pure spiritual doctrine of Christ, they inevitably complicate, obscure, and corrupt it. Following Newton, Clarke believed that the doctrine of the Trinity is the most evident, the most entrenched, and the most troublesome corruption of the revelation of Christ. Clarke's antitrinitarianism was fueled by his Newtonian devolutionary view of history. For Clarke, as for Newton, ecclesiastical history is the story of the gradual devolution of revealed religion, and the primary form this devolution takes is the gradual corruption of the pristine monotheistic understanding of the Godhead.[85]

---

85. Like Herbert of Cherbury, Clarke has to account for the inconsistency of historically generated religious particulars with the true principles of natural religion. Cherbury is forced to account for the fact that his five basic principles of human religiosity are demonstrably not universal by maintaining that they were consistently obscured by priestcraft and are therefore lost to history (Herbert of Cherbury, *De Veritate*, trans. Meyrick H. Carré [Bristol: University of Bristol, 1937], 23). Locke insists that Cherbury's five notions are not, in fact, universal. See

Although Boyle had initially established his lectureship to prove "the Christian Religion, against notorious infidels, viz. Atheists, Theists, Pagans, Jews, and Mahometans," Clarke—the most popular Boyle lecturer—could only muster that, of all the religions, "only the Christian religion has any just pretense or tolerable appearance of Reason."[86] Clarke believed that the Church of England, like all churches, was subject to corruption, given its location in history. His endorsement of Christianity in general, and the Church of England in particular, is therefore highly qualified: the Church of England is heretical and corrupt, but it is still the clearest representation of the religion of nature on offer. Boyle would surely have rolled over in his grave had he been aware that his lectureship had been given over to antitrinitarians! In Clarke's estimation, however, he was inclined toward antitrinitarianism by his desire to be a good Protestant.

Clarke took for granted the Reformed vision of religion which places human religious expression at odds with pure spiritual worship. With Calvin, religion is seen as "a human response to the reality of God, but since men are corrupt, religion, too, shares in this corruption."[87] Within the Puritan tradition, this idea takes the form of "belligerent, untiring opposition to 'human invention.'"[88] The goal of Puritanism was to "expurgate novelty from English Protestantism" over and against "a persistent Anglican advocacy of invention."[89] In the late seventeenth century, deists took up the Puritan cause against Anglican innovation. Their voices, however, were drowned out by the chorus of Latitudinarian divines who agreed with them about the dangers of innovation. These divines fanned the flames of the entrenched association of Catholicism and idolatry which the Puritans helped to create. At the turn of the eighteenth century, leading Anglicans such as Clarke were able

---

Harrison, "Religion," 70. Harrison, for his part, insists that the problem with Cherbury's thesis is that it isn't falsifiable. When confronted with counterexamples, Cherbury simply retorts that human corruption has obscured his principles (Harrison, "Religion," 71).

86. Clarke, Discourse, 13.

87. Carlos Eire, "True Piety Begets True Confession: Calvin's Attack on Idolatry," in John Calvin & the Church: A Prism of Reform, ed. Timothy George (Louisville: Westminster/John Knox, 1990), 267; War Against the Idols: The Reformation of Worship from Erasmus to Calvin (Cambridge: Cambridge University Press, 1986), 232.

88. Bozeman calls this opposition "a cardinal feature of the Puritan movement in all its phases" (Theodore Dwight Bozeman, To Live Ancient Lives: The Primitivist Dimension in Puritanism [Chapel Hill, NC: University of North Carolina Press, 1988], 51).

89. Bozeman, To Live, 76, 56.

to draw attention away from the reality that Anglican worship was histori-cally conditioned by decrying the "superstitions" of Rome.

Clarke's anti-Catholicism can only be understood with reference to the French Edict of Fontainebleau (1685). The edict was one of the decisive events of the period in English civil life. Over 200,000 evicted Huguenot refugees made their way to England, bringing with them tales of oppression and violence at the hands of Catholic clerics and magistrates.[90] The manner in which Clarke celebrates religious freedom and yet zealously defends the traditional Protestant association of the Church of Rome with the beast of St. John's Apocalypse was characteristic within the Williamite establishment of his day.[91] Within the establishment, appeals for toleration and anti-Cath-olic propaganda were mutually reinforcing principles:[92] Since Catholicism had proved itself inimical to religious freedom, it was argued that tolera-tion would inevitably lead to the suppression of the unparalleled freedoms enjoyed by the English.[93]

Clarke condemns Roman Catholicism because he believes it is the antith-esis of the religion of Christ, which consists "in the Worship and Love and imitation of God, and in universal Charity and Good-Will towards *Men*."[94] According to Clarke, the kingdom of Rome has,

---

90. See Myriam Yardeni, *Le refuge protestant* (Paris: Presses Universitaires de France, 1985).

91. Clarke, *One Hundred*, 2:99; *The Works*, 2:632. Clarke complains that the root of Rome's ailment is that it makes "void the Commandments of God through [the] Traditions of men."

92. Locke insists that those who impose their religion on others have no right to be tolerated (John Marshall, *John Locke, Toleration, and Early Enlightenment Culture* [Cambridge: Cambridge University Press, 2006], 681). Locke's refusal to tolerate English Catholics has been one of the most troubling aspects of Locke's thought for modern commentators. But for Locke and other defenders of the Protestant establishment, Catholic allegiance to a foreign temporal power made Catholics a threat to their religion, their liberty, and their state (Marshall, *John Locke*, 687). Gilbert Burnet was the first to argue along these lines in his *Six Papers* (Marshall, *John Locke*, 686).

93. In a sermon preached before the House of Commons on the day of thanksgiving for Marlborough's victory near Mons (1691), Clarke expresses the hope that God will continue to grant the English victory "till the *Liberties of Europe* be establish'd by a firm and lasting Peace" (Samuel Clarke, *A Sermon Preach'd before the Honourable House of Commons, Church of St. Margaret Westminster* [London: 1709], 25).

94. Clarke, *One Hundred*, 1:100; *The Works*, 2:635. Claydon observes that "The Protestant share of Europe's population shrank from nearly half to around a quarter between 1600 and 1700." Clarke, like his contemporaries, had no problem citing examples of "territories surren-dered, liberties withdrawn, and persecutions launched" (Tony Claydon, "Latitudinarianism and Apocalyptic History in the Worldview of Gilbert Burnet, 1643-1715," *The Historical Journal* 51, no. 3 [2008]: 587). "The fiercest and most violent Persecutors in the Church of *Rome*," claims Clarke, "constantly *profess*, and it is probable Many of them really *believe*, that they are *doing*

By the Establishment of its New Doctrines and practices ... formed a violent Schism ... separating and dividing themselves totally from all Christians, who desire to *hold fast* That *Form of sound words*, that Doctrine which *was once delivered unto the Saints* by Christ and his Apostles, and which is *now* conveyed down to *us* in the Sacred Writings ... In consequence of this *Great Separation*, by which the Church of *Rome* has thus *hedged* itself *in*, and formed itself into a *Sect*, exclusive of and destructive to all such as desire to obey *God rather than Men*; they have in all places, where-ever they have had Power, openly set themselves to destroy and extirpate, by all the Methods of Violence and Cruelty, all who would not *fall down and worship* this *Image which they have set up.* [95]

For Clarke, Christians must ultimately choose between the spiritual religion of the apostles and carnal idolatry, and this decision takes the concrete form of a decision to choose either the reformed Church of England, or popery.[96] Popery obscures revealed religion by overwhelming it with human innovation. Popish rituals equally obscure the law of nature, for superficial rites provoke carnality rather than inward renewal.[97] Furthermore, the Church of Rome also requires people to accept human tradition and human pronouncements as equal to Scripture.[98]

God good *Service*, when they are destroying his Servants with the most inhumane Cruelties" (*One Hundred*, 2:309; *The Works*, 2:105). Although Clarke refuses to tolerate Catholics in England, he does not endorse violence against them. He calls upon those who hold fast to the Reformed religion to continue to act charitably toward them and "convince them of their errors" (*One Hundred*, 1:99; *The Works*, 2:634).

95. Clarke, *One Hundred*, 1:97–98; *The Works*, 2:632–33.

96. In Clarke's mind there are but two options for Christians: the love of God or the love of the world. And for Clarke, popery is love of the world: "yet in all *Popish times principally*, and in all Other *corrupt* Ages ... *Dominion and Pomp and Power*, instead of *Truth and Righteousness and Charity*, have been esteemed as Marks and Characters of Christ's *Holy Catholick Church*" (*One Hundred*, 1:390; *The Works*, 1:370).

97. Samuel Clarke, *The Great Duty of Universal Love and Charity: A Sermon Preached before the Queen* (London: 1708), 2, 4.

98. The belief that Rome is liturgically and doctrinally innovative helped to create the standard Anglican tripartite model for church history, which identified a golden age of the primitive church, an age of decline marked by innovation and superstition, and an age of renewal and reform, which began in the sixteenth century. The canons of 1571 direct the clergy to preach the doctrines of Scripture as explicated by the Catholic fathers and ancient bishops, and the canons of 1603 and 1604 appeal to the judgement of the ancient fathers and the practice of the primitive church. John English points out that Elizabethan divines generally considered

Clarke believed it was appropriate for Christians to endorse the Apostles' Creed because he regarded it as scriptural.[99] For Clarke, the problem with the Nicene definition of the Trinity—as expressed in the Nicene-Constantinopolitan and Athanasian Creeds and endorsed by the Church of England—is that it proceeds beyond the "naked original simplicity" of the gospel and ventures into the realm of speculative, metaphysical reasoning.[100]

---

the golden age to have lasted five or six centuries. English also observes, however, that from the mid-seventeenth century onward, most Anglicans saw the golden age as having lasted a mere three hundred years (John English, "The Duration of the Primitive Church: An Issue for Seventeenth and Eighteenth Century Anglicans," *Anglican and Episcopal History* 73, no. 1 [2004]: 35). English's account of the gradual diminution of the epoch of the pristine church confirms that scholars found it increasingly difficult to protect the church from their belief that the form of history is one of decline. It also comes as no surprise that antitrinitarianism took root in England in the middle of the seventeenth century given that the updated configuration implied that the fall of the church took place around the time of the Council of Nicaea. For an introduction to English antitrinitarianism, see Philip Dixon, *Nice and Hot Disputes: The Doctrine of the Trinity in the Seventeenth Century* (London: T & T Clark, 2003). Dixon rightly interprets the antitrinitarian theology of Whiston and Clarke as an attempt to revive primitive Christianity (*Nice*, 180–89).

99. Clarke, *The Scripture-Doctrine*, ix–xii; *The Works*, 4:ix–xii.

100. Clarke's rejection of the Nicene definition and, specifically, his rejection of the idea that God is three persons (*hypostases*) in one being (*ousia*) follows that of Newton. For an introduction to Newton's antitrinitarianism, see Stephen Snobelen, "Isaac Newton, Heretic: The Strategies of a Nicodemite," *The British Journal for the History of Science* 32, no. 4 (1999): 381–419; "To Discourse of God: Isaac Newton's Heterodox Theology and his Natural Philosophy," in *Science and Dissent in England, 1688–1945*, ed. Paul Wood (Aldershot, UK: Ashgate, 2004), 39–66. Clarke succinctly expresses his rejection of the Nicene definition in anti-metaphysical and subordinationist terms in Propositions XXV, XXVII, and XXXIV of his *Scripture-Doctrine of the Trinity*. Proposition XXXIV reads as follows: "The *Son* whatever his metaphysical Essence or Substance be, and whatever divine Greatness and Dignity is ascribed to him in Scripture; yet in This he is evidently *Subordinate* to the *Father*, that *He derives* his *Being* and Attributes from the *Father*, the *Father* Nothing from *Him*" (*The Scripture-Doctrine*, 304; *The Works*, 4:155). Pfizenmaier has gone to great lengths to defend Clarke's orthodoxy. Pfizenmaier is justified in arguing that the application of the term "Arian" to Clarke is a misnomer since he claimed to be a disciple of the ante-Nicenes rather than Arius and since he affirmed the eternal generation of the Son (Thomas Pfizenmaier, *The Trinitarian Theology of Dr. Samuel Clarke [1675-1729]: Context, Sources, and Controversy* [Leiden: Brill, 1997], 3–4, 119; Clarke, *The Scripture-Doctrine*, 279; *The Works*, 4:141; Samuel Clarke, *A Letter to the Reverend Dr. Wells* [London: 1714], 28; *The Works*, 4:233). Pfizenmaier alternates between affirming the continuity of Clarke's position with that of the ante-Nicenes, on one hand, and Basil of Ancyra and the Homoiousion party, on the other (*The Trinitarian*, 136, 172). This is appropriate since the Homoiousions were, in many respects, the conservative party. Pfizenmaier refuses to acknowledge, however, that the theological positions of all of the parties in the Arian controversy, including the Homoiousions, were marked by doctrinal development for the simple reason that the debate required all those involved to articulate their views with greater precision than was previously required using language that was appropriate to the new controversial context. Moreover, Pfizenmaier believes that because Clarke avoids the extremes of the two other parties in the debate, the Homoion Arians and the Eunomians, he is as good as orthodox. But this completely disregards the decisive importance of the Council of Constantinople. Clarke hated the Constantinopolitan-Nicene definition and, within his post-Constantinopolitan

Like those living in the state of nature, the authors of the Nicene definition abandoned the primitive simplicity of true religion and fell headlong into idolatry.[101] Although Clarke appeals to Athanasius and Basil of Caesarea to justify his own subordinationist Christology, the fathers he appeals to are predominantly Ante-Nicenes.[102] "The *generality* of the Writers *before* the Council of *Nice*," says Clarke, "were in the whole clearly on *my Side*."[103] Clarke, however, concedes that this testimony is not authoritative. In the tradition of Tyndale and Cranmer, Clarke believes that the testimonies of the fathers are only useful inasmuch as they clarify the meaning of Scripture.[104]

---

context, this fact, and this fact alone, renders him unorthodox. Pfizenmaier, sympathetic as he is to Clarke's "primitive" and "anti-metaphysical" articulation of Trintiarian doctrine, never comes to terms with the reality that orthodoxy is historically contingent. Clarke's Trinitarian doctrine might have passed as orthodox in the second century, but Clarke didn't live in the second century. It is appropriate to speak of Clarke as an antitrinitarian because he rejected and fought vigorously against the prevailing Trinitarian orthodoxy, grounded, as it was, in the Nicene definition. Clarke's rejection of the language of substance (*ousia*) also has further implications that Pfizenmaier fails to address. First, Clarke is liable of being regarded as an *Appolinarian* since he insists that the Holy Spirit is, under no circumstances, to be called by the name "God" (Clarke, *The Scripture-Doctrine*, 303; *The Works*, 4:154). Second, Clarke's theology also moves in the direction of tritheism not only because of his emphasis on the distinction of persons but because he rejects the notion of *perichoresis*, the mutual indwelling of divine persons (Clarke, *The Scripture-Doctrine*, 304; *The Works*, 4:155). For a nuanced account of the developing theological positions of the different parties in the Trinitarian debates of the fourth century, see R. P. C. Hanson, *The Search for the Christian Doctrine of God, The Arian Controversy, 318–381* (London: T & T Clarke, 2005).

101. Clarke, *The Scripture-Doctrine*, 454; *The Works*, 4:208. Clarke's attempt to present an interpretation of Christian doctrine devoid of "metaphysical reasonings" is an important plank in his proto-ecumenical platform. Like many other churchmen, Clarke promoted comprehension by attempting to make Church of England doctrine as palatable as possible to dissenters and skeptics. See William Gibson, "Dissenters, Anglicans, and the Glorious Revolution: *The Collection of Cases*," *The Seventeenth Century* 22, no. 1 (2007): 168–84. Clarke states that it is necessary to paraphrase the New Testament "to represent the doctrine of our Saviour in its Original Simplicity, without respect to any Controversies in Religion" (Samuel Clarke, preface to *A Paraphrase on the Four Evangelists*, 4th ed. [London: 1722]; Benjamin Hoadly, ed., preface to *The Works of Samuel Clarke*, vol. 3). Clarke shows a clear awareness that Christian doctrinal controversies were the seeds of the New Pyrrhonism. The great irony, however, is that by forcefully advocating his own version of the Trinity, Clarke merely contributed to the doctrinal confusion that proved so detrimental to the fortunes of Christianity. See Richard H. Popkin, *The History of Scepticism from Savonarola to Bayle* (Oxford: Oxford University Press, 2003), 64–79.

102. Clarke insists that the works of these four writers, in particular, confirm that in the primitive era the term "God" refers to God the Father alone. In his published works, Clarke refers to Origen twenty-four times, Justin twenty-one times, Novatian nine times, and Tertulian six.

103. Clarke, *A Letter to the Reverend*, 28; *The Works*, 4:233. Clarke is right to identify that Ante-Nicene views of the Trinity are often tinged by subordinationism. See Pfizenmaier, *The Trinitarian*, 91.

104. See Ferguson, *An Eighteenth*, 67. On Cranmer's appeal to the fathers, see Jean-Louis Quantin, *The Church of England and Christian Antiquity: The Construction of a Confessional Identity*

In his 1712 work *The Scripture-Doctrine of the Trinity*, Clarke makes his case for his subordinationist Christology by skillfully discrediting all that would place authority in anything but Scripture and demonstrating that this doctrine is transparently taught in Scripture. "Protestants are obliged," says Clarke, "to have recourse to no other Authority whatsoever, but to that of Scripture only."[105] Clarke defends this conclusion by appealing to the "incomparable" John Tillotson, the "learned and judicious" William Wake, and the "excellent" William Chillingworth.[106] Clarke quotes Chillingworth at length and is sure to include Chillingworth's biblicist rationale:[107]

> I see plainly and with mine own eyes, that there are Popes against Popes, Councils against Councils, some Fathers against others, the same Fathers against themselves, a Consent of Fathers of one age against a Consent of Fathers of another age, the Church of one age against the Church of another age.[108]

For Chillingworth, the appeal to tradition is discredited by lack of unanimity. Clarke, for his part, emphasizes that this lack of unanimity is symptomatic of a deeper problem: it confirms that tradition is human rather than divine testimony.

This distinction between human and divine testimony is the basis of Clarke's affirmation that the New Testament is unique among books. In an early work entitled *Some Reflections on that Part of a Book called Amyntor*, Clarke

---

in the 17th Century (Oxford: Oxford University Press, 2009), 24–27.

105. Clarke, *The Scripture-Doctrine*, x; *The Works*, 4:iv. Clarke's biblicism appears peculiar in light of the extremely rationalistic vision of Christianity he endorses in his Boyle Lectures, but it is actually consistent with it. In order to uphold the conviction that the New Testament is the supreme doctrinal authority, he has had to recast it as a storehouse of self-evident philosophical propositions.

106. In the eighteenth century, Chillingworth had become famous for the mantra, which Clarke quotes with approval, "The Bible, I say, the BIBLE only, is the Religion of Protestants." Clarke, *The Scripture-Doctrine*, x–xi; *The Works*, 4:v.

107. Clarke was confident that his Protestant appropriation of the "rule of faith" and his antitrinitarian doctrine were consistent with those of Chillingworth himself. Clarke's private manuscripts contain a copy of a letter from Chillingworth to a friend collated with the original. The letter strongly suggests that Chillingworth, like Clarke, rejected the Nicene definition. William Chillingworth, A letter from Chillingworth to an unknown recipient, Add. MS 7113, no. 3, Cambridge University Library, Cambridge, UK.

108. Clarke, *The Scripture-Doctrine*, xi–xii; *The Works*, 4:v. In the original, the entire passage is written in italics.

defended the apostolic fathers against the deist John Toland.[109] Clarke, however, is measured in his endorsement. He insists that they are palpably inferior to the works of the New Testament and that the authority they possess for
Christians is proportional to this lesser status. "Though the Matter of these
Writings be such, as that they do therefore deserve very great Veneration and
Respect," says Clarke, "yet is there plainly something *humane*, something of
infirmity, something of *fallibility* in them, for which they are with all Reason
thought inferior to the Writings of the Apostles."[110] Clarke insists that the
Church of England is right to affirm the canonicity of the books of the New
Testament as those books written "by the *Apostles themselves* … or which …
were *dictated, reviewed, and approved by them*."[111] And the basis of this apostolic authority, for Clarke, is the authority of God in Christ.

> Whatever our Lord himself taught (Because his Miracles proved
> his divine Authority,) was infallibly *True*, and to Us (in matters of
> Religion) the *Rule* of Truth. Whatever his Apostles preached, (because
> they were inspired by the same Spirit, and proved their Commission
> by the like Testimony of Miracles,) was likewise a Part of the Rule
> of Truth. Whatever the Apostles *writ*, (because they writ under the
> Direction of the same Spirit by which they preached) was in like
> manner a part of the Rule of Truth. Now in the *Books of Scripture* is
> conveyed down to us the Sum of what our Saviour taught, and of what
> the Apostles preached and writ.[112]

Unlike the apostolic fathers, the apostles were guided by the infallible Spirit
of God and were, themselves, mere dictators of the spiritual revelation of
Christ.

---

109. Clarke's work is a refutation of John Toland's *Amyntor: Or, a Defence of Milton's Life*
(London: 1699).

110. Samuel Clarke, *A Letter to Mr. Dodwell* (London: 1718), 273; *The Works*, 3:923. Clarke follows Newton in the way he rejects human authority as subject to corruption. Clarke's devoted
disciple John Jackson confided in him that although he had suffered greatly on account of his
defense of Clarke's *Scripture-Doctrine*, he took solace in the fact that Clarke had always taught
him "to distinguish between humane and divine authority" (John Jackson, A letter to Samuel
Clarke, Add. MS 7113, no. 9, Cambridge University Library, Cambridge, UK).

111. Clarke, *A Letter to Mr. Dodwell*, 274; *The Works*, 3:924.

112. Clarke, *The Scripture-Doctrine*, iv; *The Works*, 3:ii.

Clarke, however, struggles to reconcile his doctrine of apostolic infallibility with the particulars he encounters in apostolic texts. He is ultimately forced to concede, for example, that "in the Epistles of the Apostles, the plain and universally necessary Doctrines, are intermixed indeed with particular and more difficult determinations of certain points of Controversy," and he therefore concludes that the primitive church "used to select out of These, the universally necessary and Fundamental Doctrines, wherein to instruct All persons, who, by believing and being baptized, were desirous to secure to themselves the Promise in the Text, that, by so doing, they should be saved."[113] In other words, although it is possible to extract the marrow of the pure religion of Christ from the Epistles, the elements in the text that are evidently subject to human history must first be discarded. It comes as no surprise, therefore, that Clarke consistently focuses upon the Gospels, and particularly upon Jesus's discourses.[114] These discourses—and especially the Sermon on the Mount—are justifiably celebrated, for they do not bear the scars of history.

As a preacher, Clarke wants to hold up the piety and righteousness of the apostolic church as a beacon of light for Christians who find themselves "in these later and corrupter Ages of the Church," but after having appealed to the purity of the apostolic religion in its "primitive and purest Times," Clarke indicates that the fall of the church must be located at its inception.[115]

---

113. Clarke, *One Hundred*, 340; *The Works*, 1:322.

114. Hoadly points out that Clarke wanted to write paraphrases of all New Testament books. According to Clarke's own principles, however, such an undertaking was unnecessary since he had already paraphrased the Gospels and, even more importantly, the crystallization of the revelation of Christ, the Sermon on the Mount (Hoadly, "Preface," iii; Samuel Clarke, *A Paraphrase upon our Saviour's Sermon on the Mount* [London: 1732]).

115. Clarke, *One Hundred*, 1:415, 2:455; *The Works*, 1:394, 2:246. In his work *History and the Enlightenment*, Hugh Trevor-Roper celebrates the English deists as the heralds of modernity. His fourth chapter, "From Deism to History," doubles as a panegyric to deist Conyers Middleton. Trevor-Roper recounts the story of Middleton's trip to Rome, and he concludes that like other Protestants, Middleton observed that "the distinguishing marks of popery which strike the visitor to the Holy City—the incense, the holy water, the altar lamps, the votive pictures, the images, the processions, and the miracles allegedly wrought by them" had at first been "denounced as 'profane, damnable and impious', 'superstitious, abominable and irreconcilable with Christianity', by the early Christian Church." The history of Christianity thus became for Middleton the story of how "Pagan temples then became Christian churches," and "pagan heroes were quietly turned into Christian saints." The novelty of Middleton's position, according to Trevor-Roper, is that whereas good Anglicans maintained that the church's deviation into idolatry began in the Middle Ages, Middleton believed that "the deviation began at the moment of its establishment." Middleton's position, however, echoes that of both Newton and Clarke (Hugh

Idolatry is the constant enemy of the truth, and it has not been decisively overcome in the New Testament dispensation. Thus, Clarke styles it "the great Enemy to Christianity at the first planting of the Gospel."[116] Even the New Testament itself attests to the devolution of divine revelation in human hands. Thus, when he studies the seven epistles to the churches in Asia, Clarke bemoans that they had already fallen from their first love.[117] Ironically, although Clarke's devolutionary interpretation of ecclesiastical history calls into question the canonicity of much of the New Testament, it is actually central to his New Testament apologetic. It is because the church is inherently fallen that it must cling to Scripture. Clarke goes so far as to define the church's fall as its refusal to do so, and he quotes Matthew Hales (1609–1676) to this end: "the common Disease of Christians from the beginning" was to refuse to "content themselves with that measure of Faith, which God and the Scriptures have expressly afforded us."[118]

Like many churchmen of his day, Clarke sees even the reformed Church of England as standing in desperate need of reformation.[119] Clarke began his literary career with a call for baptismal and liturgical reform, and a revised liturgy that remained incomplete at the time of death was published posthumously.[120] His zeal for the Bible and his antitrinitarian polemics are aspects of a single enterprise—the task of restoring Christianity to its primitive standard. As a reformer, Clarke, like Tindal, hopes to restore "the true primitive, and natural Religion, implanted in Mankind from the Creation."[121] But Clarke's problem is that his great hope is set against the reality that religion

---

Trevor-Roper, *History and Enlightenment* [New Haven: Yale University Press, 2010], 79). Most English Christians regarded the corruption of Christianity as having taken place far earlier than Trevor-Roper suggests.

116. Samuel Clarke, *An Exposition of the Church-Catechism* (London: 1729), 24; *The Works*, 3:645.

117. Clarke, *One Hundred*, 1:415; *The Works*, 1:394.

118. Clarke, *The Scripture-Doctrine*, 474; *The Works*, 4:vi.

119. In the dedicatory epistle to his paraphrase, Clarke endorses his own work as remedial of the fact that "Religion and Virtue … seem to be in great Danger" (*A Paraphrase*, "The Epistle Dedicatory"; *The Works*, 3:"The Epistle Dedicatory"). The fear that the church was in great danger was evidently not restricted to High churchmen.

120. Samuel Clarke, *The Whole Duty of a Christian, Plainly Represented in Three Practical Essays, on Baptism, Confirmation, and Repentance*, 2nd ed. (London: 1704); *The Book of Common Prayer Reformed According to the Plan of the Late Dr. Samuel Clarke* (London: 1774).

121. Tindal, *Christianity*, 379.

is intractably historical.[122] Because Clarke, like Newton, finds that the primitive church was, at its inception, subject to the devolutionary force of history, the primitive religion he appeals to is, like the state of nature, ultimately hypothetical. The Christianity Clarke demonstrates to be deductively true in his Boyle Lectures is a Christianity that cannot be located within human history, for only uncorrupted Christianity accords with reason.[123] Since even the apostles failed to secure the revelation of Christ against historical corruption, Clarke can hardly have expected that he and his antitrinitarian friends would succeed.

THE OLD TESTAMENT: THE DEVOLUTION OF NATURAL RELIGION

Clarke defends the New Testament by emphasizing its spiritual quality, but he still struggles with the fact that much of the New Testament bears the scars of history. This problem is even more acute with respect to the Old Testament than the New. Clarke affirms that the Old Testament can be used to illustrate the principles of natural religion. He equally maintains, however, that, as a testament to the idolatry of ancient Jewish religion, it bears troubling marks of human corruption. Rather than deny this corruption, Clarke chooses to emphasize it to bring into relief the spiritual quality of the revelation of Christ. It is appropriate to speak of Clarke's Old Testament as a sacrificial lamb: it is given over to the vicissitudes of history for the sake of the greater good, Clarke's New Testament apologetic.

Clarke almost always preached from the New Testament.[124] His few extant sermons from the Old Testament maintain that echoes of natural-religious

---

122. Clarke and his disciples saw it as their divine mandate to purify the reformed Church of England from Trinitarian abominations. On February 26, 1715, Jackson wrote to Clarke the following words: "See yt ye Eyes of Ye Clergy begin to be opened" (John Jackson, A letter to Samuel Clarke, 26 February, 1715, Add. MS 7113). When Clarke despaired ever achieving his objective, he fell back upon the remnant theology of the Reformed tradition: "The great Design of God in *all* institutions of religion from the beginning of the World, has been to *separate* to himself, out of the corrupt and degenerate Bulk of Mankind, *a peculiar people, zealous of good works*" (*One Hundred*, 2:274; *The Works*, 2:73).

123. Clarke, *Discourse*, 13–15.

124. A mere 28 of 173 sermons (16 percent) contained in his collected works are on Old Testament texts. See *The Works of Samuel Clarke*, vols. 1 and 2.

principles can still be located within Old Testament texts.[125] The divine attributes Clarke gleans from the Old Testament are those he has already proved in his *Demonstrations*. Thus, for example, Clarke's sermon on Malachi 3:6 provides him the occasion to defend his thesis of divine immutability; his sermon on 1 Kings 8:27, his thesis of divine omnipresence; his two sermons on Psalm 147:5, his thesis of divine omnipotence; and his sermon on Job 37:16, his thesis of divine omniscience.[126] Similarly, the moral maxims Clarke extracts from the Old Testament are principles that have been previously expounded in his *Discourse*.[127]

Clarke's use of the Old Testament is analogous to his use of the extra-canonical Apostolic Fathers. He is free to appeal to the Old Testament, in an ad hoc manner—and he does so to the extent that its testimony is not flagrantly contradicted by reason—but this appeal is discretionary. While the New Testament, at the very least, adds Christian particularity to the monotheism of natural religion, the Old Testament contributes nothing of the sort. It contains merely the tattered vestiges of natural religion. Clarke therefore refers to the Old Testament not as "revelation," but as the "Jewish law" or the "Jewish dispensation."

For Clarke, the significance of the Old and New Testaments is generated by their location within a dispensational scheme which regards Christianity as superseding Judaism.[128] Thus Clarke says in a sermon on Paul's Epistle to

125.   Stephen perceptibly captures the difficulty of Clarke's approach. Stephen asks, "How was a religion, resting upon abstract demonstration, to be fused with a religion resting upon, or at least involving, a certain series of historical beliefs? The records of a particular tribe, or family of nations, may be an insufficient basis for a religion which is to sum up the experience of the whole human race" (*History*, 123).

126.   Clarke, *One Hundred*, 1:39–45; *The Works*, 1:39–45. First Kings 8:27: "behold, the Heaven, and Heaven of Heavens, cannot contain Thee" (Clarke, *One Hundred*, 1:46–52; *The Works*, 1:46–52). Psalm 147:5: "Great is our Lord, and Great is his Power" (Clarke, *One Hundred*, 1:53–65; *The Works*, 1:53–65). Job 37:16: "Of Him that is perfect in Knowledge" (Clarke, *One Hundred*, 1:66–72; *The Works*, 1:66–72).

127.   A good example of this approach is Clarke's sermon on the fear of the Lord, based on Job 23:15 (see Clarke, *One Hundred*, 1:147–51; *The Works*, 1:147–51).

128.   Manuel observes that when, in the eighteenth century, ancient "Judaism was no longer necessary for a rational religion in Europe, the Jews lost their place in the order of things and soon stood as naked aliens in a secular society" (Manuel, *The Broken Staff*, 191). Sutcliffe argues that when philo-Semitism waned, anti-Semitism was the victor. See Adam Sutcliffe, "Judaism and the Politics of Enlightenment," *The American Behavioral Scientist* 49, no. 5 (2006): 702–15. Contemporary scholars distinguish between anti-Judaism and anti-Semitism. See Padraic

the Romans that the letter is "professedly about the casting off the Jews, and the coming in of the Gentiles."[129] Paul's argument is that

> The *Jewish* religion having proved insufficient to make Men truly holy, as natural Religion had before done, there was therefore a necessity of setting up another institution of Religion, which might be more available and effectual to that end. Now the setting up a new institution of Religion, necessarily implying the abolishing of the old, it follows that Christianity was not to be added to *Judaism*, but that *Judaism* was to be changed into Christianity, *i.e.* that the *Jewish* Religion was from thence forward to cease, and the Christian to succeed in its Room.[130]

Clarke's valuation of Jewish religion is pragmatic rather than principled. He rejects it because he finds that it was morally impotent.

For Clarke, the corruption of the Old Testament cannot simply be attributed to problematic transmission history: the Sermon on the Mount offers "Exhortations to a more exalted, spiritual, and perfect manner of performing those Duties, than was before insisted on even by the *true* intent of the Law."[131] The true intent of the law, for Clarke, is that it should promote the same virtues as natural religion and Christian revelation.[132] While Clarke is willing to preach from the Old Testament inasmuch as he finds vestiges of natural religion contained therein, the function that it often plays in Clarke's work is not to illumine the truths of natural religion, but to obscure them. This leads Clarke to refer to the Jewish religion as the antithesis of the Christian revelation. While the old covenant calls for "positive and carnal Ordinances," the new covenant makes plain the "great duties of the moral

O'Hare, *The Enduring Covenant: The Education of Christians and the End of Antisemitism* (Valley Forge, PA: Trinity, 1997), 5–33. This progression from philo-Semitism to anti-Semitism is evident in Clarke's work.

129. Clarke, *One Hundred*, 2:521; *The Works*, 2:310.

130. Clarke, *One Hundred*, 2:523; *The Works*, 2:313.

131. Clarke, *One Hundred*, 2:519; *The Works*, 2:308.

132. In this, one can detect the classic Reformed distinction between the moral, judicial, and ceremonial laws. Like Calvin and the Puritans, Clarke believes that while the judicial and ceremonial laws have been superseded, the moral law remains. Clarke affirms that the Old Testament, inasmuch as it testifies to moral law, gives echoes of the mathematical principles of natural religion.

and eternal law of God, which are absolute and in their own nature most acceptable to God."[133] While the fundamental duty of Jewish religion is the "anxious observance of the burdensome ceremonies of the Mosaick law," the Christian revelation calls for inward and moral obedience.[134] For Clarke,

> The Duties of the Christian Religion are almost wholly moral and Spiritual, respecting the inward Disposition of the Heart and Mind; whereas on the contrary, the Ceremonies of the *Jewish* Law were for the most part external, and, as the Apostle to the *Hebrew* stiles them, carnal ordinances, respecting chiefly the outward purification of the Body; therefore the Apostle calls the Christian Religion *Spirit*, and the Jewish Religion *Flesh*.[135]

For Clarke, the fleshly character of the Jewish law inhibited the Jews from producing the inward spiritual virtues required by natural and revealed religion.

Clarke follows Spencer and Newton by justifying the "carnal ordinances" of the Jewish law as gracious divine acts of accommodation. Clarke tolerates the Jewish law as "an institution of Religion adapted by God in great condescension to the weak apprehensions of that people."[136] But he also rails against false apostles "who in a contentious manner endeavored to oblige *all Christians* to observe the *Ceremonies* of the Law of *Moses*."[137] For Clarke, Judaizers are heretics not merely because the Jewish dispensation has come to an end, but because religions that promote "carnal ordinances" are intractably at war with true religion.[138] Since the law of Moses, like these Judaizers,

---

133. Clarke, *One Hundred*, 1:464; *The Works*, 1:441.

134. Clarke, *One Hundred*, 2:522; *The Works*, 2:311.

135. Clarke, *One Hundred*, 1:522–23; *The Works*, 2:312. See also Clarke, *One Hundred*, 1:558–59; *The Works*, 1:535.

136. Clarke's low opinion of the Jewish dispensation is succinctly expressed in a sermon on Galatians 4:4–5. Clarke paraphrases Galatians 4:3 as follows: being under the law, "We of the *Jewish* dispensation, *were in bondage to the elements of the world*." By this Paul means to say that "the *Jewish* Law was an Institution of Religion adapted by God in great condescension to the weak apprehensions of that people; but when the fullness of time was come, God sent his Son Jesus Christ to institute a more perfect form of Religion, after the settlement of which in the World the former dispensation was to cease" (*One Hundred*, 2:523; *The Works*, 2:313).

137. Clarke, *One Hundred*, 2:252; *The Works*, 2:51.

138. Clarke, *One Hundred*, 2:252; *The Works*, 2:51. "All ceremonial observances," says Clarke, "have no intrinsick Goodness in the nature of the things themselves" (*One Hundred*, 2:174).

promotes "carnal ordinances" which suppress the practice of inward virtue, Moses must equally be regarded as an idolater, and the God of the Jews a promoter of idolatry!

Clarke ultimately is unable to affirm the Old Testament as Christian Scripture. The outworking of his scheme leaves him only with the feeble argument that the Old Testament—the Jewish revelation—plays a positive role for Christians by highlighting the excellency of both natural religion and Christian revelation, which he narrowly defines as "the *Doctrine* of Christ and his Apostles."[139]

Clarke's appraisal of the Old Testament is refracted through the lens of his negative appraisal of Catholicism, but it can equally be said that his supersessionism fuels his hatred of popery. In both cases Clarke appeals to natural religion to strengthen the spiritualist foundation of his religious vision.[140] Natural religion functions as the mathematical standard against which all religious expressions can be adjudicated, and because the revelation of Christ accords perfectly with natural religion, it can equally be used in this way as an adjudicatory standard. Thus, when Clarke turns to the Old Testament and to church history, he finds that the role of Israelite religion is to corrupt natural religion, and the role of Catholicism is to corrupt revealed religion.[141]

THE TRINITY AND THE OLD TESTAMENT

Clarke's *The Scripture-Doctrine of the Trinity* ignited a firestorm, and the controversy confirms that Clarke's devaluation of the Old Testament did not go unnoticed by his contemporaries. The first tract written against Clarke's

---

139. Clarke, *One Hundred*, 1:307; *The Works*, 1:293.

140. Natural religion remains always the same: "Under the several Dispensations of God's true Religion in all Ages and in all Nations from the beginning of the World, either in Obedience to the Light of Nature, with *Enoch* and *Noah* and *Job* and the Patriarches; or under the Law, with *Moses* and the Prophets; or under the Gospel, after the Example of the Apostles and Disciples of our Lord, have in Piety and Devotion, in Righteousness, Equity and Charity, in Holiness and Purity of Life, served God and kept his Commandments, either from the beginning of their Lives or from the time of their Forsaking their Sins by Repentance" (Clarke, *One Hundred*, 1:341; *The Works*, 1:323).

141. For Clarke, the Old Testament stands alongside other pagan histories as a testimony to the corruption of natural religion by human hands. When Clarke reads the Old Testament, he finds exactly what he finds when he reads the classics. We might even say that, for Clarke, the Old Testament has become secular history: like other secular histories of antiquity, it contains vestiges of natural religion, but like other secular histories, its primary function is to prove the principle of religious devolution. Like the classics, the primary positive role it plays, therefore, is to attest to the need for the pure spiritual revelation of Christ.

work was an anonymous work entitled *An Essay towards an impartial account of the Trinity, and the deity of our Saviour, as contained in the Old Testament.* The premise of this work is that while Clarke claims to have presented a comprehensive discussion of the relevant scriptural data, all 1,251 texts he discusses are from the New Testament. The work therefore argues that once the Old Testament is brought into consideration, Clarke's subordination-ist *Scripture-Doctrine* falters. Clarke was uninspired by the argument, and he did not bother to reply either to it or to the other early pamphlets that attacked his work.[142]

When the illustrious Edward Wells (1667–1727), vice-chancellor of Oxford University, entered the fray, however, Clarke was forced to take note. Like Clarke's first opponent, Wells begins his pamphlet by taking Clarke to task for failing to consider the testimony of the Old Testament. Most of Wells's work, however, is a criticism of Clarke's narrow biblicism and particularly his refusal to accept the testimony of the church fathers.[143] Wells may well have detected a lack of respect for historical testimony underlying Clarke's aversion to both the Old Testament and the fathers, but he fails to precisely articulate this view. Clarke responded to Wells by saying that he was greatly surprised that such an able scholar as Wells was unable to muster a more sub-stantial argument against him: "Is this," asks Clarke, "the Arguing of a Man accustomed to Mathematical Studies?"[144] Clarke rebuts Wells's criticism con-cerning the Old Testament by insisting that while the Old Testament contains predictions concerning the coming of the Christian Messiah, it does not con-tain the doctrine of the Trinity, and he boasts that neither Wells nor anyone else can produce a single Old Testament text that does.[145] Indeed, Clarke isn't

---

142. In his letter to Wells, Clarke says that he remained silent for a year and a half because the only responses his work had elicited were completely unintelligible (*A Letter to the Reverend*, 3; *The Works*, 4:225).

143. Ferguson, *An Eighteenth*, 65. Clarke worries that reliance on patristic testimony causes Christians to refuse to think for themselves. Clarke is happy to appeal to the fathers when it suits him, but his biblicism inhibits him from regarding their testimony as authoritative. The authoritative work on the Anglican appeal to antiquity is Quantin, *The Church of England*.

144. Clarke, *A Letter to the Reverend*, 50; *The Works*, 4:242.

145. Clarke, *A Letter to the Reverend*, 7; *The Works*, 4:226. Clarke sees no need to try to under-stand individual passages by considering them in light of the "whole Scope and general Tenour of Scripture," as Wells maintains, for understanding the "whole Scope and general Tenour of Scripture" is simply a matter of understanding the particular meanings of all the particular passages in Scripture. Thus, for Clarke, there is no need to first attend to the Old Testament

even sure why Wells would want to try. Such a testimony is unnecessary for "the New Testament itself is clear enough to give us the sense of the words."[146] In the preface to *The Scripture-Doctrine*, he had boasted that he had "examined thoroughly" the nature of the Trinity "by a serious study of the Whole Scripture," and on this basis he insists there is no need to consult either the church fathers or the prophets.[147] Clarke's rhetoric betrays him: for Clarke, the terms "Scripture" and "New Testament" are synonymous.

Wells responded quickly to Clarke's defiant letter, insisting that "the Doctrin of the Trinity is in several Texts of the O.T. reveal'd in a manner Suitable to the Then Dispensation."[148] James Knight developed Wells's argument in his *The True Scripture Doctrine of the Holy Trinity*. Knight insists that

> The Gospel was contained and published to the *Jews*, under the Vail of the Law: And the Bulk of that People saw not through the Vail, but rested in the Letter and Ceremonies of the Law; yet, notwithstanding this Blindness, the Gospel was there, and consequently the Fundamental Doctrine of the Gospel Dispensation, the Trinity in Unity.[149]

Clarke replied that while Knight could only muster forty Old Testament texts in favor of his feeble definition, he had over three hundred New Testament texts in favor of his.[150] For Clarke, the gold standard of mathe-

---

in order to understand the New (*A Letter to the Reverend*, 67; *The Works*, 4:245). Clarke fails to address the fact that the Old Testament was the primary source that the Ante-Nicenes used in the construction of Trinitarian theology. This reliance upon the Old Testament is most starkly observed, however, in the Nicene controversies themselves, which were dominated by discussions concerning the meaning of Proverbs 8:22–23.

146. Ferguson, *An Eighteenth*, 67.

147. Clarke, *The Scripture-Doctrine*, "Preface"; *The Works*, 4:"Preface."

148. Edward Wells, *A Letter to the Reverend Dr. Clarke* (Oxford: 1713), 3–4.

149. James Knight, *The True Scripture Doctrine of the Most Holy and Undivided Trinity* (London: 1715), 20.

150. Ferguson, *An Eighteenth*, 74. This suggests that Clarke holds not only that the process of constructive theology is simply a matter of finding proof texts, but also that the true theological definition is the definition that lines up with the most proof texts. Clarke is driven to this peculiar conclusion because his epistemology and his hermeneutic make him unable to deal constructively with the diverse voices found within Scripture.

matical certainty generates the surprising conviction that numerical superiority wins the day!

The pamphlet exchange between Wells, Clarke, and Knight confirms that
although the controversy began as an argument concerning the authority
and integrity of the Nicene definition, the Old Testament itself was on trial.
In the early eighteenth-century context, the Christian doctrine of the Trinity
had come to be seen as the most important distinguishing feature of the
Christian religion—and perhaps the only feature which set it apart from
natural religion. For defenders of historic Christianity, to concede to Clarke
that the Old Testament had nothing to add to the construction of Trinitarian
theology was therefore to concede that it was something less than Christian
Scripture. What Clarke's opponents failed to see, however, was that it was
mathematically impossible for Clarke to alter his position. Clarke's exegesis
was bound to an underlying presupposition about the mathematical nature
of truth. Clarke's theory of linguistic signification is helpfully described as
a theory of singular referentiality. For Clarke, each word in any given language must be assigned but one referent. It is thus impossible for a single
word—in this case, the word "God"—to refer to three persons at the same
time.[151] Clarke is convinced that his antitrinitarian position is buttressed by
arithmetic: $1 = 1 / 1 \neq 3$. On this account, his exegetical method places New
Testament words under the microscope and then assigns them either to the
Father, to the Son, or to the Holy Spirit. When Clarke studies the term "God"
in the New Testament, he finds that it almost invariably refers to God the
Father—and on those few occasions when it actually does refer to Jesus Christ,
it refers to him differently, in a derivative and inferior sense. Clarke beams
with confidence that the New Testament, as it now stands, expresses the
doctrine of the early church in mathematical form.

---

151. Clarke, *The Scripture-Doctrine*, 304; *The Works*, 4:155. Clarke's logic is the direct antithesis
of the logic underlying the Nicene definition, which Lonergan describes as follows: "Whatever
propositions are true of the Father are also true of the Son, except that the Father is Father
and not Son and that the Son is Son and not Father" (Bernard Lonergan, *A Second Collection*
[Toronto: University of Toronto Press, 1996], 251). According to the Nicene definition, all three
divine persons are simultaneously at work in every divine action. From this it follows that every
divine person is being referred to, at least in a derivative way, when any one divine person is
mentioned in Scripture. Clarke's insistence that each New Testament word be assigned a single
person is a repudiation of this feature of Nicene orthodoxy.

When Clarke applies his standard of mathematical certainty to the Old Testament, he finds little worth salvaging. But the point isn't so much that the Old Testament has been tried and found wanting. The point is that engaging it has become unnecessary: Clarke doesn't need to look at the Old Testament for Trinitarian proof texts because he already knows he will find only confused and degraded Jewish ramblings that will afford little assistance in his quest for doctrinal perspicuity. Clarke's opponents couldn't possibly expect him to use the Old Testament in his constructive theology since, for Clarke, the Old Testament is a figure of historical devolution, the ancient equivalent of the innovative Trinitarian theology he seeks to overcome. They might just as well have expected Clarke to attend a Roman Mass to uncover the true Eucharistic doctrine instituted by Jesus Christ on the night he was betrayed.

CONCLUSION

In his *Historical Memoirs of the Life of Samuel Clarke*, Whiston challenged the notion that Clarke was a creative scholar. His philosophy was, Whiston maintains, "generally no other than Sir Isaac Newton's Philosophy; tho' frequently applied by Dr. Clarke, with great Sagacity, and to excellent purposes, upon many Occasions."[152] Clarke appropriates Newton's conviction that providence is most clearly seen in the mathematical regularities of natural law, and, like Newton, he therefore aspires to defend the Christian religion by demonstrating the consistency of Scripture with mathematics. With Newton as well as with Clarke, mathematics is a tool that can be used to sift through the wreckage of history to identify vestiges of natural religion. But whereas Newton interprets mathematics and vernaculars as distinct languages, Clarke blurs this distinction. Newton attempts to uphold the Old Testament by digging beneath the surface of linguistic signifiers to uncover mathematical data and thereby salvage texts that have been corrupted by the devolutionary force of history. This is not possible for Clarke. Because he believes vernaculars can have the property of being mathematical, he has no recourse but to devalue propositions and texts that fail this standard.

---

152. William Whiston, *Historical Memoirs of the Life of Dr. Samuel Clarke* (London: 1730), 122. Whiston regarded Clarke as Newton's closest friend (*Historical*, 96).

Clarke's willingness to grant that unquantifiable elements of human discourse can be considered mathematical enables him to bind linguistic statements to mathematical certainties and therefore powerfully defend the elements of revealed religion as consistent with natural religion. Clarke's concept of mathematical reasoning, therefore, is an important development within Newtonian philosophy that enables it to be skillfully employed for apologetic ends. Clarke's application of mathematical reasoning to the Christian religion, however, comes at an enormous cost. To affirm the consistency of Christian and mathematical reasoning, Clarke is forced to deny that the Christian religion is a "historically positive" religion. For Clarke, the Christian religion is the spiritual revelation of Jesus Christ, a religion without history or progeny: in the end, the Jewish religion that precedes it and the Christian tradition that follows it are to be understood not as expressions of true religion but corruptions of it.

Clarke gave his parishioners and his readers little reason to uphold the Old Testament. On occasion Clarke found Old Testament texts that bear only the superficial marks of devolution and could therefore be used to reflect upon the principles of natural religion. On the whole, however, the "carnal ordinances" of the Jewish law suppress the formation of Christian virtue. Clarke categorically rejected the idea that the Old Testament has a constructive role to play in Christian theology.

Given this meager valuation, it comes as no surprise that Wells and his allies believed Clarke had left the Old Testament for dead. Though their controversy with Clarke concerned the Christian doctrine of the Trinity, the question of the status of the Old Testament as Christian Scripture quickly became central to the debate. Clarke's opponents failed to perceive that Clarke's rejection of the Nicene definition and his devaluation of the Old Testament were both rooted in his devolutionary philosophy of history. They were not, however, the only ones to worry that the Newtonians threatened to topple the authority of Christian orthodoxy and Christian Scripture. Nor were they alone in their failure to identify the root of the ailment. John Hutchinson, the noisiest opponent of Newtonianism, was soon to follow suit on both accounts.

3

—

A STOREHOUSE OF HIEROGLYPHS: JOHN HUTCHINSON'S OLD TESTAMENT

In 1724 John Hutchinson published *Moses's Principia*, the first of twelve volumes of physico-theology intended to reassert the authority of the Old Testament over the lives of his countrymen. Robert Spearman (1703–1761) claimed these works made "no inconsiderable noise in the learned world,"[1] and a century later, Edward Churton (1800–1874) was still able to say that Hutchinson was "a man of some note among the philosophers of the eighteenth century."[2] If we are to believe Hutchinson, none other than Samuel Clarke read his second volume and sent a gentleman to him "with high Compliments of the Performance, and Discoveries made in that book."[3] Like

---

1. Robert Spearman, *A Supplement to the Works of John Hutchinson* (London: 1765), i.

2. Edward Churton, ed., *Memoir of Joshua Watson*, 2nd ed. (Oxford: 1861), 39. Churton summarizes Hutchinson's contribution as follows: "He became the founder of a school of theology and philosophy which held that the Divine Author of the universe revealed to mankind at the beginning a system of physical truth, which Moses republished in writing. His writings were voluminous, and dealt much in types and emblems, to which, however, it is impossible to deny the praise of great ingenuity" (*Memoir*, 40).

3. John Hutchinson, *A Treatise of Power Essential and Mechanical* (London: 1732), 309. Spearman claims that Hutchinson's natural-philosophical defense of the Trinity struck "Dr. Samuel Clarke so forcibly, that he sent a gentleman to Mr. Hutchinson, with compliments upon the performance, but that there was one proposition which he hoped was not true, and desired a conference with him about it" (Spearman, *A Supplement*, ix). Hutchinson claims that he refused to meet with Clarke since he "had been too forward in Writing about Subjects he knew nothing of." And if we are to believe Hutchinson, Clarke "lived about a year after, and never rested himself, nor never let me rest about it, till as I am informed, he began about three Months before his Death, to study *Hebrew*, which did not agree with his Constitution; so he had not Time to relent, nor even to know what he had been doing" (Hutchinson, *A Treatise*, 310). Hutchinson also says that he was informed that, like Clarke, Newton saw the second part of *Moses's Principia* before he died and "expressed himself much concerned at the attempt, but did not relent" (Hutchinson,

Clarke, however, Hutchinson's place in the history of eighteenth-century thought has been largely forgotten. If Hutchinson is remembered at all, he is grudgingly acknowledged as the fountainhead of the movement that bears his name or finds his place in the footnotes of Newtonian scholarship as Newton's most peculiar adversary.[4]

Despite his opposition to Newton and Clarke, Hutchinson wholeheartedly agrees with them that divine providence is supremely evident in the mathematical operations of nature because they are not subject to devolutionary history. Hutchinson's Old Testament apologetic therefore attempts to demonstrate that revealed religion accords with natural religion. To this end Hutchinson interprets Hebrew words as emblems that reveal the providential workings of nature. Because he believes that the historical realm is subject to devolution, however, he finds he must remove Hebrew words from their historical contexts and recast them as primordial hieroglyphs. This causes insurmountable problems for his apologetic. First, the extent to which Hutchinson is able to successfully excise the Old Testament from the historical realm is also the extent to which he makes it irrelevant for Christian conduct. Second, because Hutchinson must remove Hebrew words from Scripture and recast them in a different idiom to salvage them, he may actually be guilty of following the Newtonians in casting the Old Testament aside.

HUTCHINSON'S NATURAL PHILOSOPHY

Hutchinson spent most of his adult life in the service of Charles Seymour, Duke of Somerset (1662–1748). Churton relates that Hutchinson "passed many of his early years as the steward of some northern collieries, and seems to

---

A Treatise, 309). Kuhn relates that it "amused the Hutchinsonians to no end that Clarke, supposedly just before he died, began to study Hebrew." Albert Kuhn, "Glory or Gravity: Hutchinson vs. Newton," Journal of the History of Ideas 22, no. 3 (1961): 311.

4. Characteristic in this regard are G. N. Cantor, who offered a brief discussion of Hutchinson's criticisms of Newtonian natural philosophy in a chapter entitled "Anti-Newton," and John Henry, who reprinted the first volume of Moses's Principia in a five-volume series on Newtonianism merely to "represent the opposition to Newton and Newtonianism in Britain." G. N. Cantor, "Anti-Newton," in Let Newton Be! A New Perspective on his Life and Works, ed. John Fauvel et al. (Oxford: Oxford University Press, 1988), 215; John Henry, Newtonianism in Eighteenth-Century Britain: Moses's Principia (Bristol: Thoemmes Continuum, 2004), xxvii. Leighton rightly complains that scholars have tended to focus on the anti-Newtonian character of Hutchinsonianism. C. D. A. Leighton ("Knowledge," 160).

have been led to his first attempts in natural science by observations of things found in the bowels of the earth."[5] In 1700 Hutchinson traveled to London in this capacity to engage a lawsuit "of considerable consequence."[6] He undertook several experimental pursuits in his free time during his first years in London.[7] Like Clarke and other second-generation Newtonians, Hutchinson was captivated by the possibility of rendering human knowledge mathematical. To this end he created a contraption "for the more exact Measuring of Time, both in Motion and at Rest," and he boasted that he had successfully "mathematized" the science of timekeeping. When the guild of London clockmakers refused to grant him a patent, Hutchinson insisted that it was on account of their ignorance of the new mathematical sciences.[8] The lawsuit that ensued was decided in favor of the clockmakers, and Hutchinson was forced to direct his experimental ambitions elsewhere.[9] Hutchinson later boasted that he also managed to earn an audience with the members of the

.5. Churton, *Memoir*, 20.

6. Spearman, *A Supplement*, ii.

7. Some of Hutchinson's notes on his early experiments can be found in the Catcott Collection. John Hutchinson, Early natural-philosophical experiments, Add. MS B 2, 6063, Bristol Central Library, Bristol, UK. Hutchinson boasts that "as soon as I was engaged in this town, several of our philosophers sought my acquaintance ... introduced me into the Royal Society, and there asked me infinite numbers of questions" (Hutchinson, *A Treatise*, 242). Hutchinson also confesses that throughout the course of his many conversations with the members of the Society it became evident that they did not see eye to eye. This, at least, is the story that Hutchinson tells to account for the fact that he was never elected to the Society (*A Treatise*, 239–40). Levine and English both think that Hutchinson knew Newton personally (Joseph Levine, *Dr. Woodward's Shield: History, Science, and Satire in Augustan England* [Berkeley: University of California Press, 1980], 42–43; John English, "John Hutchinson's Critique of Newtonian Heterodoxy," in *Church History: Studies in Christianity and Culture* 58, no. 3 [1999]: 582).

8. John Hutchinson, *Reasons for the Bill, Entitled, a Bill for Securing to Mr. John Hutchinson the Property of a Movement Invented by him* [...] (London: [1712?]).

9. Spearman gives a fascinating account of Hutchinson's struggle to have his timekeeping device acknowledged by the establishment. According to Spearman, it was intended to solve one of the great problems of eighteenth-century experimental science, the longitudinal problem. Spearman claims that in 1712 Newton and "other persons qualified" approved of Hutchinson's contraption, and that Hutchinson "even obtained testimonials under their hands, of the perfection and usefulness of his machine." Nevertheless, when the application was made to Parliament, Hutchinson was wrongfully "dropped by those who had promised to support his pretensions" (Spearman, *A Supplement*, x). A similar account of Whiston's difficulties having his proposed solution to the longitude problem recognized by Newton and Parliament can be found in James E. Force, *William Whiston*, 22. Interestingly, even John Harrison, the country clockmaker who ultimately solved the problem with his invention of the chronometer, struggled to have his invention acknowledged. See Jonathan Siegel, "Law and Longitude," *Tulane Law Review* 84 (2009): 1–66.

Royal Society, but that he declined membership since he would have had to embrace the Newtonian theory of the vacuum, which he believed was laden with atheistic implications.[10]

Hutchinson met John Woodward shortly after his arrival in London and was employed by Somerset and Woodward simultaneously for a number of years.[11] Woodward had been appointed Professor of Physick at Gresham College in 1692. He was elected to the Royal Society on Robert Hooke's recommendation in 1693 and quickly became one of its most powerful figures.[12] Widely recognized as one of the nation's leading antiquarians and geologists, his claim to fame was *An Essay Towards a Natural History of the Earth* (1695), which employed Newtonian universal gravitation to defend the historicity of the Mosaic account of the deluge.[13] As Levine points out, some regarded it as giving "full evidence of the certainty of every single natural proposition that Moses has laid down."[14] Like other early Newtonians, he hoped to extend the

---

10. Such an encounter, if it occurred, took place under Newton's presidency, which lasted from 1703 until 1727. Hutchinson gives a convoluted account of his interactions with the Newtonians in the second half of *A Treatise of Power Essential and Mechanical*.

11. After he settled in London, Hutchinson continued to travel widely to manage the Duke's estates. He also found employment collecting "fossils" (geological specimens) and gathering geological data for Woodward's geological research. Woodward sent Hutchinson to the Welsh highlands in search of confirmation for his theory of the deluge. Hutchinson managed to collect several boxes of materials, including "shells and other curiosities," and sent them back to Woodward. The contents may well have been the specimens they later quarreled over. Hutchinson sent a number of letters to Woodward that document the course of his travels. John Hutchinson, Letters from Hutchinson to Woodward, MSS Gough Wales 8, Bodleian Library, Oxford, UK. Hutchinson relates that while he was abroad, he was "continually making, and successively made new Observations and Collections, and sent the Collections generally by Sea to him, and at my return picked out those Specimens which were most proper for Evidence, digesting them into Classes, (for he did not know one Species from another) numbering them and describing them in my Catalogue" (Hutchinson, *A Treatise*, 241–42). Hutchinson's travels led to the publication of a pamphlet entitled *Observations made by J. H. Mostly in the year 1706* (London: [1710?]).

12. Woodward, Newton, and Clarke would have known each other well not merely because all were prominent members of the Royal Society, but because they were all members of Clarke's parish (Mr. Allen, A Letter from Mr. Allen to John Woodward, 15 December 1725, Add. 7647, 24, Cambridge University Library, Cambridge, UK). Newton and Woodward had a stormy relationship, but Hutchinson claims that they were reconciled in 1713–1714 (Hutchinson, *A Treatise*, 243).

13. Woodward had claimed that the record of geological strata confirmed both the veracity of the Mosaic account of the deluge and the Newtonian theory of gravitation because sediment and fossils could be found in layers that could be classified according to the relative weight of the deposits contained therein, with the lightest objects found in the upper layers of strata (John Woodward, *An Essay towards a Natural History of the Earth*, 3rd ed. [London: 1723], Preface).

14. Levine, *Dr. Woodward's*, 34.

purview of Newtonianism, and he intended to publish a sequel that would divulge "the Structure and Use of the Parts of Animals" and "employ gravity to make those parts move."[15] He promised to show the completed work to Hutchinson, but Hutchinson began to doubt Woodward's sincerity. When Woodward left the room in haste one day, Hutchinson opened the draft Woodward was working on, and "his worst suspicions were confirmed; he found ... only a few heads of chapters and many blank pages" and concluded Woodward was a great pretender.[16] Hutchinson lost all confidence not only in Woodward but also in the Newtonianism Woodward claimed could solve the riddles of nature.[17] Hutchinson's subsequent falling out with Woodward marks the beginning of Hutchinsonianism.[18] Hutchinson took it upon himself to write the natural-philosophical treatise Woodward was unable to deliver: Moses's Principia is both the sequel to Woodward's Essay and its refutation.

Hutchinson's adverse experiences with the clockmaker guild, the Royal Society, and Woodward were episodes in an abortive attempt to earn the acceptance of a natural-philosophical establishment that should be broadly characterized as "Newtonian." Hutchinson's hostility to Newtonianism follows in the wake of this rejection.[19] Woodward played a leading role in provoking this hostility, and it comes as no surprise, therefore, that Hutchinson claims in his Principia that his primary target is Woodward rather than Newton, who was guilty by association.[20] Hutchinson's stated object is not

15. John Hutchinson, Moses's Principia (London: 1724), 38. Hutchinson was later to follow Woodward by attempting to use his corpuscularian ethereal theory to account for all the movements of the human body (John Hutchinson, The Philosophical and Theological Works of the Late Truly Learned John Hutchinson, Vol. 5: An Attempt to Explain the Oeconomy of the Human Frame upon the Principles of the New Philosophy, ed. Robert Spearman and Julius Bate [London: 1749]).

16. Levine, Dr. Woodward's, 97. For Hutchinson's tumultuous relationship with Woodward, see Hutchinson, Moses's, 78–97.

17. Spearman claims that it was a work Woodward "engaged to draw up, but seems never to have had any real intention of doing, only designing to make this a pretence to engage Mr. Hutchinson more earnestly in collecting mineral materials" (Spearman, A Supplement, iv).

18. When Hutchinson and Woodward fell out, the dispute quickly shifted from an argument about the contents of Woodward's folio to a legal dispute about the ownership of the fossils and documented geological observations. Hutchinson ultimately sent a solicitor to Woodward, but the matter was closed upon Woodward's death (Hutchinson, A Treatise, 243–44).

19. See note 10 above.

20. Hutchinson rejected Newtonian natural philosophy as he encountered it in Woodward's work. There are no references to Newton's work in Moses's Principia. It is only in later works that Hutchinson shows any evidence of having read Newton. In his twelve volumes I have found seven references to Newton's Opticks (Hutchinson, A Treatise, 200, 234, 236, 246, 252, 265;

merely to "set aside [Woodward's] pretended discoveries" and ridicule "Gravity and all his Performance," but also to show the world that Woodward "stole and distributed my observations, and intended to rob me of my collection."[21] Hutchinson's natural philosophy is the fruit of his personal dispute with Woodward.[22]

Confident that he had vanquished Woodward ("our Undertaker") with *Moses's Principia*, Hutchinson set his sights on even more illustrious targets: Clarke ("the Reviver") and Newton himself ("our Author").[23] Although it was Woodward who instigated Hutchinson's rejection of the natural-philosophical culture he inhabited, Newton and Clarke became Hutchinson's primary targets in Hutchinson's later works.[24] Hutchinson complains that Newtonian

---

Glory or Gravity, Essential or Mechanical [London: 1733], 93) and four references to his *Principia* (Hutchinson, *A Treatise*, 234, 245, 258, 306).

21. Hutchinson, *A Treatise*, 243. Hutchinson was embittered by the fact that Woodward always "set [him] down in print as his footman" rather than his partner (Hutchinson, *Moses's*, 96).

22. Hutchinson claims that Woodward confessed in private that "we know nothing of the Manner of the Formation of the Antediluvian Earth by Revelation" but the slightest of things. This confirmed for Hutchinson that, despite appearances, Woodward wasn't actually interested in allowing the words of Moses to govern his natural philosophy (Hutchinson, *Moses's*, 96). Hutchinson's disciples affectionately called him the "Mosaic philosopher" (William Jones, *The Memoirs of the Life, Studies, and Writings of the Right Reverend George Horne* [London: 1795], 22).

23. Hutchinson refers to Woodward simply as "our Undertaker" throughout *Moses's Principia* (see pages 74, 75, 77, 79–80, 88, 90, 95–96, 98). Aston assumes the term refers to Newton (Nigel Aston, "From Personality to Party: The Creation and Transmission of Hutchinsonianism, c. 1725–1750," *Studies in the History and Philosophy of Science* 35 [2004]: 628). Hutchinson is more cautious in his treatment of Newton, whose reputation as England's greatest philosopher was beyond question. Hutchinson calls Newton "our Author," "our mathematical Author," or "our philosophical Author" (*A Treatise*, 174, 181, 205, 211, 227, 240, 243–46, 248, 251–53, 256, 259, 265, 270, 272, 279, 282–83, 297, 302, 309). In later volumes Hutchinson refers to Newton by name (John Hutchinson, *Moses's—Sine Principio: Represented by Names, By Types, By Words, By Emblems* [London: 1729], 81; *The Covenant in the Cherubim: So the Hebrew Writings Perfect* [London: 1734], 269, 272; *Glory or Gravity*, 62; *The Religion of Satan, or Antichrist, Delineated* [London: 1736], 115; *The Use of Reason Recovered* [London: 1736], 158; *A Treatise*, 181, 282). Hutchinson's editors evidently added Newton's name to the second edition of *A Treatise of Power* as it is not found in the first edition of the work. Hutchinson calls Clarke "the Reviver" or the "Reviver of Jupiter" because he claims that Clarke's God is none other than the ancient pagan Jupiter (John Hutchinson, *A New Account of the Confusion of Tongues* [London: 1731], 105; *A Treatise*, 251, 253, 258, 261, 272, 275, 282, 296, 303, 309, 311). Hutchinson refers to Clarke by name in *Glory or Gravity, the Mechanical or Second Part* (London: 1749), 62, 90–91; *The Religion*, 115; *The Use*, 25. See also Robert Spearman and Julius Bate, eds., *Abstract from the Works of John Hutchinson* (London: 1753), 165. Hutchinson refers to Woodward more cordially as "my Partner" in *A Treatise of Power*. In this work Hutchinson suggests that Woodward's suspect orthodoxy is confirmed by his association with the notorious deist John Toland (*A Treatise*, 19, 243, 245, 251, 278).

24. Hutchinson's *A Treatise of Power*, for example, explicitly sets out to refute both Newton's natural philosophy and Clarke's Trinitarian theology. Hutchinson may have been convinced that no further controversy with Woodward was necessary since he had decisively refuted him in

natural philosophy is too empirical and not empirical enough;[25] that it is too mechanistic and not mechanistic enough;[26] that it is both pantheistic and materialistic;[27] and, above all, that it is rationalistic rather than scriptural.[28] To establish his peculiar brand of Scripture-philosophy, Hutchinson

---

his first work. Woodward's credibility as a scholar was widely questioned in the last years of his life. Like Whiston, he became a favorite object of Scribblerian invective, mostly on account of his defense of the authenticity of his beloved "Roman" shield. See Levine, *Dr. Woodward's*, 2–4, 114–32, 255–58.

25. Hutchinson complains that the preference Newton and other "moderns" have for empirical data leads them to ignore the Scriptures, and that they have a naïve confidence in their ability to interpret sensory data (*Glory or Gravity*, 3–4). Ironically, Hutchinson's confidence in his own interpretation of sensory data led the editor of his collected works to boast that Hutchinson's "method of judging from appearances, in such a course of experiments, must be acknowledged to be far superior to any of those upon which Sir *Isaac Newton* built his Gravitational System" (Spearman, *A Supplement*, ix).

26. Hutchinson worries that Newton is too mechanistic because he believes that God only exists where matter is present (*A Treatise*, 9; *Moses's Principia*, Part II [London: 1727], 10–11). On the other hand, Hutchinson rejects Newtonian natural philosophy as a failure because it is unable to provide a "real material Cause" to "carry on any Motion or Action in any article" (Hutchinson, *Moses's*, iii). Hutchinson's complaint that Newton makes matter co-equal with God echoes George Berkeley's argument in *De Moto* (1721). In 1751 Berkeley told a friend, "As for Mr. Hutchinson's writings, I am not acquainted with them. I live in a remote corner, where many modern things escape me. Only this I can say, that I have observed that author to be mentioned as an enthusiast, which gave me no prepossession in his favour" (A Letter from George Berkeley to Johnson, July 25, 1751, Letter 377 in *The Correspondence of George Berkeley*, ed. Marc Hight [Cambridge: Cambridge University Press, 2013]). It is likely, nevertheless, that Berkeley did acquire some knowledge of Hutchinson before he died, since he spent his last years in Oxford attending to the education of his son during the heyday of Oxonian Hutchinsonianism, and since his son, George Berkeley Jr., was an intimate friend of George Horne and William Jones and was to become, if not a Hutchinsonian, then certainly a great Hutchinsonian ally.

27. Hutchinson believed that Newton's God constitutes infinite space (*A Treatise*, 148). Hutchinson was not the first to interpret Newtonianism in pantheistic terms. See John Toland, *Letters to Serena* (London: 1704), 234. Leibniz also found Newtonianism to be pantheistic, and Clarke and Leibniz argued endlessly about the meaning and implications of Newton's obscure statement that space constitutes God's "sensorium" (Samuel Clarke and Gotthold Ephraim Leibniz, *Correspondence*, ed. Roger Ariew [Indianapolis: Hackett, 2000], 5n8, 6, 8, 16, 20, 25, 34, 55, 59, 80, 109). Hutchinson equally complained that Newtonianism is materialistic. Because it "claimed powerful invisible properties act in empty space," Newtonianism leaves no room for God's agency in creation (Hutchinson, *Moses's*, 38). See also Patricia Fara, "Marginalized Practices," in *Eighteenth-Century Science*, ed. Roy Porter, vol. 4 of *The Cambridge History of Science* (Cambridge: Cambridge University Press, 2003), 503–6.

28. Hutchinson's greatest fear is that Newtonian natural philosophy puts confidence in human reason rather than biblical authority. Hutchinson complains that "as long as gravity stands, *Moses* cannot be explain'd" (*Moses's*, 98). Hutchinson's criticisms of Newton, even those that appear contradictory, should be taken seriously. Hutchinson was not the only one to oppose Newton on either natural-philosophical or theological grounds. See Scott Mandelbrote, "Eighteenth-Century Reactions to Newton's Anti-Trinitarianism," in *Newton and Newtonianism: New Studies*, ed. James E. Force and Sarah Hutton (Dordrecht: Kluwer Academic, 2004), 93–112. Many of Hutchinson's criticisms echo those of Berkeley, the forcefulness of which only came to

attempted to refute the prevailing natural-philosophical opinions of his day. He focused his attacks upon Newton and Clarke because of their overwhelming influence.[29] For Hutchinson, Newton and his protégé stand at the head of a vast army of apostate natural philosophers who threaten to destroy biblical authority and, indeed, civilization itself.

Contra Clarke, Hutchinson insists that the doctrine of the Trinity is imprinted on the Old Testament text, and, contra Newton, he insists that the heavens bear a Trinitarian rather than monotheistic divine signature. Hutchinson's violent rejection of Newton's theory of universal gravitation is theologically motivated. He worries that it is the foundation of Newtonian antitrinitarianism.[30] Hutchinson attributes to Newton the view that God's dominion is only exercised where he is physically present.[31] Hutchinson is convinced, therefore, that by making gravity ubiquitous, Newton's intent is to make God ubiquitous. And since Newton and Clarke reserve the name "God" for God the Father alone, this means there is literally no place left for the Son or the Holy Spirit to dwell, and they are accordingly consigned to creaturely status.[32] Hutchinson affirms the position he ascribes to Newton

---

be acknowledged in the nineteenth century. See W. G. L. Randles, *The Unmaking of the Medieval Christian Cosmos, 1500–1760: From Solid Heavens to Boundless Aether* (Aldershot, UK: Ashgate, 1999), 132; Michael Buckley, *The Origins of Modern Atheism* (New Haven: Yale University Press, 1987), 118.

29. Hutchinson may well have seen the first edition of Newton's *Principia*, which begins with a Horatian ode by Edmund Halley. It is replete with pagan allusions and boasts that "Newton is better than Moses" (Stephen Snobelen, "The Theology of Isaac Newton's Principia Mathematica: A Preliminary Survey," *Neue Zeitschrift für Systematische Theologie und Religionsphilosophie* 52, no. 4 [2010]: 386). The ode claims that natural-philosophical wisdom is superior to historically conditioned wisdom, and indeed, that natural philosophy allows human beings to transcend the decrepitude of human existence (Edmund Halley, "Ode to Newton," *The Principia: Mathematical Principles of Natural Philosophy*, trans. Bernard Cohen and Anne Whitman [Berkeley: University of California Press, 1999], 380).

30. Hutchinson, *A Treatise*, 154–61. For a discussion of the extent to which Newton's heterodox leanings were known to the public, see Larry Stewart, "Seeing Through the Scholium: Religion and Reading Newton in the Eighteenth Century," *History of Science* 34, no. 2 (1996): 123–65; Mandelbrote, "Eighteenth-Century Reactions to Newton's Anti-Trinitarianism," in *Newton and Newtonianism: New Studies*, ed. James E. Force and Sarah Hutton (Dordrecht: Kluwer Academic, 2004), 93–111.

31. In Grant's words, Newton "made God's literal omnipresence the foundation of his physics, the basis for the maintenance of its mathematical laws and therefore of lawful cosmic operation" (Edward Grant, *Much Ado About Nothing: Theories of Space and Vacuum from the Middle Ages to the Scientific Revolution* [Cambridge: Cambridge University Press, 1981], 254).

32. Hutchinson argues that Newton "could not avoid the Trinity, without making one person infinitely extended, so that there could be Room for no more Persons but one" and that "our Author has made [God] no right Hand nor no left Hand; for by making his Substance infinitely

inasmuch as he holds that, "'tis necessary, that the mental Powers, and Powers of Action in a ruling Substance, should be extended as far as that Substance has Occasion to rule."[33] But whereas Newton endorses a monotheistic omnipresence, Hutchinson insists that God makes himself present in creation as Father, Son, and Holy Spirit by taking the form of fire, light, and wind.[34] For Hutchinson, fire, light, and wind are merely different conditions of an ubiquitous cosmic ether called "the Names," or "the *Elohim*," that is responsible for all of the motion in the cosmos.[35] This ether is simultaneously mechanical and spiritual. It is made of small corpuscles that penetrate the pores of particles of gross, inert matter, and it carries the active and activating presence of the Triune God. As such, it is the agent through which the Triune God governs his creation.[36]

Hutchinson's ethereal theory was designed to replace Newton's theory of universal gravitation, but Hutchinson's rhetoric must not be taken at face value. The many points of contact between Newton and Hutchinson's

---

extended, he has left no Room for him, to place Matter, Creatures, Hell or Devils out of his Substance" (*A Treatise*, 179, 181).

33. Hutchinson, *A Treatise*, 158; Hutchinson insists that the essence of God must constitute infinite space (*A Treatise*, 163). See also Hutchinson, *Moses's Principia, Part II*, 37–39.

34. Wilde summarizes Hutchinson's ethereal theory as follows: "Fire at the Sun, by its great agitation, puts the surrounding ether into the action of light which radiates outward, gradually losing its motion until it 'congeals' into spirit or air at the circumference of this system" (C. B. Wilde, "Hutchinsonianism, Natural Philosophy and Religious Controversy in Eighteenth Century Britain," *History of Science* 18 [1980]: 4). A contemporary summary of Hutchinson's ethereal theory can be found in Spearman, *A Supplement*, vii–ix.

35. Hutchinson, *Glory or Gravity*, 22–23. Hutchinson's most comprehensive defense of the Trinity is found in *A Treatise on Power*. In this work, Hutchinson makes use of natural philosophy to defend the Trinity in the same manner he employs it throughout his work to defend the Old Testament. His ethereal theory confirms the veracity of the Nicene definition because it is a single substance found throughout the cosmos that exists in three aspects (*A Treatise*, 315). One eighteenth-century thinker who was heavily influenced by Hutchinson's ethereal theory was William Blake. See Ted Holt, "Blake's 'Elohim' and the Hutchinsonian Fire: Anti-Newtonianism and Christian Hebraism in the Work of William Blake," *Romanticism: The Journal of Romantic Culture and Criticism* 9 (2003): 20–36.

36. Hutchinson wants to distinguish his Trinitarian ether from God's very presence, but he insists that the ether is God's chosen means of dispersing his presence and exercising his governance throughout his creation. Hutchinson associates each person of the Trinity with a different form of corpuscularian ether because he believes the biblical witness compels him to do so: the Bible describes the Holy Spirit as "breath" or "air," the Son as "light," and the Father as the "Sun." For Hutchinson, the progression of the Trinitarian ether from Sun to light to air is an emblem of the eternal generation of the Son and the Spirit by the Father. This theory, however, struggles to avoid modalism, since the corpuscles of the Sun, light, and air do not inhere one another.

ethereal theories are grounded in their common and unquestioned belief in "the existence of an all-pervasive material medium, which serves as an agent of change in the natural world."[37] In his "Hypothesis," Newton had speculated that human movement was made possible by the ability of the soul to exert "an immediate power over the whole aether in any part of the body to Swell or Shrink it at will," and Woodward's unfinished project was clearly intended to actualize Newton's proposal.[38] While Hutchinson's natural philosophy was primarily concerned with cosmology rather than medicine, he was clearly building upon the assumption he shared with Newton and Woodward that matter is inert unless it is acted upon by spirit by means of its engagement with ethereal particles.

Although Newton had speculated, at various points, that universal gravitation was the result of God's direct engagement with an all-pervasive ether, Hutchinson understood Newton's theory to be bound to the idea that matter has the ability to magically move itself. Hutchinson believes his theory is superior to Newton's "occult" theory because it delivers a thoroughgoing mechanistic account of the movement of all physical bodies, whether cosmic or terrestrial, and that it therefore proves that the cosmos is a finely tuned perpetual motion machine.[39] On this account his ethereal theory may appear to leave no room for God's active governance of his creation. Hutchinson,

---

37. See B. J. T. Dobbs, *The Janus Faces of Genius: The Role of Alchemy in Newton's Thought* (Cambridge: Cambridge University Press, 2002), 20. Dobbs's groundbreaking work *The Janus Faces of Genius* offers a fascinating account of the various causal interpretations of gravity that Newton wrestled with throughout his life. Dobbs concludes that Newton was unhappy with his life's work because he had not found the vegetative principle or the cause of gravity, but she relates that in his later years he came to believe that there was a link between light and electricity, that the electrical ether was a source of particulate activity, and that Christ's mediation ensures the uniform gravitational motions of the heavenly bodies (Dobbs, *The Janus*, 247–48). Ethereal theories built upon corpuscularian motion and transmutation were common and were developed in conversation with ancient Stoic texts. The Stoics, as Dobbs points out, had "postulated a continuous material medium, the tension and activity of which molded the cosmos into a living whole and the various parts of the cosmic animals into coherent bodies as well. Composed of air and a creative fire, this Stoic *pneuma* was fused with the concept of the "breath of life" (Dobbs, *The Janus*, 27). Other contemporary theorists who endorsed corpuscularian ethereal theories include Boerhaave and Berkeley. See G. N. Cantor, *Optics after Newton: Theories of Light in Britain and Ireland, 1704–1840* (Manchester: Manchester University Press, 1983), 91–98.

38. Rob Iliffe, *Priest of Nature* (Oxford: Oxford University Press, 2017), 118.

39. Hutchinson, *Moses's*, 20. The desire to describe the laws of nature in mechanistic terms had been gaining momentum since the beginning of the Renaissance. Collingwood therefore calls the mechanistic view of nature "the Renaissance view," despite the fact that its apogee was the eighteenth century. Collingwood distinguishes this Renaissance view from the ancient

however, convinced his followers that his theory, rather than Newton's, proved the existence of a generally provident God. Hutchinson's disciples were convinced that he had extended God's dominion to the far reaches of the universe by demonstrating that all motion must be attributed to God alone since the mechanical ether which God inhabits as Trinity and through which he actively directs his creation is, like all matter, passive.[40]

Perhaps even more remarkable than Hutchinson's ability to present himself as the great defender of general providence was his ability to present himself as the era's most able defender of the Bible. Like his opponents, Hutchinson's belief that epistemological certainty can only be derived from nature leaves little room for competing authorities. And yet, Hutchinson's greatest legacy was not his natural philosophy but his Old Testament apologetic. Hutchinson claims to achieve what Clarke thought was impossible: the use of the Old Testament to render certain knowledge.[41] Like Newton, Hutchinson believed that the only sure way to defend the Old Testament is to bind it to natural philosophy, because this enables the mathematical certainty derived from the Book of Nature to be transferred to the Book of Scripture. The primary mechanism Hutchinson employs to this end, however, is not numerical data. He looks instead to the emblem.

THE COVENANT IN THE CHERUBIM

In 1522 Andrea Alciato (1492-1550) wrote to a friend to announce the creation of a new genre of literary composition, and in 1531 he published his first and most popular book of emblems, known as *Emblemata*.[42] Alciato's composition

---

vitalist and modern evolutionary perspectives. See R. J. Collingwood, *The Idea of Nature* (Oxford: Clarendon Press, 1945).

40. Many scholars in Hutchinson's day believed it was necessary to prove that matter was passive to leave room for God's governance of his creation, including George Berkeley. In the seventeenth century, van Helmont had argued that it is impossible for physical objects to have a direct effect on one another. Van Helmont's notion that the activity of material bodies can be attributed to nonmaterial forces bears close resemblance to Hutchinson's notion that all motion can be attributed to a cosmic ether (Allison Coudert, *The Impact of the Kabbalah in the Seventeenth Century: The Life and Thought of Francis Mercury van Helmont [1614-1698]* [Leiden: Brill, 1999], 9).

41. Hutchinson's opponent Thomas Sharp (1693-1758) complained that "no mere man, but himself, ever pretended to absolute certainty in all his explanations of Moses" (Thomas Sharp, *Mr. Hutchinson's Exposition of Cherubim* [London: 1755], 3). Thomas, prebend of Durham Cathedral, was the father of famous evangelical abolitionist Granville Sharp.

42. "Rarely," writes Manning, "can the birth date of a genre be established so precisely, and its 'father' so clearly identified, than in the case of the emblem" (John Manning, *The Emblem*

spawned a new discipline known as emblematicism, which quickly became one of the dominant literary traditions of the Renaissance.[43] The book was an instant success and went through hundreds of editions. It inspired thousands of imitations across all major European languages. The feature of Alciato's work that authors found most attractive was his threefold composition of *picture, motto* (or lemma), and *epigram* (explanatory text).[44] Underlying this structure is the notion that the motto is necessary for the proper interpretation of the picture in question, and this proper interpretation is articulated in the epigram. Emblematicism, therefore, is built upon the conviction that the right interpretation of the world requires words.

Hutchinson's interpreters have largely failed to identify the central importance of emblematicism in his work, perhaps in part because they have taken *Moses's Principia* to be at the center of the Hutchinsonian corpus. In actual fact Hutchinson reserves this place for his 1734 work *The Covenant in the Cherubim: So the Hebrew Writings Perfect*. Hutchinson begins the work by boasting, "I have shewed many great things apart; I must now shew their Concurrence or Connection, their Dependence upon each other."[45] In Hutchinson's eyes, his own philosophical system is encapsulated by the title of the work: "The Covenant Is in the Cherubim So the Hebrew Writings Perfect." This idea is developed in the sprawling text that comprises the rest of the work. It is also encapsulated in a single picture, which Hutchinson asked the printers to include at the beginning of the work.

The Covenant in the Cherubim: So the Hebrew Writings Perfect conforms to the traditional threefold emblematic structure of picture, motto, and epigram. It is impossible to see the picture that stands at the head of the work

---

[London: Reaktion, 2002], 38).

43. Manning insists that "One cannot understate the variety as well as the pervasiveness of emblematic modes of thought and expression during this period. Without exaggeration, from Catholic Spain to the Protestant Netherlands and from England to Russia the emblem impinged on every aspect of European Renaissance and Baroque life—and death. Over 2,000 titles of printed books in who knows how many editions, manuscripts and various printed ephemera are only part of the surviving legacy of a phenomenon that decorated every aspect of domestic and civil life, however noble, however menial" (Manning, *The Emblem*, 16).

44. The popularity of the threefold structure was such that modern commentators, including Praz, Large, and Freeman, maintain that only works that conform to this threefold structure should be regarded as Emblem books (Peter Daly and Mary Silcox, *The English Emblem: Bibliography of Secondary Literature* [London: K. G. Saur, 1990], xvii).

45. Hutchinson, *The Covenant*, 2.

as anything but emblematic. It depicts an Aaronic priest offering a sacrifice beneath two sculpted cherubim that protrude from the lid of the ark.[46] The long, detailed, lines that form the contours of their robed bodies draw the eye to the focal point of the picture, an ethereal figure of Christ whose dominion over the cherubim, the ark, and the priest is represented by his elevated status.[47] The emblematic motto is the title of the work. It serves as a descriptive summary of the picture and as a germinal truth, which is expanded by means of an epigram—the expansive explanatory text that follows.

Hutchinson begins this epigram with an a priori argument. He argues that "God is invisible, in another System, and comes not under Sense."[48] If we had been present at creation, we would have seen God at work and therefore would have sufficient reason for believing in him. But since we weren't present, it seems that it is impossible for us to know God, since "we have no Idea of any thing, but what comes in by our Senses, or what is borrowed from them, to give Ideas of revealed Things *mutatis mutandis.*"[49] What we need, therefore, is an account about the beginning, from the beginning, that is passed down to us physically "by Tradition or Writing."[50] From this it follows not merely that we need revelation, but that we need *Hebrew* revelation, since Hebrew is Adam's language, the *prima lingua*. The Hebrew writings are shown to be perfect by their hidden mysteries concerning "the Essence-Existing, of the Personality, of the Covenant, and of what has been before us, and what will come after our Time, recorded by the infinite Wisdom of God."[51]

The more than five hundred pages of text that follow present an a posteriori defense of this basic idea. Hutchinson demonstrates by means of his "reasonable" exposition of Scripture that these aforementioned mysteries are hidden in the Old Testament in emblematic and specifically hieroglyphic

---

46. The picture, which is the only image in Hutchinson's corpus, appears four times throughout his published works. It was first included after page 120 of Hutchinson's 1733 work *Glory or Gravity*. The picture is also found after page 424 of *The Covenant in the Cherubim*. It was also selected as the frontpiece for Hutchinson's 1736 work *The Religion of Satan*. Sharp claims that the piece was also selected by Hutchinson's editors to serve as the frontpiece of his collected works and that they called it "The Christian Covenant in Hieroglyphics" (Sharp, *Mr. Hutchinson's*, 5).

47. See Figure 3.1 on the following page.

48. Hutchinson, *The Covenant*, 4.

49. Hutchinson, *The Covenant*, 5.

50. Hutchinson, *The Covenant*, 5–6.

51. Hutchinson, *The Covenant*, 6.

FIGURE 3.1
"THE CHRISTIAN COVENANT IN HIEROGLYPHICS"
BY HUBERT-FRANÇOIS GRAVELOT

form. The emblem Hutchinson focuses on is the angelic creature known as the cherubim which adorned the ark of the covenant. Hutchinson holds that the sacred status of the ark can be attributed to the mystery of the divine covenant hidden within these sculpted forms. The cherubim, says Hutchinson, were "an Exhibition of the Throne in Heaven, of the Persons upon it, and exhibited what was transacted, and to be transacted there, of the making and executing of the Covenant."[52] Hutchinson elaborates three features of the covenant here expressed. First, the covenant "which was made before the World" takes the form of a decree "to create this System and Man" in such a way as to leave the divine signature upon creation in the form of an ethereal Trinitarian imprint. Second, the course of salvation history was established by means of the decision to give the Second Person distinct rule "oeconomically." The decision was made that "a Man was to be the Son of Jehovah, and to be joined to the second Person, and taken into the Essence."[53] Third, this establishment of the Son's authority before the creation of the world became the basis of the angelic worship of the Godhead. For Hutchinson, the primary function of the cherubim, therefore, is to represent the three persons of the Trinity and to testify to their preeminence over all things.[54]

It is appropriate to attribute to Hutchinson the view that a refusal to interpret the cherubim as divine emblems is to acknowledge that they are useless antiquarian curiosities. Hutchinson is convinced that they must be interpreted as emblems if they are to fulfill their divinely mandated apologetic role, the role of testifying to God's dominion over creation and his authorship of Scripture. The thesis of Hutchinson's work is that since the central truths of the Christian religion and natural philosophy are hidden within the figures of the cherubim, and since the cherubim are found in the Old Testament, the Old Testament is proved to be a divine original.

EMBLEMS AND HIEROGLYPHS

In his seminal work *The Emblem*, John Manning points out that the threefold structure of picture, motto, and epigram was hardly the exclusive property of emblem books. Furthermore, he notes that emblem books were subject to

---

52. Hutchinson, *The Covenant*, 431.
53. Hutchinson, *The Covenant*, 240.
54. Hutchinson, *The Covenant*, 415–16.

various layouts, sometimes containing two, four, six, eight, or more parts.[55] And what is more, the picture is sometimes lacking.[56] Manning's constructive analysis diverts attention away from the structure of emblem books to the broader emblematic tradition, which he describes as the outworking of "emblematic contemplation." He defines emblematic contemplation as the consideration of "even the most mundane or trivial aspect of everyday life" in order to interpret it as useful or moral.[57] This broad articulation allows Manning to capture the full extent of emblematicism within the Renaissance context. Each emblem was, in Manning's words, "not so much 'made up' as found."[58] In other words, since the process of emblem creation was merely the selection of pre-established symbolic relationships, it confirmed not merely the divine meaning of particulars, but also that of the entire world. It is thus that Hutchinson's demonstration that the covenant is in the cherubim confirms the perfection of Hebrew Scripture. Once the cherubim have been established as divine emblems, the way is opened for countless other scriptural emblems to be discovered and interpreted. And this is precisely what Hutchinson does over the course of his twelve volumes of physico-theology: he relentlessly pursues the providential significance of natural-philosophical

---

55. Manning, *The Emblem*, 18.

56. Manning, *The Emblem*, 18.

57. Manning, *The Emblem*, 30. As Manning puts it, "Many aspects of daily experience were self-consciously presented as part of an emblematic theatre, in which no event could be presented without an accompanying gloss" (*The Emblem*, 29).

58. Manning, *The Emblem*, 48. In the emblematic tradition, choice was exercised in two ways. First, emblematicists were voyeurs. They scanned the created order and selected an object or image from among myriad potentially emblematic forms. The justification of his choice (the content of the epigram) is itself the second choice that had to be made. Emblematicists recognized that epigram construction was the process of choosing a specific meaning from among many possible meanings. The epigram itself therefore "exerts a gentle pressure on the reader towards the choice" of the author (Manning, *The Emblem*, 86–87). The emblematic tradition was fueled by a network of interrelationships between authors, publishers, and patrons, which led to extensive reworking of existing materials. Different images could be placed in front of different editions of the same epigram, and images were not tied to a single meaning (Manning, *The Emblem*, 86). The generation of new emblem books depended upon images and texts being brought together in unexpected and creative ways (Manning, *The Emblem*, 107). In Protestant countries, this newfound freedom was fueled by the doctrines of universal priesthood and *sola scriptura*. Protestants "found encouragement to look to emblems in nature, in scripture, and in emblem books to enhance his knowledge of spiritual matters, and to assist his meditations" (Barbara Kiefer Lewalski, *Protestant Poetics and the Seventeenth-Century Religious Lyric* [Princeton: Princeton University Press, 1979], 187).

objects found in the Old Testament by interpreting them as divine emblems.[59] On this account, his works that do not explicitly conform to Alciato's threefold structure must nevertheless still be located within the emblematic tradition.[60]

Like other emblematicists, Hutchinson believes he has the license to select which objects he chooses for emblematic contemplation. In Hutchinson's hands, the emblematic interpretation of physical objects is buttressed by a Lockean sensualist epistemology.[61] This should come as no surprise given that Locke's *Essay* was written as an epistemological manual for the Royal Society, the immediate context of Hutchinson's natural-philosophical formation.[62] Like Locke, Hutchinson premises his epistemology on the rejection of innate ideas; he believes all knowledge begins with sensory experience.[63] Hutchinson thus insists that "The Method directed perhaps to Man at first ... was to meditate upon the works of God," and that "this was the Work for which their Sabbath was set apart."[64] God never intended to give humans unmediated knowledge of his substance, dimension, or figure. He has, however, ordained that humans are to learn about him by means of created things by making "similitudes."[65] Humans must compare matter with God while recognizing that all comparisons are partial and imperfect. As we observe number, extension, duration, mechanism, and impulse motion, we interpret them as the effects of divine wisdom, power, and goodness and are therefore able to draw connections between the physical and spiritual realms.[66] To form ideas of the

59. According to Sharp, Hutchinson's disciples defend the emblem of the cherubim as "one of the uncontested explanations given by the Author" (*Mr. Hutchinson's*, 5).

60. The fact that interpreters of Hutchinson have failed to locate him within the emblematic tradition is a glaring deficiency in Hutchinsonian scholarship. In his *Moses's—Sine Principio*, for example, Hutchinson explicitly calls an object he interprets an Emblem no fewer than forty-five times.

61. Kuhn, "Glory," 307.

62. Hans Aarsleff, *From Locke to Saussure: Essays on the Study of Language and Intellectual History* (Minneapolis: University of Minnesota Press, 1982), 58.

63. Robert Spearman, *An Abstract from the Works of John Hutchinson* (London: 1753), 41.

64. Hutchinson, *Moses's Principia*, Part II, xxxvi.

65. Hutchinson, *A Treatise*, 28.

66. Hutchinson, *Moses's Principia*, Part II, 30–31. Wilde puts it this way: "just as God had so framed the Hebrew language that man might understand the physical world, so he had formed the physical world in such a way that through it man could acquire, by analogy, some knowledge of spiritual things" (Wilde, "Hutchinsonianism," 3–4).

unobservable, we need observable, sensory experience.[67] While we cannot see the face of God and live, by contemplating the physical world, humans can, like Moses, at least get a glimpse of his back (Exod 33:20–23).

For Hutchinson, as for other emblematicists, physical objects need human words to give voice to their praise (Ps 19:1).[68] Human words are necessary to articulate the providential meaning of natural-philosophical objects. Hutchinson does not merely believe in "convincing analogies between the visible system of nature and the invisible system of Providence."[69] He believes objects, as emblems, contain "the Presence of what [is] represented in them."[70] The authentic interpretation of physical objects is found, rather than created, because the objects he studies are already located within a vast web of meaning created by the Divine Artificer himself. Hutchinson insists that natural-philosophical objects are far more than what they are apparently. Fine particles of fire, light, and air appear to be nothing more than corpuscles in motion, but from the Old Testament we learn that they are emblems of Trinitarian persons.

Hutchinson's use of biblical words to draw out the divine meaning of physical objects locates him within the emblematic tradition. But this observation fails to capture the extent to which emblematicism marks Hutchinson's exegesis. Although Hutchinson, in *The Covenant in the Cherubim*, takes it upon himself to present his readers with a picture of the ark and the cherubim, his favored approach is to explore the emblematic meaning of biblical objects by interpreting biblical words as hieroglyphs. In Hutchinson's works, these hieroglyphs function as pictures, the Bible verses from which they are extracted function as mottos, and the commentaries themselves serve as epigrams. Hutchinson is only able to apply his emblematic method to biblical

---

67. G. N. Cantor, "Revelation and the Cyclical Cosmos of John Hutchinson," in *Images of the Earth: Essays in the History of the Environmental Sciences*, ed. L. J. Jordanova and R. S. Porter (Chalfont St. Giles, UK: British Society for the History of Science, 1979), 5.

68. For a discussion of the Hutchinsonian interpretation of Psalm 19, see chapter 3.

69. Kuhn, "Glory," 304.

70. Hutchinson, *The Covenant*, 415. Newton hated Platonism, for he found that, like Jewish kabbalah, it had contaminated the pristine theology of the early church with metaphysical speculations. Matt Goldish, *Judaism in the Theology of Sir Isaac Newton* (Dordrecht: Kluwer Academic, 1998), 112. This being said, commentators have observed that Newtonian metaphysics bear strong Platonic influences. See, for example, Edward Slowik, "Newton's Neo-Platonic Ontology of Space," *Foundations of Science* 3 (2013): 419–48. See also Douglas Hedley and Sarah Hutton, *Platonism at the Origins of Modernity: Studies on Platonism and Early Modern Philosophy* (Dordrecht: Springer, 2008).

words, however, because he believes that Hebrew words are divinely insti-tuted pictographic representations of the objects they refer to.

The Renaissance tradition of hieroglyphics can appropriately be called emblematicism's twin. Both disciplines took part in the Renaissance *ad fontes* project, and both used historical facts, archaeological records, and classical literary evidence to uncover *prisca theologia*. Alciato himself studied hiero-glyphs in Bologna,[71] and his friend Aldus Manutius (1449–1515) was at the cut-ting edge of hieroglyphic research, being the first to put *Horapollo* into print.[72] The bond between emblematicism and hieroglyphics was evident from the outset: the emblems Alciato explored are often drawn from ancient litera-ture, and sometimes the pictures he contemplates are Egyptian hieroglyphs.[73]

The earliest extant English emblem book, which was also the most popular, Francis Quarles's (1592–1644) *Emblemes and Hieroglyphikes* (1635), ensured the continued coinherence of emblematicism and hieroglyphics in England.[74] Like Marsilio Ficino (1433–1499), Pico della Mirandola (1463–1494), and the many intellectuals influenced by their work, Quarles held that, as mystic ideographs, hieroglyphs are able to enclose within themselves the essence of physical and spiritual things. This ability is achieved by means of their hybridity: as linguistic signs they denote particular things, and as pictures they contain within themselves the very things they denote. This hybridity does not, however, distinguish hieroglyphs from emblems but rather draws them together within a single symbolic frame, for the task

---

71. Manning, *The Emblem*, 58.

72. Manning, *The Emblem*, 45. See George Boas, ed. and trans., *The Hieroglyphics of Horapollo* (Princeton: Princeton University Press, 1993).

73. Alciato's work has much in common with Piero Valeriano's influential work *Hieroglyphica* (Basil, 1556; Manning, *The Emblem*, 54). Alciato's extensive use of hieroglyphs contributed to the popular notion that the emblem and the hieroglyph were cognate forms (Manning, *The Emblem*, 59).

74. Some early Renaissance theorists distinguished between hieroglyphs and emblems, but Valeriano's use of the term "hieroglyph" as a synonym for "symbol" meant that the distinction between emblems and hieroglyphs was often unclear (Lewalski, *Protestant*, 180–81). Quarles follows Valeriano in treating the terms "hieroglyph" and "symbol" as synonyms. Quarles's work went through more than fifty editions from the sixteenth to the nineteenth century. It was immediately welcomed to England as a "striking new type of devotional emblem book that could capture the senses and the mind, and stir the imagination and affections" (Karl Höltgen, "Francis Quarles's Emblemes and Hieroglyphickes: Historical and Critical Perspectives," in *The Telling Image: Explorations in the Emblem*, ed. Ayers Bagley, Edward Griffin, and Austin McLean [New York: AMS, 1996], 3).

that emblem writers placed before themselves was to convince their readers that the mottos they chose were not imposed upon the pictures they chose, but were, rather, somehow embedded within them. It comes as no surprise, therefore, that in Quarles's work it is not easy to determine which entries are hieroglyphs and which are emblems. Hutchinson's conviction that "emblems and hieroglyphicks" fulfill the same methodological role is therefore further confirmation that his work must be located within the European and English emblem traditions.[75]

HUTCHINSON'S HIEROGLYPHIC METHOD

Much has been made about the importance of personal contact between Christians and Jews that accompanied the rise of Christian Hebraism in early modern Europe, but—however important this was for select individuals— Hebrew was not a living language.[76] It was, even for Jews, an ancient and archaic tongue. As such it was often regarded as free from the complexities of linguistic utterance and semantic shift.[77] This conviction led many scholars, including Hutchinson, to literally "objectify" Hebrew words: it was hardly a stretch for them to come to regard them as ancient artifacts and thus to interpret them as static word-pictures—hieroglyphs.

Seventeenth- and eighteenth-century Hebraists had at their disposal a large number of grammatical and lexical works. Hutchinson utilizes Hebrew lexicons far more than he consults grammars.[78] In his work with the Hebrew language, Hutchinson's emphasis falls almost entirely on etymology, and his exegesis therefore proceeds almost entirely by means of term definition. The

75. Hutchinson, *A New Account*, 6.

76. See, for example, Allison Coudert, "Christian Kabbalah," in *Jewish Mysticism and Kabbalah: New Insights and Scholarship*, ed. Frederick Greenspahn (New York: New York University Press, 2011), 162.

77. Given his conviction concerning the incomparability of the Hebrew tongue, Hutchinson might well have embarked on a program of educational reform that involved not merely the dissemination of Hebrew learning, but also the vernacularization of it. Nevertheless, Hutchinson's failure to endorse vernacularization is not merely attributable to the fact that the idea had not yet come of age. Hutchinson's system is incompatible with it. Spoken tongues are intractably historical, but the *prima lingua* must be free from the foment of history.

78. Nevertheless, Hutchinson occasionally defends his reading of the text on the basis of Hebrew grammatical constructions. Thus, for example, he argues that John Partridge has wrongly understood the usage of קרא in Jeremiah 7:11 because he failed to consult "a Grammar" and thus failed to recognize the form of the present participle. It is unclear however, whether "Grammar" includes syntax for Hutchinson (Hutchinson, *The Covenant*, 284).

sense of a Hebrew word is the sense in which it was originally used, and this sense is confirmed by consulting lexicons.[79] Influential American cleric and educator Samuel Johnson (1696–1772) remarked that "no man in these latter ages, has ever appeared to have studied so laboriously, and to have understood so thoroughly the Hebrew language and antiquities, as Mr. Hutchinson."[80] But because his labor is expressed almost solely in term definition, the extent of his proficiency remains unclear. Any skeptic who dared to question his competency could hope to make little headway not merely because of Hutchinson's prickly personality, but because his underlying assumption is that Hebrew is not like other languages. Because Hebrew is not like other languages, it is not to be read like other languages.[81] Hebrew, the *prima lingua*, was created by God, and it is therefore unique.[82] That Hebrew bears a unique divine imprint is evident even in the meaning of the Hebrew word *dabar* (דָּבָר), which can be translated either as "word" or "thing." Conventional associations govern other languages, but Hebrew is a language of symbolic correspondences: as divine pictograms, Hebrew hieroglyphs capture the essences of the things they represent as "proper names." God's intent was to furnish his people with the divinely established identities of created things, and the Hebrew language was the gift he gave them toward this end.

79. Hutchinson, *A New Account*, 61. Hutchinson consults at least twelve different Hebrew lexicons throughout the course of his works, but it is unclear whether he has a consistent rationale to help him navigate conflicting definitions.

80. Thomas Bradbury Chandler, *The Life of Samuel Johnson, D.D.* (New York: 1824), 76.

81. John Hutchinson, "The Names and Attributes of the Trinity of the Gentiles," in *A New Account of the Confusion of Tongues* (London: 1731), 4. See also Kuhn, "Glory," 307–8.

82. The great sixteenth-century Hebraist Reuchlin expressed this sentiment as follows: "when reading Hebrew I seem to see God himself speaking" (Johann Reuchlin, *Breifwechsel*, ed. L. Geiger [Tübingen: 1875], 105; quoted in Jerome Friedman, "The Myth of Jewish Antiquity: New Christians and Christian-Hebraica in Early Modern Europe," in *Jewish Christians and Christian Jews*, ed. Richard H. Popkin and Gordon Weiner [Dordrecht: Kluwer Academic, 1994], 37). Sixteenth- and seventeenth-century language theorists were consumed by the quest to uncover the *prima lingua* (Peter Harrison, *The Fall of Man and the Foundations of Science* [Cambridge: Cambridge University Press, 2007], 193). Although some argued that the *prima lingua* was Latin, Chinese, or Egyptian, most scholars agreed that it was Hebrew. Katz maintains that "by the middle of the seventeenth century, Hebrew was the unopposed ancient mother of languages for most English thinkers" (David S. Katz, *Philo-Semitism and the Readmission of the Jews to England, 1603–1655* [Oxford: Clarendon Press, 1982], 65). The challenge, of course, was to discover how to make Hebrew divulge its ancient secrets. For an introduction to the quest for the *prima lingua*, see Allison Coudert, "Eavesdropper in the Garden of Eden: The Search for the Ursprache and the Genesis of the Modern World," in *The Language of Adam/ Die Sprache Adams*, ed. Allison Coudert (Wiesbaden: Harrassowitz Verlag, 1999), 7–24.

As an exegete, Hutchinson endeavors "to open the Nature of the Sacred writings."[83] By this he means that his goal is to match created objects with corresponding Hebrew referents. John English helpfully identifies three of the dominant techniques Hutchinson employs to accomplish this goal. The first is to uncover the roots of Hebrew words. According to Hutchinson, the root of the word "firmament" (*rka*) means to "expand, extend, distend, stretch" or "to make thin" or "to press," and he therefore argues that firmament should be translated "expansion."[84] He then draws upon different biblical and classical uses of the word "expansion" to argue that, as "a thin fluid that is widely distributed or extended, and the action of this substance, moving or pressing material objects toward the extremities of the universe," the term "expansion" refers to the cosmic ether.[85] Hutchinson's second technique is to derive the meaning of Hebrew words from grammatical observations. This technique is clearly seen in Hutchinson's insistence that *Elohim*, or *Aleim*, is to be translated not merely as "God" but as a reference to the Trinity because of its plural ending.[86] Hutchinson's third technique is to bring together words with similar consonantal patterns. For example, the Hebrew words *sam* ("placed," "put" or "disposed"), *shem* ("name"), and *shamaim* ("the heavens") are mutually interpreted. Thus, when *sam* is properly defined as "place," it establishes that "place" and "name" and "the heavens" are identical. This allows Hutchinson to argue, once again, for the existence of a ubiquitous ether that God *placed* in *the heavens* as an emblem of the divine *name*.[87]

---

83. Hutchinson, *The Covenant*, 2.

84. English, "John Hutchinson's," 589. English's analysis is helpful because it treats Hutchinson's exegetical techniques as subservient to his larger project to de-historicize the Hebrew tongue (English, "Hutchinson's," 589–93). Interpreters of Hutchinson run the risk of making too much of individual exegetical techniques. Gürses Tarbuck, for example, sees the elimination of vowel points as the central tenet of early Hutchinsonianism. While this may be true for certain early Hutchinsonians, it is certainly not true of Hutchinson himself (Derya Gürses Tarbuck, "The Hutchinsonian Defence of an Old Testament Trinitarian Christianity: The Controversy Over Elahim, 1735–1773," *History of European Ideas* 29 [2003]: 393–409).

85. English, "John Hutchinson's," 588–89.

86. English, "John Hutchinson's," 589.

87. English, "John Hutchinson's," 589. Hutchinson's treatment of Hebrew words as specimens that can be dissected and broken down into component parts would have appeared entirely appropriate to many of his contemporaries. Preeminent language theorist John Wilkins had earlier proposed that since "the Hebrew *Tongue*" consisted of the "fewest Radicals," it could serve as the basis of a philosophical language (John Wilkins, "Epistle to the Reader," in *An Essay Toward a Real Character, and a Philosophical Language* [London: 1668]).

For Hutchinson, natural-philosophical objects present natural philosophers with the occasion to ponder theological and metaphysical truths which
are embedded in creation. The importance of emblems and hieroglyphs is
that they facilitate the unveiling of these truths. The proper pursuit of the
natural philosopher is therefore biblical commentary. For Hutchinson, the
Hebrew Bible is a storehouse of ancient hieroglyphs, and he takes pride in
demonstrating that words, which appear mundane, are pregnant with divine
meaning. Hutchinson begins his commentary on Genesis 1:14 as follows: "As
every Word, nay every Letter here, is of the utmost Importance, nothing
deficient nor nothing superfluous, we shall consider the meaning of these
Words, which have not been settled, Word by Word."[88]

The function of Hebrew hieroglyphs in Hutchinson's method is to
facilitate the emblematic interpretation of created things, without which
the divine order of the cosmos would remain hidden from view. Thus,
Hutchinson's justification for his emblematic interpretation of the cherubim is the fact that the word "cherubim" is an ancient Hebrew word.[89] When
people use the Hebrew tongue, they name objects as God intended them to
be named, and when they do so, the objects reveal and revel in the glory of
God. Like Newton and other universal language progenitors, Hutchinson is
driven by the taxonomic quest to locate proper names. Like Newton, he has,
however, become convinced that no vernacular will be able to achieve this
goal. As fallen languages given over to historical devolution, vernaculars are

---

88. Hutchinson, *Moses's Principia, Part II*, 354.

89. Hutchinson's justification in exploiting the spiritual significance of sacred objects is
exactly the same as his justification for his emblematic interpretations of the objects of the
natural world. For example, he takes the common onion to be a microcosm of the universe
(Hutchinson, *A New Account*, 24). He suggests that the planetary orbs exist "within one another"
because this conforms to the pattern both of the Copernican system (the macrocosm) and of
the onion (the microcosm). For Hutchinson, emblem interpretation is simply the process of
identifying preexisting patterns of correspondence imprinted on creation by the divine artificer (Hutchinson, *A New Account*, 228). Hutchinson chooses to consider the onion as emblem
because it corresponds to a Hebrew hieroglyph found in Numbers 6:5. Although his discussion of the original meaning of the hieroglyph is brief (he admits that we cannot be sure
whether the Israelites were eating onions or garlic in Egypt), its location in Hebrew Scripture
is what justifies Hutchinson's choice to interpret it as an emblem (Hutchinson, "The Names
and Attributes," 23–24). Sloane notes that the correspondence between the microcosm and the
macrocosm "was one of the ubiquitous metaphors of the Renaissance" (Mary Cole Sloane, *The
Visual in Metaphysical Poetry* [Atlantic Highlands, NJ: Humanities, 1981], 61). See also Don Parry
Norford, "Microcosm and Macrocosm in Seventeenth-Century Literature," *Journal of the History
of Ideas* 38 (1977): 409–28.

unable to uncover the essences of things because they are unable to reveal the intrinsic relation between created things and the Creator.

Hutchinson begins *Moses's Principia* by insisting upon the definitive importance of Hebrew Scripture on this basis: "The Revelation of Moses of the Creation and Formation of Matter ... was not intended to relate any Thing or Circumstance to us, but what we could not perceive without it; and yet has not omitted any Thing we could not otherwise know."[90] Although humans may well be able to learn a myriad things about created things without Moses' help, they are entirely dependent upon him to bequeath their spiritual and providential import. They are, accordingly, equally dependent on the one who has managed to uncover Moses's esoteric knowledge. "As I am the first," says Hutchinson, "who has dared to shew the Excellences and Beauties of the *Hebrew* Tongue, and the Imperfections of the rest, my present Readers ought to make me some Allowance."[91] Having identified the original referent for each Hebrew hieroglyph, the "Excellences and Beauties of the Hebrew Tongue" are made known, and what was once a merely mundane object becomes a window to the divine.

IDOLATRY, LINGUISTIC DEVOLUTION, AND SCRIPTURE

Hutchinson is at pains to argue that the Mosaic writings are the direct transcription of God's revelation to Moses, transcribed in the divinely appointed hieroglyphic form.[92] Hutchinson believes direct revelation is necessary to ensure the purity of the Mosaic account because he endorses a devolutionary philosophy of history.[93] If Moses were found to have inherited his knowledge

---

90. Hutchinson, *Moses's*, 1.

91. Hutchinson, *A New Account*, 102.

92. "All the Pretences of Tradition from *Adam* to *Moses*," says Hutchinson, "signify nothing; *Adam* could know nothing without Revelation, and if there could be a Revelation to *Adam*, why not to *Moses*? What Occasion for having it spoil'd by Tradition, and imperfectly recorded?" John Hutchinson, *An Essay toward a Natural History of the Bible, especially of some Parts which relate to the Occasion of revealing Moses's Principia* (London: 1725), 10, 27. Markley observes that universal histories tend to celebrate "often to the point of obsession, the authority of the Mosaic account of history" (Robert Markley, "Newton, Corruption, and the Tradition of Universal History," in *Newton and Religion: Context, Nature, and Influence*, ed. James E. Force and Richard H. Popkin [Dordrecht: Kluwer Academic, 1999], 122).

93. Although his apologetic forces him to treat revelation as ahistorical, Hutchinson doesn't explicitly reject the historicity of revelation. He even says that "God was pleased to reveal many Things to *Adam* before his Fall, and some afterwards, and to several of his Descendants" (*An*

from Adam, Hutchinson would have to concede that his knowledge was subject to corruption. It is equally essential for Hutchinson that God did not merely speak to Moses, but that he also provided a protective covering for his revelation to enable it to be transmitted to posterity. Hutchinson's devolutionary philosophy of history compels him to interpret Hebrew characters as hieroglyphs. All other human languages show the effects of historical devolution; only Hebrew hieroglyphs are able to protect divine knowledge from the corrosive waves of time.

Following Newton and Clarke, Hutchinson articulates his devolutionary philosophy of history as a history of idolatry. Hutchinson believes idolatry began in the garden of Eden and is inherent in humankind's necessary reliance on sensory experience. Hutchinson confesses that had Adam "not been informed, and endowed with unblemished Faculties, he might have guess'd, as the latest *Heathens* did, and their Scholars do" that "the Light, Orbs, Waters, Creatures ... had Powers to move one another or move of themselves."[94] What kept Adam and Eve from believing motion to be inherent in ethereal matter was God's direct revelation that all motion is attributable to God himself. The fall is conceived as a rejection of this revelation. Instead of attributing motion to God, Eve trusted in "the Powers in the Names," and therefore in her own creaturely wisdom.[95] The story of the fall is thus retold as Adam and

---

Essay, 3). The descendent Hutchinson is most interested in, of course is Moses, since his primary object is to defend the Mosaic writings.

94. Hutchinson, *A Treatise*, 43. Hutchinson's interpretation of light as the active principle that sparked the various processes of spontaneous creation recorded in Genesis locates him firmly within the alchemical tradition. As Dobbs observes, "Tract after tract on the alchemical process used illumination to explain God's actions with respect to matter at the beginning of time" (Dobbs, *The Janus*, 40). Hutchinson's interest in light as an active principle also echoes that of Newton: "Newton was concerned from the first in his alchemical work to find evidence for the existence of a vegetative principle operating in the natural world, a principle that he understood to be the secret, universal, animating spirit of which the alchemists spoke. He saw analogies between the vegetable principle and light, and between the alchemical process and the work of the Deity at the time of creation. It was by the use of this active vegetative principle that God constantly molded the universe to his providential design" (Dobbs, *The Janus*, 5). See also note 37.

95. Dobbs, *The Janus*, 47. "The Names" is the term Hutchinson uses to designate the cosmic Trinitarian ether. "The Names" is a rabbinic term, and Hutchinson's use of it suggests kabbalistic influences (Katz, *Philo-Semitism*, 72). Although Hutchinson consistently denigrates Judaism in general and rabbinic Judaism in particular, he was clearly familiar with Kabalistic literature and sometimes quotes it authoritatively. See, for example, Hutchinson, *The Covenant*, 242.

Eve's decision to become the first freethinkers—and, specifically, to believe in Newtonian universal gravitation![96]

Hutchinson's primary interest, however, is not Adam and Eve's idolatry, but that of the Israelites.[97] This emphasis is, as Katz suggests, undoubtedly enflamed by anti-Semitic sensibilities. The primary reason, however, that Hutchinson must de-emphasize pre-Mosaic idolatry is that his object is to protect Moses from chronological degradation. For Hutchinson, it isn't enough merely to demonstrate that Moses received direct revelation from God. For Moses and his message to be free from corruption, Moses must stand outside of the devolutionary sequence of history. The only surefire way to protect Moses from his detractors, therefore, is to present him as the font of *prisca theologia* that stands at the dawn of time.[98] Hutchinson is at pains to emphasize that Moses was the first person to learn the art of writing. He stands at the dawn of recorded history, and his writings are therefore the most direct access humans have to the primordial divine counsel.[99] Hutchinson's hatred for John Spencer, whom he calls one of the wickedest men to have ever professed Christianity, results from the fact that Spencer's historical inversion removes the Mosaic writings from the protective covering of prehistory.[100]

---

96. Spearman, *An Abstract*, 79; Wilde, "Hutchinsonianism," 10. For Hutchinson, to believe in gravitation is to disbelieve that the world is emblematically ordered. To interpret physical things as emblems is to interpret them as icons that testify to the divine activity in the world and to the inactivity of lifeless matter. "That it was a great part of the first Man's Duty, to contemplate the Models, or Emblems, the Garden afforded, the Emblems in, and the Operations of the Machine, the Names, and through them the Power of those who created and formed them" (Hutchinson, *The Religion*, 4).

97. The only time Hutchinson speaks about pre-Mosaic idolatry is his observation that the first account of images in the Bible is that of Laban's idols (Hutchinson, *An Essay*, 82).

98. If Hutchinson emphasized the progress of pre-Mosaic corruption, he would be placing Moses after Adam and Eve on a chronological axis, and this would entail that Moses is subject to history and therefore subject to devolution.

99. Hutchinson holds that after Moses had been on the mount of the Lord, he "was instructed how to write" (*An Essay*, 9). According to Hutchinson, "There were no letters before *Moses*. I need say nothing of his natural Faculties, or of his personal Virtues; of his Affection to his Brethren, of his Courage, of his Meekness, of his Faith; his private Actions ... nor of those Faculties being supernaturally supported till his Death ... my Business is to speak of him as a Prophet" (*The Covenant*, 6).

100. Hutchinson, *The Covenant*, 93. Saving the Old Testament from Spencer is something Woodward had also hoped to do (Iliffe, *Priest of Nature*, 199).

Hutchinson holds that the story of how the prelapsarian worship of the *Elohim* became gradually obscured is the story of how divine revelation was gradually given over to corruption after Moses. Yet Hutchinson also wants to emphasize that the Mosaic account is the great antidote to human idolatry. Hutchinson therefore argues that in the generations after Moses, many Israelites were able to hold fast to their belief in the *Elohim* thanks to their knowledge of the Mosaic writings.[101] For Hutchinson, the decisive step toward idolatry was the exile, for it is at this time that the Jews lost their knowledge of Hebrew and it "was never after spoken in any Place."[102] By the time Nehemiah returned to Jerusalem, everyone had forgotten the Hebrew tongue.[103] Once the divinely ordained Hebrew names were replaced by those of common vernaculars, the Jews became hopelessly engulfed in idolatrous notions, for only Hebrew hieroglyphs describe created objects as entirely passive, dependent upon the divine mover.[104] Thus, when Hutchinson takes up arms against Clarke's antitrinitarianism, he concedes Clarke's basic point that in English the word "God" never signifies more persons than one. Rather than demonstrating against the consubstantiality of the divine persons, however, this merely confirms that English is a bastardization of the *prima lingua*! Had Clarke turned to the Old Testament and done his Hebrew exegesis properly instead of "quibbling about the English Word God," he would have identified that the word *Elohim* "always signifies three Persons."[105]

---

101. Hutchinson also holds that the heathens knew the Mosaic writings. There are many instances, says Hutchinson, "where Strangers, some from the utmost of the then inhabited Parts of the Earth ... conferr'd freely with the *Israelites*, and no Difficulty appear'd" (*A New Account*, 73).

102. Hutchinson, *A New Account*, 80. Thus, concludes Hutchinson, "all the best authors do earnestly contend to have Hebrew escape a confusion at Babel, but suffer it to be led captive in the Babylonian captivity" (*A New Account*, 27). According to Hutchinson, the first mention of inhabitants from different nations using different tongues, and indeed failing to understand one another, is the account in 2 Kings 18:26 and Isaiah 36:11, in which the servants of Hezekiah requested that the servants of the king of Assyria speak to them in Syrian rather than in Hebrew, which the people understood (*A New Account*, 74). This story makes it clear, even at this point, however, that "The Heathens had not left the *Hebrew* so far" since they retained the ability to converse in it (*A New Account*, 75).

103. Hutchinson, *A New Account*, 77. This catastrophic loss meant that the Jews were no longer able to decipher their own hieroglyphs (*A New Account*, 8).

104. Hutchinson, *A New Account*, 115. Servetus expressed this sentiment in the following terms: "The Hebrew tongue, when translated into any other tongue, is defective and the spirit is almost lost" (Michael Servetus, *Biblia Sacra ex Santis Pagnini Talatione* [Lyons, 1542], "Introduction"; quoted in Friedman, "The Myth," 39).

105. Hutchinson, *Glory or Gravity*, 228. Hutchinson also complains that Clarke takes his definition of God (the being that is "every where as well as always") from Philo rather than from

Within Hutchinson's devolutionary scheme, Greek and Latin are regarded as superior to English since, as ancient languages, they are closer to the primordial source. Hutchinson thus argues that unlike the English word "God," the Greek word θεός retains the Hebraic idea of consubstantiality.[106] Even Greek sits awkwardly within Hutchinson's devolutionary scheme, however, as an early corruption of the *prima lingua*. "We have nothing to do with Translations or Paraphrases of the Apostate *Jews*," says Hutchinson,

> Nor with Words, Terms, or Definitions, writ by Heathens since the Confusion of Tongues, when the Writers knew nothing of the Subjects before us. We are only to explain the Meaning of the Words, Terms, or Definitions, writ by the Prophets, and even the *Greek* by the Hebrew.[107]

The truth that the Greek language, which Hutchinson calls the language of the pagans, manages to retain is already present in the Old Testament. In the Hebrew, however, this truth is expressed in pristine hieroglyphic form. "The New Testament," claims Hutchinson, "says nothing but what *Moses* and the Prophets said; as the Prophets say nothing but what *Moses* saith, so *Moses* by Hieroglyphicks, or Words, says all things."[108] Hutchinson accordingly feels no need to apologize for meddling "as little as possible with the *Greek language*."[109]

By unveiling the hieroglyphic mysteries of Hebrew, Hutchinson intends to "settle the chief Points in Religion, so that it shall not be in the Power of Man to disturb them." He believes this requires not only that he "shew the Perfection of the Writings and Language I am construing, but the Imperfection of all other Languages, and of all human Writings," and thus "to exalt the Works of

---

Scripture (*Glory or Gravity*, 90). According to Hutchinson, "modern Fools" and "apostate Jews" agree that the word "God" refers to the absolute power vested in one person (*The Covenant*, 102-3).

106. Hutchinson, *Glory or Gravity*, 228.

107. Hutchinson, *A Treatise*, 5-6.

108. Hutchinson, *The Covenant*, 11. Since Moses says "all things," it appears that God's revelation to Moses brings to an end the necessity of further revelation. Hutchinson seems not to acknowledge this implication as he continues to affirm the scriptural status of the New Testament and the necessity of interpreting it: "I pretend not yet to be sufficiently prepar'd to explain the New Testament" (*Glory or Gravity*, 232). This admission confirms that for Hutchinson, Old Testament interpretation has very little to do with New Testament interpretation. The Testaments are different species altogether and require different exegetical and apologetic methods. I will argue that later Hutchinsonians rejected this position and held that the Old Testament could only be adequately defended as Scripture on the same terms as the New Testament. See chapter 6.

109. Hutchinson, *Moses's Principia, Part II*, xlix.

God, and depress those of Men."[110] For Hutchinson, "the books in the *Hebrew* Tongue were writ by inspired Men ... and so are infallible." In order to emphasize this infallibility, Hutchinson believes he must downgrade the authority of other writings. Hutchinson insists that "the Knowledge containd in [the Hebrew books] is not to be acquir'd from any other Writing, nor by any other Means."[111] For Clarke, the degradation of the Old Testament is a necessary consequence of his elevation of the message of the New Testament to the status of spiritual revelation. For Hutchinson, the exact opposite is true. By elevating the Mosaic writings to the status of primordial divine counsel, Hutchinson threatens the canonical status of the New Testament. If Clarke is guilty of regarding only the New Testament as Scripture, Hutchinson, by the same account, regards only the Old Testament as such.

EMBLEMATIC DECONTEXTUALIZATION

In the emblematic tradition, any human language and any written text can theoretically be utilized to draw out the divine meaning of created things. Hutchinson, though, insists that Hebrew alone is endowed with emblematic potency. This, however, is only the beginning of Hutchinson's truncation of the emblematic tradition. Hutchinson does not treat every Hebrew character as equally emblematic. In fact, Hutchinson is only interested in the emblematic potential of a select group of Hebrew words: words that refer to natural-philosophical objects. On this account, Hutchinson's scriptural reflections are largely confined to the first chapters of the book of Genesis.[112] And given this interest in natural philosophy, Hutchinson is not interested in all of the Hebrew words contained in these first few chapters: he only offers emblematic interpretations of a select few.

Because Renaissance Hebraism tended to view Hebrew words as ancient artifacts, it promoted the decontextualization of Hebrew words. Working

---

110. Hutchinson, *A New Account*, 8.

111. Hutchinson, *A New Account*, 8–9.

112. One nineteenth-century Anglican who took Hutchinson's interpretation of Genesis very seriously was Samuel Taylor Coleridge. Coleridge confesses, "his interpretation of the first nine verses of Genesis xi seems not only rational in itself, and consistent with after accounts of the sacred historian, but proved to be the literal sense of the Hebrew text." Coleridge also adds: "His explanation of the cherubim is pleasing and plausible: I dare not say more" (W. G. T. Shedd, ed., *The Complete Works of Samuel Taylor Coleridge* [New York: 1871], 2:454).

as he did within this tradition, Hutchinson focused upon the excavation of *prisca theologia* from these ancient artifacts. Like so many Renaissance Hebraists before him, he inevitably finds that he can only be successful in this pursuit when he extracts them from their literary contexts and examines them as specimens. Because Hutchinson, having pursued his method, fails to recontextualize Hebrew words within Scripture, it is appropriate to speak of him as embracing a hermeneutic of literary decontextualization.

Hutchinson begins each section of *Moses's Principia* and *Moses's Principia II* by presenting the Bible verse he plans to interpret. Hutchinson gives each verse visual prominence by presenting it in large italicized font as an emblematic motto at the head of his explanatory text. The reader of *Moses's Principia*, a commentary that covers only the first thirteen verses of Genesis 1, is forced to follow Hutchinson's circuitous reflections upon the Hebrew text without being given the Hebrew words that form the backbone of his exegesis.[113] Hebrew words appear in Hebrew script for the first time in *Moses's Principia II* (which now extends to verse seventeen), scattered throughout the biblical texts Hutchinson interprets and his compendious commentary on them. Hutchinson's refusal to translate these select Hebrew hieroglyphs into English highlights their function as emblematic pictures. It is also a pronounced step toward interpretive decontextualization. Hutchinson, no doubt, wants to remind his readers that the words he has chosen to emphasize are not like other words: they are hieroglyphs. Whether the other Hebrew words—those that remain translated in the vernacular—are also to be regarded as hieroglyphs is unclear. They are not elevated to hieroglyphic status and are accordingly given little comment. Nor do they play a prominent role in the interpretation of the select hieroglyphs. Their sole purpose,

---

113. Hutchinson's musings on the Genesis creation narrative bear the imprint of kabbalistic philosophy. In particular, Hutchinson follows Isaac Luria in making divine light the agent of creation. Hutchinson also follows Luria in calling this light by the divine name. Furthermore, Hutchinson's opinion that light is the emblem of the Second Person in the Trinity bears kabbalistic (as well as Neoplatonic) influences. Luria often describes the light as having emanated from God, and Hutchinson picks up this language in his discussions of the way in which light emanates from the sun (God the Father; Hutchinson, *Moses's*, 16–20; *A Treatise*, 12–13). See Shaul Magid, *From Metaphysics to Midrash: Myth, History, and the Interpretation of Scripture in Lurianic Kabbala* (Bloomington, IN: Indiana University Press, 2008), 16–33; see also James David Dunn, *Window of the Soul: The Kabbalah of Rabbi Isaac Luria* (San Francisco: Red Wheel, 2008).

it appears, is to function as a backdrop that brings into relief the imagistic quality of the hieroglyphic images that radiate divine light.

In *Moses's—Sine Principio*, which extends the commentary to Genesis 2:8–3:22, the emblematic images, Hebrew hieroglyphs, continue to be interspersed throughout the mottos and epigrams. The commentary continues to be given in the vernacular, but the Scripture verses at the head of the text are now presented in Latin.[114] This choice is curious given that Hutchinson had little confidence in the linguistic proficiency of his readers.[115] As Hutchinson writes in a context in which Latin had been eclipsed by the vernacular as the language of scholarship, his decision to Latinize the biblical text drives it into obscurity. What is more, Hutchinson offers his readers little guidance in interpreting these Latin texts. The message he implicitly communicates is that readers only need to concern themselves with the hieroglyphs he has selected for them. The Latin words retreat into the background in order to bring the select Hebrew hieroglyphs forward and into relief.

The presentation of the biblical text in Latin, however, is not the final step in Hutchinson's decontextualization. Hutchinson's exegesis of the second and third chapters of Genesis is restricted to the introduction of *Sine Principio*. In the main body of the work Hutchinson no longer finds it necessary to present the texts he plans to interpret. The biblical texts that had stood at the head of his commentary as mottos are replaced with the Hebrew hieroglyphs he has selected in the introduction of his work. This shift in the presentation of the material completes the process of decontextualization. The hieroglyphs Hutchinson brings under the microscope no longer have a literary context. They are simply free-floating word-pictures. Hutchinson's exegesis in *Moses's Principia* was already dominated by lexical considerations. There can be no doubt, however, that *Sine Principio* completes the transition from biblical commentary to lexicography. Strictly speaking, this decontextualization of Hebrew words is not a movement away from emblematicism because

---

114. A stark visual contrast is seen when samples from the three works are placed consecutively: (1) "And Darkness was upon the Face of the Deep" (Hutchinson, *Moses's*, 4); (2) "And חשך Darkness was upon the Face (Faces) of תחם the Deep" (Hutchinson, *Moses's Principia, Part II*, 118); (3) "Et הנחש serpens erat ערום calidior סכל omni Bestia agri quam secerat Jehovah Elohim" (Hutchinson, *Moses's—Sine Principio*, civ).

115. Elsewhere Hutchinson laments that there are "few now who can read, and not many who will read any thing that is either difficult or tedious" (*Moses's—Sine Principio*, 2).

Hutchinson retains emblematicism's foundational conviction that words are necessary for the providential interpretation of things. The Hebrew words Hutchinson interprets are emblems since they are word-pictures. And Hutchinson, in good emblematic fashion, explores the meaning of these word-pictures using other words.

Because they are word-pictures, his definitions bear little resemblance to those found in lexicons but rather are extended, circuitous reflections upon biblical, classical, and contemporary authors that frantically seek to uncover the wisdom that lies hidden beneath the hieroglyphic veneer of the words.[116] Hutchinson regularly treats a single term for more than twenty pages because he believes "The Perfection of the Descriptions" found in Hebrew hieroglyphs "are never to be exhausted; they treat of Subjects which will be the Objects of Contemplation for Eternity."[117] Sometimes Hutchinson includes a string of quotations in these long, circuitous reflections. And sometimes the string of quotations comprises biblical references. Most of the time, however, Hutchinson proceeds by quoting the work of a prominent scholar and then reflecting extensively upon it. The emblematic world Hutchinson inhabits is a world in which the vestiges of *prisca theologia* are ubiquitous. They can be found in the words of any and every author, whether classical or contemporary, pagan or Christian. The Bible plays an important role in this world, but it is not clear that the role it plays is distinct from that of other sources. At the very least, the Bible provides the foundation for Hutchinson's natural-philosophical reflection in his three commentaries on Genesis. The nine volumes of physico-theology published subsequently, however, are not commentaries but lexical reflections upon various natural-philosophical subjects. And in these works, the role and authority of biblical and classical authors appears synonymous. Although Hutchinson's emblematicism is scriptural because the emblems he interprets largely originate in Scripture, Scripture itself does not play a privileged role in the interpretation of these emblems.

---

116. The breadth of Hutchinson's engagement with Renaissance scholarship is impressive by any standard. Given his modest means, he must have gone to great lengths to find copies of the numerous works he regularly quotes.

117. Hutchinson, *The Covenant*, 189. In this, Hutchinson's approach is the direct antithesis of Clarke's. For Clarke, the definition of a term, and indeed, the exegetical process, is exhausted when its true referent is identified.

This separates Hutchinson's exegesis from that of the church fathers, as well as that of later Hutchinsonians.

The fear that patristic figural exegesis decontextualizes biblical words fuels the contemporary criticism that it frequently violates the literal sense of Scripture. When the fathers interpret a particular Scripture word or image as a figure, it is argued, it is removed from its original context, and a meaning from a foreign context is imposed upon it.[118] Whether or not a particular reading is guilty of decontextualization, however, is a complex question given that the context of any given Scripture word is multivalent and functions on several levels.[119] Otherwise put, decontextualization depends upon the context in question. Thus, the figural reader that sets out to interpret a word in scriptural context does not decontextualize the word so long as her interpretation interprets that word canonically. The figural reading of the fathers often avoids decontextualization in precisely this way.

Origen, in his homilies on Genesis, for example, reins in his reflections on the meaning of particular words by interpreting them in canonical context. Given Origen's notorious predilection for allegorical speculation, we would expect him to seize upon words that are pregnant with metaphysical potential, such as "light" or "firmament," and launch into Neoplatonic speculation. But this is precisely what he refuses to do. When he ponders

---

118. The classic statement of this opinion is R. P. C. Hanson, *Allegory and Event: A Study of the Sources and Significance of Origen's Interpretation of Scripture* (London: SCM Press, 1959). For a more sympathetic treatment of Origen's interpretive method, see Henri de Lubac, *History and Spirit: The Understanding of Scripture according to Origen*, trans. Anne Englund Nash and Juvenal Merriell (San Francisco: Ignatius, 2007).

119. The scriptural context of any given word includes the phrase in which the word is found, the sentence in which the phrase is found, the pericope in which the sentence is found, the paragraph in which the pericope is found, the book in which the paragraph is found, the collection of books in which the book is found, the testament in which the collection of books is found, and the canon of Scripture itself. Strictly speaking, the only way to protect against decontextualization is to atomize Scripture words, for the decision to recontextualize a word within any given textual level always follows a decision to decontextualize it, whether the interpretation is considered either literal or figural. Nor is it simply the case that the decontextualization of Scripture words that accompanies literal translations is necessarily inferior in extent to the decontextualization that accompanies figural translations. No human word is self-interpreting. Human words always depend upon other words and usages to grant them meaning. Thus, the text-critical scholar is sometimes forced to decontextualize a particular word by drawing its meaning from its usage in another biblical book. And the figural reader is sometimes only required to look elsewhere in the same pericope to define the term in question.

the significance of the lights of heaven in Genesis 1:14–15, he observes that they have been established

> "For signs and seasons and days and years," that they might give light from the firmament of heaven for those who are on the earth, so also Christ, illuminating his Church, gives signs by his precepts, that one might know how, when the sign has been received, to escape "the wrath to come," lest "that day overtake him like a thief," but that rather he can reach "the acceptable year of the Lord." Christ, therefore, is "the true light which enlightens every man coming into this world."[120]

Origen interprets the term "light" in canonical context to render a tropological interpretation of it. He proceeds from the lights of heaven to the light of Christ, and this allows him to employ the lights of heaven as a guide for holy living.

Hutchinson's interpretation of the term "light" in the first chapter of Genesis echoes that of Origen inasmuch as Hutchinson interprets light figurally as a reference to Christ. Nevertheless, the location of Hutchinson's Christ is not that of Origen's. In the first place, Origen's Christ is found in the first chapter of John's Gospel. Hutchinson's Christ, on the other hand, rides on the waves of a cosmic ether and inhabits John's Gospel only to the extent that Hutchinson's readers bring echoes of John's Gospel with them to Hutchinson's text. This Christ must remain trapped within this cosmic ether for the same reason that Hutchinson's Old Testament must be descriptive of it. Hutchinson refuses to place Christ in the New Testament because, if he did so, he would be returning Christ to the scriptural context. And Scripture, Hutchinson knows, is unable to uphold its own authority. Nor is it able to uphold Christian doctrine. Hutchinson requires a more certain authority to serve as the basis of his scriptural and doctrinal apologetics, and he finds it in cosmological theory.

Within Hutchinson's Newtonian context, his decontextualization of Hebrew hieroglyphs in order to recast them as natural-philosophical emblems is his attempt to affirm that the authority of the Old Testament

---

120. Ronald E. Heine, *Homilies on Genesis and Exodus* (Washington, DC: The Catholic University of America Press, 2002), 54. Scriptures referenced in this brief passage include 1 Thess 1:10; Matt 3:7; Luke 3:7; 1 Thess 5:4; Isa 61:2; John 1:9.

consists in its ability to describe the world as providentially ordered. This being said, Hutchinson's method ultimately calls into question the scriptural authority he seeks to defend. Hutchinson decontextualizes Hebrew words by transforming them into natural-philosophical hieroglyphs because he believes he must remove them from Scripture to save them from Scripture because Scripture is subject to the devolutionary force of history.

JOHN HUTCHINSON, NEWTONIAN

Matt Goldish observes that Hutchinson's Hebraic method follows Louis Cappel "(1585–1658) and a long line of Hebraists who sought to recapture the pristine simplicity of the Hebrew language.[121] Goldish also observes that although Newton scholars have failed to consider the importance of Hebrew etymologies in establishing Newton's universal history, "His method has a great deal of similarity to the method of Hutchinson."[122] Along similar lines, C. D. A. Leighton maintains that the facile characterization of Hutchinson as "anti-Newton" may "seriously mislead" because it fails to place Hutchinson's biblical apologetic at the center of his thought.[123] Hutchinson's rejection of Newton is his rejection of universal gravitation and its attendant theological implications. The forceful rhetoric that accompanies this rejection obscures the fact that Hutchinson upholds several of Newton's most important suppositions. Among these is Newton's underlying devolutionary philosophy of history, which Hutchinson continues to express in Newtonian terms. Like Newton and Clarke before him, the problem for Hutchinson is ultimately history itself.

Newton and Hutchinson believe that contact with human history invariably corrupts divine knowledge. This belief is the complement to their

---

121. Goldish, *Judaism*, 54.

122. Goldish, *Judaism*, 55. Newton often wrote words in Hebrew to highlight the importance of the individual characters, and Yahuda MS 16 shows that he understood that Hebrew consonants could sometimes be flexible. Goldish therefore concludes that "His method has a great deal of similarity to the method of Hutchinson" (Goldish, *Judaism*, 55). Isaac Newton, Rough draft portions of and notes for "Theologiæ Gentilis Origines Philosophicæ" and "The Original of Monarchies," Yahuda MS 16, National Library of Israel, Jerusalem, Israel. Goldish, however, rejects any idea of a genetic link between Newtonian and Hutchinsonian Hebraism: "Newton permitted almost no one to see his theological manuscripts, so the Hutchinsonians could hardly have been aware of his derivations" (*Judaism*, 55). I am less prepared than Goldish to insist that no such link exists.

123. Leighton, "Knowledge," 160.

conviction that God's providence is his governance of nature by means of mathematical laws. For Newton and Hutchinson, providential discernment must be guided by Scripture, and it must be natural-philosophical in orientation.[124] The Old Testament apologetics of both Newton and Hutchinson therefore attempt to corroborate the biblical witness with the preexisting natural order. Newton and Hutchinson insist that the truths of revealed religion can only be true if they conform to nature. In this light, it can be argued that they both make nature, rather than revelation, the touchstone of their scriptural apologetics.

The confidence that Newton and Hutchinson place in nature as the grounds of truth is expressed in their preference for things rather than words. Hutchinson's insistence that Hebrew characters are word-pictures appears to problematize this distinction, but in actual fact, it presupposes it. It is because Hutchinson doubts that biblical words, as human linguistic utterances, can function as vehicles of divine truth that he interprets Hebrew characters as hieroglyphs. Newton, for his part, seeks to extract numbers from the biblical witness because he similarly doubts that human linguistic utterances can effectively transmit divine truth. Newton and his rival share the common belief that they must dig beneath the lifeless husks of linguistic signifiers to uncover the life-giving kernels of divine truth contained in nonlinguistic forms.

Whereas noteworthy philosophers such as Locke and Clarke were satisfied that vernaculars can be sufficiently (through probably not fully) mathematized, Newton and Hutchinson held that a more radical solution is in order. To this end they interpret Hebrew characters in ways that allow them to overcome the constraints and corruptions of human language. Both explore the possibility that Hebrew words can be reconceived as hieroglyphic monuments of natural-philosophical and religious truth.[125] Although Newton ultimately focused his attention on the potential of mathematical objects to serve as a language of nature, his attempt to save the Old Testament through numbers is not a rejection of Hutchinson's conviction that human language

---

124. See Hutchinson, A Treatise, 39.

125. As universal historians, Hutchinson and Newton share a surprising number of specific doctrines. As we have seen, for example, they both emphasize that early natural-philosophical inquiry and sun worship were properly directed toward the divine but came to be idolatrous through the attribution of motion to nature.

is hopelessly subject to the vicissitudes of history. Newton's numeritization of the Old Testament and Hutchinson's hieroglyphic method are parallel attempts to de-historicize the Old Testament to protect it against corruption, and against deistic detractors.

Hutchinson's de-historicization of the Old Testament shares two additional features with that of Newton. First, it generates a truncated view of providence. Like Newton, Hutchinson never repudiates the idea that God is at work in and through human history, and yet, like Newton, his work forcefully promotes the view that providence is supremely evident in the consistent mechanical workings of nature. Although Hutchinson evidently brings this view with him to the study of the Old Testament, it is also a view that he believes the Old Testament text compels him to affirm. Hutchinson has no doubt that the Old Testament is to be regarded as authoritative on account of the natural-philosophical wisdom that lies hidden beneath the Hebrew text.

The second feature that accompanies both Hutchinson and Newton's de-historicization of the Old Testament is an inability to interpret the text tropologically.[126] Given that Hutchinson worked so hard to remove the biblical text from the realm of human history, this inability to speak authoritatively regarding human conduct is entirely predictable. Hutchinson, like Newton, transforms the Old Testament into a fountain of demonstrable natural-philosophical truths, but in the process, he makes it a moral wasteland. Since Hutchinson gives his Christian readers little reason to regard Scripture as necessary for the sustenance of Christian life and virtue, his Old Testament apologetic is severely compromised.

CONCLUSION

According to emblematicism, words and things can be used to interpret one another to cultivate the good life. Emblematicism celebrates human words as able to articulate the divine and moral significance of things, but it also insists that things are indispensable for the articulation of these truths—truths that words struggle to capture on their own. Hutchinson's inability to offer tropological readings of the Old Testament is surprising given that

---

126. In this, Hutchinson's approach is radically different from Origen and other patristic writers. In the passage quoted earlier, for example, Origen continually refers to Christ in his reflections upon light so that he can offer tropological readings of the text.

emblematicism plays a central role in his thought. Hutchinson's scriptural apologetic is grounded in the conviction that the providential interpretation of things requires textual mediation. In the course of his work, however, this conviction is constrained and contorted. To begin, the only things Hutchinson is willing to interpret emblematically are natural-philosophical objects. Furthermore, he maintains that the only words capable of divulging the divine meaning of things are Hebrew words. Then again, even Hebrew words, it seems, are unequal to the task—as long as they are interpreted as mere words, that is. Hutchinson therefore refashions Hebrew words as primordial artifacts. This is a clear indication that, like Newton, he ultimately doubts that words are able to divulge the providential meaning of the things he interprets.

Hutchinson's attempt to highlight the uniqueness of the Hebrew Old Testament and his elevation of select Hebrew words to the status of hieroglyphs are apologetic moves necessitated by his devolutionary philosophy of history. To defend the divine origination of the Old Testament, Hutchinson believes he must decontextualize Old Testament words by removing them from the historical and therefore the linguistic realm. This decontextualization is deeply problematic. While select Hebrew hieroglyphs are elevated to the status of divine emblems, the status of the remaining Old Testament text is unclear. The greatest irony, however, is not that Hutchinson's method encourages scholars to leave the text of the Old Testament behind. The greatest irony is that it invites them to cast aside his own writings too.

When, in 1749, Hutchinson's devoted disciples, editors Robert Spearman and Julius Bate (1710–1771), compiled the twelfth and final volume of Hutchinson's collected works, they appended a Hebrew lexicon based upon Hutchinson's voluminous writings. The definitions found in their little lexicon were, for Hutchinson's early disciples, the pure distillation of his meandering natural-philosophical explorations, and they would fight, tooth and nail, to defend them. With the lexicon in hand, aspiring Hebrew scholars could hope to plumb the depths of Hutchinson's writings, Scripture, and of course nature itself. Yet according to Hutchinson's own principles, this appended lexicon is actually *all* they needed.[127] Devoted followers could enhance their knowledge of the terms in the lexicon by tracing Hutchinson's circuitous discussions found throughout his writings, but such labor is surely discretionary. Spearman and Bate's lexicon grants Hutchinson's readers the ability to uncover the great natural-philosophical and religious truths of the cosmos, and this indispensability makes every other document—including the Bible and Hutchinson's writings—redundant.

---

127. It comes as no surprise that Hutchinson's followers were devoted lexicographers. The most celebrated Hutchinsonian lexicographer was John Parkhurst, whose *An Hebrew and English Lexicon without Points* (London: 1762) and *A Greek and English Lexicon to the New Testament* (London: 1769) went through several editions.

4
—

AN EQUAL WITNESS: GEORGE WATSON'S OLD TESTAMENT

"Hutchinson's persuasiveness," remarks Nigel Aston, "was not assisted by his inaccessibility as an author."[1] In this, Hutchinson was very much like Newton, and, like Newton, the dissemination of his ideas therefore depended upon popularizers. By the end of his life Hutchinson had gathered a small group of zealous disciples, including Alexander Catcott Sr. (1692-1749), James Holloway (1690/1-1759), Robert Spearman (1703-1761), and Julius Bate (1710-1771).[2] Hutchinson's name would surely have vanished into obscurity were it not for their tireless efforts to promote his work. The wide array of polemical materials these early Hutchinsonians produced—pamphlets, commentaries, natural-philosophical works, lexicons, and sermons—focused the discussion concerning the merits of Hutchinson's philosophy on the identity of the Hebrew language as the *prima lingua* and confirms that they continued to uphold Hutchinson's emblematic vision. Following Hutchinson, they

---

1. Nigel Aston, "From Personality to Party: The Creation and Transmission of Hutchinsonianism, c. 1725-1750," *Studies in History and Philosophy of Science* 35 (2004): 629. See also David S. Katz, "Christian and Jew in Early Modern English Perspective," *Jewish History* 8 (1994): 66-67. Not everyone who struggled to understand Hutchinson was willing to condemn him for being an obscure writer. John Wesley, for one, remarked that Hutchinson's writings are "quite too elegant for me" (quoted in Derya Gürses Tarbuck, "John Wesley's Critical Engagement with Hutchinsonianism, 1730-1780," *History of European Ideas* 37, no. 1 [2011]: 42).

2. Of the early Hutchinsonian apologists, Aston gives Bate pride of place: "there is a strong case for arguing that Bate fashioned 'Hutchinsonianism' as a distinct ideology as a result of co-editing Hutchinson's collected works and writing numerous pamphlets in defence of his master's mystical theology and his distinctive interpretation of the Hebrew text of the Bible. He thereby brought Hutchinson to the notice of far more people than had been the case in Hutchinson's lifetime" (Nigel Aston, "Bate, Julius [1710-1771]," *Oxford Dictionary of National Biography*, accessed March 9, 2015, http://www.oxforddnb.com.myaccess.library.utoronto.ca/view/article/1664).

interpreted Hebrew characters emblematically as primordial hieroglyphs that sheltered the knowledge of the natural world from the devolutionary force of history.

The most important shift in the history of Hutchinsonianism took place in Oxford in the 1750s. Following the lead of University College fellow George Watson, the Oxonians left behind Hutchinson's hieroglyphic method, choosing to focus instead on the final form of the biblical text. This shift was accompanied by a rejection of the devolutionary philosophy of history that made Hutchinson's hieroglyphic method necessary. The two pillars of early Hutchinsonian philosophy were scriptural emblematicism and devolutionary history. For Watson and the Oxonian Hutchinsonians, the two pillars were scriptural emblematicism and figural history. Watson and the Oxonians extended Hutchinson's emblematic method to all Scripture words, and this propelled them to interpret both natural-philosophical and historical entities as scriptural figures. The figural reading of Scripture led Watson and the Oxonians to uphold the Church of England, the English commonwealth, and countless other elements of human society as providentially ordered. Watson's scriptural emblematicism was the basis of establishmentarian Hutchinsonianism, which rose to prominence in the second half of the eighteenth century.

THE CONSTRUCTION OF HUTCHINSONIANISM

The early Hutchinsonians were zealous defenders of Hutchinson's hieroglyphic method and his larger scriptural apologetic, which sought to defend the Old Testament by binding it to natural-philosophical truths. Probably the best account of early Hutchinsonianism comes from the preface of little-known Hutchinsonian James Moody's *The Evidence for Christianity Contained in the Hebrew Words* Aleim *and* Berit (1752). According to Moody, the genesis of Hutchinsonianism, as a movement, was Catcott Sr.'s sermon "The Supreme and Inferior Elahim," preached before the corporation of Bristol and the Lord Chief-Justice Hardwick on August 16, 1735. As Moody describes it, Catcott's sermon on the text "I said ye are gods" (Ps 87:6) "took occasion to shew that the *English* word *God* singular, was no way expressive of the

Hebrew אלהים *Aleim,* which is plural, and which is a name or noun derived from ALE, which as a verb signifies *to confirm by oath.*"[3] According to Catcott,

> The Persons in Jehovah had, before the world was made, performed an action which had denominated them ALEIM or *Covenanters*: That the substance of this Covenant was to redeem mankind, which was to be effected by the sufferings and death of the second person; for, and in the stead of man, in case man fell.[4]

Catcott's sermon generated what Derya Gürses Tarbuck calls "the *Elahim* controversy," which erupted when Arthur Bedford (1668–1745), Catcott's predecessor as vicar of Temple Church, responded with a pamphlet entitled *Observations on a Sermon* (1736).[5] Bedford was puzzled by Catcott's peculiar etymology and defended the received scholarly opinion that *Elohim* was "derived from the *Arabick* verb *Alaha,* which signifies to *worship religiously,* and ... signifies *that Being, who alone is religiously to be worshipped.*"[6] Bedford's reply was the opportunity for the publicity Hutchinson and his followers longed for: they quickly responded with a number of aggressive refutations.[7]

---

3. James Moody, *The Evidence for Christianity Contained in the Hebrew Words* Aleim *and* Berit (London: 1752), ix. Alexander Catcott Sr., *The Supreme and Inferior Elahim,* 2nd ed. (London: 1742), 8. Catcott's work can be seen as a refutation of Clarke's influential argument that the English word "God" always refers to but one being (Samuel Clarke, *The Scripture-Doctrine of the Trinity* [London: 1712], 1–83).

4. Moody, *The Evidence,* x.

5. Derya Gürses Tarbuck, "The Hutchinsonian Defence of an Old Testament Trinitarian Christianity: The Controversy Over Elahim, 1735–1773," *History of European Ideas* 29 (2003): 396. Although there were Hutchinsonians who were not engaged in the controversy, Gürses Tarbuck is right to identify it as central to the formation of early Hutchinsonian identity.

6. Arthur Bedford, *Observations on a Sermon Preach'd before the Corporation of Bristol* (London: 1736), 15.

7. Hutchinson's final work was a vindictive anonymous reply to Bedford's *Observations*: John Hutchinson, *Remarks Upon the Observations on a Sermon Preach'd before the Corporation of Bristol, and the Lord-Chief-Justice Hardwick* (London: 1737). Catcott defended his deceased master with an *Answer to the Observations* (London: 1737), Bedford replied with *The Examination of the Remarks Upon, and Mr. Catcot's Answer to the Observations Upon his Sermon* (London: 1737), and Catcott replied again with *An Answer to the Observations on a Sermon Preach'd before the Corporation of Bristoll* [...] (London: 1737) and *The State of the Case between Mr. Bedford and Mr. Catcott, in Answer to Mr. Bedford's Examination* (London: 1738). Julius Bate and Daniel Gittins then entered the fray in defense of Catcott: Julius Bate, *The Examiner Examined* (London: 1739); Daniel Gittins, *An Answer to a Pamphlet Entitled, An Examination of Mr. Hutchincon's Remarks, and Mr. Catcott's Answer* [...] (London: 1739); and *Observations on some Sermons Preach'd at the lady Moyer's Lectures* (London: 1741). Bedford's final defense of his position is contained in Arthur Bedford, *A Defence of the Doctrine of the Holy Trinity, and the Incarnation of the Son of God, from the Testimony of the*

These refutations confirm that Catcott and his allies were seeking to faithfully reproduce and popularize Hutchinson's hieroglyphic method.[8]

For Gürses Tarbuck, the central issue of the *Elahim* controversy is Hebrew pointilization.[9] But while Hutchinson and his disciples passionately defended the un-pointed text as Gürses Tarbuck maintains, their rejection of vowel points was but one component of their hieroglyphic method.[10] Once vowel points are eliminated, the hard work of hieroglyphic decipherment remains. First, the consonantal accretions must be removed to identify the primeval roots of the Hebrew words, and then these roots must have their correspondences within the Hutchinsonian natural-philosophical scheme.

Most Ancient Jews. In Eight Sermons, Preached at the Lady Moyer's Lecture (London: 1741). Moody claims that Mr. Langford and Mr. Lookup wrote in defense of Bedford, but I have been unable to locate their works.

8. Moody reminds his readers that Catcott ended his sermon by endorsing Hutchinson's work and giving a "generous and open confession of his obligation to Mr. H. as an author, which shewed at once, the gentleman, the scholar, and the christian." For both Moody and Catcott, Hutchinson was "the first who, since inspiration ceased, began to recover the true sense of the Hebrew S. S." (Moody, *The Evidence*, xii–xiii).

9. Gürses Tarbuck concludes that the ability of Hutchinsonian opponents to utilize comparative linguistics to establish the original text "triumphed over the Hutchinsonian, spiritual method of interpreting what was to them a fixed and certain unpointed text" ("The Hutchinsonian," 408). Gürses Tarbuck emphasizes Benjamin Kennicott's role in bringing about the demise of Hutchinsonianism. Nevertheless, Kennicott's prodigious effort to create an updated edition of the Hebrew text was looked upon with askance by many of his contemporaries. "The great expectations that were formed respecting this edition of the Hebrew Bible were somewhat disappointed on its appearance. Perhaps however they had been unreasonably high. Amid the immense mass of various readings which he had collected with so great labour, few were found to be of any value in the emendation of the text. The majority were at once seen to be the mere *lapsus* of transcribers" (Samuel Davidson, *Lectures of Biblical Criticism, Exhibiting a Systematic View of that Science* [Edinburgh, 1839], 224). Ironically, Kennicott's own perspective on transmission history is remarkably like that of his Hutchinsonian opponents. Like the Hutchinsonians, Kennicott believes the Masoretes had corrupted the Hebrew Old Testament, and, like the Hutchinsonians, his primary object is to convince scholars that he possesses the means to overcome this corruption. See William McKane, "Benjamin Kennicott: An Eighteenth-Century Researcher," *Journal of Theological Studies* 28 (1977): 460.

10. The debate between the Hutchinsonians and their opponents was not the first of its kind. In the sixteenth century, Elias Levita had already raised a significant controversy when he challenged the antiquity of Hebrew vocalizations, and by the seventeenth century the antiquity of vocalizations had become one of the primary issues that Hebrew scholars were forced to confront. In one of the great scholarly debates of the century, Louis Cappel challenged Johann Buxtorf Sr.'s defense of the originality of the pointing and was vigorously opposed by Buxtorf the Younger. Johann Anselm Steiger, "The Development of the Reformation Legacy: Hermeneutics and Interpretation of the Sacred Scripture in the Age of Orthodoxy," in *Hebrew Bible / Old Testament, Vol. 2: From the Renaissance to the Enlightenment*, edited by Magne Sæbø (Gottingen: Vandenhoeck & Ruprecht GmbH & Co., 2008), 748.

The *Elahim* controversy fizzled out in the early 1740s, but the fortunes of Hutchinsonianism were revived by the publication of Hutchinson's collected works.[11] In 1746, 1747, and 1748, Spearman and Bate published *Proposals for Printing, by Subscription, the Philosophical and Theological Works of the Late Truly Learned Mr. Hutchinson*. Remarkably, they managed to acquire the subscriptions necessary to publish all twelve volumes of Hutchinson's physico-theology by the end of 1749.[12] The publication of Hutchinson's collected works served as a second birth for Hutchinsonianism.[13] In the years following the publication of Hutchinson's collected works, Hutchinsonians produced a number of related natural-philosophical works.[14] Benjamin Holloway's (1690/91–1759) *Originals Physical and Theological* (1751) illustrates that the Hutchinsonians continued to approach natural philosophy through Hutchinson's emblematic lens. The subtitle of the work is "An Essay towards

---

11. In 1750 Warburton remarked in a letter to Bishop Hurd that the controversy was still well known in intellectual circles (William Warburton, *Letters from a Late Eminent Prelate [W.W.] to one of His Friends* [London: 1809], 58–59).

12. A list of the subscribers can be found at Spearman and Bate, *Proposals for Printing by Subscription the Philosophical and Theological Works of the Late Truly Learned Mr. Hutchinson* [...] (London: 1748), 30.

13. Gürses Tarbuck points to Thomas Sharp's *Two Dissertations Concerning the Etymology and Scripture-Meaning of the Hebrew Words* Elohim *and* Birth (London: 1751) as the instigator of the second stage in the *Elahim* controversy, as it provoked fierce rejoinders from Hutchinsonians, including Aboab, Bate, Holloway, and Moody. David Aboab, *Remarks on Dr. Sharp's Two Dissertations* (London: 1751); Julius Bate, *The Scripture Meaning of Aleim and Berith* (London: 1751); Benjamin Holloway, *Remarks on Dr. Sharp's Pieces on the Words* Elohim *and* Berith (Oxford: 1751). Tarbuck remarks that the only support given to Sharp in the debate was from the German immigrant George Kalmar, who was mercilessly ridiculed by the Hutchinsonians because of his lack of proficiency in the English language. George Kalmar, *Mr. Bate's Answer to Sharp's Two Dissertations Answered* (London: 1751); *A Short Reply to Mr. Holloway's Remarks on Dr. Sharp's Two Dissertations* (London: 1751); *Censurer Censured: Or a Defence of Dr. Sharp's Two Dissertations &c. Being a Reply to Mr. Aboab's Remarks* (London: 1751). The second stage of the controversy was, like the first, but one aspect of a larger debate concerning the merits of Hutchinson's collected works that precedes the publication of Sharp's *Dissertations*. Catholic vicar Simon Berington and Bate exchanged pamphlets in 1750–1751, and a number of other Hutchinsonian works were published in these years. Simon Berington, *Dissertations on the Mosaical Creation* [...] (London: 1750); Bate, *A Defence of Mr. Hutchinson's Tenets in Philosophy and Divinity* [...] (London: 1751); Duncan Forbes, *Some Thoughts Concerning Religion, Natural and Revealed* (Edinburgh: 1750); Walter Hodges, *Elihu: Or an Enquiry into the Principle Scope and Design of the Book of Job* (London: 1750 and 1751).

14. These include Benjamin Holloway, *Originals Physical and Theological, Sacred and Profane. Or an Essay Towards a Discovery of the First Descriptive Ideas in Things* (Oxford: 1751); George Horne, *The Theology and Philosophy in Cicero's Somnium Scipionis Explained* (London: 1751); *A Fair, Candid, and Impartial State of the Case between Sir Isaac Newton and Mr. Hutchinson* (London: 1753); Andrew Wilson, *The Principles of Natural Philosophy* (London: 1753); Samuel Pike, *Philosophia Sacra: Or, the Principles of Natural Philosophy; Extracted from Divine Revelation* (London: 1753).

a Discovery of the first descriptive Ideas in Things, by the Discovery of the simple or primary ROOTS IN WORDS." Holloway's work confirms that the Hutchinsonian interest in the Hebrew language must not be confined to the theological realm. Holloway picks up exactly where Hutchinson left off—in more ways than one. First, he employs the emblematic method Hutchinson undertook in his final work on Genesis, *Moses's—Sine Principio*. Each section begins with an image—a Hebrew hieroglyph—that is followed by an epigram, which illumines the manner in which the hieroglyph reveals the hidden structure of the universe. Second, Holloway begins his commentary on Genesis exactly where Hutchinson left off in the middle of Genesis chapter 3, and continues on, in the first volume, through to the middle of Genesis chapter 14. Holloway's employment of Hutchinson's method illustrates that the early Hutchinsonians were interested in more than simply defending Hebrew as the *prima lingua*. Their object is to defend the divine authority of the Old Testament by means of Hutchinson's scriptural emblematicism. Like Hutchinson, they believed the only way to save the Hebrew language, and the Old Testament, was to defend the Pentateuch as a prehistorical linguistic monument, thereby binding it to the immovable truths of nature and protecting it from the corrupting force of history.

HUTCHINSON AND OXONIAN HUTCHINSONIANISM

Early Hutchinsonians such as Holloway and Walter Hodges (d. 1757), provost of Oriel College, circulated Hutchinsonian pamphlets in Oxford as early as 1734.[15] In the third and fourth decades of the eighteenth century, however, Bristol was the center of Hutchinsonianism.[16] After the publication of Hutchinson's collected works in 1748-1749, the center shifted to Oxford. In 1751 William Stevens (1732-1807) wrote to Alexander Catcott Jr. (1725-1779) that "the people at Oxford are involved in ... [a] grand undertaking."[17] In 1753 parliamentarian Horace Walpole (1717-1797) wrote to a friend that

---

15. Derya Gürses Tarbuck, "Academic Hutchinsonians and Their Quest for Relevance, 1734-1790," *History of European Ideas* 31 (2005): 410; *Enlightenment Reformation: Hutchinsonianism and Religion in Eighteenth-Century Britain* (London: Routledge, 2016), 87.

16. With Catcott as headmaster, Bristol Grammar School produced several zealous young Hutchinsonians (Aston, "From Personality," 631).

17. Gürses Tarbuck, *Enlightenment*, 88. The Hutchinsonians were assisted in this undertaking by the help of poet and Hutchinsonian sympathizer Christopher Smart, who played a leading

Methodism is quite decayed in Oxford, its cradle. In its stead, there prevails a delightful fantastic system, called the sect of the Hutchinsonians, of whom one seldom hears anything in town. After much inquiry, all I can discover is, that their religion consists in driving Hebrew to its fountainhead, till they find some word or other in every text of the Old Testament, which may seem figurative of something in the New. As their doctrine is novel, and requires much study, or at least much invention, one should think that they could not have settled half the canon of what they are to believe—and yet they go on zealously, trying to make and succeeding in making converts.[18]

The Oxonians enlisted the help of the student newspaper and wrote more than one hundred pamphlets from 1761–1784.[19]

The shift from Bristol to Oxford is the backdrop of perhaps the most important problem that Hutchinsonian studies must face: the relationship between the early Hutchinsonianism that flourished in Bristol and the late Hutchinsonianism that had its rise at Oxford. Admittedly, there were personal connections between the Bristol and Oxford societies, and some Oxonians, including Holloway and Hodges, followed the lead of the Bristolians by vigorously promoting Hutchinson's hieroglyphic method. As Hutchinsonianism took root in Oxford, however, the character of Hutchinsonianism was decisively altered by its new surroundings. In particular, Hutchinson's hieroglyphic method is not employed in the sermons and writings of most Oxonians, including Thomas Patten (1714–1790), Denny Martin (a.k.a. Dr. Fairfax; 1725–1800), Catcott Jr., Nathan Wetherell (1726–1808), George Horne, William Jones of Nayland, and Watson. Some scholars have therefore called into question the relationship between the Oxford Hutchinsonians (Horne and Jones in particular) and Hutchinson. But although the Oxonians distanced themselves from Hutchinson's hieroglyphic method, they continued to affirm Hutchinson's interest in natural philosophy and the Hebrew language,

role in the student newspaper, *The Student*. See Karina Williamson, "Smart's Principia: Science and Anti-Science in Jubilate Agno," *Review of English Studies* 30 (1979): 409–22.

18. Horace Walpole, *Correspondence*, ed. W. S. Lewis et al. (New Haven: Yale University Press, 1937–1983), 35:156.

19. Gürses Tarbuck, *Enlightenment*, 88.

and, most importantly, they continued to take for granted his emblematic orientation.[20]

At the beginning of the twentieth century, Overton maintained that Horne and Jones were only "partially Hutchinsonian," arguing that they must be seen, fundamentally, as High-Church ecclesiastics.[21] Overton also insisted that Horne and Jones were much more attracted to Hutchinson's spiritual interpretation of Scripture than his cosmology.[22] As Carroll points out, however, "il est indéniable qu'ils adoptèrent avec enthousiasme et développèrent les principes de sa cosmologie."[23] Carroll's work, which to date represents the most comprehensive study of the theological vision of Horne and Jones, defines Hutchinsonianism as a theophanic vision of creation which seeks to defend a providential ordering of creation through analogies that are drawn between physical and spiritual realities.[24] Carroll believes that Horne and Jones only endorse Hutchinsonian natural philosophy to the extent that it promotes this vision. Thus, although Carroll disagrees with Overton's analysis in several particulars, Carroll consistently endorses his conclusion that Horne and Jones enlisted Hutchinsonianism in the service of the ancien régime as an affirmation of the goodness of the established order. Hutchinsonian doctrine and natural philosophy are accordingly interpreted as subservient to High churchmanship: "Pour ces chrétiens de la "Haute Eglise", l'hutchinsonisme était quelque chose ... surajouté."[25]

With his 2001 article "Knowledge of Divine Things: A Study of Hutchinsonianism," C. D. A. Leighton brought Carroll's analysis of

---

20. Reno puts this in a characteristically colorful way: "Once you get rid of the anti-Newtonian polemics and its quirky Hebrew philology all that is left of Moses's Principia is Hutchinson's emblematic approach to biblical exegesis. This is exactly what Horne and Jones emphasized. Figural interpretation made the Hutchinsonians Hutchinsonian." Rusty Reno, "The Theological Roots of Modern Conservatism," 381–96 in The Identity of Israel's God in Christian Scripture, ed. Don Collett, et al. (Atlanta: SBL Press, 2020), 392.

21. J. H. Overton, A History of the English Church: The English Church from the Accession of George I to the End of the Eighteenth Century (1714-1800) (London: 1906), 205.

22. Overton, A History, 204; See also X. William Carroll, "Hutchinsonisme: Une vue de la nature come Théophanie au cours du dis-huitième siècle" (PhD diss., University of Strasbourg, 1968), 22.

23. Carroll finds this enthusiasm for Hutchinsonian cosmology rather unfortunate, as it tainted the reputations of two of eighteenth-century England's greatest minds ("Hutchinsonisme," 22).

24. Carroll, "Hutchinsonisme," 288–92.

25. Carroll, "Hutchinsonisme," 300.

Hutchinsonianism as theophanic vision to a twenty-first-century English readership. First, Leighton complains that while writers have tended to treat Hutchinsonianism as a set of doctrines about the physical sciences with religious significance, "as a practice, Hutchinsonianism had all appearances of scholarly religion, rather than science."[26] Next, he argues that the religious character of Hutchinsonianism moves it "from a peripheral position in the history of Enlightenment/Counter-Enlightenment debate" concerning the foundations of human knowledge.[27] For Leighton, this debate was dominated by the question of the "security to be had from one or other form of revelation."[28] The defining feature of Hutchinsonianism, thus, for Leighton, is its adoption of the "pre-eminently acceptable epistemology of the day, that of Locke," which "it developed and adapted ... to construct what appeared to be an effective defense of revelation against rationalist assault."[29]

As Leighton rightly points out, the use of a sensualist epistemology in the defense of revelation was hardly unique to the Hutchinsonians. It was also employed to this end by a group Berman calls Irish "right-wing Lockeans," which included Henry Dodwell (1641–1711), William King (1650–1729), and Edward Synge (1659–1741).[30] Leighton maintains that "perhaps the most important figure among them" was Peter Browne (d. 1735), who "took Locke's epistemology beyond Locke's own position, rejecting even reflection as a supplement to sensation," and then extended this position theologically in service of "a doctrine of analogy."[31] Leighton claims that it was "among the

---

26. C. D. A. Leighton, "'Knowledge of Divine Things': A Study of Hutchinsonianism," *History of European Ideas* 26 (2000): 161.

27. Leighton, "Knowledge," 161.

28. Leighton, "Knowledge," 162.

29. Leighton, "Knowledge," 162. Other scholars, including Kuhn (1964), Carroll (1968), and Wilde (1980), have also identified the importance of Lockean sensualism for Hutchinsonianism. Albert Kuhn, "Glory or Gravity: Hutchinson vs. Newton," *Journal of the History of Ideas* 22 (1961): 318; Carroll, "Hutchinsonisme," 245–46; C. B. Wilde, "Hutchinsonianism, Natural Philosophy and Religious Controversy in Eighteenth Century Britain," *History of Science* 18 (1980): 3. Conservative Lockeanism and theophanic vision are but different articulations of the notion that sensory input can be enlisted in the service of revealed religion by means of the principle of analogy. And because Leighton, like Carroll, identifies this conviction as the central tenet of Hutchinsonianism, he follows Carroll in subsuming Hutchinsonianism within the High-Church Counter-Enlightenment.

30. Leighton, "Knowledge," 162. This leads Leighton to employ Berman's phrase "conservative Lockeans," which Berman applies to both Berkeley and Burke.

31. Leighton, "Knowledge," 162.

Hutchinsonians ... that the Irish Counter-Enlightenment churchmen exerted their widest influence."[32] Leighton maintains that while Hutchinson's "view of the Hebrew language had sensationalist roots," Hutchinson's own writings were probably not the major channel through which the Hutchinsonians received the teachings of the Irish Counter-Enlightenment.[33] "In truth," says Leighton, "Hutchinsonians seem to have had as little recourse to Hutchinson's own writings as possible."[34] For Leighton, the central tenet of Hutchinsonianism is the rejection of natural religion, and its central influence is the "Irish school."[35]

Leighton is justified in his appraisal of Horne and Jones as sensualists and in his observation that they engaged Hutchinson critically and cautiously. Nevertheless, as Leighton works through the implications of these findings, he forges a doubtful account of a "Hutchinsonianism *sans* Hutchinson."[36] Horne and Jones's relationship to Hutchinson is evidently very different from that of the early Hutchinsonians. Whereas the early Hutchinsonians zealously defended their master as the most brilliant philosopher the world had

32. Leighton, "Knowledge," 164. Given that these scholars were extremely radical in their appropriation of the sensualist ideal, it is curious that Leighton calls them Counter-Enlightenment figures.

33. Leighton, "Knowledge," 165.

34. Leighton, "Knowledge," 165. It is perhaps because he wishes to defend this startling claim that Leighton avoids the "more zealously Hutchinsonian" Jones of Nayland and focuses on Horne and William Van Mildert, whom he considers to have endorsed a more moderate form of Hutchinsonian doctrine ("Knowledge," 166).

35. Leighton, "Knowledge," 166. There can be no doubt that the Hutchinsonians reacted violently against systems of natural religion that seemed to call into question the necessity of biblical revelation. Nevertheless, the Hutchinsonian system was itself a form of natural religion. Like proponents of natural religion, the Hutchinsonians believed that the only true religious principles were principles grounded in the nature of things. And like so many of their contemporaries (including many deists), they also held that these true religious principles are consistent with biblical revelation. The classic deist articulation of this position is Matthew Tindal's *Christianity as Old as Creation* (London: 1730).

36. Leighton, "Knowledge," 171. Leighton bases his analysis on an anachronistic characterization of religion and philosophy as distinct disciplines that are inherently at odds with each other. This characterization is curious, for if ever there were a movement that challenges the bifurcation of theology and philosophy it is Hutchinsonianism. Although Leighton maintains that his characterization of the Hutchinsonians as "religious" rather than "philosophical" thinkers allows their importance to be recognized, it has the effect of muting their testimony by relegating it to the periphery of intellectual history. This characterization of the Hutchinsonians as "religious" forces Leighton to dismiss their continued natural-philosophical interests as unimportant. For Leighton, "conservative Lockeanism" and indeed "High churchmanship" are little more than counter-arguments leveled against the rising tide of infidelity.

ever seen, Horne and Jones are measured and methodical in their appropriation of Hutchinson's ideas. Jones admits that Hutchinson was "a character *sui
generis*, such as the common forms of education could never have produced."[37]
Jones cleverly uses this inconvenient truth to full advantage as he seeks to
introduce his fellow Oxonians to Hutchinson's writings. He points out that
his full knowledge of Hutchinson's "mean character" had propelled him—as
it should propel others—to painstakingly analyze Hutchinson's ideas so as
to endorse them only as much as is necessary.[38]

There is no doubt that, as Leighton maintains, the Oxonian Hutchinsonians
enthusiastically endorsed a sensualist epistemology. Jones deems Descartes's
attempt to deduce certain knowledge of physical causes a priori "very excep-
tionable" and concedes that there are no a priori arguments for the existence
of God.[39] Jones conceives of knowledge acquisition as a two-step process:
when the mind receives impressions, it is passive, but when it forms ideas,
it is active.[40] The process of idea-formation depends upon the imagination to
give pictures of truth. These pictures are the means through which God "communicates to the mind of man the knowledge of spiritual things, by means
of a certain resemblance, which the Creator hath wisely ordained between
the objects of *sense* and the objects of *faith*."[41] Horne likewise affirms that

> The visible works of God are formed to leads us, under the direction
> of his Word, to a knowledge of those which are invisible; they give
> us ideas, by analogy, of a new creation rising gradually, like the old
> one, out of darkness and deformity, until at length it arrives at the
> perfection of glory and beauty.[42]

---

37. William Jones, *A New Preface to the Second Edition of Memoirs of the Life, Studies, Writings,
& c. of The Right Rev. George Horne* (London: 1799), xxiii.

38. Jones argues that "Had this man been a splendid character, and a great favourite with
the world, we might have received his doctrines with our mouths open, and our eyes shut: but
our dangers are quite of another kind. From *him* nothing is to be taken upon trust: every thing
must be sifted and examined to the uttermost. And so let it: for thus it will be better understood"
(*A New Preface*, xxx–xxxi).

39. William Jones, *An Essay on the First Principles of Natural Philosophy* (London: 1762), 8. See
also Carroll, "Hutchinsonisme," 245.

40. William Jones, *The Nature, Uses, Dangers, Sufferings, and Preservatives, of the Human
Imagination*, London: 1796), 4. Jones's insistence that sensation must be reflected upon in order
to generate ideas suggests that Browne and the "Irish school" were not his primary influences.

41. William Jones, *A Free Enquiry into the Sense and Signification of the Spring* (London: 1772), 1.

42. George Horne, *A Commentary on the Book of Psalms* (London: 1776), 1:xxxix.

The sensualism of the Oxonians, however, need not be attributed either to Locke or to the "Irish School."[43] Unlike either Locke and the members of the "Irish School," the Oxonians made sensualism the basis of an emblematic method, which they inherited directly from Hutchinson.[44]

Gürses Tarbuck's 2005 article "Academic Hutchinsonians and Their Quest for Relevance, 1734–1790" is an important challenge to Leighton's vision of an Oxonian Hutchinsonianism *sans* Hutchinson. To date it represents the only published effort to engage the intellectual foment of 1750s Oxonian Hutchinsonianism. This engagement places Gürses Tarbuck's analysis of Horne and Jones on solid ground. Oxford in the 1750s is the hinge of the move-ment—the link between early Hutchinsonianism and the establishmentarian Hutchinsonianism that flourished into the second quarter of the nineteenth century, and it is therefore impossible to understand Hutchinsonianism without properly attending to it. As Gürses Tarbuck puts it, there is a gap in our knowledge of the relationship between "early and late Hutchinsonian attitudes" because few have explored "the transition that the movement went through."[45]

Gürses Tarbuck agrees with Leighton that the young Oxonians endorsed Hutchinsonian attitudes selectively within a "wider, not exclusively Hutchinsonian, set of ideas," and that they welcomed "other intellectuals to join their speculation and to incorporate a sanitized Hutchinsonian thinking with contemporary thought."[46] Contra Leighton, however, she insists that the

---

43. I am of the opinion that one of the reasons scholars often regard Locke as a fundamen-tally creative thinker is that he consistently fails to acknowledge his sources because he believes that authentic knowledge must be self-generated rather than received from tradition. Locke did not spawn the idea that sensory data is necessary for the acquisition of knowledge. Nor were the members of the "Irish School" the first to apply a sensualist epistemology to divine things. The notion that concrete particulars are necessary for the generation of divine knowledge is fundamental both to precritical biblical exegesis and to Christian mysticism. Meister Eckhart, for instance, observed that the world would not have been created if the soul were able to come to know God without it. Raymond Blakney, ed. and trans., *Meister Eckhart: A Modern Translation* (New York: Harper & Row, 1941), 161.

44. The notion that the Hutchinsonians are Lockeans is curious given that Jones claims that although Locke may well have been an upright individual, his philosophical principles have been incredibly destructive of religion (William Jones, *A Letter to the Church of England, Pointing out Some Popular Errors of Bad Consequence* [London: 1798], 30–31.).

45. Gürses Tarbuck, "Academic," 410.

46. Gürses Tarbuck, "Academic," 410, 422. Although Tarbuck acknowledges that the Oxonians were influenced by the "Irish school," she opposes Leighton's notion of a Hutchinsonianism *sans*

concerted effort of the Oxonians to supplement Hutchinson's perspective
does not imply a rejection of it. To the contrary, the Oxonians made use of
other writers to make Hutchinson's ideals palatable to contemporary scholars.[47] Interpretations of Hutchinsonianism tend to emphasize either natural
philosophy or Hebraic scholarship. Gürses Tarbuck's interpretation rightly
affirms the importance of both. She argues that the two key elements of 1750s
Oxonian Hutchinsonianism are Hebraic scholarship and natural philosophy,
and that these elements point not to the "Irish school" but to Hutchinson himself.[48] The Oxonians wholeheartedly embraced Hutchinson's natural-philosophical system. A Fair, Candid, and Impartial State of the Case between Sir Isaac
Newton and Mr. Hutchinson (1753) is a case in point. It is Horne's diplomatic
attempt to moderate the controversy the Oxonians instigated through their
vocal endorsement of Hutchinson's anti-Newtonian natural philosophy.[49]

Although natural-philosophical study was central to Oxonian
Hutchinsonianism, Hebraic study was arguably even more prominent.[50] Zeal
for the prima lingua took several colleges by storm during the 1740s and 1750s,
and the Hutchinsonians were leading the charge. There were, Jones relates,
"many good and learned men of both Universities, but chiefly in and of the
University of Oxford," who had "become zealous advocates in favour of the
new scheme of Mr. Hutchinson."[51] Jones sat down with fellow students Horne,
Wetherell, and Martin "for one whole winter, to examine and settle as far

Hutchinson: "for the later group of followers Hutchinson's system of thought lost little of its
importance." Tarbuck, "Academic," 423.

47. Gürses Tarbuck also acknowledges, however, that "The realization among this Oxford
group that a full-blooded Hutchinsonian system was on the margins of orthodox thinking led
them to develop a more integrated approach which arguably contributed to the gradual break-
down of Hutchinsonianism as a coherent body of thought" ("Academic," 408). Tarbuck's conclusion that the effort to integrate Hutchinsonianism into mainstream Anglicanism ultimately
compromised "the distinctiveness and unity of the movement" is incontrovertible ("Academic,"
427).

48. Gürses Tarbuck, "Academic," 421–22.

49. The most influential Hutchinsonian natural-philosophical treatise ever written was by
an Oxonian: Alexander Catcott Jr.'s A Treatise on the Deluge (London: 1761). Like Hutchinson himself, Catcott Jr. traveled widely gathering geological specimens, and his work echoes Hutchinson's
reflections found in Moses's Principia: Part II (London: 1727).

50. C. D. A. Leighton, "Hutchinsonianism: A Counter-Enlightenment Reform Movement,"
The Journal of Religious History 23 (1999): 173.

51. William Jones, Memoirs of the Life, Studies, and Writings of the Right Reverend George Horne,
D. D. Late Lord Bishop of Norwich (London: 1795), 22. Jones describes the proselytizing zeal of the
Oxonians as follows: "When a student hath once persuaded himself that he sees truth in the

as they were able, all the Themata of the Hebrew language; writing down their remarks daily."[52]

The central importance of natural philosophy and Hebrew scholarship for the Oxonian Hutchinsonians importantly highlights the continuity of their enterprise with that of early Hutchinsonianism. The point that must be made, however, is not just that the Oxonians pursued Hutchinson's two great interests, as Gürses Tarbuck maintains. Their indebtedness to Hutchinson runs deeper still. Following Hutchinson, Watson, Horne, and Jones all interpret biblical particulars as emblems that unveil the providential order of the natural world.[53]

The biblical hermeneutic of the Oxonians must be described as emblematic rather than merely analogical. The failure to properly account for Hutchinson's influence upon the Oxonians corresponds to a failure to appreciate the mediatorial role that Scripture plays in their work in creating and sustaining comparisons between physical and spiritual things. Once this is properly recognized, Hutchinson's pervasive influence becomes apparent in their work. The Oxonians were convinced that it is only by treating Scripture words as emblems that correspondences between material and spiritual things are revealed to human intellects. The Oxonians are to be regarded as Hutchinsonians not merely because they appropriated Hutchinson's interest in natural philosophy and his fascination with the Hebrew language but because the foundation of their work is Hutchinson's own scriptural emblematicism. Scriptural emblematicism is the *sine qua non* of Hutchinsonianism.

---

principles of Mr. Hutchinson, a great revolution succeeds in his ideas of the natural world and its oeconomy" (*Memoirs*, 36).

52. Jones, *Memoirs*, 46. Hebrew scholars Jones, Horne, Wetherell, and Martin took for granted many of Hutchinson's basic tenets concerning the Hebrew language, including its priority, divine origin, and imagistic quality. Despite these similarities, the students were all hesitant to utilize Hutchinson's etymological method. This hesitancy is discussed further in chapter 4. The sources they used in their study were the standard Hebrew lexicons of the day, including Marius, Buxtorf, Pagninus, and others.

53. The fact that individual Hutchinsonians shared a common hermeneutic did not go unnoticed by early commentators. Thus Teale remarks: "It has been already remarked that one of the peculiarities of the Hutchinsonians was to adopt a figurative rather than literal interpretation of Scripture, especially of those passages which refer to the natural world. This mode of interpretation runs through most of Jones's writings, while several of them were composed for the express purpose of elucidating it" (William Henry Teale, "The Life of William Jones, M. A., Perpetual Curate of Nayland," in *Biography of English Divines: The Life of Launcelot Andrewes, D. D., Bishop of Winchester* [London: Joseph Masters, 1849], 361).

WATSON AND OXONIAN HUTCHINSONIANISM

Watson matriculated to University College in 1740. He received his bachelor of arts in 1743. He was elected to a scholarship from the Bennet foundation in 1744, received his master of arts in 1746, and was chosen for a fellowship at University College in 1747.[54] Watson served University College as fellow and tutor until 1758, and it was in these capacities he exerted a decisive influence on the next generation of Hutchinsonians, including Horne and Jones. Much of what we know concerning Watson's life and work comes from Jones's *Memoirs of the Life, Studies, and Writings of the Right Reverend George Horne* (1795). In this work, Jones begins his account of the happy days he spent at Oxford with Horne by mentioning his friendship with Catcott Jr. Catcott Jr., Jones tells us, "possessed a very curious collection of fossils, some of which he had digged and scratched out of the earth with his own hands at the hazard of his life."[55] Jones confesses that when he saw them he was "without any particular knowledge of the subject," but that Catcott taught him Hutchinson's philosophy to help him understand the significance of his geological specimens.[56]

Catcott Jr.'s influence led Jones to call into question the prevailing Newtonian natural philosophy he had been taught as an undergraduate, and Jones became convinced that he could not hope to order his thoughts concerning the natural world without fluency in the *prima lingua*. Jones set off in search of a Hebrew tutor. His quest led him to Watson, whom Jones introduces in the following terms:

> In the same College with us, there lived a very extraordinary person. He was a classical scholar of the first rate, from a public school, remarkable for an unusual degree of taste and judgment in Poetry and Oratory; his person was elegant and striking, and his countenance expressed at once both the gentleness of his temper and the quickness of his understanding. His manners and address were those of a perfect gentleman: his common talk, though easy and fluent, had the

54. Joseph Foster, ed., *Alumni Oronienses: The Members of the University of Oxford, 1715–1886* (Oxford: 1891), 4:1510. See also Richard Sharp, "Watson, George (1723–1773)," *Oxford Dictionary of National Biography*, accesses March 13, 2015, http://www.oxforddnb.com.myaccess.library.utoronto.ca/view/article/28835?docPos=2.

55. Jones, *Memoirs*, 23.

56. Jones, *Memoirs*, 24.

correctness of studied composition: his benevolence was so great, that all the beggars in Oxford knew the way to his chamber-door: upon the whole, his character was so spotless, and his conduct so exemplary, that, mild and gentle as he was in his carriage toward them, no young man dared to be rude in his company. By many of the first people in the University he was known and admired: and it being my fortune to live in the same staircase with him, he was very kind and attentive to me, though I was much his junior: he often allowed me the pleasure of his conversation, and sometimes gave me the benefit of his advice, of which I knew the meaning to be so good, that I always heard it with respect, and followed it as well as I could. This gentleman, with all his other qualifications, was a Hebrew scholar, and a favourer of Mr. Hutchinson's Philosophy; but had kept it to himself, in the spirit of Nicodemus.[57]

When Jones asked Watson to teach him the elements of Hutchinson's philosophy, Watson desisted because he perceived that "these things are in no repute."[58] Jones boasts, however, that he managed to convince Watson to become his tutor nonetheless. Jones relates that in this capacity, Watson "acquitted himself with so much skill and kind attention, writing out for me with his own hand such grammatical rules and directions as he judged necessary, that in a very short time I could go on without my guide."[59]

Although Jones was already inclined to favor Hutchinsonian philosophy when he began to study with Watson, Watson provided him with its underlying scriptural framework. Jones quickly took it upon himself to win over his best friend, Horne, to Hutchinson's principles but found Horne "very little inclined to consider them."[60] Horne eventually became a passionate defender of Hutchinson, but Jones confesses that he had "no title to the merit

---

57. Jones, *Memoirs*, 25–26.

58. Jones, *Memoirs*, 26. Watson told Jones that he was worried that teaching him the principles of Hutchinsonianism would compromise Jones's friendships and prospects at upward mobility.

59. Jones, *Memoirs*, 26–27. Jones admits, "I had nearly worked myself to death, by determining, like Duns Scotus in the Picture-Gallery, to go through a whole chapter in the Hebrew before night" (*Memoirs*, 27).

60. Jones, *Memoirs*, 24.

of forming him into what he afterwards proved to be."[61] That distinction rests, once again, with Watson. Jones introduced Horne to Watson after Jones had matriculated with an MA in the spring of 1749 and was set to leave Oxford to pursue an ecclesiastical career in the Diocese of Peterborough. Horne became so enthusiastic about the prospect of studying Hebrew with Watson that he "stayed for the advantage of following his studies at Oxford, under the direction of his new teacher" rather than "going home to his friends in the vacation."[62]

When Horne wrote to his father in the fall to apologize for failing to return over the summer, he praised Watson in terms reminiscent of Jones:

> I am obliged for the happiness I have enjoyed of late to a gentleman of this society, and shall always bless God that his providence ever brought me acquainted with him. He is a Fellow of our house and though but six-and-twenty, as complete a scholar in the whole circle of learning, as great a divine, as good a man, and as polite a gentleman, as the present age can boast of.[63]

---

61. Jones, *Memoirs*, 25.

62. Jones, *Memoirs*, 27. One of the primary difficulties for the young students was that the Hebrew concordances and lexicons their studies required were often well beyond their means. Jones relates that when Horne began to study Hebrew, he "set his heart" upon the concordance of Marius de Calasio, which had recently been republished by the sometime Hutchinsonian William Romaine. The problem for the young Horne, however, was that it was an extremely expensive work—"so high as ten guineas at that time." Jones relates that as Horne "knew not how to purchase it out of his allowance, or to ask his father in plain terms to make him a present of it," he told him the following story: "In the last age, when bishop Walton's Polyglott was first published, there was at Cambridge a Mr. Edwards, passionately fond of oriental learning; who afterwards went by the name of Rabbi Edwards: a good man, and a good scholar: but being then rather young in the University, and not very rich, Walton's great work was far above his pocket. Nevertheless, not being able to sleep well without it, he sold his bed, and some of his furniture, and made the purchase. In consequence of witch, he was obliged to sleep in a large chest, originally made to hold his clothes. But getting into his chest one night rather incautiously, the lid of it, which had a bolt with a spring, fell down upon him and locked him in past recovery; and there he lay well nigh smothered to death. In the morning, Edwards, who was always an exact man, not appearing, it was wondered what was become of him: till at last his bed-maker ... being alarmed, went to his chambers time enough to release him: and the accident, getting air, came to the ears of his friends, who soon redeemed his bed for him. This story Mr. Horne told his father; and it had the desired effect. His father immediately sent him the money; for which he returns him abundant thanks, promising to repay him in the only possible way, viz. that of using the books to the best advantage" (*Memoirs*, 35–36).

63. Jones, *Memoirs*, 27–28.

As we might expect, Watson imparted to Horne far more than linguistic competence. Horne confesses

> To have been persuaded, that the System of Divinity in the Holy Scripture is explained and attested by the scriptural account of created nature; and that this account, including the Mosaic Cosmogony, is true so far as it goes: and that the Bible in virtue of its originality is fitter to explain all the books in the world than they are to explain it.[64]

Although Jones's interest in Hutchinsonian natural philosophy led him to study Hebrew with Watson, it was Horne's desire to study Hebrew with Watson that led him to embrace Hutchinsonian natural philosophy. This interesting contrast highlights the interplay of natural philosophy and biblical study characteristic of Hutchinsonian scriptural emblematicism. What we see in the work of Horne and Jones, as in the work of the early Hutchinsonians, is a fluid movement between textual and empirical study, and the creative integration of empirical and humanistic impulses.

Horne and Jones, like the early Hutchinsonians, are convinced that textual study is empirical study given that texts are physical objects, and that empirical study demands textual study given that empirical objects depend upon texts to give voice to the praise they render unto God. As Hutchinsonians, they consider Hebraic studies to be consistent with their sensualist epistemology because they consider it a "language of ideas." This, Jones says, is one of the central ideas Watson imparted to his students. Watson taught them that

> The Hebrew language, and the Hebrew antiquities, lead to a superior way of understanding the mythology and writings of the Heathen classical authors: and that the Hebrew is a language of ideas; whose terms for invisible and spiritual things are taken with great advantage from the objects of nature; and that there can be no other way of conceiving such things, because all of our ideas enter by the senses: whereas in all other languages, there are arbitrary sounds without ideas.[65]

64. Jones, *Memoirs*, 30.
65. Jones, *Memoirs*, 31.

This ideographic interpretation of the Hebrew tongue, proposed by Hutchinson and mediated by Watson, compelled the young Oxonians to pay utmost attention to the meaning of the individual words of the Hebrew text.[66] Watson managed, nevertheless, to pass to his students Hutchinson's reverence for Hebrew words without endorsing his peculiar etymological method.[67] Watson's published scriptural reflections, and those of his students, are governed by a nonetymological scriptural emblematicism.

WATSON'S SCRIPTURAL EMBLEMATICISM

Watson published only five works in his lifetime—three sermons and two essays.[68] His first published work, a sermon entitled "Christ the Light of the World," was preached before the University of Oxford at St. Peter's on Saturday, October 28, 1749. Like Hutchinson, Watson begins his first published work by declaring that his object is to defend the authority of Scripture, and like Hutchinson, he does so through the emblematic interpretation of the Old Testament. The text for Watson's sermon is Psalm 19:4-5: "In them hath he set a Tabernacle for the Sun, which is as a Bridegroom coming out of his Chamber." Following Hutchinson, his reflections are dominated by the quest to uncover the meaning of particular Hebrew words. Watson zeros in on the term "Sun." He argues that "The *Sun* here spoke of, in the full and Prophetical Sense of the Expression, is ... *Christ*, and the Psalm from which the Text is taken a glorious and animated Description of his *Rising* and the blessed *Effects* of it."[69] Watson's sermon can be interpreted according to Alciato's traditional

---

66. Watson's careful attention to the nuances of Hebrew words in their interpretation closely resembles that of the patristic interpretive practice O'Keefe and Reno call "intensive exegesis" (John J. O'Keefe and Russell R. Reno, *Sanctified Vision: An Introduction to Early Christian Interpretation of the Bible* [Baltimore, MD: The Johns Hopkins University Press, 2005], 45-50).

67. Watson may well have spoken with Horne and Jones in secret about Hutchinsonian etymologies, but all three were hesitant to discuss them in their published work.

68. George Watson, *Christ the Light of the World: A Sermon Preached before the University of Oxford at St. Peter's* (Oxford: 1750); *A Seasonable Admonition to the Church of England: A Sermon Preached before the University of Oxford at St. Mary's* (Oxford: 1755); *Aaron's Intercession, and Korah's Rebellion Considered: A Sermon Preached before the University of Oxford* (Oxford: 1756); *The Doctrine of the Ever-blessed Trinity Proved in a Discourse on the Eighteenth Chapter of Genesis* (London: 1756); *A Letter from the Author of a Late Discourse on the XVIIIth Chapter of Genesis, to the Monthly Reviewers* (London: 1758).

69. Watson, *Christ*, 7. For a study of Watson's treatment of Psalm 19 in eighteenth-century context, see David Ney, "Allegory and Empiricism: Interpreting God's Two Books in Newtonian England," *Journal of Theological Interpretation* 7, no. 1 (2016): 37-52.

threefold emblematic structure: the sun is the image, Psalm 19:4–5 is the motto, and the sermon itself is the epigram.

Although Watson eagerly embraced Hutchinson's scriptural emblematicism, he does not slavishly follow Hutchinson. For Hutchinson, the metaphysical import of scriptural terms is only faintly impressed upon the final form of the text given that it is subject to corruption. His favorite term, *eloheim*, for example, must be stripped of historical accretions to be rendered *elahim*, and then broken down into radical form to be rendered *ela* (*ale*). Hutchinson and his early followers, however, had an additional problem. It is far from obvious how *ela* can be redeployed as a natural-philosophical concept. Hutchinson's natural-philosophical system is therefore called upon to bridge the gap between the term *ela* and the natural world. One might equally say that his system manipulates the natural world to render the term *ela* descriptive of it: Hutchinson's insistence that *ela* refers to a primordial covenant between Trinitarian persons must be supplemented by his ethereal speculations concerning air, light, and fire to render *ela* emblematic. Hutchinson's scriptural emblematicism therefore depends upon a twofold manipulation, which is, conveniently, necessitated by the fact that history has obscured the accordance of Scripture and nature.

For Watson, however, no such manipulation is necessary. The scriptural term "Sun" is allowed to stand as it is found in the final form of the text. Watson therefore finds it unnecessary to subject the physical object "Sun" to metaphysical speculation. In this, Watson's approach can be seen as less scholarly than that of Hutchinson. Hutchinson's emblematicism makes his readers dependent on his surprising natural-philosophical insights to reorder their ideas concerning the natural world in scriptural terms. Watson's approach liberates the reader from such dependence. Watson has clearly done the hard work of scholarly engagement with the Hebrew text, but his labor is rarely explicitly noted in his work.[70] As for his observations concerning the natural world, they are neither scholarly nor esoteric; his

---

70. Watson's lexical and grammatical reflections are selectively included in his footnotes—available only as supplemental insights for keen readers. The one exception to this approach that I have found is the Hebrew term *Geber*, which Watson discusses on page 15 of his sermon *Christ the Light of the World*.

reflections upon the physical properties and effects of the sun, we shall see, are observations a child could be expected to make.

Watson takes for granted that sensible objects are necessary for the generation of authentic knowledge, whether natural objects or the words of Scripture. He says that Christ is, in Psalm 19, "as in other Places of holy Writ, represented to our Senses under the Image of the material Sun, doing in the spiritual or moral World what That does in the natural."[71] Only because the sun is a sensible object can it elevate our thoughts to divine things. For Watson, there is only one road to spiritual contemplation, and that road passes through the natural world. "We must therefore," says Watson, "briefly enquire what the Light does there, and apply it spiritually as we go along."[72] Scripture mandates empirical study because it calls Christ "the light of the world."[73] Indeed, a refusal to consider what light is and does in the natural world is to close the door on God's appointed means of instruction concerning his Son. Watson ponders the role of light in the natural world as that which God has "appointed to be the Author and Supporter of animal and vegetable Life" in order to understand how Christ can be said to be the one upon whom

Our Spiritual Life, our Growth in Grace, our Fruitfulness in good Works, our final Attainment of Perfection wholly depend. Does the natural Light in Spring-time call forth dead and rotten Seeds to the Birth, cause naked Roots and Branches to sprout out afresh, and enliven and renew the Face of the Earth? So shall it also be in the Morning of the Resurrection.[74]

---

71. Watson, *Christ*, 7. Watson's willingness to interpret both the sun and the light that emanates from the sun as christological emblems stands in contrast to Hutchinson's clear demarcation between the sun as that which represents the Father, and light as that which represents the Son.

72. Watson, *Christ*, 17.

73. This should come as no surprise, since Hutchinson's hermeneutic called interpreters to assign Scripture words to natural-philosophical objects. Hutchinson maintained that the Hebrew words for air, fire, and light have biblical and therefore spiritual referents. But he also treated the biblical words as invitations to consider the empirical properties and functions of air, fire, and light. Hutchinson did not oppose the zeal with which his contemporaries were studying natural phenomena. He merely wished to remind those toiling away in their laboratories that they must not forget to attend to the Bible if they hope to find the hand of God.

74. Watson, *Christ*, 17.

This reflection leads Watson to draw upon Paul's discussion of resurrection bodies in 1 Corinthians 15. In this passage Paul considers the mystery of plant germination, and he observes that a kernel of wheat "is not quickened, except it die" (1 Cor 15:36). "So will it be with our Bodies," says Watson, paraphrasing Paul, "They must die before they can be quickened, be sown in Corruption e'er they can be raised in Incorruption: And as the material Light is the Cause of this Resurrection in the natural World, so shall the Light divine be in the spiritual."[75] This observation encourages Watson to reflect upon many other ways in which the "Properties and Effects" of the "visible Sun" are precisely those of the "Sun of Righteousness."[76]

That Watson's exegetical method compels him to strongly endorse empirical study confirms that, as a Hutchinsonian, he does not see biblical interpretation and natural philosophy as separate fields of study. Hutchinson's voluminous writings betray his conviction that he alone is able to demonstrate the accordance of the Book of Nature and the Book of Scripture, and he therefore carries the overwhelming responsibility of recasting Scripture as a natural-philosophical textbook. Watson is similarly motivated to demonstrate the emblematic accordance of God's two books. But unlike Hutchinson, he is content to affirm the apparent though limited accordance he finds between the scriptural text as he finds it and the natural world as he observes it.

CANONICAL READING AND
PROVIDENTIAL HISTORY

Watson's biblical hermeneutic extends Hutchinson's emblematic interpretation of select Hebrew hieroglyphs to the entire text of the Christian Scriptures. In his hands, therefore, it is not merely individual Scripture words but rather the biblical canon as a whole that fulfills the mandate of the emblematic motto: it mediates the providential interpretation of natural and historical particulars (images) in order to generate edifying epigrams. In *Christ the Light of the World*, Watson's canonical hermeneutic leads him to interpret natural objects as scriptural figures, but in *A Seasonable Admonition to the Church of England* (1756) and *Aaron's intercession, and Korah's rebellion considered* (1756), he extends the figural reach of Scripture to historical objects.

---

75. Watson, *Christ*, 18.
76. Watson, *Christ*, 18.

Although there is some ambiguity in Watson's hermeneutical method, the goal of his labors is not in doubt. He seeks to unveil the providential significance of natural-philosophical and historical particulars by interpreting them, in canonical context, as scriptural figures.

Watson spends almost half of *Christ the Light of the World* defending his central claim that the "Sun of righteousness" is Christ, and he presents no fewer than seven justifications for his decision to do so.[77] From these justifications it is clear that Watson believes the meaning of the term "Sun of righteousness" is determined primarily by the way it is employed by canonical authors.[78] This insistence leads Watson to leave behind the traditional Hutchinsonian affirmation of the uniqueness of the Hebrew tongue and, therefore, Hebrew Scripture. Thus, when he turns to the tiny New Testament Epistle of Jude, Watson observes that what Jude

> Hath written upon this occasion is full of divine energy; the sentiments have in them all the depth and majesty that is peculiar to the divine writings; and the expressions, with which they are clothed, are the inimitable language of the Spirit of God.[79]

---

77. First, Watson maintains that he is compelled to interpret Christ as the "Sun of righteousness" because "Christ is the chief or principal Subject of the Psalms in general." The Psalter, says Watson, "can be looked upon as nothing less than a rich Storehouse of Christian Knowledge" in lieu of the fact Christians have been given the key to the Psalter, which is Christ (Watson, *Christ*, 8). "To him every page relates," and "has its full Completion in him" (*Christ*, 9). Second, Watson argues that he is bound to his christological interpretation by St. Paul's precedent, for St. Paul says that the gentiles received the news that Christ is the light of the world when they received the preaching of the apostles (Rom 10; *Christ*, 9). Third, Watson argues that the title of the psalm, "For the Conqueror," is a reference to Christ since we are told in the book of Revelation that Christ, the true David, is the final conqueror (*Christ*, 10–11). Fourth, it is evident to Watson that Christ is the object of verses 7–12, as he is the spiritual end of the law. Watson argues that the transition from verse 6 to verse 7 is awkward when a christological interpretation of verses 4–6 is refused (*Christ*, 11). Fifth, Watson argues that the term "*Sun* or *Light* is above all others the *Title* by which [Christ] was always distinguished" (*Christ*, 11). Watson proceeds to list several biblical characters who give him this name, including Balaam, David, Isaiah, Malachi, Zachariah, Simeon, St. John, and John the Baptist (*Christ*, 12). Sixth, Watson argues that two other key terms used to describe the sun—"bridegroom" and "strong man"—are also, throughout the Scriptures, used to refer to Christ (*Christ*, 13–15). Lastly, Watson argues that the validity of his christological interpretation is buttressed by the fact that "most of the antient * Fathers, and best † Interpreters ... apply this Psalm to Him" (*Christ*, 15).

78. For Hutchinson, the historical transmission of a Hebrew term can only have the effect of corrupting and obscuring its primordial meaning, but for Watson, the meaning of a term is given in its reception history.

79. Watson, *A Seasonable*, 1.

Newton thinks he can defend all of Scripture by proving the divine origin of a particular set of biblical words: prophetic language. Hutchinson thinks that select Hebrew hieroglyphs can carry the burden of his scriptural apologetic. But although Watson shares Hutchinson's passion for Hebraic scholarship, he affirms the providential import of all Scripture words, whether Hebrew or Greek.

Watson's only extant treatment of a New Testament text is his sermon *A Seasonable Admonition to the Church of England.* The text for the sermon is Jude 5: "I will therefore put you in remembrance, though ye once knew this, how that the Lord, having saved the people of the land of Egypt, afterward destroyed them that believed not." Because this New Testament text is an explicit reflection upon Old Testament history, Watson is able to use it to defend his conviction that the meaning of New Testament texts cannot be isolated from the Old Testament. This does not mean, however, that he believes the Old Testament should be given more weight than the New, just as his decision to turn to the New Testament to generate the meaning of the term "Sun of righteousness" does not imply that the New Testament is to be given more weight than the Old. In Watson's hermeneutic, the Old and New Testaments are equal and mutually dependent conversation partners.

Watson describes Jude 5 as an "awakening admonition" written "to put the Christian Churches upon their Guard in a Time of manifest Danger, and thereby prevent the ruinous Consequences of a general Apostasy."[80] Although this general admonition might well have come from a number of eighteenth-century apologists, Watson's apologetic method is starkly uncharacteristic. Rather than turn to Newtonian science or the commonplace appeals to miracles or messianic fulfillment, Watson defends the Christian religion with what he calls the most "awful and affecting" argument of all. Jude's letter is less than a page long in most Bibles, and his argument in defense of Christianity is contained within one brief sentence. But Watson reads it in the most comprehensive terms possible as an appeal to

> the whole stupendous scheme of God's immutable Counsels, with respect to All who would, upon Tryal, accept of it, and of Judgement, without Mercy, to All who, in their State of Probation, would finally

---

80. Watson, *A Seasonable*, 1.

reject it; in a Word, the vast and comprehensive Plan, which God saw to be good, and therefore decreed *before all Time*, and the invariable Method of his Administration *in Time*, to execute and accomplish it.[81]

For Watson, Jude's argument is "much insisted upon by the Apostles; they frequently repeat it, they recommend it with Earnestness."[82] Jude 5 is not an isolated text, able to hold the entire weight of a grand apologetic. It can only fulfill its apologetic function when it is interpreted in canonical context as part of a larger New Testament apologetic. And this larger apologetic is but one aspect of the larger scriptural vision, which promotes the Christian religion by appealing to the providential character of history.

Watson believes that the immediate problem Jude is addressing, forgetfulness of the history of the exodus, is but one instance of a larger failure to perceive the scriptural vision of the providential order of history. He therefore argues that Jude's specific complaint is not so much that Christians have forgotten the historical facts that constitute the exodus, but that they have "neglected to make the proper use of the above-mentioned history." Their sin was to fail to consider it "as an infallible Relation of great and glorious Transactions, wherein the almighty Power and loving Kindness of *Jehovah* were most marvelously displayed, and for which his Name was to be praised throughout all succeeding Generations."[83]

Watson is convinced that the purpose of the Old Testament is not merely to give a providentially ordered account of past historical events. To accept the Old Testament as an equal partner in the canon is to acknowledge the Old Testament as that which enlivens Christian participation in this providential order. Watson is supremely interested in the *use* of Israelite history, and he describes this use in tropological terms. He argues that Jude's words have the "same Import" as Paul's words to the Corinthians: "*all these Things happened unto them for* Examples ... *and they are written for our Admonition.*"[84] Watson also holds that Paul and Jude agree that identifying the tropological

---

81. Watson, *A Seasonable*, 2. Watson's use of the idea of the "State of Probation" points to Bishop Butler's influence. See Joseph Butler, *The Analogy of Religion, Natural and Revealed*, 3rd ed. (London: 1740), 103–15.

82. Watson, *A Seasonable*, 2.

83. Watson, *A Seasonable*, 3.

84. Watson, *A Seasonable*, 3.

import of Scripture is not simply a matter of finding parallels between scriptural and contemporary particulars. Before the exegete can do so, scriptural
particulars must be set in providential context, which means placing them
in canonical context. The book of Exodus tethers the book of Jude to God's
providential order, which, having been identified, can be extended by means
of tropological appropriation to the present day.

The reason Watson believes he can make use of Jude, and the history of
the Exodus, to admonish his countrymen is that "God's government (as has
been observed) is an universal, not partial one."

> The Scheme of the divine Administration … must be *universal*, because
> it is founded and proceeds upon the Plan of *Redemption*, concerning
> which the Prophet declares, that *The Lord (is) good to All, and his tender
> Mercies (are) over all his Works*; and the Apostles, that *Jesus Christ is the
> Propitiation for our Sins, and not for ours only, but also (for the Sins) of the
> whole World*; that *God is no* Respecter *of* Persons, *but in* every Nation,
> *he that* feareth *him, and* worketh Righteousness is *accepted with him*.[85]

Watson appeals here to Psalm 145:9, 1 John 2:2, and Acts 10:34–35 to defend
the notion that the history of the exodus is a particular instance of God's universal and beneficent government. When Exodus is interpreted in canonical
context, the history of the exodus is set within the "Plan of *Redmeption*," and
is able to function as a guide for members of the Church of England. The
process of locating the Exodus within this larger providential scheme, far
from minimizing its importance, actually enhances it. By confirming "the
impartiality of God's dealings with mankind," the exodus is recognized as
"the fittest pattern that could be given to succeeding generations," and "the
greatest temporal deliverance that ever was wrought for the Church." From
this standpoint, Watson is able to interpret Exodus tropologically to expound
"awakening Truths" such as assurance of providential care, the necessity of
faith, and the inevitability of judgement, which in turn "lead *us* to reflect in
what Situation we ourselves stand towards God."[86]

Watson develops this tropological approach to biblical history in a sermon
on Numbers 16:47–48 entitled *Aaron's Intercession, and Korah's Rebellion*

85. Watson, *A Seasonable*, 4.
86. Watson, *A Seasonable*, 16.

Considered.[87] In his preface to the sermon, Watson returns to his preeminent concern to defend the Old Testament as Christian Scripture. He paraphrases Romans 15:4—"whatsoever things were written aforetime were written for our learning"—and observes first that *"the apostle's assertion is general, evidently involving in it all the Scriptures of the old testament,"* and second that we can only hope to benefit from Old Testament texts if *"they are applicable to all times, and we, in particular, apply them to our own times and to ourselves, in order to avoid whatever is displeasing to God, and to do his blessed will."*[88]

Watson begins his sermon with a reaffirmation of his providential vision of the Old Testament. He promises his listeners that if they follow him in considering "the *design* of the history," they will see "how nearly [they] are concerned in it" because they have "*divine* Authority to affirm, that the *things* which happened to Israel of old, under that figurative dispensation, *happened unto them for* examples to *us*, the Christian Church in the latter days."[89] As is his custom, Watson begins with a clear outline for his sermon. He promises first to describe the "historical relation" of the text, which in this case involves an articulation of the "*occasion* of Aaron's interposition, and the *consequence* of it." Next, he will "Shew the merciful *design*" of the history, and specifically "what it was intended to represent." Finally, he will articulate the "farther instruction that arises from the history."[90]

Watson's exposition of the "the historical relation" of the text is what we might expect from any modern preacher—an outline of the story of Aaron's intercession in its narrative context. Although Watson discusses the role of Korah and his followers in bringing about the devastating plague described in the text, he is particularly interested in Aaron's interposition on behalf of the people of Israel when he "exposed himself for their sake to the irresistible displeasure of his God" by standing "mid way between the wrath and them, between the *dead* and the *living*." Watson praises this bold intercession as

---

87. The text in Watson's Authorized Versions reads as follows: "And Aaron took as Moses commanded, and ran into the midst of the congregation, and behold the plague was begun among the people; and he put on incense, and made an atonement for the people—and he stood between the dead and the living, and the plague was stayed."

88. Watson, *Aaron's*, i.

89. Watson, *Aaron's*, 1–2.

90. Watson, *Aaron's*, 2.

"so full of faith and love as to deserve the admiration of all ages."[91] Although the preacher might be expected, at this point, to proceed from this reflection directly to an admonition, this is precisely what Watson refuses to do. True to his word, he proceeds from his exposition of the "historical relation" of the text to consider its meaning in light of its location within the canon of Scripture. Watson concludes that the significance of Aaron's intercession, like that of Moses or David, is that it is a figure of the "great mediation" of Christ.[92] It is only once this figural relation is established that Watson proceeds to the third part of his sermon and offers a tropological and specifically ecclesial reading of the text.

Some further comments regarding Watson's method are in order. Watson's insistence that expositors present the "historical relation" of the text before pursuing figural and tropological readings confirms he has left behind Hutchinson's devolutionary philosophy of history. Watson does not flee from the historical particulars in the text but insists they must be duly acknowledged and interpreted. As he states at the outset, his task is to consider the history in question. His figural and tropological approach is not a movement away from historical study but the consummation of it. Watson refuses to believe that men and women are isolated from history by an "ugly, broad ditch."[93] Through figural reading, historical particulars are upheld as shining lights that guide contemporary Christian life. The second step in Watson's method—teasing out the significance of the "historical relation" of the text—is a process in which historical particulars are interpreted as figures within the order of Scripture by means of engagement with other scriptural texts. Watson's third step in his interpretive method is an extension of his second step. Like the second step, the task of drawing out "farther instruction" is the process in which historical particulars are located within a larger providential framework through their interpretation as scriptural figures. The difference is that whereas the particulars that are interpreted as figures are found within Scripture in Watson's second step, the particulars interpreted in the third step are taken directly from the world.

91. Watson, *Aaron's*, 4.
92. Watson, *Aaron's*, 4.
93. Gotthold Ephraim Lessing, "The Proof of the Spirit and of Power," in *Lessing's Theological Writings*, ed. and trans. Henry Chadwick (Stanford, CA: Stanford University Press, 1956), 55.

It must be admitted, however, that there are two potential interpretations of Watson's method. The first interpretation mutes the mediating role
of Scripture because it ascribes to Watson the view that canonical mediation is not always necessary. According to this view, Watson divides tropological readings into two categories. First, there are tropological readings
derived directly from the "historical relation" of a given scriptural passage,
and, second, there are those that are derived from the canonical reading of
this relation. The basis of this view is Watson's statement that tropological
readings are "partly deducible from the *history itself*, and partly from the *spiritual exposition* of it."[94] He proceeds to offer three edifying readings derived
directly from the text. First, Numbers 16:47–48 teaches the necessity of "an
outward consecration to the priesthood, and that in the way of *God's* institution." Second, it teaches the order of "*subordination* he himself has appointed
amongst the persons *so* consecrated." Finally, it teaches "the great duty of
universal obedience to all *lawful* authority."[95] Here Watson interprets the fact
that God's wrath "waxed more than ordinarily hot against these *self-commis-
sioned holy ones*" as an explicit condemnation of English dissent.[96]

The difficulty that accompanies this rendering of Watson's hermeneutic
is that it runs counter to the sequence of his method in which the third step
in the interpretive process, that of extracting tropological import from the
text, follows the second step, that of canonical reading. Indeed, since the
edifying readings Watson claims to derive directly from his initial historical
exposition also follow after his canonical reflections, one would expect these
edifying readings to be informed by his canonical reflections. And this is
precisely what we find. After a brief discussion of Korah's rebellion against
Moses and Aaron, Watson reflects upon Paul's warning against rebellion in
Romans 13:2: "Whosoever therefore resisteth the power, resisteth the ordinance of God: and they that resist shall receive to themselves damnation."
Watson interprets the Old Testament description of Korah's destruction in
the "pit and fire" as "*figurative representations*" of the damnation of which Paul
speaks, which is elsewhere described as an "*invisible pit*" and "*unquenchable*

---

94. Watson, *Aaron's*, 12.

95. Watson, *Aaron's*, 11–12.

96. Watson, *Aaron's*, 13.

fire."[97] Watson insists that the Christian doctrine of hell compels Christians to "pray for *grace* and *lowliness* of *spirit*" and to submit "themselves to their appointed governors, even as to him who appointed them."[98] Watson relies upon the canon to clarify the relation between biblical and contemporary particulars, and this suggests that Watson's tropological readings are, at least in some way, dependent upon canonical mediation. For Watson, the canonical reading of the text in question is a bridge that unites the world of the text and the world of the interpreter.

Watson's dependence upon the canon to establish tropological meaning is confirmed by his "spiritual exposition" of Numbers 16:47-48, which concludes the third and final section of his sermon. He begins this exposition by applying his canonical reflections upon the necessity of Christ's mediation to the death of Korah and his followers. Death, in canonical context, Watson finds, includes not merely physical death but also "eternal death"—"everlasting exclusion *from the* presence *of the* Lord, *and from the* glory *of his* power."[99] He points out that "no mere man, *can by any means* redeem *his* brother" from the bonds of this eternal death,[100] and he reiterates that "the interposition *of Christ* alone is sufficient for the accomplishment of this merciful work."[101] Watson's ensuing reflections upon the necessity of Christ's interposition are marked by rhetorical flourish and literary refinement, and they crescendo to a celebration of the salvation wrought by the intercession of Jesus Christ on the cross.

Admittedly, as he pursues the third step in his method, Watson often appears to echo rather than extend his previous canonical reflections. Nevertheless, his tropological orientation is consistent. Watson concludes with what he calls "an application of the great and leading subject of this discourse." Watson continues: "The way to profit by an example, is to make the case our own," and we will have made it our own

> When what is recorded of Israel for *our* use shall be fulfilled in *us* as well as them, when all the particulars of this history, how awful

---

97. Watson, *Aaron's*, 19.
98. Watson, *Aaron's*, 19-20.
99. Watson, *Aaron's*, 22.
100. Watson, *Aaron's*, 23.
101. Watson, *Aaron's*, 23.

soever, shall have a much more awful accomplishment such as neither I can describe to you, nor you can fully conceive. When, instead
of the earthly pit opening its mouth to swallow up Korah and his
company, the infernal pit of everlasting destruction shall disclose its
bottomless depth, to receive alive into it the great adversary, and all
that have taken part with him against God, every rebel against Christ
and the Christian covenant.[102]

According to Watson, Christians must make the particulars of Old Testament
history examples unto themselves, yet they must also recognize that these
particulars can only be recast as examples when they are reinterpreted in
canonical context as scriptural figures.[103] It is thus that he maintains that
the contemporary spiritual significance of Korah's rebellion and death only
comes to light when it is reinterpreted as a figure of rebellion against God
and eternal damnation.

Watson favors the figural reading of Old Testament particulars because
he finds it to be the most natural way of uncovering their contemporary
import.[104] Once the textual particulars have been rendered as figures through
canonical interpretation, the interpreter is free to extend these figures into
contemporary life. Along these lines, Watson proceeds to beg "*rebels* to claim
the benefit of an *act of grace*."[105] He urges deists and dissenters to "come in
now, while the act of grace affords a protection," and above all he praises

---

102. Watson, *Aaron's*, 26–27.

103. Thus, when Watson argues that Old Testament particulars are ordered toward Christian
admonition in *Christ the Light of the World*, he reminds his readers that the Greek word the
Authorized Version translates as "examples" is more accurately rendered as "types" (*A Seasonable*,
3).

104. The way Watson's hermeneutic brings together typology and tropology is entirely
characteristic of pre-modern exegesis. As Lindbeck puts it, "Traditionally expressed, one could
perhaps say that typological tropology or tropological typology was the chief interpretative
strategy for making the Bible contemporary, for absorbing one's own world into the world of
the text" (George Lindbeck, "Postcritical Canonical Interpretation: Three Modes of Retrieval,"
in *Theological Exegesis: Essays in Honor of Brevard S. Childs*, ed. Christopher Seitz and Kathryn
Greene-McCreight [Grand Rapids: Eerdmans, 1998], 31). Treier persuasively argues that this
traditional marriage between figuration and tropology confirms that exploring biblical types is
not simply "a prophetic matter of extrapolating the *indicative*," but rather "also involves discerning the *imperative*: prudential discernment of such realities in light of their divinely prepared
application to God's people in the present" (Daniel Treier, "Typology," in *Dictionary for Theological
Interpretation of the Bible*, ed. Kevin Vanhoozer et al. [Grand Rapids: Baker Academic, 2005], 826).

105. Watson, *Aaron's*, 26.

God that "To the *redeemed* of the Lord this history is a sure *earnest* of their deliverance."[106] For Watson, the "ugly, broad ditch" that separates Aaron's intercession and Korah's rebellion and contemporary English life is obliterated by figural reading. Once Aaron's intercession and Korah's rebellion have been recast as figures, the particulars of Watson's own context attach themselves to these figures. This is what allows him to reinterpret the story in tropological and therefore providential terms as a warning to those who would resist the authority of the established church.

CONCLUSION

Christ the Light of the World was Watson's most influential work. Most notably, it had an enormous impact on Horne and Jones.[107] Jones relates that it was the inspiration behind Horne's magnum opus, his *A Commentary on the Book of Psalms* (1776).[108] After his exposition of Psalm 19 in this commentary, Horne pauses to acknowledge his debt to Watson's sermon: "If the reader shall have received any pleasure from perusing the comment on the foregoing psalm ... he is to be informed, that he stands indebted, on that account, to a discourse entitled, CHRIST THE LIGHT OF THE WORLD."[109] In *A Course of Lectures on the Figurative Language of the Holy Scripture* (1787), Jones is equally generous in his tribute:

> An excellent sermon, which ought never to be forgotten and which I carried through the press, when I was an under graduate at Oxford, was published on *Christ the Light of the World*, from a verse of the 19th Psalm, by my admired, beloved and lamented friend, the late Rev. *George Watson*.[110]

The great appeal of Watson's sermon was that it provided Horne and Jones a means to pursue scriptural emblematicism without recourse to Hutchinson's peculiar hieroglyphic method. The final two chapters of this book will explore

---

106. Watson, *Aaron's*, 30.

107. Horne and Jones weren't the only Hutchinsonians to celebrate the work. See Fowler Comings, *The Printed Hebrew Text of the Old Testament Vindicated* (Oxford: 1753), 100–101n.

108. Jones, *Memoirs*, 28.

109. Horne, *A Commentary*, 1:87n.

110. William Jones, *A Course of Lectures on the Figurative Language of the Holy Scripture* (London: 1789), 47–48n.

their specific appropriations of Watson's method. Horne and Jones endorsed Watson's scriptural emblematicism because they were drawn to the way it informs and upholds a providential vision of *both* nature and history.

As he pursues his threefold method in *Aaron's Intercession*, Watson proceeds from Aaron's intercession on behalf of the people of Israel to Christ's intercession on behalf of Christians and, finally, to a call to repentance. The same trajectory, which proceeds from the text in question, to canonical context, to contemporary context, is evident in *Christ the Light of the World*. In *Christ the Light of the World*, Watson's exposition proceeds from the sun to Christ, and then finally to a reflection upon the resurrection of the people of God. In both cases the Christian canon mediates the providential reading of scriptural particulars, whether natural or historical. Whether Watson interprets historical actions in the Old Testament text, such as Aaron's intercession, or natural-philosophical objects, such as the sun, the result is the same. Through his canonical method, Watson locates them within the orb of God's providence, and once they are so located, they become, as Scripture figures, relevant to contemporary life. Watson's method establishes equilibrium between nature and history because it functions indiscriminately with respect to natural and historical objects, and this equilibrium undercuts the Newtonian and early Hutchinsonian devolutionary interpretation of history. With Watson, nature is no longer set apart as that which alone can offer a sure foundation for the Christian religion.

After Watson, however, Hutchinsonians continued to grapple with the relationship between Scripture and providence. This struggle can, at least in part, be placed at Watson's feet. Watson's suggestion that tropological readings can be drawn directly from the literal reading of texts betrays the conviction that there is a prior providential order to which both scriptural and the contemporary world belong. On the other hand, Watson's more prevalent practice of drawing tropological readings from the canonical reading of texts implies that Scripture itself, in its two-testamental expression, is the order that is logically and perhaps even ontologically prior to the providential order that governs the world.[111] The final two chapters of this book will

---

111. The notion that God created words before he created the physical universe has a long pedigree in rabbinic Judaism. Early modern scholars such as Newton and Hutchinson would have been aware of it through their engagements with kabbalistic literature and, perhaps,

highlight these different interpretations of Watson's work which became operative in Hutchinsonianism. The next chapter, which focuses on Watson's disciple George Horne, argues that Horne adopts the view that tropological readings can be established directly from the literal reading of particular texts and that this suggests he believes in an overarching providential order within which Scripture must be placed. The final chapter, which focuses on Watson's disciple William Jones of Nayland, argues that Jones upholds an alternative viewpoint on both accounts. Jones insists that tropological readings must be mediated by the Christian canon, and this implies the view that Scripture itself is the providential order through which God governs the world. I will argue that this difference has important implications for the providential interpretation of history. Horne's approach opens the door to a renewed appeal to the Newtonian devolutionary philosophy of history. Jones's approach, on the other hand, makes such an appeal unnecessary.

---

through Maimonides. See T. M. Rudavsky, *Maimonides* (Chichester, UK: Wiley-Blackwell, 2010), 73. Ephraim Radner's *Time and the Word: Figural Reading of the Christian Scriptures* (Grand Rapids: Eerdmans, 2016) is, to my knowledge, the only contemporary Christian proposal for Scripture's ontological priority.

5

—

A MONUMENT OF THE DIVINE ORDER: GEORGE HORNE'S OLD TESTAMENT

Although I maintain that scriptural emblematicism is the *sine qua non* of Hutchinsonianism, I do not deny that the other elements, such as natural philosophy or establishmentarian politics, are also important to the movement. Nevertheless, it is impossible to account for Hutchinsonianism as a coherent movement that lasted for over a century if natural philosophy or churchmanship is regarded as foundational, since the positions of individual Hutchinsonians with respect to these matters were wildly different. There were a number of dissenters among the early Hutchinsonians, and the status of early Hutchinsonianism with respect to the Church of England establishment was accordingly tenuous. The Oxonians and their progeny, on the other hand, were fierce establishmentarians. And while early Hutchinsonians were vehemently opposed to Newtonianism, the Oxonians and their descendants were equally passionate in their defense of Newton.

The about-face on both accounts is attributable to the fact that the Oxonians rejected Hutchinson's devolutionary view of history and replaced it with a providential view. This transition began with Watson, but it was left to George Horne and William Jones of Nayland to solidify the new Hutchinsonian framework. Horne, more than anyone else, established the pro-Newtonian and pro-Church of England orthodoxy that came to define the movement and establish its credibility among scholarly-minded Anglicans. His positions of influence within the University of Oxford and the Church of England enabled him to play a leading role in forging the establishmentarian churchmanship that birthed nineteenth-century High churchmanship.[1] As a biblical interpreter, Horne's work on Old Testament interpretation was widely read throughout the eighteenth and nineteenth centuries, but his measured emblematicism ultimately contributed to the loss of the unique Hutchinsonian scriptural vision.

Horne was only able to embrace the Newtonian scientific establishment and the Church of England establishment because he had embraced a providential view of history. This transition is evident in Horne's rejection of Hutchinson's hieroglyphic method and his accompanying affirmation that the received Old Testament text has been preserved from obfuscation by divine providence. And yet, despite this strong affirmation, the role that Scripture plays in fostering a providential interpretation of particulars is not as pronounced in Horne's thought as we might expect. The role Scripture plays is restricted because his scriptural hermeneutic, like his Newtonianism and his establishmentarianism, becomes subservient to his larger providential interpretation of history.

HORNE'S HUTCHINSONIANISM

It is appropriate to speak of Horne as a Hutchinsonian on account of his scriptural emblematicism. This being said, some interpreters have found his scriptural emblematicism hard to detect because it is subsumed within Horne's larger providential vision. This measured emblematicism is, understandably, the source of the doubts some interpreters have had about his Hutchinsonian credentials.

Horne's relationship to Hutchinson was already a matter of some controversy at the end of the eighteenth century. When Horne died in 1792, it fell to Jones, who calls himself "one of his Lordship's chaplains, and long his most intimate and confidential friend," to write an account of his life.[2] As Jones surveys the life, studies, and writings of his dearest friend, he ascribes

---

1. Churton maintained that "Bishop Horne, long before he was bishop, had as much influence on the minds of young men at Oxford, as ever Newman or Pusey have lately had" (Edward Churton, A Letter to W. Gresley, May 25, 1846, Gresley Papers, GRES 3/7/68; quoted in Peter Nockles, The Oxford Movement in Context: Anglican High Churchmanship, 1760–1857 [Cambridge: Cambridge University Press, 1994], 13n44).

2. William Jones, ed., The Works of the Right Reverend George Horne, D. D. (London: 1818), Title Page.

two important events to the workings of providence: Horne's election to the mastership of Magdalen College in 1768, and his encounter with Hutchinson's writings in 1749, which led him away from his study of the Greek tragedians to the study of divinity.[3] Jones relates that Horne quickly earned the reputation of being a Hutchinsonian while still an undergraduate—"which is the name of those who studied Hebrew and examined the writings of Hutchinson 'the famous Mosaic Philosopher' and became inclined to favour his opinions in Theology and Philosophy."[4]

As we have already noted, Horne embraced Hutchinsonianism through Watson's influence. Like Watson, Horne refuses to elevate Hutchinson above other scholars—Horne was happy to supplement his reading of Hutchinson with other sources. Like Watson, Horne enthusiastically embraced Hutchinson's natural-philosophical system, and like Watson, Horne held Hebraic studies in the highest regard. The feature of Horne's Hutchinsonianism that most clearly bears Watson's influence, however, is Horne's aversion to the Hutchinsonian hieroglyphic method. As early as 1753, Horne commented that many readers "highly approved of [Hutchinson's] general plan" without agreeing with him "in every particular etymology, or interpretation."[5] For Jones, Horne's critical embrace of Hutchinsonianism is confirmed by his willingness to question the value of Hutchinsonian etymologies and his disinterest in the controversies they generated.[6]

---

3. William Jones, *Memoirs of the Life, Studies, and Writings of the Right Reverend George Horne, D.D.* (London: 1795), 21.

4. Jones, *Memoirs*, 22. Horne was regarded as a Hutchinsonian by other Oxonians. Benjamin Kennicott's *A Word to the Hutchinsonians* (London: 1756) was a direct attack on the homilies of three scholars, including one of Horne's.

5. George Horne, *A Fair, Candid, and Impartial State of the Case between Sir Isaac Newton and Mr. Hutchinson* (London: 1753), 5.

6. "Mr. Hutchinson," explains Jones, "fell into a new and uncommon train of thinking in Philosophy, Theology, and Heathen Antiquity; and appears to have learned much of it from the Hebrew, which he studied in a way of his own: but as he laid too great a stress in many instances on the evidence of Hebrew etymology, his admirers would naturally do the same; and some of them carried the matter so far, that nothing else would go down with them; till by degrees they adopted a mode of speaking, which had a nearer resemblance to cant and jargon, than to sound and sober learning. To this weakness, those persons were most liable, who had received the fewest advantages from a learned education. This was the case with some sensible tradesmen and mechanics, who by studying Hebrew, with the assistance of English only, grew conceited of their learning, and carried too much sail with too little ballast. Of this Mr. Horne was very soon aware; and he was in so little danger of following the example, that I used to hear him display the foibles of such persons with that mirth and good humour which he had ready at hand upon all occasions ... he never, through the whole course of his life, was a friend to the etymological

When Jones published the second edition of the *Memoirs* of Horne in 1799, he was clearly exasperated. Although he had only wished "to give a true idea of that good man, as it presented itself to [his] memory and affections; and to produce an edifying book, rather than a formal history," he acknowledges that the work had offended some of his readers.[7] "Some few exceptions," says Jones, "have been made to the performance by little cavillers, which are not worth mentioning." He observes that what brought him "into the most serious difficulty of all" was the fact that he had represented Horne as a Hutchinsonian.[8]

Jones employs two strategies to defend this portrayal. The first is to emphasize Horne's moderation.

I never said, nor did I ever think, that Bishop Horne owed every thing to *Hutchinson*, or was his implicit follower. I knew the contrary: but this I will say, because I know it to be true, that he owed to him the *beginning* of his extensive knowledge; for such a beginning as he made placed him on a new spot of high ground; from which he took all his prospects of religion and learning; and saw that whole road lying before him, which he afterwards pursued, with so much pleasure to himself, and benefit of the world.[9]

Jones's detractors, of course, would not have denied that Horne owed to Hutchinson "the *beginning* of his extensive knowledge."[10] They evidently thought that Horne had *begun* his career as a Hutchinsonian but had

part of the controversy; as it appears from his writings; in which Hebrew etymology, however he might apply to it *for himself*, is rarely if ever insisted upon. In some of his private letters ... he declared his mind very freely on the inexpediency of squabbling about words, when there were so many *things* to be brought forward, which were of greater importance, and would admit of less dispute" (Jones, Memoirs, 59–60).

7. William Jones, *A New Preface to the Second Edition of the Memoirs of the Life, Studies, Writings & c. of the Right Reverend George Horne* (London: 1799), i.

8. Jones, *A New Preface*, i–ii. Jones evidently perceived this matter as central to Horne's legacy. *A New Preface to the Second Edition* deals almost exclusively with the question of Horne's Hutchinsonianism.

9. Jones, *A New Preface*, ii.

10. This conclusion was reasonably drawn, for the last time Horne mentions Hutchinson in print is his 1756 pamphlet *An Apology for Certain Gentlemen in the University of Oxford* (Oxford: 1756). Jones, however, interpreted Horne's silence very differently. Watson, as we have seen, urged Jones not to pursue Hutchinsonianism because it would be detrimental to his friendships and hinder his chances at preferment. For Jones, Horne's silence concerning his Hutchinsonianism is nothing but a prudential acknowledgement of the wisdom of Watson's advice. The establishment

later repudiated Hutchinsonianism. Jones, however, insists that Horne's Hutchinsonianism is the foundation of his work. Jones's interpretation depends on a particular understanding of the nature of Hutchinsonianism—a particular understanding that clearly bears Watson's influence. Following Watson's lead, Jones rejects the facile association of the hieroglyphic method and Hutchinsonianism. This enables him to minimize the application of the hieroglyphic method as discretionary and affirm Horne's scriptural emblematicism as his Hutchinsonian inheritance.[11]

Horne consistently affirmed that Scripture words relay the emblematic import of objects of nature to contemporary readers. In his magnum opus, his *Commentary on the Psalms* (1776), he affirms that

> The visible works of God are formed to lead us, under the direction of his Word, to a knowledge of those which are invisible; they give us ideas, by analogy, of a new creation rising gradually, like the old one, out of darkness and deformity, until at length it arrives at the perfection of glory and beauty.[12]

Horne insists that humans are dependent upon the Word of God to expose the spiritual significance of objects of nature. When he considers human nature, he begins by observing that "man is often in Scripture compared to a merchant."[13] And when he gazes at flowers, he cannot help but do so through the lens of the Sermon on the Mount:

> THE LILY.
> Emblem of Him, in whom no stain
>   The eye of Heav'n could see,
> In all their glory monarchs vain
>   Are not array'd like me.[14]

It is, however, in his scriptural meditations upon light that Horne's work most clearly bears the mark of Hutchinson. Horne begins his commentary

---

viewed Hutchinsonianism with suspicion, and Horne was evidently hindered by his association with Hutchinson. His first important ecclesial post didn't come to him until 1771.

11. Jones, *A New Preface*, vii.

12. George Horne, *A Commentary on the Book of Psalms* (Oxford: 1776), 1:xxxix.

13. Jones, *The Works*, 2:388.

14. Jones, *The Works*, 1:237. Horne's poem "The Lily" is a reflection upon the words of Matthew 6:28.

on Psalm 19:1, "The heavens declare the glory of God," by paying tribute to Hutchinson's ethereal theory. "The heavens," says Horne, are composed of "that fluid mixture of light and air, which is every where diffused about us; and to the influences of which, are owing all the beauty and fruitfulness of the earth, all vegetable and animal life, and the various kinds of motion throughout the system of nature."[15] This consideration of the physical properties and functions of light enables Horne, following Watson, to ponder anew "the manifestation of the Light of Life, or Sun of Righteousness, and the efficacy of evangelical doctrine."[16]

That Horne continued to enthusiastically embrace Hutchinson's scriptural emblematicism in his mature *A Commentary on the Psalms* confirms that Horne had not repudiated the Hutchinsonianism of his youth. This being said, Horne's scriptural emblematicism is palpably more restrained than Jones's. Whereas Jones dives headlong into the waters of scriptural emblematicism, Horne gives the impression that he is merely dipping in his toes. This difference must be understood not only quantitatively, but also qualitatively. Horne's providential reading of the Scriptures, which is often expressed in emblematic terms, is grounded in his strong affirmation of the providential order of the world, but for Jones, Scripture itself is the ground upon which the providential interpretation of particulars is established.

PROVIDENCE AND NATURE

Horne took for granted that the mechanical workings of nature play a crucial role in testifying to the existence of providence. This comes as no surprise given that he was formed in an intellectual context which was enamored by

---

15. Horne, *A Commentary*, 1:81.

16. Horne, *A Commentary*, 1:81. Hutchinson's influence on Horne is seen in the way Horne devotes much of his commentary on the Psalm to pondering celestial motions. Watson's influence is evident in the way the spiritual import of these motions is rendered by means of canonical readings of particular Hebrew terms. Horne ends his commentary on the psalm with a tribute to Watson and *Christ the Light of the World*: "If the reader shall have received any pleasure from perusing the comment on the foregoing psalm, especially the first part of it, he is to be informed, that he stands indebted on that account, to a Discourse entitled, CHRIST THE LIGHT OF THE WORLD, published, in the year 1750, by the late Reverend Mr. GEORGE WATSON, for many years the dear companion and kind director of the author's studies; in attending to whose agreeable and instructive conversation, he has often passed whole days together, and shall always have reason to number them among the best spent days of his life; whose death he can never think of, without lamenting it afresh; and to whose memory he embraces, with pleasure, this opportunity to pay the tribute of a grateful heart" (*A Commentary*, 1:87).

the new mechanical philosophy. Watson convinced Horne that because it was authentically mechanistic, Hutchinsonianism was apologetically superior to Newtonianism. Horne's first published work, *The Theology and Philosophy in Cicero's Somnium Scipionis Explained* (1751), confirms that for Horne, endorsing Hutchinson meant rejecting all other natural-philosophical authorities. The ridicule it heaps on Newton and Clarke is as caustic as Hutchinson's invective. Horne laughs at the notion that the best ancient philosophers were empirical metaphysicians, and he disparages the Newtonian argument that Christianity can stand on *"the certainty, and infallibility of mathematical principles."*[17] Most of all, however, Horne takes up Hutchinson's crusade against the ancient pagan idea of *anima mundi*, which he attributes to Newton on account of his belief in an absolute vacuum and action at a distance.[18] For Horne as well as for Hutchinson, that Newton does not believe in a "clockwork" universe renders his natural philosophy apologetically deficient and theologically suspect. It must be noted, further, that Horne's rejection of the prevailing Newtonian philosophy extends to the question of method. Horne takes for granted the emblematic assumption that Cicero's text is an appropriate field for natural-philosophical discovery.

Horne's next published work, *A Fair, Candid, and Impartial State of the Case between Sir Isaac Newton and Mr. Hutchinson* (1753), represents a startling contrast to his previous work. Whereas *The Theology and Philosophy in Cicero's Somnium Scipionis Explained* demonizes Newtonianism as antithetical to all true (Hutchinsonian) natural-philosophical principles, it presents Newtonianism and Hutchinsonianism as complementary natural-philosophical systems.[19] "The piece," comments Jones,

---

17. George Horne, *The Theology and Philosophy in Cicero's* Somnium Scipionis *Explained* (Oxford: 1751), 4.

18. Horne, *The Theology*, 12, 14.

19. Although it is hard to ignore the novelty of Horne's interpretation, the groundwork for it was laid by influential Newtonian Scotsman Colin Maclaurin. Interpreters of Newton working in the second half of the eighteenth century largely read Newton through Maclaurin's *An Account of Sir Isaac Newton's Philosophical Discoveries* (London: 1748), and what they found in it was, in Aston's words, "a profoundly anti-metaphysical stance that led [Maclaurin] to denounce system builders from Aristotle to Leibniz" (Aston, "From Personality," 639). Horne quotes Maclaurin to defend the idea that the mathematical foundation of Newtonianism must be complemented by further study. "Geometry," says Maclaurin, "can be of little use in philosophy till DATA are collected to build on," and it is, therefore, "the province of mathematics to put the LAST hand to physics" (Horne, *A Fair*, 22). Horne bemoans the fact that Hutchinson's work has been neglected

Certainly is what it calls itself, *fair, candid,* and *impartial*; and the merits of the cause are very judiciously stated between the two parties: in consequence of which, a reader will distinguish, that Newton may be of sovereign skill in measuring *forces* as a Mathematician; and yet, that Hutchinson may be right in assigning *causes*, as a Physiologist.[20]

Jones attributes Horne's about-face to the fact that he "soon saw the impropriety of the style and manner, which as a young man he had assumed for merriment." Once "he had taken time to bethink himself, he resumed and reconsidered the subject."[21]

A Fair, Candid, and Impartial State of the Case helped to establish the conciliatory approach to Newton that marked establishmentarian Hutchinsonianism.[22] The Oxonians, as Aston observes, worked hard to "repackage the message" by incorporating into their work a "wider range

---

because "Sir Isaac's philosophy is considered certain and infallible because it is founded upon and proved by mathematics." Horne also decries the fact that the followers of Newton have bestowed "such extravagant encomiums upon him as they have done" that they have fashioned him "as a writer who had made such amazing and stupendous *physical* discoveries into the *agency* of nature" (Horne, *A Fair*, 6, 41). Like the scholars of the new Newtonian studies, Horne levels these complaints not against Newton but against Newton's disciples. Newton himself, remarks Horne, "complained he was killed by the kindness of his friends," for it was "contrary to his own declarations" that they insisted that, "he had made such amazing and stupendous *physical* discoveries into the *agency* of nature" (Horne, *A Fair*, 42). Although Horne genuinely believes that Hutchinson's work complements Newton's, his intent is not to argue that mathematical discourse must be grounded in Scripture. Such a view would merely duplicate the error of the Newtonians that wish to ground natural-philosophical discourse in mathematics. Hutchinson's scriptural philosophy is one thing, and Newtonian mathematical physics is another. Each discourse has its own distinct methods and objects of inquiry. Horne traces Hutchinson's pursuit of natural-philosophical knowledge to Adam himself, for Adam, "by the material elements of a visible world, to the knowledge of one that is immaterial and invisible ... found himself excited by the beauty of the picture, to aspire after the transcendent excellence of the divine original" (George Horne, *Discourses on Several Subjects and Occasions*, 3rd ed. [Oxford: 1787], 69). Horne believes that no human being can claim comprehensive knowledge of the natural world, let alone the divine. The contributions of even the best mathematicians and natural philosophers are but pieces of a larger puzzle, and those who, through party allegiances, dismiss the insights of rival natural philosophers foolishly spurn the opportunity to inherit a fuller picture of the natural world and therefore the divine mind than they would otherwise be able to obtain.

20. Jones, *Memoirs*, 39.

21. Jones, *Memoirs*, 38–39.

22. That being said, Horne's work does not bear this distinction alone. See, for example, Samuel Pike, *Philosophia Sacra: Or, the Principles of Natural Philosophy* (London: 1753).

of orthodox references" and omitting the "anti-Newtonian rhetoric altogether."[23] Horne's about-face was consistent with the developing logic of the Oxonian providential vision. In order to defend the indispensability of the hieroglyphic method, it was necessary for early Hutchinsonians to dismiss all natural-philosophical knowledge acquired through alternative channels as misguided and corrupt. On this account, even the smallest concession to Newton destabilized Hutchinson's entire system. Since the Oxonians, however, were not invested in defending Hutchinsonian hieroglyphics, they had no reason to fear Newton or any other natural philosopher, for that matter.

There are at least two other reasons why it was appropriate for Horne to leave behind his anti-Newtonianism. The first has to do with the nature of emblematicism. Although Alciato's book of emblems was a touchstone for later emblematicists, his emblematic associations never atrophied into dogmatic truths. As we have seen, emblematicism was marked from the beginning by a fluidity of association and a willingness to consider the emblematic potential of every object it encountered. By embracing Newton's natural philosophy as potentially able to testify to divine providence, Horne was being consistent with the receptive emblematic manner. The second reason it was appropriate for Horne to leave behind his anti-Newtonianism is his growing confidence that God's providence extends over both created things and human history.

Watson had taught that the Church of England was under attack on two fronts. First, established truths were being called into question (including the Trinity, the efficacy of the sacraments, the spiritual sense of the Bible, and justification by Christ), and second, established "divine" institutions were being jettisoned (including holy matrimony, episcopacy, church hierarchy, and church discipline). The religious vision Horne inherited from Watson was founded upon the conviction that the institutions that formed the foundation of English society were the given means God had ordained to bestow grace upon his people by ordering their lives. By the middle of the eighteenth century, Newtonian natural philosophy was undoubtedly one such institution. Thanks to the tireless efforts of Whiston, Desaguliers, and others, Newtonianism was enthusiastically embraced by the gentry and the

---

23. Nigel Aston, "From Personality to Party: The Creation and Transmission of Hutchinsonianism, c. 1725–1750," *Studies in History and Philosophy of Science* 35 (2004): 641.

middling classes. Scholars pursuing all manner of studies regarded themselves as Newtonians, as did the entrepreneurial barons of the new industry. Horne's providential view of human history grants him a willingness to
interpret everything he encounters as infused with the light of God. It doesn't
bother Horne in the least that Newton's principles were newly discovered:
Horne is happy to concede that they were unknown to the greatest ancient
natural philosophers. He insists that Newton not be given preeminence in
either empirical or religious matters. Horne is prepared, nonetheless, to
affirm with his countrymen that Newton's mathematical principles are both
demonstrably true and apologetically useful.

For Horne, putting Newton in his rightful place means regarding him not
as a physicist, but as a mathematician. Horne quotes Newton's *Principia* on
several occasions to defend this opinion. He reminds his readers that Newton
described his objective in the following terms:

> I shall at present go on to treat of the motion of bodies mutually
> attracting each other; considering the centripetal forces *as attrac-*
> *tions*; tho' perhaps in a PHYSICAL *strictness* they may more truly be
> called *impulses*. But these propositions are to be considered as *purely*
> MATHEMATICAL; and therefore, *laying aside all* PHYSICAL *consid-*
> *erations*, I make use of a *familiar way of speaking*, to make myself *the*
> *more easily understood by a mathematical reader.*

Horne's analysis of Newton's physical and metaphysical speculations certainly lacks the nuance of modern studies such as *The Janus Faces of Genius*,
but Horne is accurate in his assessment inasmuch as Newton continually
flirted with and sometimes embraced agnosticism concerning the cause of
universal gravitation.[24]

---

24. In *A Fair, Candid, and Impartial State of the Case,* Horne rejects Hutchinson's belief that
Newton attributes active powers to nature, and he quotes Newton to this end: "I likewise call
attractions and impulses in the *same sense* accelerative and motive; and use the words attrac-
tion, impulse, or propensity of any sort towards a centre, *promiscuously*, and *indifferently one*
for another; considering those forces not PHYSICALLY, but MATHEMATICALLY: wherefore, *the*
reader is not to IMAGINE, that by those words I *any where* take upon me to define the *kind* or the
manner of any action, the CAUSES or the PHYSICAL *reason* thereof, or that I attribute FORCES
in a TRUE and PHYSICAL sense to certain centres (which are only mathematical points;) when
at any time I HAPPEN to speak of centres as *attracting*, or *endued with attracting powers*" (Horne,
A Fair, 35–36). Isaac Newton, *The Mathematical Principles of Natural Philosophy*, trans. Andrew
Motte (London: 1729), 1:8–9.

Horne's is a well-ordered universe in which diverse human researches find their proper and distinctive place. He celebrates the "widely different nature and genius of each science," and when he considers mathematical and natural-philosophical discourse, he concludes that they work together in perfect harmony. Natural philosophy "is conversant about causes," and mathematics "effects." Natural philosophy "finds out agents," and mathematics "adjusts the proportions of the powers of those agents."[25] On this basis, Horne argues that Hutchinson's natural-philosophical speculations complement and, indeed, perfect Newton's mathematical work. Indeed, says Horne, "Isaac never intended or thought of any thing farther than illustrating actions and effects, leaving the agents to be discovered by succeeding philosophers."[26] Horne continues: "Mr. Hutchinson has made farther enquiries—that he has attempted from scripture and experiment" that prove "Sir ISAAC's conjectures" and enable him identify the agents that generate the motions represented by Newton's mathematical laws.[27] Together, Newton's *Principia* and *Moses's Principia* give the modern English interpreter a wondrously full picture of a providentially ordered universe. Suddenly Newton and Hutchinson have become the best of friends.

PROVIDENCE AND THE CHURCH

Horne's willingness to embrace Newton enabled him to overcome Hutchinsonian natural-philosophical dogmatism. This being said, Horne's broadening perspective is most clearly seen in the way that, following Watson, he affirms the providential significance of history. For Horne, the providential order of history is given in the doctrine and institution of the church, and under Horne's leadership, the Hutchinsonians earned the reputation as vociferous defenders of the church establishment. Establishmentarianism, however, is not to be regarded as the foundation of Horne's theological vision.

---

25. Horne, *A Fair*, 8. Horne quotes Clarke to defend his interpretation of Newton. Clarke challenges Leibniz in the following way: "If Mr. Leibnitz or any other philosopher can explain these phaeonomena by the laws of mechanism, far from meeting with any *opposition* he will receive the *thanks* of all the learned world" (*A Fair*, 54). Hutchinson, by claiming to have uncovered the mechanical cause of all celestial movements, presented himself as the philosopher the "learned world" had been waiting for, and Horne seems to approve of this appraisal.

26. Horne, *A Fair*, 53.

27. Horne, *A Fair*, 23.

His establishmentarianism is grounded in his providential interpretation of history.

In his *Memoirs* of the life of Horne, Jones remarks that in the early years of the movement, many dissenters embraced Hutchinsonianism.[28] Jones observes—and he seems somewhat surprised by this fact—that these dissenters, despite "all the information they had acquired, did not appear (as might reasonably have been expected) to be much softened in their prejudices against the constitution of [the Church of England]." Jones relates that "with some of these, Mr. Horne frequently fell into company," and that it was therefore likely "that he might come by degrees to be less affected, than he ought to be, to the Church of which he was a member."[29] Horne, however, broke with the dissenting Hutchinsonians, and Jones attributes this break to the most unlikely of influences: the controversial Church of Ireland bishop Robert Clayton (1695–1748).[30] Horne wanted Jones to write an answer to Clayton's *An Essay on Spirit* (1750), and the two friends worked together for over a month on the project using the library of Sir John Dolben (1684–1756), who was overseeing Jones's assistant curacy at Finedon in Northamptonshire.[31] Clayton had downplayed the importance of Trinitarian orthodoxy to promote comprehension, and the fact that he employed Arian doctrine as an olive branch to dissenters led Horne and Jones to "look into the controversy" as centrally concerned with the issue of nonconformity.[32] Their researches inclined them to believe that heresy always works its leaven against the established order of the church. They therefore came to believe that the surest preservative against heresy was the preservation of the church establishment.

The association between early Hutchinsonianism and dissent was tied to the esoteric nature of Hutchinson's method and philosophy. The early Hutchinsonians were violently antagonistic to all who rejected their kabbalah, and their antagonism was accordingly directed toward established doctrinal and natural-philosophical conclusions. Because it was the divines rather than the natural philosophers who took up the mantle to refute

---

28. Jones, *Memoirs*, 64.

29. Jones, *Memoirs*, 64.

30. See F. C. Mather, *High Church Prophet: Bishop Samuel Horsley (1733–1806) and the Caroline Tradition in the Later Georgian Church* (Oxford: Clarendon Press, 1992), 10.

31. See William Jones, *A Full Answer to an* Essay on Spirit (London: 1753).

32. Jones, *Memoirs*, 67.

Hutchinson, the revolutionary impulse of Hutchinsonianism was directed against the church. Jones confirms that the relationship between early Hutchinsonianism and dissent was solidified by the protracted controversies surrounding Hutchinson's ideas: many early Hutchinsonians harbored jealousy "against their superiors both in Church and State, on account of the unfair and angry treatment (I may say, persecution) some of them had suffered, and the dislike and aversion which their principles had met with from persons of established reputation."[33] Horne himself was attacked on account of his association with Hutchinson. Nevertheless, the early controversies surrounding Hutchinsonianism centered on the validity of the hieroglyphic method, and on this matter Horne's allegiance was not with Hutchinson. Since he believed the method obscured the salutary elements of Hutchinson's philosophy, he had no reason to take up arms against the establishment.

It is easy to see where the revolutionary foment of early Hutchinsonianism might have led. Their hieroglyphic method was, as we have seen, firmly entrenched in a devolutionary interpretation of religious history. The Church of England was therefore intrinsically suspect for them, as it was for Newton, as the product of historical devolution. Hutchinson, like Clarke and other devolutionists, may well have affirmed the necessity of conforming to the Church of England as the best option on offer, but such conservatism is contingent upon discretionary criteria of adjudication and it is therefore tenuous. Given that Hutchinson, like Newton and Clarke, insists that all religion, not merely Roman Catholicism, is subject to devolution—and all Christians, not only Roman Catholics, have obscured the true import of the Scriptures—there is little to stop his philosophy from moving in an explicitly dissenting and perhaps deistic orientation. Horne, more than anyone else, was responsible for the fact that this possibility failed to actualize.

Although Watson presented the outlines of what would later be considered a High-Church ecclesiology, he was never able to fully develop his ecclesiological position. When he left Oxford in 1758, he slipped into obscurity, and it fell to Horne, his most impressive pupil, to establish the ecclesiological orientation of the movement. Horne gradually rose to the highest echelons

---

33. Jones, *Memoirs*, 64.

of the University of Oxford administration: he was elected junior proctor of the university in 1758, received his doctor of divinity in 1764, was elected president of Magdalen College in 1768, and was elected vice-chancellor of the university in 1776.[34] Ecclesiastical preferment was slower in coming. In 1771 he was elected chaplain in ordinary to his Majesty, in 1781 he was promoted to the deanery of Canterbury, and he was finally consecrated bishop of Norwich in 1790.[35] Yet even before his consecration, his position of influence allowed him to solidify the Hutchinsonian commitment to the established church.

Horne's establishmentarianism became the provenance of Tories in the nineteenth century, but in Horne's day establishmentarianism was not tied to a particular political party.[36] Horne occupies what can be described as a centrist or orthodox position. He upholds the legitimacy of the Hanoverian monarchy and Church of England not because of his allegiance to a particular party but because he believes that, as established, they are providentially ordained.[37]

---

34. Joseph Foster, ed. *Alumni Oxoniones: The Members of the University of Oxford, 1715–1886* (London: 1888), 2:692.

35. See Joseph Meadows Cowper, *The Lives of the Deans of Canterbury, 1541–1900* (Canterbury: 1900), 194–97. Of the Oxonian coterie, Horne was the only one elevated to the bench.

36. The notion that the eighteenth-century church was composed of different warring parties owes much to W. J. Conybeare's influential essay "Church Parties." As Andrews remarks, however, "Attempting to classify and define the nature and makeup of such 'parties' is a task that cannot be achieved without a great deal of subjectivity and ahistorical labeling" (Robert Andrews, *Lay Activism and the High Church Movement of the Late Eighteenth Century* [Leiden: Brill, 2015], 20–21n45).

37. Few works have altered the face of eighteenth-century studies like J. C. D. Clark's *English Society, 1660–1832*. Clark's work opened "a new phase in English historiography which questioned much of the received picture of English society as secular, modernizing, contractarian and middle class." For Clark, the eighteenth century "has an integrity of its own which belongs neither to 'pre-modernity' nor to 'modernity,'" the defining feature of which is "the close relationship of monarchy, aristocracy and church" (Clark, *English Society*, 14, i). Clark insists that "if symbolic dates have any value, then not 1642, not 1688, not 1714 or 1776 but 1832 is the more meaningful," for it is in 1832 that the *ancien régime* finally collapsed. Nevertheless, Clark insists that what was lost in 1832 was not "'the old world' *tout court*" but "the hegemonic status and the integrity of a certain body of ideas, beliefs, customs, and practices" (Clark, *English Society*, 16). Although scholars wishing to uphold the traditional emphasis upon the radical Enlightenment have contested Clark's work, it has compelled many to acknowledge that the religious establishment enjoyed widespread if tacit support in the eighteenth century. Sanna argues, "At the practical level it is a little difficult to sustain the thesis that eighteenth century England was a confessional polity, even if it was still one in theory. Yet, few recent books have caused more fluttering in academic dovecotes. Indeed at the end of the 1980s scarcely one among professional historians of Hanoverian Britain was averse to acknowledge the need to incorporate religion in his work" (Gugileimo Sanna, "The Eighteenth Century Church of England in Historical

When Horne stood before the university on Friday, January 30, 1761, "the day appointed to be observed as the Day of the martyrdom of Charles I," and paid tribute to Charles I, "a blessed martyr," he was employing Royalist rhetoric that, since the Glorious Revolution, was bitterly contested. Although Jacobites appealed to the martyrdom of Charles I to justify the restitution of the house of Stuart, Latitudinarians had used Charles's death to rhetorical advantage by emphasizing the necessity of submission to governing authority—in other words, the Williamite and then Hanoverian regimes.[38] Earlier in the century, Horne's sermon might have allied him with the Latitudinarian cause. But in his late eighteenth-century context, such a tribute to Charles would have been regarded rather generically as a token of Horne's endorsement of the given establishment. The object of Horne's sermon was to draw comparisons "between the Lord and the royal martyr" and to urge men "to eradicate out of the minds of men those diabolical principles of resistance to government in church and state."[39] For Horne, Charles I has become both a figure of Christ and a figure of the establishment.[40]

It must be emphasized that Horne's Royalism says nothing about his parliamentary allegiance. Although radical "Whiggishness" was associated with

---

Writing," in *Cromohs Virtual Seminars: Recent Historiographical Trends of the British Studies [17th-18th Centuries]*, ed. M. Caricchio and G. Tarantino, 1-6, accessed July 22, 2015, http://www.cromohs.unifi.it/seminari/sanna_church.html). Clark's emphasis on the strength of the religious establishment in the eighteenth century has led to a resurgent interest in eighteenth-century High churchmanship. Mather observes that the Latitudinarian, or "Low church," wing of the church was already on the wane in the 1740s and 1750s and that Latitudinarians ultimately "lost their battle for the soul of the Church of England" (Mather, *High Church*, 21). Following Clark, Mather questions the assumption that "those who remained in the Established Church were excluded from ecclesiastical preferment as tainted with Jacobitism and for the most part fell into obscurity" (*High Church*, 1). As he traces the ascendency of High churchmanship in the mid-eighteenth century, Mather pays tribute to the influence of Archbishop Thomas Secker (1693-1768) as "the principal enemy of 'Low church controversialists'" (*High Church*, 10). Aston claims that the Hutchinsonians played a crucial role in reinvigorating High churchmanship even before Secker (Nigel Aston, "Horne and Heterodoxy: The Defence of Anglican Beliefs in the Late Enlightenment," *The English Historical Review* 108, no. 429 [1993]: 898.

38. Horne, *An Apology*, 41. The Hutchinsonians, like the non-jurors, advocated passive obedience to a regime that blocked their promotion (Mather, *High Church*, 227).

39. Horne, *An Apology*, 41.

40. Horne, *An Apology*, 5. Horne teems with confidence that the given order has been established by God in direct opposition to High churchmen such as Francis Atterbury, who allowed their desire to restore primitive order to become the seeds of insurrection. The defense of the Hanoverians on the basis of the appeal to the martyrdom of Charles I became a favorite Hutchinsonian refrain.

dissent, the moderate Rockingham Whigs, for whom the great Edmund Burke (1729-1797) played the role of chief spokesman, upheld the traditional Whig defense of the legitimacy of the Hanoverian regime, even though they were often outspoken critics of it.[41] When Burke looked at English society, he saw, if not a confessional state, then certainly something closely resembling one.[42] And what he saw across the channel was equally not merely the destruction of an ancient monarchy, but the collapse of a confessional state.[43] For Burke, the horror of regicide and the descent into despotism were not the decisive events of the Revolution in France. They followed unremarkably from the decisive act of the National Assembly, the confiscation of church property.[44] Burke insists that the protection of individual property is integral to human society as providentially ordered.[45] Seen in this light, the government's protection of *church* property has symbolic significance for the maintenance of providential order and is integral to it. The fact, therefore, that it was church property that was confiscated made the Revolution doubly appalling to Burke, and it led him to condemn it as—in Turner's words—the "self-consciously

---

41. The Rockingham Whigs were not the only ones to critique the establishment while defending its legitimacy. Gibson remarks that although "it has settled into the foundations of British historical orthodoxy that the bishops of the Hanoverian era were servile lap dogs for their Whig masters," he documents a number of clear instances where principled bishops opposed and defeated government motions (William Gibson, *The Church of England, 1688-1832: Unity and Accord* [London: Routledge, 2001], 64. And for Gibson, these "displays of independence by bishops in the Lords raises a significant problem for the traditional interpretation of the Hanoverian bench" (*The Church*, 71).

42. Burke insists that, "Nothing is more certain, than that our manners, our civilization, and all the good things which are connected with manners and with civilization, have, in this European world of ours, depended for ages upon two principles; and were indeed the result of both combined; I mean the spirit of a gentleman, and the spirit of religion. The nobility and the clergy, the one by profession, the other by patronage, kept learning in existence, even in the midst of arms and confusions, and whilst governments were rather in their causes than formed. Learning paid back what it received to nobility and to priesthood; and paid it with usury, by enlarging their ideas, and by furnishing their minds. Happy if they had all continued to know their indissoluble union, and their proper place! Happy if learning, not debauched by ambition, had been satisfied to continue the instructor, and not aspired to be the master!" (Edmund Burke, *Reflections on the Revolution in France*, ed. Frank M. Turner [New Haven: Yale University Press, 2003], 67-68).

43. Burke refused to be caught up in the euphoria for the Revolution that swept up many European commentators. In August 1789, he mused that he found "something in it paradoxical and Mysterious," and he predicted all of the major events that were to transpire, including regicide and military despotism. Frank Turner, introduction to Edmund Burke, *Reflections on the Revolution in France* (New Haven: Yale University Press, 2003), xix.

44. Turner, "Introduction," xxx.

45. Turner, "Introduction," xxi.

arbitrary and tyrannical rejection of experience, tradition, historical precedent, religion, and natural social hierarchy."[46]

Burke's publication of *Reflections on the Revolution in France* in 1789 provoked a furious controversy not only concerning the legitimacy of the French
Revolution but also, importantly, concerning the relationship of church and
state in England.[47] This comes as no surprise given that, while the work is
presented as a response to the enquiry of a young French nobleman, Burke's
real opponent is the popular Unitarian minister Richard Price (1723–1791).
On November 4, 1789, Price delivered a political discourse before the Society
for Commemorating the Revolution (of 1688) and argued that the revolution
of 1688 was the analogue of the revolution in France.[48] This confirmed for
Burke that the central issue at stake was the interpretation of the English
Constitution, which he insists is but a modest departure from previous
arrangements rather than, as Price claimed, the establishment of the people's "right to choose their own king."[49]

At the time of his *Reflections*, Burke's own political fortunes had already
suffered bitter disappointment, and he was desperate for allies. When Bishop
Horne published an endorsement of Burke's *Reflections* in 1791, Burke was
ecstatic to receive the affirmation of so eminent a spokesman. In *A Charge
Intended to Have Been Delivered to the Clergy of Norwich*, Horne cuts short his
reflections on "the proper opinions to be held with regard to the constitution of the state" because

---

46. Turner, "Introduction," xxiii–iv.

47. Burke's impassioned and uncompromising condemnation of the Revolution left some
of his fellow Whigs puzzled, and to this day critics have wondered about the consistency of his
position as outspoken defender of the American Revolution and bitter enemy of the French
Revolution. Burke insists, however, that the British Crown's treatment of the colonists is analogous to the French populace's treatment of the French Crown: both are in clear violation of
the "ancient constitution" which has, as its pillars, the "spirit of a gentleman, and the spirit of
religion" (Burke, *Reflections*, 67).

48. The work was written to Charles-Jean-Francois Depon, a young French acquaintance
of Burke's (Burke, *Reflections*, 3n1).

49. Turner, "Introduction," xxxvii. For Burke, Price's nonconformity had already compromised his position as a spokesman for the Revolution, and Burke was not alone in this opinion.
For Burke and others, Price's nonconformity made him complicit in the revolutionary rejection
of the French establishment.

All farther reflections on this subject are rendered needless by a late work of a learned and eloquent layman, who hath very effectually exposed those wild opinions lately risen up to disturb the peace of mankind; and hath called us back to the measures of common sense and experience, at a time, when we were hasting towards anarchy, under the specious name of liberty; pointing out to us a more excellent way, which if we follow we shall do well. As Christians and Englishmen, we are unquestionably obliged to those, who are not afraid to declare themselves against the overbearing violence of licentious principles, and the torrent of calumny which followeth so close after them: and it is to be hoped, *our* zeal will be stirred up by so laudable an example.[50]

On December 9, 1791, Burke wrote a letter to Horne thanking him for his generous endorsement. "I have been honoured," begins Burke, and

I flatter myself thro' your Lordships indulgence, with your truly Episcopal Charge to the Clergy of your Diocess. It appears to me full of Wisdom, and piety, and of doctrine not only sound in itself, but for the time most seasonable. I should say a great deal more, which however would be short of what I think, of the merits of that piece, and of my reverence to the Character of the writer, if your Lordships polite and generous acceptance of my feeble endeavours in our Common Cause might not appear as some ingredient in my admiration of the author of his work. I ought not to be too much ashamed neither of receiving some Bias on my Judgement from the Sentiments of my Gratitude. In one respect I shall be justified in expressing the highest opinion of whatever comes from the Bishop of Norwich, by its being known, that I am in unison with the publick Voice.[51]

As an establishmentarian, Burke views Horne's position as bishop as an inherently political one, and he pays tribute to Horne as one who speaks with "the publick Voice." Burke's exchange with Horne is intriguing because

50. George Horne, *A Charge Intended to Have Been Delivered to the Clergy of Norwich* (Norwich: 1791), 33.

51. Edmund Burke, "Edmund Burke to George Horne, 9 December, 1791," in *The Correspondence of Edmund Burke*, ed. Alfred Cobban and Robert Smith (Cambridge: Cambridge University Press, 1967), 6:455–56.

it confirms Clark's opinion that the *ancien régime* was upheld by those across the political spectrum. It also confirms that upholding this ideal is a wholly inadequate marker to identify the politics or churchmanship of individuals at the dawn of the French Revolution.

Scholars have tended to view Horne's theological position entirely in terms of ideological categories and to interpret him, therefore, as "Tory," "High Church," or "right wing." There can be no doubt that Horne held positions that, in the nineteenth century, would have clearly allied him with such parties. Within Horne's own context, however, these terms should be applied cautiously.[52] To describe Horne's position in ideological terms is to ignore his self-understanding. Horne dissociates himself from the term "High Church" for the same reason that he dissociates himself from the term "Hutchinsonian": he refuses to be enlisted in any cause that might be interpreted as sectarian. From his position at the center of the ecclesial-political establishment, Horne used his influence to build bridges with those at the margins. His willingness to align himself with churchmen of diverse loyalties confirms that he made his personal theological opinions subservient to his establishmentarianism.[53] He was happy to associate with Low-Church

---

52. Andrews acknowledges the point that the Hutchinsonians and other High churchmen saw themselves as "orthodox" rather than as members of a High-Church party, but he nevertheless insists that they should be called High churchmen despite the fact that they did not have a party allegiance. He rightly maintains that someone can be a High churchman even at a time when no High-Church party exists (Andrews, *Lay*, 20–21n45). Nockles is also willing to regard Horne and other establishmentarian ecclesiastics as "High churchmen," and he does so in order to challenge the notion that the Tractarians brought High-Church principles to a church that had fallen away from the Caroline tradition (Nockles, *The Oxford*, 12–26). Even as he does so, however, Nockles is keenly aware of the important distinctions that separate late eighteenth- and early nineteenth-century High churchmen from the Tractarians. The danger that accompanies the application of the term "High Church" to eighteenth-century ecclesiastics is that it is easy to take current understandings of High churchmanship, which are based upon nineteenth-century categories, and impose them on previous eras. In particular, since the Oxford Movement, the term has been used to refer to a specific party within the Church of England with anti-establishmentarian sensibilities. But since establishmentarianism was central to the High churchmanship of previous generations, the application of the term to eighteenth-century churchmen runs the risk of obscuring this important distinction (Nockles, *The Oxford*, 90). Sack argues that the defense of the Church of England establishment was the central element in English conservatism prior to 1832. See James J. Sack, *From Jacobite to Conservative: Reaction and Orthodoxy* (Cambridge: University of Cambridge Press, 1993).

53. While Horne's agreement with Burke does not disconfirm the existence of a High-Church party in the second half of the eighteenth century, it suggests that the existence of such a party must be established on the basis of something other than political theory. Mather, for one, discusses several controversies of the late eighteenth century that he believes helped to consolidate such a party. First, there was the battle with the Methodists concerning "breaches of

evangelicals.[54] He worked eagerly with them on issues of societal reform. He happily adopted their rhetoric of conversion.[55] He nurtured a friendship with John Wesley (1703-1791),[56] and he even entrusted the education of his daughter Sally to Hannah More (1745-1833).[57]

F. C. Mather observes that under Horne's leadership, the Hutchinsonians became "the nearest thing to a coherent body on the High Church side of the eighteenth-century Church of England."[58] It may ultimately be appropriate to regard Horne and his allies as High churchman. But the danger that accompanies this attribution is that it can obscure what was more fundamental about their churchmanship—namely, their establishmentarianism. Although the Hutchinsonians may well have distinguished themselves from

---

parish order and the holding of irregular services, with which was connected an attack on the 'enthusiasm' and moderate Calvinism of the Anglican Evangelicals" (Mather, *High Church*, 17). Second, there was the even more urgent task of reaffirming the "Catholic teaching concerning the Sacrament of the Lord's Supper against the reductionism of the advanced Latitudinarians" (Mather, *High Church*, 17-18). For Mather, "A prolonged controversy over Prayer Book revision was the third main dispute in which High Churchmanship developed its identity" (*High Church*, 20). Admittedly, Horne's involvement in these controversies gives further reason to call into question his identity as a leader of the High-Church party. Horne, as we have seen, was very friendly to evangelicals, and as Mather himself acknowledges, "Horne created an entente between High churchmanship and Calvinism when he defended six Calvinistic Methodists expelled from St. Edmund Hall in 1768 for praying and preaching in private houses, and he collaborated with Augustus Toplady to resist alterations in the liturgy and articles in 1772-3." See C. J. Abbey, *The English Church and Its Bishops, 1700-1800* (London: 1887), 2:125-27.

54. It is not clear that pre-Tractarian evangelicals should be regarded as "Low-churchmen." Mather finds that the term was first applied to evangelicals in 1833. The label "Low church" was originally used to describe the Erastianism of Hoadly, which the evangelicals vigorously opposed. Mather, *High Church*, 32.

55. In other words, Horne's theology also contains elements that, while "orthodox" in his own context, came to be associated in the nineteenth century not with High churchmen, but with evangelicals. George Horne, *Letters on Infidelity*, 2nd ed. (Oxford: 1786), 213, 295.

56. See Derya Gürses Tarbuck, "John Wesley's Critical Engagement with Hutchinsonianism 1730-1780," *History of European Ideas* 37 (2011): 35-42.

57. George Horne, Journal entry, April 28, 1786, Add. MS 8134, A3, p. 52, Cambridge University Library, Cambridge, UK. Describing Horne's churchmanship as "orthodox" is appropriate for at least three reasons. The first is that he spurned innovation and strove, as far as he was able, to uphold the consensus of the catholic tradition. The second is that his establishmentarianism was, within his context, entirely "orthodox," as most of his fellow clergy saw the church and state as two institutions that formed a single entity. The third is that Horne's establishmentarianism was, as we have seen, grounded in a concern to preserve the Christian doctrinal tradition and especially Trinitarian orthodoxy (Gibson, *The Church*, 27).

58. Mather observes that the Hutchinsonians "formed a compact coterie, whose members corresponded and helped one another whenever possible. Though their numbers were few they exerted a large and growing influence in the Church during the first half of George III's reign" (Mather, *High Church*, 13).

other clerics by the sheer intensity of their establishmentarian apologetic, the fact that orthodox churchmen from across the political spectrum were strong establishmentarians confirms that establishmentarianism is not the distinguishing feature of Hutchinsonianism.

Hutchinsonian sensualism played an important part in leading Horne to the conviction that it is necessary to defend the establishment as providentially ordered. But although Horne occasionally appeals to Charles I as a figure of Christ, his establishmentarian apologetic does not often appear to be the outworking of a figural scriptural hermeneutic. While his emblematic interpretation of Scripture is the means through which Horne discerns the providential order of nature, it does not play the same role in his reflections upon the providential order of history. Indeed, it is tempting to ascribe to Horne the view that the providential order of history is apparent and therefore does not rely upon Scripture words. Horne's establishmentarianism was so widespread that it does not necessarily point to the unraveling of the scriptural basis of Hutchinsonianism. But there can be no doubt that as Hutchinsonianism gradually came to be understood exclusively in terms of political and ecclesial commitments, scriptural emblematicism came to be regarded as useful for the maintenance of the established order, then discretionary, and, finally, irrelevant.[59]

PROVIDENCE AND SCRIPTURE

One of the basic difficulties with Hutchinson's defense of the Old Testament was that he tried to elevate the status of the Old Testament while insisting all the while that the text of the Old Testament is fundamentally corrupt. The early Hutchinsonians were unable to resolve this tension, for while they were vociferous defenders of the Hebrew tongue, they continued to promote Hutchinson's theory of textual corruption.[60] Early Hutchinsonians found that the surest way to highlight the wonder of Hutchinson's hieroglyphic decipherment was to emphasize the corruption of the Old Testament text.

---

59. The fortunes of Hutchinsonian scriptural emblematicism in the nineteenth century are engaged in the epilogue of this work.

60. Bate, for one, insists that Hutchinson's quarrel was not with the Christian grammarians and lexicographers but with the Jews. The Jews intentionally obscured the christological import of the original Hebrew words, for although "the Scriptures were wrote for Evidence of Christ—they renounce Christ" (Julius Bate, *The Examiner Examined* [London: 1739], 62).

When the Oxonians quietly moved away from Hutchinson's etymological method, they no longer found it necessary to parade Old Testament textual obfuscation. In fact, the Oxonians became the eighteenth-century's great defenders of Old Testament textual integrity.

Horne's pamphlet exchange with noted Old Testament textual critic Benjamin Kennicott (1718–1783) played an important role in this about-face.[61] Because Horne argued that textual transmission was guided by divine providence, his defense of the Old Testament, like his defense of the providential order of nature and of the church establishment, displays an increased willingness on the part of Hutchinsonians to affirm the providential order of history. This being said, Horne's defense of the Old Testament suggests that he has come to instrumentalize Scripture as a means of defending this overarching providential order.

Like Hutchinson, Kennicott insisted that the Old Testament had a central role to play in the defense of Christianity against atheists and infidels; like Hutchinson, Kennicott's object was to reclaim the Old Testament as a Christian text; like Hutchinson, he held that the single most important factor hindering the Old Testament from fulfilling this role was textual corruption; and like Hutchinson, he insisted that the importance of his own work could only be discerned when the sheer extent of textual corruption was made known.[62] "Since the last Translation was made," says Kennicott,

> Many *imperfections* and *errors* in it have been discovered by learned men. And several passages have been lately pointed out, in which the *older* English Translations had *better* expressed the sense of the originals, both in the Old and in the New Testament. But, notwithstanding these blemishes, and even mistakes; and though it is certain,

---

61. Ruderman observes that the controversy with Kennicott forced the Hutchinsonians to affirm the integrity of the rabbis as divinely appointed caretakers of the Old Testament text (David B. Ruderman, *Jewish Enlightenment in an English Key* [Princeton: Princeton University Press, 2000], 35).

62. Kennicott insists that "*All Scripture was given by inspiration of* God—and, that the Volume of the Old Testament, as well as that of the New, is to be reverenced, and received by *Christians* for their *instruction in righteousness*" (Benjamin Kennicott, *The Sabbath: A Sermon Preached in His Majesty's Chapel, Whitehall* [London: 1781], 5). Kennicott, like his Hutchinsonian opponents, is well aware that upholding the Old Testament as Christian Scripture means affirming its ability to direct Christian behavior. Following seventeenth-century Sabbatarians, Kennicott insists that, "ALL MANKIND are bound to observe A SABBATH DAY" (*The Sabbath*, 14).

that great improvements might be now made in translating the whole
Bible, because the Hebrew and Greek languages have been much cultivated, and far better understood, since the year 1600: yet we shall
then only see the great *Expediency*, or rather the *Necessity*, of a more
exact English Bible; when we reflect, that the *Heb. Text* itself is now
found to be wrong in many instances, some of which are of considerable consequence.[63]

Kennicott's lifelong work, which built upon the text-critical labors of Louis
Cappel and Jean Morin (1591–1659), was to "organize a census of hundreds
of biblical manuscripts" to present "a systematic collation of variant readings."[64] After almost thirty years of work, Kennicott finally published his
Vetus Testamentum Hebraicum (1776–1780).

Horne was opposed to Kennicott's project from the beginning.[65] Horne
may well have been willing to keep the matter to himself, but in 1756
Kennicott published *A word to the Hutchinsonians: Or remarks on three extraordinary sermons lately preached before the University of Oxford by The Reverend Dr.
Patten, The Reverend Mr. Wetherall and The Reverend Mr. Horne.* In this pamphlet, Kennicott argues for the inherent reasonableness of textual criticism
to overcome the problem of textual corruption, and he complains that the
"Hutchinsonians are men who, despising reason and learning, and indulging
their minds in all the wildness of imagination and unbounded whim, make
Words signify what they please, turn *the plainest History* into *sublime Prophecy*,
and compel *Sentences* to be oracular, in various ways, *with all such meanings
as were never meant*."[66]

Kennicott evidently perceived that the popularity of Hutchinsonianism
at Oxford was an obstacle to his massive project. For Kennicott, that the

---

63. Benjamin Kennicott, *Remarks on Select Passages in the Old Testament* (Oxford: 1787), 6.

64. Stephen Burnett, "Later Christian Hebraists," in *Hebrew Bible / Old Testament, Vol. 2:
From the Renaissance to the Enlightenment*, ed. Magne Sæbø (Göttingen: Vandenhoeck & Ruprecht,
2008), 796. McKane observes that "the purpose of his massive collation is, paradoxically, to
destroy the credence of those variants which are the consequence of imperfect transmission,
and to reinstate the text in its originality and purity by discerning which of the variants preserve that text" (William McKane, "Benjamin Kennicott: An Eighteenth-Century Researcher,"
The Journal of Theological Studies 28, no. 2 [1977]: 458).

65. Jones, *Memoirs*, 97.

66. Kennicott, *A Word*, 42.

Hutchinsonians irresponsibly made "*Words* signify what they please" is indicative of the fact that they fail to appreciate that the words they interpret have been subject to the corrosive waves of time. The great irony here is that Kennicott is troubled that the Hutchinsonians no longer endorse the devolutionary philosophy of history which he shares with the founder of the movement.

Horne responded to Kennicott with *An Apology for Certain Gentlemen in the University of Oxford* (1756). Horne begins this work by complaining that he and his compatriots had been unjustly derided as schismatics.[67] He insists that while all those who claim that Christ is "*the end of the law, and the fullness of the Gospel*" are branded as Hutchinsonians, he and his compatriots are not party men. Far from being "a *sect*, or schismatical combination of separatists from other Church of *England* Christians," they are "fully persuaded of the necessity of being in the *unity* of the *church*, to obtain salvation."[68] Horne then proceeds to outline eight objections to Kennicott's work, which dispel the accusation that Hutchinsonians are anti-intellectual brigands.[69]

Like any good apologist, however, Horne is not merely content to defend himself. He uses the pamphlet to go on the offensive against Samuel Clarke and his disciples. He insists that there is a powerful link between anti-trinitarianism and natural religion, for those who are zealous to promote Christianity as moral religion invariably come to devalue faith in Christ.[70] The implication of Horne's argument is clear: by accusing the Hutchinsonians of turning "the plainest history into sublime prophecy" concerning Christ, Kennicott shows himself to be an ally of those who repudiate Christian orthodoxy.[71] Horne ends his piece with a defense of the way in which he and his compatriots read the Old Testament in christological terms, and he insists that "*prophecy is a sign only to those that believe, who by reason of use have their* [spiritual] *senses exercised and the eyes of their understanding enlightened, to see wonderful things in God's law.*"[72]

---

67. Horne, *An Apology*, 1–3.
68. Horne, *An Apology*, 3.
69. Horne, *An Apology*, 6–23.
70. Horne, *An Apology*, 48–51.
71. Kennicott, *A Word*, 42.
72. Horne, *An Apology*, 58. St. Paul's example in this respect is important for Horne, but Horne does not suggest that he is only licensed to offer figural readings that have been previously

Contemporary scholars have tended to assume that Kennicott vanquished Horne because his text critical approach was ultimately victorious, but the effectiveness of the Hutchinsonian critique of Kennicott's project must not be underestimated.[73] The Hutchinsonians were, in Ruderman's estimation, "the most vocal opponents" of Kennicott's scheme, and they helped to provoke a "huge storm" that ultimately involved the king himself.[74] Horne's most important contribution to the controversy was his subsequent work, *A View of Mr. Kennicott's Method* (1765).[75] Curiously, Horne's earlier emphasis on the necessity of christological interpretation is conspicuously absent from this work. He argues not that the Hutchinsonian interpretive method is inherently superior to Kennicott's, but that Kennicott's method is dangerous for the Christian religion since it is liable to be misunderstood by the masses and maleficently used by Socinian dissenters. The tone of Horne's muted criticisms stands in sharp contrast to his earlier work and confirms that, as an experienced churchman and administrator, Horne has become skilled in the art of diplomacy.[76] Horne's shift in tone also suggests that he no longer sees

---

sanctioned by him. Horne finds that "there is enough of the old Testament applied to the new to enable us to apply the rest, if we have but humility to receive the key of knowledge from Christ and diligence to use it" (*An Apology*, 58).

73. Ruderman, for one, finds that Jones's portrait of Kennicott is fair. Ruderman points out that there were several methodological problems that troubled Kennicott's enterprise (David Ruderman, *Jewish*, 52–55).

74. Ruderman, *Jewish*, 24.

75. George Horne, *A View of Mr. Kennicott's Method of Correcting the Hebrew Text* (London: 1765). Jones summarizes Horne's argument against Kennicott in his *Memoirs*, pages 97–107. Katz sees the Hutchinsonians as anti-Semites, but the anti-Semitic impulse of early Hutchinsonianism disappeared when the Oxonians rejected Hutchinson's devolutionary philosophy of history. Horne and Jones deny the idea that the Old Testament text is in need of improvement because "the Masoretical Jews had guarded and secured the Text of their Bible in such a manner, that no other book in the world had ever been so guarded and secured" (Jones, *Memoirs*, 98). See David S. Katz, "Christian and Jew in Early Modern English Perspective," *Jewish History* 8 (1994): 68. Manasseh ben Israel "was convinced that as long as the Old Testament was venerated by Christians, there would always be a place of honour for the Jews." It comes as no surprise, therefore, that as the Old Testament became increasingly marginalized in eighteenth-century England, anti-Semitism was the victor. In particular, the cutting-edge work of Orientalist Sir William Jones and others on the priority of Sanskrit "eliminated the Jews as a necessary component in the history of mankind, and reduced them to … freaks who could be persecuted and expelled" (Katz, "Christian," 69).

76. Jones celebrates "the friendly way in which Dr. Kennicott and Dr. Horne lived together, forgetting all their former disputes, yet without changing their opinions on either side" (Jones, *Memoirs*, 108). Mrs. Horne and Mrs. Kennicott were intimate friends and may well have had a part in reconciling their husbands. A collection of thirty-four letters from Mrs. Kennicott to Mrs. Horne, three from Mrs. Kennicott to Dr. Horne, and three from Dr. Kennicott to Mrs. Horne,

the controversy primarily as a battle between opposing hermeneutical methods or Christologies. As he surveys the ecclesial landscape from his position of power within the establishment, his primary objective is pragmatic: to uphold the providential order by upholding the integrity of the established scriptural text. Contra Kennicott, he therefore argues that the hard work of noting significant textual variants has already been done, and the integrity of the given Old Testament text has already been aptly defended.[77]

In *A View of Kennicott's Method*, Horne argues that further prodding into the textual history will only serve to compromise the status of the text and thereby the status of the Christianity.[78] But although he worries the project will be detrimental to established religion, Horne no longer condemns it as inherently problematic. Indeed, Horne even claims that he is willing to be convinced that the project is valuable in the service of Christianity. Horne's moderation does not imply that Horne has rejected the emblematic interpretation of his youth. What it does suggest, however, is that Horne's Hutchinsonian hermeneutic has been subsumed within his larger providential vision. Horne has come to regard figural and specifically christological interpretation instrumentally. It is only necessary to the extent that it preserves providential order. This argument is borne out by the study of Horne's renowned two-volume commentary on the Psalms.

HORNE'S MEASURED EMBLEMATICISM

Horne's *Commentary on the Psalms*, like Hutchinson's *Principia* and Watson's *Christ the Light of the World*, begins with an impassioned defense of the emblematic interpretation of the Old Testament. But Horne is ultimately willing to interpret only a few psalms emblematically. Although he expressly follows Watson's threefold approach on certain occasions, the mediatorial role that the Christian canon plays in Watson's method is muted in Horne's work. Much of the time Horne is confident that the devotional significance

---

has been preserved in the Magdalen College archives. Papers of George Horne, MC: PR29 MS 2/1, fols. 66–136, Magdalen College Archives, University of Oxford, Oxford, UK.

77. Horne, *A View*, 21.

78. Jones relates that Horne "thought it would be of disservice to turn the minds of the learned *more* toward the *letter* of the Bible, when they were already too much turned away from the *spirit* of it. The best fruits of divine wisdom may be gathered from the word of God, in any language, and in any edition. To what the Scripture itself calls the *spirit* of the Scripture, the learned of late days were become much more inattentive than in past ages" (Jones, *Memoirs*, 108).

of individual Psalms can be exploited by relating the passage directly to contemporary circumstances. This confirms that for Horne, Scripture does not establish the providential order of the world but is, itself, subject to it.

Horne's two volume *Commentary on the Psalms* was, in Jones's estimation, his greatest achievement.[79] Jones concludes his *Memoirs* of Horne with a transcription of his epitaph for Horne, which praises Horne for "Depth of Learning," "Brightness of Imagination," "Sanctity of Manners," and "Sweetness of Temper."[80] The most effusive praise, however, is reserved for Horne's commentary: "His Commentary on the psalms will continue to be / A Companion to the Closet, / Till the Devotion of Earth shall end in the Hallelujahs of Heaven."[81] Although the *Commentary* was Horne's most popular work, Jones admits that there were several scholars who opposed it from the beginning.

There are good and learned men, who cannot but speak well of the work, and yet are forward to let us know, that they do not follow Dr. Horne as an interpreter. I believe them; but this is one of the things we have to lament: and while they may think this an honour to their

---

79. Jones says that "the first edition in quarto was published in the year 1776 when the author was vice-chancellor; and it happened, soon after its publication, that I was at Paris. There was then a Christian University in the place! and I had an opportunity of recommending it to some learned gentlemen who were members of it, and understood the English language well. I took the liberty to tell them, our church had lately been enriched by a Commentary on the Psalms; the best, in our opinion, that had ever appeared; and such as St. Austin would have perused with delight, if he had lived to see it. At my return the author was so obliging as to furnish me with a copy to send over to them as a present; and I was highly gratified by the approbation with which it was received. With those who could read English, it was so much in request, that I was told the book was never out of hand; and I apprehend more copies were sent for. Every intelligent Christian, who once knows the value of it, will keep it, to the end of his life, as the companion of his retirement" (Jones, *Memoirs*, 122).

80. Here Jones refers to himself as Horne's "other chaplain." He relates that "one of his Lordship's chaplains attended him to his grave, and then returned in sorrow to Norwich: his other chaplain paid the tribute due to his memory in a plain monumental inscription" (Jones, *Memoirs*, 173). See also William Henry Teale, "The Life of William Jones, M. A., Perpetual Curate of Nayland," in *Biography of English Divines: The Life of Launcelot Andrewes, D. D., Bishop of Winchester* (London: Joseph Masters, 1849), 392.

81. Jones, *Memoirs*, 173–74. Jones insists that the *Commentary* is Horne's finest work: "His Commentary on the Psalms was under his hand about twenty years. The labour, to which he submitted in the course of the work, was prodigious: his reading for many years was allotted chiefly to this subject; and his study and meditation together produced as fine a work, and as finely written, as most in the English language" (*Memoirs*, 121).

judgement, I am afraid it is a symptom that we are retrograde in theological learning.[82]

One reader who was willing to praise the work while all the while questioning its underlying hermeneutic was John Wesley. When he "met with" the
Commentary, he declared that he supposed it was "the best that ever was
wrote." And yet, he also confessed, "I could not comprehend his aggrandizing the *psalms*, it seems even above the New Testament."[83]

While Wesley paid tribute to the commentary and yet found Horne's
christological method bewildering, Unitarian minister Theophilus Lindsey
(1723–1808) rejected the commentary outright as "imaginative." As a disciple
of Clarke, Lindsey emphasized the necessity of the rational interpretation
of the literal sense by individual interpreters.[84] He insists that by using the
Psalms as the basis of his ecclesiological and theological reflections, Horne
violates the literal sense and demonstrates that he believes that "anything
may be made out of any thing." Horne, complains Lindsey, finds "all his own
peculiar notions and doctrines, largely and continually displayed in these
sacred songs; whilst others can discover nothing of the sort, neither in them,
nor throughout the whole Bible."[85]

82. Jones, *Memoirs*, 120.

83. John Wesley, *An Extract of the Rev. Mr. John Wesley's Journal, from Sept. 4, 1782, to June 28,
1786* (London: 1789), 14; *The Works of the Rev. John Wesley*, 3rd ed. (London: 1829), 4:245. Wesley
had a high regard for Horne and appreciated the perspicuity of his writing. See also Gürses
Tarbuck, "John Wesley's," 42. For other contemporary endorsements of Horne's work, see
Robert MacCulloch, *Lectures on the Prophecies of Isaiah* (London: 1791), xv–xvi; David Simpson,
Strictures on Religious Opinions (Macclesfiled: 1792), 65–66n; John Gillies, ed., *The Psalms of David,
with Notes Devotional and Practical* [...] *extracted* [...] *from Dr. Horne's Commentary on the Book of
Psalms* (Edinburgh: 1796), preface; Lindsey Murray, "Review of A Selection from Bishop Horne's
Commentary on the Psalms," *European Magazine and London Review* 61 (1812): 39–40.

84. According to Lindsey, who is largely recognized as the founder of the Unitarian Church
of England, "Few men in any age have, by their writings cast more light on the dark parts of the
word of God, or more laboured to restore his true worship, than Dr. *Samuel Clarke*" (Theophilus
Lindsey, *The Apology of Theophilus Lindsey* [London: 1782], 82). Lindsey sees Clarke as one of the
chief spokesmen of a Unitarian tradition that dates back to the Reformation. Lindsey interestingly also identifies Newton as a Unitarian (Theophilus Lindsey, *An Historical View of the
State of the Unitarian Doctrine and Worship from the Reformation to Our Own Times* [London: 1783],
366–95, 401–4).

85. Theophilus Lindsey, *Vindiciæ Preistleian: An Address to the Students of Oxford and Cambridge*
(London: 1788), 315.

Objections to Horne's method were provoked by his bold defense of the Psalms in his introduction to his commentary, which begins by "aggrandizing" the Psalms as "the epitome of the Bible ... adapted to the purposes of devotion." Horne quotes Richard Hooker (1554–1600) to the effect that "this little volume, like the paradise of Eden, affords us in perfection, though in miniature, everything that groweth elsewhere."[86] Here Horne draws upon the microcosm-macrocosm distinction that was central to Renaissance Neoplatonism to defend the principle of emblematic mediation. As the "epitome" of the Bible "adapted to the purposes of devotion," the Psalms play the role of the emblematic motto—they relay the biblical message to the contemporary context through devotional idiom.

Despite this bold defense of the Psalms, Horne is extremely cautious in his application of the emblematic method he celebrates. He assures his readers that while he plans to interpret the Psalms by means of figural reading, which he calls the ancient art of spiritual interpretation, he is equally indebted to the labors of modern interpreters who have "set themselves to investigate with diligence and ascertain with accuracy their literal scope and meaning." Indeed, Horne says, "All who desire to understand the Scriptures, must enter into their labours." "But let us also bear in mind," urges Horne,

> That all is not done, when this is done. A work of the utmost importance still remains, which is the business of Theology to undertake and execute; since, with respect to the Old Testament, and the Psalter more especially, a person may attain a critical and grammatical knowledge of them, and yet continue a Jew, with the veil upon his heart; an utter stranger to that sense of the holy books, evidently intended, in such a variety of instances, to bear testimony to the Saviour of the world; that sense, which is style, by divines, the PROPHETICAL, EVANGELICAL, MYSTICAL, or SPIRITUAL sense.[87]

To refute the notion that spiritual and philological interpretation are incommensurable, Horne's intent is to liberally use the methods and insights of each insofar as they assist him in his overarching devotional purpose: "To

---

86. Horne, *Commentary*, ii.
87. Horne, *Commentary*, vii.

bring them in some measure together," he says, "is the design of the following work."[88]

Horne can be regarded as tipping his hat to spiritual interpretation, since
he suggests philological interpretation is barren without it. Spiritual interpretation, says Horne, is what renders the Psalms "profitable for doctrine, for
reproof, for correction, for instruction in righteousness."[89] Horne is, however,
equally insistent that spiritual interpretation creates fictitious allegories
when it roams free from the mooring of the literal text.[90] Horne is therefore at pains to emphasize that the Davidic history is the foundation upon
which messianic interpretations must be established.[91] "Very few psalms,"
says Horne,

> Appear to be simply prophetical and belong only to Messiah without
> the intervention of any other person. Most of them, it is apprehended,
> have a double sense, which stands upon the ground and foundation
> of the ancient patriarchs, prophets, priests, and kings.[92]

Horne insists that modern interpreters are not constrained to extract messianic import only in those instances where the New Testament does so,[93]
but he equally holds that many Psalms have no messianic import.[94] Horne
finds this concession unproblematic for at least two reasons. First, because

---

88. Horne, *Commentary*, iii.

89. Horne, *Commentary*, xvii.

90. Horne, *Commentary*, xxiv.

91. Horne, *Commentary*, xxi. Horne's insistence that the literal and spiritual senses must both
be addressed is evident in his treatment of King David. Horne is careful to protect the integrity
of David as a historical person, and this leads Horne to consistently distinguish between David
and Christ, and thereby the historical and ecclesial readings of the text. In Psalm 6 he observes,
for example, that "David makes a solemn appeal to God, the searcher of hearts, as judge of
his innocence, with regard to the particular crime laid to his share." This appeal, however, is
very different than that of Christ, who alone "could call upon Heaven to attest his universal
uprightness" (*Commentary*, 23).

92. Horne, *Commentary*, xxi. Horne's endorsement of the "double sense" of messianic proph-
ecy is consistent with the emerging consensus. See David Ney, "Reconciling the Old and New
Testaments in the Eighteenth-Century Debate over Prophecy," in *Change and Transformation:
Essays in Anglican History*, ed. Thomas P. Power (Eugene, OR: Pickwick, 2013), 85–112.

93. Horne, *Commentary*, xiv.

94. Wesley observes that Horne considers some Psalms to be far more important than
others. He complains that "some of them he hardly makes any thing of; the eighty-seventh in
particular" (Wesley, *An Extract*, 14; *The Works*, 245). I maintain that this unequal treatment is
attributable to Horne's selective application of his emblematic method.

he reads the Psalms canonically, he insists that individual psalms that lack messianic import acquire their devotional significance from their providential location within the Psalter, which is "written upon a divine, preconcerted, prophetical plan."[95] Second, Horne insists that the Psalms do not need to have messianic import because they are "very delightful and profitable ... in their literal and historical sense, which well repayeth all the pains taken to come at it."[96] While the spiritual sense is only sometimes necessary, the literal sense is always indispensable to the interpreter.

Horne's appropriation of Watson's threefold emblematic method is clearly seen in his commentary upon Psalm 7:5: "Let the enemy persecute my soul, and take it; yea, let him tread down my life upon the earth, and lay mine honour in the dust." Horne begins by reflecting upon the "evils which David imprecates on himself" but quickly turns to consider the manner in which "Christ, for our sakes," submitted "to the imputation of guilt." Since Christ was "innocent in himself," however, "he persued and overtook his enemies, he conquered the conquerors, and trampled them under his feet." Horne applies his christological reading to tropological ends: "He enableth us, through grace, to do the same."[97] Following Watson, however, Horne draws devotional import directly from the literal sense of the text. Having reflected upon David's "solemn appeal to God" in Psalm 7:3, Horne observes that "any person, when slandered, may do the same."[98] Indeed, says Horne, "Believers in every age have been persecuted in this way; and the King of saints often mentions it as one of the bitterest ingredients in his cup of sorrows."[99] The Christian reader of the Psalm, then, can find Christ in the text on the same basis that he finds himself in the text—namely, points of contact with David's personal experience. Christ's experience may assist Christians in drawing devotional application from the text, or it may not, depending on the nature of the case. On this account, interpreters of the Psalms will sometimes find that canonical, and specifically christological, reading is necessary, and sometimes find that it is not.

---

95. Horne, *Commentary*, xii.
96. Horne, *Commentary*, xiii.
97. Horne, *Commentary*, 24.
98. Horne, *Commentary*, 23.
99. Horne, *Commentary*, 23.

That Horne was measured in his scriptural emblematicism was apparent to Jones. Jones celebrates the Puritans as "excellent spiritual interpreters of the word," and he bemoans the fact that when his fellow establishmentarians rejected their overzealous piety, they also rejected their interpretive method. Jones finds that interpreters such as "Clarke, Hoadley, Hare, Middleton, Warburton, Sherlock, South, William Law, Edmund Law and others since the restoration" completely neglect the spiritual interpretation of Scripture, and he praises Horne's attempt to reestablish it through his *Commentary*.[100] Jones notes that as Horne wrote the work, he was cognizant that it was a work his countrymen were "ill prepared to receive."

> This put him upon his guard; and the work is in some respects the better for it, in others not so good; it is more cautiously and correctly written, but perhaps not so richly furnished with matter as it might have been. Had he been composing a novel, he would have been under none of these fears: his imagination might then have taken its course, without a bridle, and the world would have followed as fast as he could wish.[101]

Jones insists that Horne's measured application of his favored spiritual method is prudential. As the work was oriented toward the promotion of piety within the Church of England, Horne wished to remove any roadblocks that would hinder its reception, and he discerned that the "imaginative" exploration of emblems and allegories would have been counterproductive. When he is able to extract devotional import directly from the literal text, he is quick to do so, so as not to offend his critically-minded colleagues. He equally recognizes, however, that some psalms do not readily bear this fruit, and when they do not, Horne looks to the New Testament for assistance.

As he studies the Old Testament, Horne finds it is sometimes necessary to employ figural readings to generate devotional readings, but when he studies the New Testament, he finds that no such assistance is necessary. Because devotional import can be drawn from the New Testament text by comparing it directly to contemporary circumstances, figural reading plays no part in Horne's New Testament hermeneutic. Horne finds that the New Testament

---

100. Horne, *Commentary*, 108–9.
101. Horne, *Commentary*, 122.

functions as Christian Scripture without the assistance of the Old Testament and that the Old Testament is only sometimes able to do the same. When the Old Testament struggles to stand on its own two feet, canonical reading can be happily employed as a crutch.

That Horne's measured emblematicism establishes disequilibrium between the canons is clearly borne out by the study of his late devotional essays on great biblical characters. Horne's *Considerations on the Life and Death of Abel*, *Considerations on the Life and Translation of Enoch*, and *Considerations on the Life of Noah* are part of the larger Hutchinsonian project to defend the canonicity of the Old Testament. And they are, specifically, part of Horne's concerted attempt to do so on devotional grounds. In *Considerations on the Life and Death of Abel*, it takes Horne less than a page to proceed from Abel to Christ: "The days of [Abel's] pilgrimage," says Horne, "were quickly ended, he hasted away to an abiding city ... And so the holy Jesus, King of saints and Prince of martyrs, made but a short stay amongst us in the days of his flesh."[102] In *Considerations on the Life and Translation of Enoch*, it takes Horne less than a paragraph. According to Horne, the translation of Enoch is "a rehearsal of the ascension of the holy Jesus" intended for the "building up of those before the law" and so that "we of these latter days might admire the wisdom of God in foreshowing what hath been accomplished."[103] In *Considerations on the Life of Noah*, Horne begins with the meaning of the name "Noah," which involves "in it the ideas of *rest* and *consolation*." This name, says Horne, was assigned to Noah on account of the prophecy that he "*shall comfort us concerning our work, and the toil of our hands, because of the ground which the Lord hath cursed*" (Gen 5:29).[104] The salvation which Noah provided, however, was "but a temporary reprieve" and could only

Prefigure and shadow forth, *until the seed should come, to whom the promise was made*, and in whom alone it could be fulfilled. Of the blessed Jesus may it be said emphatically, and in every sense of the words;—*This same shall comfort us concerning our work and the toil of our hands.*[105]

---

102. Horne, *The Works*, 118.
103. Horne, *The Works*, 128–29.
104. Horne, *The Works*, 138.
105. Horne, *The Works*, 139.

In all three essays on Old Testament saints, the New Testament plays a central role in drawing out the devotional import of the Old Testament text.

The Old Testament, however, plays no such role in Horne's *Considerations on the Life and Death of St. John the Baptist*. In this work Horne teems with confidence that "knowledge drawn freshly, and as it were in our view, out of particulars, knows the way best to particulars again."[106] To illustrate this point, Horne refuses to read the New Testament texts he studies in canonical context. When he reflects upon the devotional import of the life and death of John, he is careful to extract tropological import directly from the text in question rather than appealing to the larger scriptural witness. Horne often appeals to the New Testament as he studies the Old Testament but does not frequently appeal to the Old Testament as he studies the New.

Horne comes to treat the Old and New Testaments differently because of his measured emblematicism. Horne finds that certain things he encounters in Scripture are relatively transparent. When he does, he moves quickly to point out their devotional import. There are, however, certain things he encounters that he finds more obscure, and he overcomes this obscurity by calling upon his Hutchinsonianism. Horne finds more obscurity in the Old Testament than the New, and this is why he frequently offers emblematic readings of Old Testament texts but does not often employ emblematic readings of the New.

CONCLUSION

George Horne's theology is governed by a robust providentialist vision. Horne teems with confidence that creation, the church establishment, and Scripture all testify to God's beneficent government. He sets his face against deists, skeptics, dissenters, and revolutionaries because their opposition to the established order tears down what God himself has established.[107] It is appropriate to describe Horne as a conservative. But he does not merely defend the given structures and institutions of the world because he wants to preserve the establishment. He wants to preserve the establishment because he thinks the given structures and institutions bear the mark of divine providence. Like Newton, Horne worships the great *pantokrator*, the Lord God of

---

106. George Horne, *Considerations on the Life and Death of St. John the Baptist* (Oxford: 1769), ii.

107. For an introduction to Horne's apologetic work, see Aston, "Horne," 895–919.

dominion. And Horne is quite confident that he can identify just where this Lord God of dominion is at work: he is at work in making himself known to humans through their knowledge of creation, in strengthening and uphold-ing the church establishment, and by making himself known in the revela-tion of Scripture.

Horne employs scriptural emblematicism to assist him in the interpre-tation of Old Testament particulars when he struggles to understand their significance. However, he rarely, if ever, relies upon the emblematic interpre-tation of Scripture to guide his interpretation of historical particulars, and he does not call upon emblematicism to assist in the interpretation of New Testament texts. Horne is measured in his scriptural emblematicism because he believes the primary role of Scripture is to testify to the existence of an overarching providential order rather than to serve as the grounds upon which the discernment of providential order is established.[108]

Horne's measured emblematicism appears to give credence to the notion that he is merely "partly Hutchinsonian." On this account, however, so is Hutchinson. Hutchinson, we saw, is extremely selective in his emblemati-cism, reserving it only for natural-philosophical objects found in the Genesis creation account. Scriptural emblematicism plays an important role in the work of both Horne and Hutchinson, yet they are both inconsistent in their approach. The important difference between Horne and Hutchinson is that whereas Hutchinson is unwilling to interpret historical objects emblemati-cally because he believes they have been given over to devolution, Horne is confident in his ability to articulate their established providential orientation.

That Christians as theologically diverse as Wesley and Lindsey found even Horne's measured approach extravagant is indicative of the fact that the tra-ditional figural reading of the Old Testament had fallen out of favor in the second half of the eighteenth century. This constriction of figural reading

---

108. Horne's difficulty in promoting the idea of an all-encompassing providential order is that it is impossible to celebrate everything he encounters with equal vigor. The emphasis he places on the providential significance of certain things is, correspondingly, a decision not to emphasize the providential orientation of others. Admittedly, Horne's decision to zero in on the providential signification of empirical science, the church establishment, and Scripture is not arbitrary: he celebrates them because of the prominent position they occupy in the world he inhabits. Nevertheless, Horne might just as well have emphasized other elements—England's market economy, or parliamentary democracy, for example. The discretionary element in Horne's providentialism looms large.

is symptomatic of a larger shift in Old Testament interpretation. For Wesley, Lindsey, and even for Horne, the role of the Old Testament is to stand as a monument to God's providential engagement with ancient Israel. It can serve as a guide for providential discernment, but to do so it must jump across Lessing's "ugly, broad ditch." God's providential workings with Israel are not his workings with contemporary Christians. For Horne and his opponents, belief in God's providential ordering of contemporary existence therefore functions independently of the Old Testament and does not depend upon it.

Clarke, as we have seen, does not deny that the Old Testament testifies to divine providence. He simply chooses to focus on other elements that he finds more perspicuous in this regard. In order to challenge Clarke's prejudice, Horne might well appeal to his favorite figural readings of Psalms. Clarke would presumably find at least some of these readings edifying. But in the end, Horne is still held captive to Clarke's rationality. If Clarke were to retort that while he acknowledges God's providence in Israelite history, the providential significance of the historical events of the New Testament supersede those of the Old Testament, Horne would be at pains to say otherwise.

That Horne is willing to interpret the Old Testament figurally confirms his retention of the traditional Christian idea that the providential orientation of the Old Testament is unveiled by engaging it in canonical context. Yet Horne's conviction that the New Testament does not require figural reading is a departure from the traditional Augustinian understanding that "the grace of the New Testament was veiled in the law, but is revealed in the Gospel."[109] For in the traditional Augustininan understanding, the New Testament "lies hidden" in the Old, and yet the fullness of the New Testament also resides within the Old Testament because all that the New Testament says is brought to bear on all the forms presented in the Old Testament. "The same things," says Augustine, "are in the Old and the New Testaments—there overshadowed, here unveiled, there prefigured, here manifest."[110] Horne's measured approach to the Old Testament, on the other hand, is accompanied by the

---

109. As quoted in Henri de Lubac, *Medieval Exegesis, Vol 2: The Four Senses of Scripture*, trans. E. M. Macierowski (Grand Rapids: Eerdmans, 1998), 441n64.

110. As quoted in Phillip Cary, *Outward Signs: The Powerlessness of External Things in Augustine's Thought* (Oxford: Oxford University Press, 2008), 241. The Augustinian understanding of the "harmony" of the Old and New Testaments is helpfully developed in Henri de Lubac, *Scripture in the Tradition*, trans. Luke O'Neill (New York: Herder & Herder, 2000), 113–29.

conviction that only some of what God revealed in the New Testament is present in the Old Testament. This signals the return to Clarke's conviction that the New Testament is superior to it. Horne does not succumb to Clarke's devolutionary philosophy of history. Nevertheless, in the hands of many of Horne's nineteenth-century readers, Horne's measured preference for the New Testament became pronounced. His providentialism was overcome by a reinvigorated devolutionary philosophy of history which looked upon the New Testament as the pristine ideal and the Old Testament as the figure of devolution.

6

—

THE VOICE OF PROVIDENCE: WILLIAM JONES OF NAYLAND'S OLD TESTAMENT

Anglican cleric, theologian, and natural philosopher William Jones of Nayland was one of the most influential theologians of his day. Jones's career path looks almost nothing like that of his closest friend and ally George Horne. Whereas Horne was given administrative and ecclesiastical posts that eventually made him a powerful figure within the establishment, Jones spent his adult life serving as a cleric in obscure rural parishes. That he was unencumbered by administrative duties, however, meant that he became a far more prolific author than Horne.[1] In Jones's works, eighteenth- and nineteenth-century Anglicans found intellectually robust defenses of Nicene Trinitarian doctrine and church tradition, as well as powerful justifications for the belief that the church establishment and natural world were providentially ordained.

Although these elements are all present in Horne's work, they function somewhat independently within Horne's providential vision. Jones, on the other hand, is able to bring them together within a coherent scriptural framework. Like Horne, Jones owes not merely his Hutchinsonianism, but also the unique character of his Hutchinsonianism, to George Watson. Following

---

1. Twenty-five years after Jones's death the editor of *Gentleman's Magazine* could still call Jones "the pious and learned author of numerous highly esteemed theological and philosophical works," and fifty-two years after Jones's death the biographer of Jones's student remarked that Jones is "so widely and universally known, that any notice of him here, beyond that which is to be derived from his letters, would be superfluous" ("Obituary: Benjamin Harenc, Esq.," *Gentleman's Magazine and Historical Chronicle*, New Series 18, no. 2 [1825]: 567; John Freeman, *The Life of Rev. William Kirby, M.A.* [London: 1852], 34).

Watson, Horne and Jones both reject the Newtonian devolutionary interpretation of history in favor of a providential one. This providential interpretation is expressed in the way Horne and Jones interpret not merely natural objects as emblems, but historical objects as well. But whereas Horne is measured in his application of the emblematic method, Jones employs a thoroughgoing scriptural emblematicism. The consistent emphasis Jones places on the necessity of the emblematic mediation of Scripture for both constructive theology and providential discernment grants Scripture an epistemological priority in his thought.

Within the Hutchinsonian apologetic tradition, scriptural emblematicism is utilized as the primary means of making the Old Testament necessary for providential discernment. Because he is only willing to use the Old Testament to render providential interpretations of cosmological objects, Hutchinson severely restricts the scope of this apologetic. Horne defends the providential basis of nature and history, but his apologetic is still hindered by his measured emblematic approach to the Old Testament. In Jones's thoroughgoing scriptural emblematicism, on the other hand, the Old Testament is the grounds of his apologetic because it generates providential interpretations of the full spectrum of natural-philosophical and historical objects. On this account, Jones's thoroughgoing scriptural emblematicism is not only what makes his Old Testament apologetic compelling, it is also the apogee of a tradition.

THE CATHOLIC DOCTRINE OF THE TRINITY

In the nineteenth century, Jones was revered as the eighteenth century's greatest defender of Trinitarian orthodoxy.[2] This reputation rests largely upon his first and what was long his most popular work, *The Catholic Doctrine of the Trinity*.[3] Although the primary object of the work is to refute the

---

2. Jones's friend Bishop Samuel Horsley said he was "a man of quick penetration, of extensive learning, and the soundest piety; and he had, beyond any other man I ever knew, the talent of writing on the deepest subjects to the plainest understanding" (quoted in William Henry Teale, "The Life of William Jones, M. A., Perpetual Curate of Nayland," in *Biography of English Divines: The Life of Launcelot Andrewes, D. D., Bishop of Winchester* [London: Joseph Masters, 1849], 418). In the second half of the nineteenth century, Daniel Waterland surpassed Jones in this respect, but Waterland was not rescued from obscurity until 1823, when Hutchinsonian William van Mildert published his collected works.

3. William Jones, *The Catholic Doctrine of the Trinity* (Oxford: 1756). The work went through seven London editions and two Dublin editions and was republished several times in the nineteenth century in the first volume of Jones's collected works. Its popularity in the nineteenth

subordinationist doctrine of Samuel Clarke, Jones makes it clear that what separates them is not merely doctrinal formulations but scriptural hermeneutics.[4] Whereas Clarke is confident he can extract doctrinal particulars directly from texts, Jones insists that texts be read in canonical context before they can be employed for doctrinal discernment. This use of Watson's principle of canonical mediation in *The Catholic Doctrine of the Trinity* is important because it serves as the foundation of Jones's subsequent application of the same principle to non-scriptural objects.

Jones begins the work with a strong affirmation of a figural understanding of the church. This affirmation embodies Jones's emphatic rejection of Clarke's devolutionary view of history. Israelite religion is not the devolution of pristine religion. Nor is Christianity that which supersedes it.[5] For Jones, the primary distinction the theologian must make is not between Jews and Christians but between ancient Jews and Christians as the one people of God and "the unchristian part of mankind, who are by far the majority" (those who "either know him not, or willfully deny him").[6] Jones complains that in his day, many have fallen under the spell of "a fashionable notion, propagated by most of our moral writers, and readily subscribed to by those who say their prayers but seldom, and can never find time to read their Bible, that all who worship any God, worship the *same* God."[7] Jones's work, then, is grounded in an affirmation of the particularity of the God of Scripture in the face of religious pluralism, and Jones is certain that those who reject this God do so because they have come to rely upon their own learning rather than the wisdom of God. Jones reiterates the favorite Hutchinsonian refrain that "all that can be known of the true God, is to be known by Revelation."[8]

---

century, however, was surpassed by *A Course of Lectures on the Figurative Language of the Holy Scripture* (London: 1787) and *A Letter to John Bull, Esq.* (London: 1793).

4. For an account of Clarke and Jones's hermeneutics in eighteenth-century context, see David Ney, "The *Sensus Literalis* and the Trinity in the English Enlightenment," *Pro Ecclesia* 29, no. 3 (2020): 293–307.

5. For the importance of a figural view of the church in combating supersessionism, see Ephraim Radner, *A Brutal Unity: The Spiritual Politics of the Christian Church* (Waco, TX: Baylor University Press, 2012), 155–65.

6. Jones, *The Catholic*, ii–iii. This second group includes modern Jews, Mahometans, Socinians, Arians, and many who call themselves Christians.

7. Jones, *The Catholic*, iii.

8. Jones, *The Catholic*, xii.

Jones defends this conviction by appealing to the doctrine of original sin. The only source of evil is the heart of "natural man," which, "remaining in that state wherein the fall left him, is so far from being able to discover or know any religious truth, that he hates and flies from it when it is proposed to him."[9] The means of restitution Scripture prescribes is that natural man should be "transformed by the renewing of his mind," a process whereby the Holy Spirit leads the human mind to become subject to divine revelation. The mind of natural man, however, "abhors restraint and subjection; and is ever aspiring, right or wrong, to be distinguished from the common herd, and to *exalt itself against the knowledge of God.*"[10]

For Jones, the theologian who is most representative of this abhorrence of subjection to Scripture is Clarke, who is "deservedly placed at the head of the *Arian* disputants in this kingdom."[11] Jones observes that the first proposition in Clarke's *Scripture-Doctrine of the Trinity*—that the one God spoken of in Matthew 19:17 is only one person—is accompanied by Clarke's affirmation that "this is the *first principle of Natural Religion.*"[12] Jones capitalizes on this admission to argue that Clarke's religion is fundamentally at odds with the Christian religion: while Clarke's natural religion is founded on the conviction that the one God is one person, the Christian religion insists that the one God is three persons.[13] Jones proceeds to condemn natural religion as "the Gospel of the *natural man,* unsanctified by divine grace, and uninstructed by any light from above."[14] According to Jones, then, Clarke's basic problem is that he imports a logical framework he has devised *as natural man* and imposes it upon Scripture.[15]

---

9. Jones, *The Catholic*, xvii.

10. Jones, *The Catholic*, xxxi. Here Jones is quoting 2 Corinthians 10:5.

11. Jones, *The Catholic*, xxxii. At the end of his life Jones was still convinced that Clarke was a serious threat to the Church of England. In an unpublished 1796 sermon, Jones takes up arms against the "learned metaphysician" that "argues upwards to a first-cause and when he has found it, concludes on the authority of human philosophy, that this first cause can be no other than a single person. Thence he goes to the Scripture, and of course either rejects the Scripture or finds his own doctrine there" (William Jones, MS Sermons by the Rev. W. Jones of Nayland, 1.14, Pusey House, Oxford, UK). In this sermon Jones also insists, against Clarke, that "Absolute titles of divinity" are conferred upon Christ in both the Old and New Testaments" (MS Sermons 1.23).

12. Jones, *The Catholic*, xxxii. Samuel Clarke, *The Scripture-Doctrine of the Trinity* (London: 1712), 241.

13. Jones, *The Catholic*, xxxii.

14. Jones, *The Catholic*, xxxiii.

15. Jones, *The Catholic*, xxxiv–xxxv.

Jones's refutation is not—like the great tomes of Clarke's great adversary Daniel Waterland—a reasoned disquisition of the logic of Trinitarian orthodoxy. The structure and argument of the work is actually closer to that of Clarke. Like Clarke, Jones thrusts scriptural text after scriptural text at the reader, seemingly in the hope of overwhelming him by cumulative weight of evidence. But whereas Clarke asks the reader to consider the merits of individual scriptural passages in themselves, Jones presents two or more passages consecutively, and more often than not he places Old Testament and New Testament texts side by side. He begins by juxtaposing Isaiah 8:13–14, which states that the Lord of hosts himself will be "a STONE OF STUMBLING and ROCK OF OFFENCE," and 1 Peter 2:7–8, which states that Christ has been made a "STONE OF STUMBLING and ROCK OF OFFENCE." From this it follows, reasons Jones, that Christ is the "Lord of Hosts himself."[16] Jones moves quickly to consider a second set of texts, Isaiah 6:5, "Mine Eyes have SEEN the King, the LORD OF HOSTS," and John 12:41, which insists that when Isaiah said this it was because "he SAW HIS (CHRISTS) GLORY, and spake of HIM."[17] The Christian must therefore conclude, says Jones, that Jesus is "the Lord of Hosts." The third set of passages Jones considers is Isaiah 44:6, in which the Lord says, "I am THE FIRST, and I am THE LAST, and BESIDES ME there is NO GOD," and Revelation 22:13, in which Jesus declares, "I am Alpha and Omega, the beginning and the End, THE FIRST and THE LAST."[18] When the titles "the first" and "the last"—as titles reserved for the one "besides whom there is no God"—are applied to Jesus, says Jones, he is confirmed to be the God besides whom there is no other. Jones's straightforward method—juxtaposing Scripture passages and then commenting on their accordance—is pursued relentlessly to defend not only the divinity of Christ but also the divinity of the Spirit, and the plurality and unity of Trinitarian persons as "Scripture doctrines."

For Jones there are not two covenants, that of works and that of grace. Nor are there two religions, that of Old Testament monotheism and that of New Testament Christianity. The basis of Jones's hermeneutic, therefore, is the conviction that the Old and New Testaments present a unified witness

---

16. Jones, *The Catholic*, 1–2.

17. Jones, *The Catholic*, 2.

18. Jones, *The Catholic*, 3.

concerning the Triune God.[19] Jones is deeply troubled by the way the Old Testament had fallen into disrepute, and his object is to offer a hermeneutic that makes the Old Testament, as well as the New, doctrinally authoritative.[20] Following Wells and Knight, he complains that Clarke's collection of "ALL *the Texts* relating to the matter" is "finished and shut up without a single Text from the *old Testament!*"[21] Jones articulates what Wells and Knight could only venture at: an interpretive method that makes the Old Testament necessary for the formation of Christian doctrine. Unlike Hutchinson, Jones's method does not depend upon the veracity of a particular natural-philosophical theory. It simply requires that the Old and New Testaments be allowed to interpret one another.[22]

This method, admittedly, does not always consist in juxtaposing Old Testament and New Testament texts. Sometimes the passages Jones juxtaposes are both from the New Testament, and sometimes they are both from the Old.[23] On rare occasions passages within a single biblical book are juxtaposed to generate unanticipated Trinitarian renderings. Jones's method exudes an interpretive freedom that minimizes the distinction between the Old and New Testaments, and therefore renders his hermeneutic consistent with his ecclesiological starting point. The doctrine Jones defends is catholic because it has been preached by the church "in all places, at all times, and

19. Jones insists that Scripture is a unified whole because it speaks with one voice concerning the nature of God in opposition to those who follow the deists in failing to attend to the whole of Scripture because they find parts of it contrary to natural religion. To this end, Jones appeals to the words of Jesus himself in John 5:46: "*Had ye* BELIEVED *Moses, says our* LORD, *ye would have believed me*" (Jones, *The Catholic*, xxxv).

20. Jones even quotes one author who claims that he "*may reject Arguments brought from the old Testament to prove the Trinity, as trifling, and proving nothing but the* Ignorance *of those that make use of them*" (Jones, *The Catholic*, 26–27; Francis Hare, *The Difficulties and Discouragements which attend the Study of the Scriptures in the way of Private Judgment* [London: 1714], 17). Jones appears to have not read Hare very carefully. Hare regards the idea that the Old Testament is impotent to prove the Trinity as one of several fashionable notions that will bring "certain Mischief, but no certain Good at all" (Hare, *The Difficulties*, 19).

21. Jones, *The Catholic*, 79. For a discussion of Clarke's controversy with Wells and Knight following the publication of *The Scripture-Doctrine of the Trinity*, see chapter 2.

22. Jones was a student of the New Testament's use of the Old. In an unpublished sermon on Hebrews, he claims that "The chief design of the Epistle to the Hebrews is to demonstrate the divinity and dignity of Christ from the old Testament to the unbelieving Jews" (Jones, MS Sermons, 1.19).

23. See, for example, Jones, MS Sermons 1.15, 17.

by all the faithful."[24] It is also catholic—that is, universal—because it takes into account not merely select decontextualized Scriptures but the entire scriptural testimony.

Jones's insistence that the entire canon of Scripture be used in constructive theology is bound to his conviction concerning the generation of scriptural meaning. For Clarke, as we have seen, the meaning of a particular scriptural word becomes apparent only when all external references and resonances are cast aside. The goal of exegesis is thus a comprehensive isolation and atomization of terms to achieve maximal denotative precision. For Jones, on the other hand, the meaning of Scripture words is obscured when they are taken in isolation from one another: atomized words are empty receptacles that are easily filled by the prejudices of natural man.[25] Jones strongly endorses Watson's notion of canonical mediation because he is keenly aware of just how easy it is for humans to impose their own preconceptions on the text. If interpreters are allowed to apply Scripture directly with their own contexts, Clarke's doctrine will likely follow. But if Scripture is allowed to mediate the interpretation of Scripture words, interpreters will be led to the catholic doctrine of the Trinity.

For Jones, the meaning of particular Scripture words must be complemented by the attributions of other Scripture words both to render an accurate appreciation of a trinity of persons within the Godhead and to uphold a Christian understanding of Scripture as inclusive of the Old Testament. Jones therefore confronts Clarke with a dilemma: either he must embrace a juxtapositional method or he must reject the Christian understanding of the canon because the isolation of textual meaning inevitably evokes contradictions that destroy the unity of Scripture. Jones insists that "if the Scripture, thus compared with itself, be drawn up into an argument, the conclusion

---

24. Jones's appeal to the notion of catholicity encapsulated by Vincentius's rule has deep roots in the Anglican tradition. See, for example, Jeremy Taylor, *The Whole Works of the Right Rev. Jeremy Taylor* (London: 1835), 3:344; William Reeves, *The Apologies of Justin Martyr, Tertullian, and Minutius* (London: 1709), 234–35.

25. The term "Lord of Hosts" in Isaiah 8:13, for example, is in danger of being interpreted by "natural man" according to the preconceived categories of natural religion unless the meaning of the term in 1 Peter 2:7–8 is brought into consideration. Jones does not deny, of course, that the meaning of the term in Isaiah 8:13 is of great importance. The fact that it refers to the one God of Israel is retained as an essential component of his Trinitarian formula.

may indeed be *denied*, and so may the whole Bible, but it cannot be *answered*."[26]
Scripture must be taken in whole or rejected in whole—it cannot be taken
in part.

THE FIGURATIVE LANGUAGE
OF THE HOLY SCRIPTURE

After serving as an assistant curate for several years, Jones was given a living
in Bethersden (Kent) in 1764, made rector in Pluckley (Kent) in 1765, and
made perpetual curate of Nayland (Suffolk) in 1776.[27] As he preached weekly
sermons in his parish, dutifully catechized his parishioners, wrote letters
to friends, and published works on subjects ranging from natural philosophy to music, Jones continued to refine his hermeneutical method, which
he describes as the practice of allowing Scripture to be "compared with
itself."[28] A full thirty years after the publication of *The Catholic Doctrine of
the Trinity*, he presented *A Course of Lectures on the Figurative Language of the
Holy Scripture* in the obscurity of his rural parish of Nayland.[29] In *A Course of*

---

26. Jones, *The Catholic*, 2. Thus Jones, in "Letters to a Predestinarian," complains chiefly
that while "we take the *whole* word of God, as the rule of our faith and obedience: *you* take a
part of it; and that part you interpret, in such a way of your own, as to endanger all the rest"
(Jones, *The Theological*, 12:341).

27. Teale, "William Jones," 356, 358, 368.

28. Jones interestingly describes this process as follows in *Zoologia Ethica*: "the only rational
method of interpreting the Scripture is to *compare spiritual things with spiritual*; to clear up one
passage of divine writ by others which relate to it: and *in the mouth of two* or three *witnesses*
of this sort every word ought to be established" (William Jones, *Zoologia Ethica: A Disquisition
Concerning the Mosaic Distinction of Animals into Clean and Unclean* [London: 1773], 2).

29. In his final work, *A Letter to the Church of England*, Jones complained, "I learned very
early in life that if any one would go through the world with peace to his mind and advantage
to his fortune, he must *hear, and see, and say nothing*; but I learned afterwards that the truth
of God is worth all the world; and in this persuasion; as I have long lived, so now I hope to
die" (William Jones, *A Letter to the Church of England, Pointing out Some Popular Errors of Bad
Consequence* [London: 1798], 32). As a young cleric, Jones had reason to expect rapid preferment
since his defenses of Church of England Trinitarian orthodoxy were widely celebrated. In
the eighteenth century, scholars were frequently elevated to the bench for similar displays
(Joseph Butler, Samuel Chandler, and Thomas Newton come immediately to mind). Bishops
may well have regarded Jones with suspicion because of his Hutchinsonianism. The prefer-
ments Jones received were extremely modest, and he had to wait a long time for them to come.
In the year before he died, Horne asked Jones to be one of his chaplains, and in 1798 Jones
was presented with the sinecure rectory of Holingbourne (Kent; Teale, "William Jones," 409).
The *British Critic* praised Jones as "an author more distinguished by eminent services than by
rewards conferred, and whose slender participation of professional emoluments renders his
attachment to the Church the more conspicuously affectionate, generous, and disinterested"
(quoted in Teale, "William Jones," 419). Jones's association with Hutchinson was still regarded

Lectures, Jones extends the canonical approach that he had used to generate Trinitarian doctrine to the question of providential discernment. The lectures demonstrate that for Jones, objects of nature and history are granted providential significance through scriptural mediation.

A *Course of Lectures* is Jones's most comprehensive articulation of his hermeneutic, and while it develops earlier expositions, it is remarkably consistent with the basic principles outlined in *The Catholic Doctrine of the Trinity*. The major themes in the introduction to *The Catholic Doctrine of the Trinity*—the figural view of the church and of history, the emphasis on the need for revelation because of Adam's fall, and the distinction between natural and spiritual men—all feature prominently in the introduction to *A Course of Lectures* and in the lectures themselves. In the introduction, however, Jones also adds a new element: the figurative language of Scripture.[30]

Jones uses the concept of figurative language to extend Hutchinson's hieroglyphic interpretation of Hebrew words to the entire scope of Scripture.[31] Jones's early fascination with the Hebrew language followed his acceptance of Hutchinson's conviction that "the language is *in itself* instructive: its words give us light into *things*, in a manner different from those of any other language in the world: and this, beyond all other arguments, convinces me of its divine original."[32] Yet this strong Hutchinsonian affirmation is contradicted by Jones's practice of scriptural interpretation. The canonical method Jones employs clearly treats Greek words and Hebrew words as equally authoritative. It comes as no surprise, therefore, that Jones claims the infidelity of his age can be attributed not merely to young graduates ignoring Hebraic studies, but because of the "general neglect in schools and seminaries of the study

---

by some to be problematic at the time of his death. Jones's obituary in the *Gentleman's Magazine* complains that Jones and his fellow Hutchinsonians were "chargeable with great eccentricity in their philosophy" ("Obituary, Anecdotes, of Remarkable Persons," *Gentleman's Magazine and Historical Chronicle* 70 [1800]: 184).

30. Jones promises that although his method will separate "the figures of the scripture into their proper kinds, with examples and explanations in each kind," he will consistently conform to "the rule of making the scripture its own interpreter" (Jones, *A Course*, 32).

31. Jones, *The Theological*, 12:225. Jones endorses the foundation of Hutchinson's Mosaic philosophy, the conviction that Hebrew was the *prima lingua*. He also endorses the attendant notion that "If the Hebrew were the original language (which, however, is disputed, as all other things are) the different languages of the world must partake of it more or less; and consequently they may be traced up to it."

32. Jones, *A Course*, 235.

of the Scriptures in their original languages."[33] When Jones complains that Joseph Priestley (1733–1804) cannot be trusted because he does not know the original languages of Scripture, his statement is but one plank in his larger argument that Priestly does not give the revelation of God due diligence.[34]

The importance of Greek and Hebrew is a historical contingency—it is because the eternal Word of God has been given in Greek and Hebrew that the languages are to be held in high esteem.[35] Because the sacredness of Greek and Hebrew is contingent upon their location in Scripture, Jones has no interest in constructing elaborate arguments to defend the notion that they are ontologically unique. In particular, Hutchinson's quest to trace the history of linguistic devolution is conspicuously absent from Jones's voluminous corpus. Jones acknowledges that a certain degree of textual corruption inevitably accompanies the passage of time. All languages are subject to history: "Words are changeable; language has been confounded; and men in different parts of the world are unintelligible to one another as barbarians."[36]

For Jones it is the power of scriptural language that sets it apart. When scriptural language is received and interpreted according to its native figurative capacity, it becomes a "language of things."

> When it is said, *God is a sun and a shield,* then *things* are added to words, and we understand that the being signified by the word *God,* is bright and powerful; immeasurable in height, inaccessible in glory; the author of light to the understanding, the fountain of life to the soul; our security against all terror, our defense against all danger. See here the difference between the language of words and the language of things. If an image is presented to the mind when a sound is

---

33. William Jones, *Memoirs of the Life, Studies, and Writings of the Right Reverend George Horne* (London: 1795), 33.

34. William Jones, *A Small Whole-Length of Dr. Priestley, from His Printed Works* (London: 1797), 3.

35. This difference points to an inversion of Hutchinson's scriptural apologetic. For Hutchinson, Scripture is authoritative because Hebrew is authoritative, but for Jones, Hebrew is authoritative only because it is contained in Scripture.

36. Jones, *A Course,* 294. Jones juxtaposes the power of the figurative language of Scripture with that of common vernaculars: "Thus, for example, if we take the word *God,* we have a sound which gives us no idea; and if we trace it through all the languages of the world, we find nothing but arbitrary sounds, with great variety of dialect and accent, all of which still leave us where we began, and reach no farther than the ear" (*A Course,* 294–95).

heard by the ear, then we begin to understand; and a single object of our sight, in a figurative acceptation, gives us a large and instructive lesson; such as could never be conveyed by all the possible combinations of sounds.[37]

Although the language of words is able to grant a modest degree of conceptual knowledge, it struggles to penetrate the divine meaning of created things. The associative capacity of scriptural language as figurative language, on the other hand, grants it the capacity to make created things speak.[38]

Jones feels no need to translate the words "sun" and "shield" into Hebrew to convey their figurative and tropological import. He may have a preference for the interpretation of Scripture in the original languages, but he does not make the interpretation of scriptural figures dependent upon them. It is enough for English speakers to have an awareness of suns and shields as objects of sense and, on this basis, he celebrates the fact that "we have the scripture in our mother tongue; a blessing which was denied to us so long as we were under the authority of the Church of Rome."[39] Jones's willingness to grant every human language the ability to function figuratively confirms that he has moved well beyond Hutchinson's Hebraic fundamentalism. The primary distinction, for Jones, is not between biblical languages and vernaculars, but between scriptural and non-scriptural words. The words of Scripture are unique because they are the words God has ordained as his favored means to communicate the figurative meaning of the world to his people.[40] The scholar could, in theory, apply Jones's figurative hermeneutic

---

37. Jones, *A Course*, 295.

38. In his 1960 essay "The Nature of Things and the Language of Things," Gadamer endorses the term the "language of things" as able to protect things against technological manipulation and desire by helping people remember that things have their own existence and are not, as Heidegger says, "forced to do anything." Gadamer finds that the term "rouses the memory (slumbering in us all) of the being of things that are still able to be what they are" (Hans-Georg Gadamer, "The Nature of Things and the Language of Things," in *Philosophical Hermeneutics*, ed. and trans. David E. Linge [Berkeley, CA: University of California Press, 2008], 72). Inasmuch as Jones's hermeneutic instrumentalizes created things by refashioning them as tools that promote Christian virtue, his usage contradicts that of Gadamer. Nevertheless, Gadamer insists that things are not self-interpreting and that "the mediation of finite and infinite that is appropriate to us as finite beings lies in language" (Gadamer, "The Nature," 80).

39. Jones, *A Course*, 5.

40. "The knowledge of human languages," says Jones, "Prepares us for the reading of human authors; and great part of our life is present in acquiring them. But the interpretation of this sacred language takes off the seal from the book of life, and opens to man the treasures of

to non-scriptural words, but such an application would generate human rather than providential interpretations. The Christian seeking to uncover the providential import of created things will be frustrated in her search for providence until she employs the figurative language of Scripture.

Jones confesses that "there is a certain obscurity in the language of the Bible, which renders it difficult to be understood," presumably because of its divine origin. This obscurity calls forth figurative interpretation. He maintains that all Christians are drawn to ask the question of the Ethiopian eunuch, "How can I understand unless some man should guide me?"[41] Jones affirms the importance of human teachers, but he insists that "something more than the guidance of man is necessary."[42] Linguistic proficiency and philological criticism are ultimately unable to overcome scriptural obscurity: "The great difficulties of the scripture arise totally from other causes and principles; namely from the *matter* of which it treats, and the various *forms* under which that matter is delivered."[43] Like the disciples on the Emmaus road, Christians are dependent upon the light of Christ to open *"their understandings, that they might understand the Scriptures."*[44] Without such illumination, Christians will remain like the unbelievers who had *"eyes without seeing, and ears without hearing"* even though they were "familiarly acquainted" with the writings of Moses and the prophets and "understood the original language in which they were delivered."[45] Jones nowhere suggests that his interpretive method will eliminate textual obscurity. He does, however, believe that his method is maximally conditioned for the procurement of providential insight since it is appropriate to the means by which God has chosen to reveal himself, the figurative language of the Holy Scripture.

---

divine wisdom, which far exceed all other learning, and will be carried with us into another world, when the variety of tongues shall cease, and every other treasure shall be left behind" (Jones, *A Course*, 316–17).

41. Jones, *A Course*, 3. Acts 8:31.
42. Jones, *A Course*, 3.
43. Jones, *A Course*, 6.
44. Jones, *A Course*, 3.
45. Jones, *A Course*, 4.

The eyes of "natural man" see only immediate physical entities, but illumined eyes perceive the spiritual significance of physical things. The role of the Scriptures, as revelation, therefore, is to "open to us an invisible world."[46]

Of all the objects of sense we have ideas, and our minds and memories are stored with them. But of invisible things we have no ideas till they are pointed out to us by revelation: and as we cannot know them immediately, such as they are in themselves, after the manner in which we know sensible objects, they must be communicated to us by the mediation of such things as we already comprehend. For this reason, the scripture is found to have a language of its own, which doth not consist of words, but of signs or figures taken from visible things. It could not otherwise treat of God who is a spirit, and of the spirit of man, and of a spiritual world; which no words can describe. Words are the arbitrary signs of natural things; but the language of revelation goes a step farther, and uses some things as the signs of other things; in consequence of which, the world which we now see becomes a sort of commentary on the mind of God.[47]

For Jones, "the professed design of the scripture" is nothing less than to grant God's children the ability to see the world the way that he sees it.[48] The figurative expressions of Scripture render the world in providential terms, and such renderings "cannot proceed without them."

If we descend to an actual examination of particulars, we find [Scripture] assisting and leading our faculties forward; by an application of all visible objects to a figurative use; from the glorious orb which shines in the firmament, to a grain of seed which is buried in the earth.[49]

Jones refuses to exclude *anything* from his comprehensive providentialist vision.[50] For Jones, providence is not an abstract principle that can be imposed

---

46. Jones, *A Course*, 8.
47. Jones, *A Course*, 9–10.
48. Jones, *A Course*, 10.
49. Jones, *A Course*, 10.
50. Jones develops this point further in a sermon entitled "Trust in Providence, the Comfort of Man's Life." "Our Saviour," says Jones, "hath extended the attention of Providence to the

without discretion upon created things. Jones believes that, as a "commentary on the mind of God," every object in creation has a unique divinely mandated ability to assist Christians in their knowledge of God and in their pursuit of Christian virtue. Jones equally believes that Christians have a divine mandate to uncover the providential ordering of everything they encounter, and Jones is convinced that the breadth of scriptural language makes this lofty object possible.

In *A Course of Lectures*, Jones guides the Bible reader through the different types of figurative expressions he finds in Scripture. He zeroes in on five types of expressions, classified according to the nature of the figures themselves: figures taken from (1) images of nature, (2) institutions of the law, (3) the persons of the prophets, (4) the history of the church of Israel, and (5) the miraculous acts of Christ and his people.[51] Detailed discussions of these figures comprise lectures two through ten. Jones's eleventh lecture on "The uses and effects of the symbolical style of the Scriptures" helpfully lays the groundwork for the application of Jones's figural method to particulars that fall outside of the five categories he discusses.

In *The Catholic Doctrine of the Trinity*, scriptural accordance is the primary tool Jones utilizes to generate Trinitarian doctrine. It is equally the case in his lectures that scriptural accordance enables Jones to proceed from created

---

lowest particulars in the creation; to the hairs of our head, and to the life of a sparrow" (William Jones, "Trust in Providence, the Comfort of Man's Life," in *Sermons on Moral and Religious Subjects* [London: 1790], 1:222). Jones therefore concludes, "His attention therefore does not only extend to single persons, but to the dust of the earth, and to single atoms" ("Trust," 222–23). Jones's conviction that the most insignificant things can carry profound divine significance points to Auerbach's famous analysis of the Christian rejection of the classical doctrine of separations of styles, which he regards as the foundation of Christian figural reading. Auerbach argues that the Christian message and early Christian literature were direct affronts to the classical doctrine of separations of style, which insisted that significant events could only be undertaken by great and divine persons and described with grand and florid rhetoric: "The true heart of the Christian doctrine," says Auerbach, was "totally incompatible with the principle of the separation of styles. Christ had not come as a hero and king but as a human being of the lowest social station. His first disciples were fishermen and artisans; he moved in the everyday milieu o the humble folk of Palestine; he talked with publicans and fallen women, the poor and the sick and children. Nevertheless, all that he did and said was of the highest and deepest dignity, more significant than anything else in the world. The style in which it was presented possessed little if any rhetorical culture in the antique sense; it was *sermo piscatorius* and yet it was extremely moving and much more impressive than the most sublime rhetorico-tragical literary work" (Erich Auerbach, *Mimesis: The Representation of Reality in Western Thought* [Princeton: Princeton University Press, 2003], 72).

51. Jones, *A Course*, 34.

particulars to divine truth. When Jones reflects upon the spiritual import of the sacrifices of the priesthood in the Old Testament, he finds that Hebrews 10:1 and 1 Corinthians 5:7 instruct Christians to believe that Christ himself is the Passover lamb.[52] In this manner, not merely the paschal lamb but, indeed, all of the particular elements in the Old Testament sacrificial system are given their divinely assigned spiritual meaning. The same can be said for the other scriptural figures Jones investigates.[53] When Christians read of the tabernacle in the book of Exodus, it strikes them as a historical curiosity, but when they are told in St. John's Gospel that the Word "tabernacled amongst us," they are confronted by the mystery that, "as the glory of the Lord was once present in the tabernacle, it was now present in the body of Christ."[54] When the Christian reads of Jonah's being "buried in the body of a fish, and cast up alive again after three days," it strikes him as "monstrous," but when it is compared with "the return of Jesus Christ from the dead," it becomes "fit and reasonable" as a sign "to instruct the people of God in the truth of their salvation."[55] Jones insists that when Scripture is interpreted with Scripture, every Scripture word can be employed as a figure which renders the world in providential terms.

---

52. Jones, A Course, 91–92.

53. Jones argues that "From the various applications of particular passages from the law, previous to the revelation of the gospel, it appears that the law was in itself a spiritual as well as a figurative system, for the forming of the heart, and the purifying of the mind" (Jones, A Course, 149). In his Lectures, the accordance of Old Testament and New Testament referents continues to be the primary lens through which spiritual import is generated. For Jones, the spiritual import of Old Testament events is already inherent in the Old Testament itself. Thus, Jones finds that the spiritual import of the "redemption of the people of God from Egypt" is a major theme in the Old Testament (A Course, 163). Contra Warburton, Jones insists that "The prophets warned the people not to rest in the redemption that was past, but to look for another, and that so much more excellent in its nature" (A Course, 164). Jones insists on pursuing figural reading only insofar as is necessary to unveil the tropological import of scriptural figures. In his dedicatory preface to a volume of sermons published in 1790, he therefore tells Horne that he has, in his lectures, been moderate in his interpretation of scriptural figures: "I have carried the apostolical mode of interpreting them as far as I thought it needful" (William Jones, preface to Sermons on Moral and Religious Subjects [London: 1790], 1:iv).

54. Jones, A Course, 128.

55. Jones, A Course, 209–10.

JONES'S THOROUGHGOING
SCRIPTURAL EMBLEMATICISM

Within the Hutchinsonian apologetic tradition, the function of emblematicism is to render providential interpretations of select objects. Because Jones is willing to apply the emblematic method to every Scripture word, it is appropriate to describe his approach as a thoroughgoing scriptural emblematicism.[56] With his thoroughgoing emblematicism, Jones is able to fulfill the latent promise of the tradition by presenting a providential interpretation of *every* object that comes under scholarly gaze, whether it be located in Scripture or in the contemporary context, whether in nature or in human history.[57]

The year after Jones died, his dear friend and fellow Hutchinsonian William Stevens published a twelve-volume edition of his collected works. He included a little piece in the eleventh volume entitled *A Key to the Language of Prophesy, with References to Texts of the Old and New Testaments*.[58] The work, which is but fourteen pages in length, is an unpublished dictionary of scriptural emblems that was probably intended for private use. Because it stabilizes the correspondence between Scripture words and their figural referents, it harkens back to the final volume of the 1748 edition of Hutchinson's works, to which a dictionary of scriptural emblems was appended. It was, as we

---

56. A prominent eighteenth-century scholar who may perhaps be regarded as having a hermeneutic that is analogous to Jones's thoroughgoing scriptural emblematicism is Jonathan Edwards. Recent work on Edwards suggests that his figural reading of the Old Testament is far more prominent than was previously recognized. For instance, Nichols argues that, for Edwards, the christological relationship that binds the Old and New Testaments is "manifest not only at finite specific points, but at every moment" (Stephen R. C. Nichols, *Jonathan Edwards' Bible: The Relationship of the Old and New Testaments* [Eugene, OR: Pickwick, 2013], 106). Nichols also finds that Edwards's figural reading of natural-philosophical objects grants them "multiple referents" in order to draw them into his overarching metaphysic (*Jonathan*, 106–7).

57. Although many eighteenth-century scholars struggled to believe that the historical realm was subject to providential order, most of Jones's contemporaries had no problem believing that the providential order of nature could be readily discerned. Figures such as Priestly, who now tend to be regarded as *avant-garde*, were often the most vociferous defenders of the providential order of nature. See Joseph Priestly, *Institutes of Natural and Revealed Religion*, 2nd ed., 2 vols. (Birmingham: 1782).

58. Stevens was Horne's cousin. The two boys grew up together in Kent and formed a lifelong friendship. Stevens's modern biographer Robert Andrews argues that late eighteenth- and early nineteenth-century High churchmanship "received much of its influence and direction from Stevens" (Robert M. Andrews, *Lay Activism and the High Church Movement of the Late Eighteenth Century* [Leiden: Brill, 2015], 1).

have seen, Hutchinson's entrenchment of emblematic referentiality that gave rise to the violent debates between Hutchinsonian etymologists and their adversaries. Although Jones repudiated these debates, scriptural figures for Jones, as for Hutchinson, are the filaments that bind Scripture words to nature, thus allowing the epistemological certainty that accompanies natural-philosophical knowledge to be transferred to Scripture.

A *Key to the Language of Prophesy* makes it clear that Hutchinson's ethereal theory underlies Jones's own emblematic vision. The first terms Jones lexiconizes are the terms upon which Hutchinson built his theory, including "Firmament," "The Sun," and "The Light of the World." These and similar terms are succinctly defined in unmistakably Hutchinsonian language.[59] Jones's definitions, however, are followed by a complement of scriptural references. The decisive difference between Jones and Clarke's doctrinal apologetic, Jones's engagement with multiple texts, is fully evident in Jones's selection of references.[60] The sheer range of references Jones includes—some of them taken from such obscure books as Joel and Jude—is remarkable. The deliberate way in which Old Testament and New Testament texts are placed side by side is also noteworthy, and it thus becomes apparent that the two or three texts that follow each definition are not intended to function in isolation from one another: the generation of meaning is to be found in their accordance.[61] Even here, as he plays the lexicographer, Jones remains faithful to the juxtapositional method outlined in *The Catholic Doctrine of the Trinity*. It is in this little lexicon that Jones's distinction not only from Clarke but also from Hutchinson is most clearly in view. Jones's approach decisively

---

59. Following Hutchinson, Jones believes these terms refer to "The Divine Power ruling over the world," "The Lord God," and "Christ" (Jones, *The Theological*, 11:185).

60. Jones's willingness to engage the Old Testament as an equal partner in Christian Scripture is also confirmed by the frequency with which he preached from the Old Testament. Of the twenty-nine sermons contained in the two-volume compilation of sermons published before his death, nine of them (31 percent) are on Old Testament texts (William Jones, *Sermons on Moral and Religious Subjects*, 2 vols. [London: 1790]).

61. The juxtaposition of scriptural texts plays a crucial role in Jones's homiletic. Jones often scrawled out Scripture references on the reverse side of his sermons in a handwritten volume of unpublished sermons located in the library of Pusey House, Oxford. Most of the time these Scripture references are found in groups of two. Thus, for example, on the back of page 21 of a sermon on the Trinity, Jones wrote two Scripture references, 1 Corinthians 10:9 and Psalm 68:56, and then joined them with a bracket. Further down the page he listed two other texts, John 20:28 next to Romans 9:5 (Jones, MS Sermons, 1.21).

overcomes Hutchinson's emblematic decontextualization. The terms Jones defines are not, as they are for Hutchinson, free-floating signifiers. Their meaning is generated by multiple texts, and because of this, by their location within a wider, historical frame of reference. Jones's juxtapositional method pushes him beyond Hutchinson's constrained emblematicism in two important ways. Jones is also able to leave behind the Hutchinsonian association of divine activity and cosmology by drawing all natural-philosophical artifacts into the scriptural world. Thus, after he discusses cosmological figures in *A Key to the Language of Prophesy*, Jones proceeds to discuss plants, animals, and minerals.[62]

The significance of Jones's willingness to interpret these objects emblematically comes to light in a collection of four sermons on (1) The Religious Use of Botanical Philosophy, (2) Considerations on the Nature and Oeconomy of Beasts and Cattle, (3) On the Natural History of the Earth and Its Minerals, and (4) On the Natural Evidences of Christianity. Jones begins the third sermon by pointing out that "Writers, who have given us descriptions of the natural world, have divided it into three grand departments or kingdoms, of *plants*, *animals*, and *minerals*."[63] Jones's argument becomes apparent only when the place of the third discourse is considered in relation to the previous two discourses: having demonstrated that plants can be used to relay divine truths in his first discourse, and that animals can be used to relay divine truth in his second, his argument that divine truth can be derived from minerals is a demonstration that *everything* in creation can function as a divine emblem. When the interpreter condescends to interpret nature figuratively, says Jones, "a vast field is open to us, as wide as the world itself."[64] In his first discourse, Jones thus observes that "herbs and flowers may be regarded by some persons as objects of inferior consideration in philosophy; but every thing must be great which hath God for its author."[65]

62. Jones, *The Theological*, 11:187–91.

63. William Jones, *Four Discourses: (1) The Religious Use of Botanical Philosophy; (2) Considerations on the Nature and Oeconomy of Beasts and Cattle; (3) On the Natural History of the Earth and Its Minerals; (4) On the Natural Evidences of Christianity*, a new ed. (London: 1799), 87.

64. Jones, *A Course*, 43.

65. Jones, *Four*, 4. Jones continues: "To [God] all the parts of nature are equally related. The flowers of the earth can raise our thoughts up to the Creator of the world as effectually as the stars of heaven; and till we make this use of both, we cannot be said to think properly of either." The effusive language Jones uses in celebration of the contemplation of nature rivals that of

Jones's juxtapositional method moves beyond Hutchinson's constrained emblematicism because he applies it not merely natural objects, but to historical ones as well.[66] Although the first four sets of figures Jones interprets in his *A Key to the Language of Prophesy* are taken from nature, the final five sets come from human society: "Different States of Men" comprises figures that capture the entire spectrum of human experience—words such as "King" and "Captive," "Master" and "Slave," "Virgin" and "Harlot," "Physician" and "Beggar";[67] "Husbandry" comprises figures that deal with the relation between humans and the earth, including "The Harvest," "The Reapers," and "The Labourer";[68] "The Body of Man, and its Clothing" includes physical descriptors of the body and clothing and terms related to the constitution of man such as "Sleep," "Death," "Bread," and "Hunger";[69] "Places and Buildings"

---

even the most lyrical Romantics: "Happiest of all is he who having cultivated herbs and trees, and studied their virtues, and applied them for his own and for the common benefit, rises from thence to a contemplation of the great Parent of good, whom he sees and adores in these his glorious works" (Jones, *Four*, 36).

66. As I argued in chapter 3, emblematicism regards the entire realm of human experience as potentially subject to emblematic illumination. Furthermore, since emblematicism insists that the interpretation of nature requires human words, it necessarily brings nature and history together into a single realm of interpretation. The fact that Jones, like Watson and Horne, is willing to interpret historical objects emblematically therefore draws Hutchinsonianism back to its emblematic roots.

67. Jones, *The Theological*, 11:191–93.

68. Jones, *The Theological*, 11:193–94.

69. Jones, *The Theological*, 11:194–97. In the modern era the pervasive unwillingness to render providential interpretations of human history and society, and the attendant tendency to focus exclusively upon the providential interpretation of nature, is closely tied to the problem of evil. Webster maintains that the existence of evil is only problematic for the belief in providence to the extent that it causes people to restrict their providentialism: "A theology of providence," says Webster, "need not and cannot wait upon demonstration of the divine righteousness, because providence is not asserted on the basis of the insignificance of evil but on the basis of the belief that God outbids any and all evil. What makes evil problematic for providence is not its existence but the fact that we resist applying belief in providence to cases of it, especially those in which we are concerned. Theological answers to this will therefore be as much ascetic as argumentative: we need to learn what it is to apply belief in providence, and how to apply it, in order to be persuaded of the viability and fruitfulness of making the application. Reconciling providence and horrors is a task within fellowship with God; inability to commend and receive the proffered reconciliation indicates estrangement" (John Webster, "On the Theology of Providence," in *The Providence of God*, ed. Francesa Aran Murphy and Philip Ziegler [London: T & T Clark, 2009], 158). Jones was willing to describe even the most difficult experiences in providential terms. On January 29, 1762, Jones wrote the following words to his friend George Berkeley Jr.: "My wife has lately been delivered of a son, whom I baptized by the name of George, but it hath pleased God to take him from me" (William Jones, A letter to George Berkeley Jr., January 29, 1762, Add. MS 39311, 109, The British Library, London: UK).

includes a handful of select figures, including place names ("Jerusalem") and general locations ("house"); and "Rites and Ceremonies of the Mosaic Law" offers figural readings of the tabernacle, the high priest, and various articles of the temple.[70] More than half of the figures Jones deals with in *A Key to the Language of Prophecy* are taken from human history, culture, and society.[71] As Jones undertakes to interpret scriptural figures, particulars from human history, culture, and society inevitably lose their devolutionary character and become emblems of divine light. In Hutchinson's work, scriptural signifiers can only hope to convey divine meaning if they are removed from history and refashioned as hieroglyphs that refer to natural-philosophical objects. Within this framework, select Hebrew hieroglyphs become the hinges between the fallen world of human history and the heavens. But because the signifiers Jones interprets figurally are not decontexualized and dehistoricized as they are interpreted, they retain their place within human history. For Jones, figural reading operates squarely within human culture and experience.

The remarkable breadth of Jones's emblematic vision is exemplified by his interpretation of the term "light."[72] Hutchinson's emblematic interpretation of "light" is confined to his christological rendering of the particle that emanates from the orb of the sun. Watson and Horne extend Hutchinson's reflections on the emblematic manner of light by considering the functions and powers of light that are exercised within the terrestrial realm. Watson marvels at the ability of light to bring seeds and buds to life, and he therefore celebrates the miracle of bodily resurrection in Christ. Horne, following Hutchinson, ponders the ability of light to penetrate "even to the inmost substances of grosser bodies," and this leads him to praise the "unbounded and efficacious ... influence of the Sun of Righteousness, when he sent out his word, enlightening and enlivening all things by the glory of his grace."[73] Although Jones pays tribute to Watson's *Christ the Light of the World* before he launches into his own emblematic interpretation of the term, his own

70. Jones, *The Theological*, 11:197–98.
71. This emphasis upon human culture is consistent with that of *A Course of Lectures*. In *A Course of Lectures*, four of five categories of figures are taken from history rather than nature.
72. See David Ney, "The Multiplicity of Scripture Words: William Jones of Nayland and Figural Reading," in *All Thy Lights Combine: Figural Reading in the Anglican Tradition*, ed. David Ney and Ephraim Radner (Bellingham, WA: Lexham Press, 2021): 156–71.
73. George Horne, *A Commentary on the Book of Psalms* (London: 1776), 1:84.

interpretation moves well beyond previous Hutchinsonian interpretations. Jones finds that in Scripture the

> natural image of the light is applied to so many great purposes ... You see, our God is light; our Redeemer is light; our scripture is light; our whole religion is light; the ministers of it are light; all Christian people are children of the light, and have light within them. If so, what an obligation is laid upon us, not to walk as if we were in darkness, but to walk uprightly as in the day, shewing the people of this world, that we have a better rule to direct us than they have.[74]

The figural import of light is no longer confined to God the Son; it now includes no less than seven specific referents.

The scriptural references Jones includes in *A Key to the Language of Prophecy* have a latent generative capacity. Since they include not merely the term that is being defined but other terms as well, they have the potential to extend the meaning of the term in question by serving as the beginning of an extended chain of references that renders providential interpretations of numerous other terms. Thus, although Hutchinson's emblematic interpretation of the word "light" allows him to offer a providential interpretation of the wave/particle we receive from the sun, Jones's emblematic interpretation is extended to include Scripture, the Christian religion, the priesthood, the laity, righteous living, and, indeed, the entire moral order of the world. This thoroughgoing scriptural emblematicism overcomes Hutchinson's restricted cosmological interpretation of providence. Even if Jones tried to restrict his providentialism, he would not find it easy to do so since his method continually draws objects of Scripture—objects of history and nature both—into a comprehensive emblematic and therefore providential frame.

THE WORLD OF SCRIPTURE

The three steps Watson outlines in *Aaron's Intercession* (the interpretation of the "historical relation" of the text, canonical reading, and tropological reading) all feature in Jones's hermeneutical method. Following Watson, Jones believes that the object of textual interpretation is to render tropological

---

74. Jones, *A Course*, 46–47.

readings of them. But unlike Watson, Jones insists that tropological readings must always be generated by the emblematic interpretation of scriptural texts. This suggests that he is interested in more than simply "applying" one set of particulars to another. Since he believes that—to quote Lindbeck—"A scriptural world is … able to absorb the universe," he conceives of the task of interpretation as that of extending the "domain and meaning" of Scripture "over the whole of reality."[75]

Following Watson, Jones begins many of his sermons with what might be described as a literal or historical rendering of the text.[76] More often than not, however, Jones's discussions of literal textual elements are interspersed throughout, set within discussions of related scriptural texts and moral lessons.[77] Watson's influence on Jones is most vivid in Jones's appropriation of the second and third steps of Watson's method. Jones wholeheartedly embraces Watson's conviction that the interpretation of Christian Scripture is tropologically oriented, and he follows Watson by insisting that tropology is generated by scriptural accordance. In particular, Jones follows Watson by insisting that Christians must interpret Old Testament particulars as figures, since it is only through their figural import that they are able to

---

75. George Lindbeck, *The Nature of Doctrine: Religion and Theology in a Postliberal Age* (Philadelphia: Westminster, 1984), 117. The notion that Christian Scripture has the ability to "absorb" the world appears in Auerbach, *Mimesis*, 72. Kathryn Greene-McReight observes, however, that the notion has gained currency due to the work of members of the "Yale school," Hans Frei, George Lindbeck, and more recently, Bruce Marshall. Although Greene-McReight is clearly intrigued by Frei's observation that the orientation of precritical interpretation was to incorporate "extra-biblical thought, experience, and reality into the one real world detailed and made accessible by the biblical story—not the reverse," she complains that Frei and his allies fail to tell us "in concrete terms what such an absorption would actually entail" (Kathryn Greene-McReight, "'We are the companions of the Patriarchs' or Scripture Absorbs Calvin's World," *Modern Theology* 14, no. 2 [1998]: 213). Following Frei's suggestion, she looks to John Calvin as one who "read the Bible as one continuous narrative, whose reality was overcome by the reality of the biblical world," and she finds this clearly articulated in Calvin's preface to his commentary on Genesis ("We are," 214). Greene-McReight observes that it is Calvin's interpretation of Genesis as not only a "history of the creation of the world" but as the "the sum of the Christian story." On this account it becomes "the story of the reader," which enables Calvin to conclude that "we are companions of the patriarchs" ("We are," 215).

76. For example, he begins his sermon on Genesis 6:5—"God saw that the wickedness of man was great in the earth, and that every imagination of the thoughts of his heart was only evil continually"—by reflecting upon the nature of the human condition before the deluge (Jones, *The Theological*, 7:363–65).

77. Like Horne, Jones affirms the necessity of literal interpretation while insisting that it stands in need of further reflection (Jones, *A Course*, 28).

engage contemporary Christian experience. Jones observes, for instance, that St. Peter applies the history of the salvation of Noah as "a *figure* of that *Salvation* which we now obtain as the *family* of Jesus Christ in the Ark of the *Church* by the *waters of Baptism*."[78] From this it follows, argues Jones, echoing the church fathers, that a "practical inference is to be made in favour of the ordinance of the Church; that as the ark could not be saved but by water, so must all the Church of Christ be baptized."[79]

The guiding principle of Jones's hermeneutic is the conviction that the tropological rendering of scriptural particulars is generated through figural reading. Unlike Horne, Jones applies this principle consistently and to the Old and New Testaments both. This is colorfully illustrated in one of Jones's final works, *A Discourse on the Use and Intention of Some Remarkable Passages of the Scripture* (1798). In the opening pages Jones offers a tropological reading of the Magnificat, and the method Jones employs is identical to the method he uses to render Noah's ark as a figure of the church. For Jones, any comparison that is to be drawn between Mary and the Christian must first be established through the mediation of Scripture. "Many good Christians," says Jones,

> who read the word of God with a desire to profit by it, and have been taught, that *whatsoever things were written aforetime were written for our learning* (Rom. xv. 4.), have their doubts concerning the use of many things they find in the Scripture; not being able to see how they can answer that general design of adding to our *learning*, and thereby leading us to more *patience* and *comfort*.[80]

Jones observes that St. Paul's comments follow his application of a passage from the Psalms to Christ, and he finds that for the apostle, this is but one instance of a general rule that "the things written aforetime are to be thus applied to Jesus Christ." Jones finds that unless they are applied to Christ, such passages "are nothing to us as Christians, neither shall we find in them the comfort they were intended to give."[81]

---

78. Jones, *A Course*, 155.
79. Jones, *A Course*, 156.
80. Jones, *A Course*, 13.
81. Jones, *A Course*, 14.

Jones relates that he once met "a clergyman of no mean learning" who "objected to the use of the *Magnificat*, in the service of the church, as a form that could have no relation to us."[82] To the contrary, Jones insists that

> Christ, who was formed in the blessed virgin, is also formed in us; and the mother of Christ, like Sarah, the mother of the promised seed, in her spiritual capacity, is a figure of the church, that blessed Jerusalem, which is the *mother of us all*: so that the words, which were spoken by her, may be used by all Christians, with the utmost truth and propriety. Each of us may truly say, *My soul doth magnify the Lord*, for he, who regarded the virgin, did regard her for my salvation; that Christ might be formed in me, as he was in her ... When the promise, made to the church of Israel in our father Abraham, was fulfilled to the blessed virgin, it was fulfilled to us, that is, to the *seed of Abraham for ever*, which seed are we at this day. Thus is the *magnificat* brought home to us, and the use of it in the church, to the end of the world, is justified.[83]

Jones's exegesis of the Magnificat illustrates that he is unwilling to follow Watson and Horne in drawing out "unmediated" tropological readings of biblical texts. Here Jones refuses to draw a direct analogy between Mary's psychological state and that of modern man, or a comparison between her relationship with God and that of the Christian. The basis of the bond between Mary and the Christian is not that the feeling of having Jesus in the womb is akin to the feeling of having Jesus in the heart, or even, more abstractly, that Mary's experience of being redeemed is similar to that of contemporary Christians! Christians can only join in Mary's song because Mary's song is the fulfillment of God's promise to Abraham. It is only on account of Abraham that Mary becomes a figure of the church and that Christians can join with her in singing, "He that sent away the rich, and accepted a lowly maiden" as a tribute to God for his condescension "to regard and magnify us poor Gentiles."[84]

---

82. Jones, *A Course*, 15.

83. Jones, *A Course*, 15–16.

84. Jones, *A Course*, 15.

As Jones interprets the Magnificat, he insists that it depends upon the Old Testament to unveil its tropological import. Although Horne is confident that he can interpret the New Testament without the assistance of the Old Testament, Jones believes that the New Testament needs the Old Testament as much as the Old needs the New. "Too many mistakes," says Jones, "are current amongst us in regard to the Old Testament; without which, the New never was and never will be understood."[85] This insistence that New Testament interpretation requires canonical mediation protects Jones against Horne's nascent primitivism. It takes away the temptation to divide history into epochs of either growth or decline. For Jones, scriptural time, and therefore historical time, consists of but one dispensation. The "matter" the Bible treats, says Jones, is the "dispensation of God, which began before this world, and will not be finished till the world is at an end, and the eternal kingdom of God is established." [86]

For Jones, the problem of the historical relation of the Old Testament to the contemporary context is no more perplexing than this problem with respect to the New Testament. The relevance of the New Testament and its status as Christian Scripture can be attributed neither to the fact that it deals with Christians nor to the fact that European culture has more in common with Greco-Roman culture than it has with ancient Hebrew culture. It is tempting to say that for Jones, the "ugly, broad ditch" that separates Christians from the early church is the same "ugly, broad ditch" that separates them from the ancient Israelites. But for Jones, no such "wide ugly ditch" exists. Jones jumps back and forth between his literal, allegorical, and tropological reflections. His fluid movement between the contemporary application and the canonical rendering has the effect both of granting the text a degree of contemporaneity, and of drawing contemporary events into

85. Jones, A Letter to the Church of England, 20.
86. Jones, A Course, 6–7.

"salvation history."[87] It is hard to read Jones without feeling the pull of Calvin's notion that Christians are "companions of the Patriarchs."[88]

Jones's hermeneutical method is driven by the impulse to absorb the entire world within the world of Scripture. His appropriation of the second step of Watson's hermeneutic, the canonical reading of particular texts, can be described as a process in which the contours of the scriptural world are established; the numerous figural threads he draws as he juxtaposes scriptural texts binds them together by establishing a shared referentiality within what can justly be called the "world" of Scripture. But because Jones interprets texts canonically to discover their tropological import, the contours of the scriptural world are extended to include the world in which Jones lives. For Jones, therefore, tropological reading is best described not as a process in which the truth of Scripture is applied to the contemporary world, but as a process in which the contemporary world is absorbed by the Scriptures.

Emblem books create a world that is morally charged by reinterpreting these objects as part of an overarching moral order. Hutchinson's work sits awkwardly within the emblematic tradition because it cuts short the chain of emblematic associations by restricting emblematic referentiality to single natural-philosophical objects. Jones's work, on the other hand, harkens back to that of Quarles and other emblematicists because he places all natural and historical objects within a universal emblematic frame.[89] And for Jones, that frame is, quite simply, the Scriptures.[90] The experience of the patriarchs is

---

87. This approach implies a philosophy of time that differs from that of Watson and Horne. For Watson and Horne, the movement from the literal text of the Old Testament, to its spiritual rendering in the New, to its contemporary application depends upon a chronological understanding of time.

88. See note 75 above. In an unpublished sermon, Jones says, "Our friends also are in that country to which we are travelling. To the Christian, considered as such, the world hath never been nor will its principles ever suffer to be, a friend. The friend of the Christian is Christ, whom the Jews in scorn called the friend of publicans and sinners: the blessed Angels are friends to those that love God: the saints departed are friends to those who are passing through the trials which they have happily escaped: the Prophets and Evangelists are friends to those who are enlightened by their writings. We are brought to a communion with these, and are intimately related to them, from the time that we are made Christians" (Jones, MS Sermons, 1.16).

89. Emblem books tend to be read anachronistically as motivated to employ natural and historical objects to render moral lessons, but this analysis fails to account for what was, in fact, a far larger ambition.

90. It is inappropriate to speak of Jones as guilty of scriptural decontextualization inasmuch as he is continually drawing non-scriptural elements into the scriptural world. Jones's Scripture words remain within the scriptural world and therefore remain Scripture words.

found to be morally relevant not because it is found to be *like* our experience but because it is found to be truly ours once our experience is absorbed within the scriptural world.

THE BOOK OF NATURE AND
THE BOOK OF SCRIPTURE

Jones's epistemological justification for his belief that Christian edification depends upon the emblematic interpretation of Scripture has two aspects: sensualism and biblicism. As a sensualist, Jones believes that providential discernment can only be achieved through engagement with sensible particulars, and as a biblicist, he holds that it is equally dependent upon Scripture words.[91] The bond between Jones's sensualism and his biblicism can be helpfully clarified by reflecting upon the relationship between the Book of Nature and the Book of Scripture in his thought. As we have already seen, eighteenth-century scholars who emphasized the distinction between God's two books, such as Clarke and the deists, found it easy to regard the Book of Nature as a superior foundation for divine knowledge than the Book of Scripture. But because Jones's thoroughgoing scriptural emblematicism makes natural-philosophical knowledge subject to Scripture, Scripture is given epistemological priority in Jones's thought.

Jones inherited from Newton, Clarke, and Hutchinson the notion that truths found in the Book of Nature are the only certain and demonstrable truths.[92] Jones therefore assumes, as they did, that his task as a scriptural

---

91. Jones's interpretive method is grounded in the conviction that "we are obliged to attain to all our knowledge of things spiritual or invisible, that is, by using the creation as a mirror in which to behold them." And he finds justification for this view in Romans 1:20: "*The invisible things of God, concerning his being and power, and the oeconomy of his are clearly seen from the creation of the world, being* understood *by things that are made*" (William Jones, *A Full Answer to the* Essay on Spirit [London: 1753], 83–84). For Jones, even our conviction that our knowledge is dependent upon physical things is dependent upon Scripture. Such is the intimate link between sensualism and biblicism in Jones's epistemology.

92. Jones was a natural philosopher of some repute, being elected to the Royal Society in 1775. Jones does include scriptural and tropological reflections in his natural-philosophical work, but much of it is strictly empirical and can be seen as the result of an intensely inquisitive intellect. In his *Physiological Disquisitions*, for instance, Jones reflects upon the nature of (1) matter, (2) motion, (3) the elements, (4) fire, (5) air, (6) sound, (7) fossils, (8) natural history, and (9) the weather. Jones's willingness to embrace the insights of a vast array of authors continues the process begun by Horne's work on Newton and Hutchinson. Jones is even willing to endorse the work of Hutchinson's archnemesis Woodward, although he does criticize Woodward for trying

apologist is to demonstrate the accordance of the Book of Nature and the Book of Scripture. This presupposition accounts for Jones's consistent defense of Hutchinsonian natural philosophy: he believes that, like all good natural philosophy, it confirms the accordance of God's two books.[93]

> When the maker of the world becomes an author, his word must be as perfect as his work: the glory of his wisdom must be declared by the one as evidently as the glory of his power is by the other: and if nature repays the philosopher for his experiments, the scripture can never disappoint those who are properly exercised in the study of it.[94]

Here Jones insists upon the equilibrium of God's two books while continuing to affirm their distinction. The danger that attends Jones's project is the same danger that troubles Hutchinson, Clarke, and Newton: the attempt to bind Scripture to nature is prone to give way to the positivistic assumption that naturalistic knowledge is superior to historically conditioned knowledge. Nevertheless, Jones's thoroughgoing scriptural emblematicism stops this possibility from materializing.

In 1787 Jones published his Fairchild Lecture entitled *A Lecture on the Natural Evidences of Christianity*.[95] The natural-philosophical apologetic Jones articulates in the work stands in stark contrast to that of the renowned apologist William Paley (1743-1805). Paley's *Natural Theology* (1802) duplicates the Newtonian apologetic of Clarke's Boyle Lectures by establishing the principles of revealed religion through logical deductions. For Jones, on the other hand, it is impossible to proceed deductively from the natural world to revelation for the simple reason that "the world, always has been, and now is, to those that are shut up under its laws, a schoolmaster to turn men away from Christ."[96] Only when the existence of revelation is presupposed can the providential significance of the world be discerned. Jones therefore begins

---

to use universal gravitation to defend his cause. See Jones, *The Theological*, 10:104–5, 256–58; William Jones, *An Essay on the First Principles of Natural Philosophy* (Oxford: 1762), 105–7.

93. For Jones's appropriation of Hutchinson's natural philosophy, see William Jones, *A Short Way to Truth: Or the Christian Doctrine of a Trinity in Unity, Illustrated and Confirmed from Analogy in the Natural Creation* (London: 1793).

94. Jones, *A Course*, 1.

95. The lecture is appended to the 1787 edition of *A Course of Lectures*.

96. Jones, *A Course*, 150.

his lecture by insisting that although he is considering the wisdom of God in the natural world, "the knowledge of the scriptures is not excluded," and he will therefore attempt "to bring them both together into one discourse; for they illustrate one another in a wonderful manner."[97]

> To those who search for it, and have pleasure in receiving it, there is a striking alliance between the oeconomy of Nature, and the principles of divine Revelation; and unless we study both together, we shall be liable to mistake things now, as the unbelieving Sadducees did, in their vain reasonings with our blessed Saviour. They *erred, not knowing the Scriptures, nor the power of God*: they neither understood them separately, nor knew how to compare them together.[98]

Here Jones articulates his intriguing appropriation of the Protestant principle of *sola Scriptura*. Following William Chillingworth, and like Clarke, Jones understands Scripture itself to be the rule of faith, but he adapts this conviction to eighteenth-century empirical sensibilities by insisting that scriptural authority does not function independently of its ability to accurately describe the world.[99]

For Clarke, the authority of the Bible is confirmed by its factually correct description of the Godhead and of ethical principles. In Clarke's apologetic, however, the Bible refers to the divine being and to moral principles independently of the Bible's relationship to the natural world. Similarly, natural religion, in itself, has the capacity to lead humans to divine truth without the aid of the Bible. Jones's defense of the accordance of God's two books, on the other hand, is issued in a single apologetic thrust. He brings together Scripture and nature in an act of interpretation which affirms, simultaneously, that the providential order in creation is inaccessible to human minds apart from the mediation of Scripture, and that the divine meaning of Scripture is imperceptible apart from its relationship to the natural

---

97. Jones, *A Course.* 435.

98. Jones, *A Course*, 435–36.

99. In good Protestant fashion, Jones places the church under the authority of Scripture: "The Church doesn't determine whether there is a Christ or a Holy Ghost," says Jones, it "only declares the faith which it has received; and instead of her *imposing*, this faith is *imposed* upon the Church by the uncontrolable authority of God in Holy Scripture" (William Jones, *A Letter to the Common People* [London: 1767], 8).

world. In this Jones unites Scripture and nature in a way that is impossible for Clarke. The providential knowledge of nature is only rendered infallible when nature is rendered in scriptural terms, and scriptural knowledge, likewise, is only rendered providential when it is brought into accordance with the natural world.

For Jones, the unity of God's two books, which is expressed in a shared emblematic capacity, stems from their common divine origin. Interpreting Scripture emblematically is warranted because creation itself, as generated by the divine Word, is ripe with emblematic potential. The task of the Christian exegete is not confined to working with the biblical text. The Christian exegete must be conversant in empirical science. The goal is to interpret Scripture with Scripture and nature with nature, but also Scripture with nature so as to draw every physical specimen of the natural world into the scriptural orbit. "Whoever mediates upon the world thus applied as a figure of truth," says Jones, "and sees that agreement between nature and revelation which revelation itself hath pointed out to us, will want no miracle to persuade him of the Christian doctrines; for nature itself is Christian, and the world a daily miracle."[100]

For Jones, the divine, emblematic meaning of the Book of Nature is given in the Book of Scripture.[101] Thus the task of scriptural catechesis can no longer be confined to theology proper. The goal is now to find the true and providential signification of every object of creation. This expansive catechetical vision is succinctly expressed in Jones's work *The Book of Nature*, a children's catechism published one year after the publication of Jones's lectures on the figurative language of Scripture.[102] In the introduction to the

---

100. Jones, *A Course*, 303.

101. Scripture abounds with "metaphorical allusions to the natural creation. Sometimes they refer us to the *heavens* and the *firmament*, to the *sun*, the *moon*, and the *stars*; which, in the emblematical language of divine revelation, are but other names for *Christ*, the *church*, and the *saints* of God" (William Jones, *A Free Enquiry into the Sense and Signification of the Spring* [London: 1772], 1–2).

102. Jones took the Christian formation of children very seriously. See Jones, MS Sermons, 2.1. Sarah Trimmer (née Kirby) has been credited with two innovative educational practices. First, she "popularized the use of pictoral material in books for children," and second, she used "animals, birds, and the natural world in stories she called fables" (Barbara Brandon Schnorrenberg, "Sarah Trimmer," *Oxford Dictionary of National Biography*, accessed July 3, 2015, http://www.oxforddnb.com.myaccess.library.utoronto.ca/view/article/27740O). Both of these innovations point to Jones's influence. Trimmer was the cousin of Jones's protégé William Kirby,

work, Jones revisits the distinction between the language of words (here he calls it the language of the mind) and the language of things, and he insists that children, since they love pictures, are predisposed to learn about God through the "language of things." His object, therefore, is to employ the figurative language of Scripture to instruct children that "the whole world is a picture and that everything we see speaks something to the mind, to instruct and improve it."[103]

Each of Jones's sixteen catechetical lessons begins with a discussion of things children are familiar with, whether animals, natural objects, or things taken from human life and society. These things are then refracted through the lens of Scripture to generate tropological interpretations of them. Although the moral lessons Jones extracts from biblical figures throughout the work are pithier than those found in his course of lectures, his favored emblematic hermeneutic remains unaltered in the catechism. Other intellectuals who took a keen interest in child development, such as Isaac Watts (1674–1748), had already identified the importance of teaching children with things as well as with words. With Watts, it turns out that reliance on things is simply a heuristic device, an accommodation to the restricted intellectual abilities of children.[104] With Jones, however, there is never any question of being able to rise above and beyond the human reliance on sensory input or the concrete forms that are presented to the human intellect in the pages of Scripture. The path to Christian virtue and divine illumination is the same for both child and sage.

---

and she worked closely with nineteenth-century Hutchinsonians. For Trimmer's approach to Christian formation, see Heather E. Weir, "Spiritual Transformation in Sarah Trimmer's *Essay on Christian Education,*" in *Change and Transformation: Essays in Anglican History,* ed. Thomas P. Power (Eugene, OR: Pickwick, 2013), 113–39.

103. William Jones, *The Book of Nature* (London: 1788), vi. Teale calls the work "an experiment to teach children the knowledge of Scripture by things instead of words" (Teale, "William Jones," 377).

104. Isaac Watts, "On Instruction by Catechism," in *The Works of the Rev. Isaac Watts* (London: 1813), 5:215. Watts praises the ability that things have to powerfully relay moral lessons ("On Instruction," 234). Watts does not, however, question the ability of words to relay Christian knowledge on their own. For Watts, words are the husk that contain the marrow of divine, immaterial truth ("On Instruction," 214). Since Scripture words, like other words, are only the husk of immaterial truth, however, Watts does not find it necessary to always rely on them. For Watts, the primary purpose of Scripture, therefore, is to offer proof texts for Christian doctrine ("On Instruction," 222).

That Jones is willing to include objects taken from human culture and society in *The Book of Nature* confirms that his thoroughgoing scriptural emblematicism has the capacity to draw both natural and historical objects into the scriptural world.[105] It also confirms that for Jones, the Book of Nature has been expanded to include the entire realm of human experience. When Jones compares the Book of Nature and the Book of Scripture, he is not following Clarke in evaluating Scripture according to the "mathematical" standard of natural philosophy. He is simply comparing Scripture, as it is read, with the world, as it is experienced. There is therefore no question of being able to prop up the Book of Nature as a primordial standard against which historical experience can be evaluated by enlightened minds. Jones's Book of Nature has been historicized.

That *The Book of Nature* is a children's catechism is not without importance. Jones recognizes that the strength of emblematic catechesis is that it is accessible to all. Opening the Book of Nature is no longer restricted to Newton the mathematician or Clarke the metaphysician. That Jones has children in mind also confirms that Jones has historicized human engagement with his historicized Book of Nature: human engagement with the Book of Nature takes place within time. It begins in childhood and continues until death and is itself bound to the order of creaturely existence. The Book of Nature, thus conceived, can no longer serve as a mechanism to help scholars escape the vicissitudes of history. With Jones, the Book of Nature has become an emblem of creaturely existence.

PROVIDENCE AND THE OLD TESTAMENT

Horne's belief in the providential order of the world serves as the foundation of his affirmation of scriptural authority. Conversely, because Jones gives the Book of Scripture epistemological priority over the Book of Nature, scriptural authority becomes the basis of his belief in providence. For Jones, the scriptural authority of a text is its ability to render the world of the reader in providential terms. Jones's Old Testament apologetic, therefore, is an attempt

---

105. In *The Book of Nature*, as elsewhere, Jones's canonical method leads him to apply words that refer initially to natural objects to historical ones (Jones, *The Book*, 18). Jones's tropological orientation plays a further role in breaking down the distinction between history and nature. The objects he takes from nature are also drawn into the historical realm when they take on an existence within the moral lives of people. See, for example, Jones, *The Book*, 26.

to convince Christians that they cannot hope to understand the divine order of the world without the aid of the Old Testament. This being said, Jones believes that this order is revealed not simply in the Old Testament, but in the whole of Christian Scripture. In Jones's configuration, it is not possible to divide the Bible into distinct theological loci, law and gospel. Nor is it possible to drive a wedge between the Old and New Testaments: a single apologetic upholds them both.[106]

Jones believes that the given order of Scripture itself calls forth this point of view. The Old Testament itself renders theological interpretations of the Mosaic law, and the New Testament extends this process of reflection by applying the law to other concrete realities, such as Christ and the church. Thus, concludes Jones, "From the various applications of particular passages from the law, previous to the revelation of the gospel, it appears that the law was in itself a spiritual as well as a figurative system, for the forming of the heart, and the purifying of the mind."[107] The Old Testament does everything that the New Testament does: it speaks truthfully about God and about the world and—what is more—it is itself the means by which human creatures find their way to God.[108] There is reason to believe that Jones would still be able to venerate the Old Testament as Christian Scripture in a world in which there was no New Testament.[109] This being said, the full force of Jones's Old

---

106. Jones is thus able to conclude that the "law and the gospel are the same religion under different forms" (Jones, *A Course*, 368–69).

107. Jones, *A Course*, 149.

108. This ability of the Old Testament to speak truthfully about the nature of the Christian God is what Seitz calls the "discrete witness" of the Old Testament (Christopher Seitz, "Scripture Becomes Religion[s]: The Theological Crisis of Serious Biblical Interpretation in the Twentieth Century," in *Renewing Biblical Interpretation*, ed. Craig Bartholomew, Colin Greene, and Karl Möller [Grand Rapids: Zondervan, 2000], 43). The concern to uphold the Old Testament "on its own terms" is, as we might expect, a top priority for theologically-minded Old Testament scholars. See also R. W. L. Moberly, *The Bible, Theology, and Faith: A Study of Abraham and Jesus* (Cambridge: Cambridge University Press, 2000). Jones's *Catholic Doctrine of the Trinity* confirms that he shares this concern. This being said, the fact that much of his work is oriented toward the Christian interpretation of creation suggests that it is appropriate to ascribe to Jones the view that proving that the Old Testament has the ability to speak truthfully concerning the nature of God is apologetically inadequate.

109. This is further evidence that Jones's hermeneutic echoes that of the early church. The fact that the early church was able to apply a figural hermeneutic to the Old Testament without the aid of the New is confirmed not only by the fact that St. Paul himself did so, but by the fact that the contours of the New Testament were not firmly established until the third century.

Testament apologetic is only expressed when the Old Testament is brought into conversation with the New.

Hutchinson's Old Testament implicitly draws upon the New Testament in its Trinitarian renderings of Hebrew words. Nevertheless, because Hutchinson forges an apologetic that is unique to the Old Testament, he severs the Old Testament from the New, and he accordingly has great difficulty convincing Christians that the Old Testament must be upheld as a guide for the Christian life. At most, Hutchinson's apologetic is able to convince empiricists that the Old Testament speaks truthfully about the divine meaning of the natural world. By drawing the Old and New Testaments together, on the other hand, Jones makes it difficult for his readers to dismiss the Old Testament as an ancient artifact and irrelevant curiosity. Through his juxtapositional method, which brings Old Testament texts into conversation with other scriptural texts, Jones demonstrates that Old Testament texts carry contemporary weight. More often than not, this method draws upon texts from the New Testament. This does not only mean, however, that the New Testament is superior to the Old. The experience of Old Testament Israel is celebrated as that which determines the experience of the New Testament church. Through canonical reading, the New Testament draws contemporary Christians into the story of ancient Israel, enabling them to make it their own.

Although the scriptural authority of the Old Testament is upheld for the Christian by the testimony of the New Testament, the scriptural authority of the New Testament equally depends upon the Old Testament. It depends upon the Old Testament quite literally because it is composed, in good measure, of Old Testament words. As Henri de Lubac observes, "All of Israel mysteriously relives in the Church—its history, its personalities, its battles, its trials, its destiny, its expectations."[110] Existentially, the New Testament also depends upon the Old because the New is limited in its reflections on human experience, including family life, human love, human labor, human warfare, human governance, and human society at large. And it is even more limited in its narrative depiction of them. The New Testament is unable to draw many of the central aspects of human existence into God's providential order for the simple fact that it does not name them. For this, it relies upon

---

110. Henri de Lubac, S.J., *Scripture in the Tradition*, trans. Luke O'Neill (New York: Crossroad 2010), 115.

the Old Testament. As Jones reflects upon the experiences of ancient Israel he concludes, "Not a single circumstance befell them, which, at some stage of our journey through life, does not happen to us."[111]

The Christian reader of the Old Testament finds much that is familiar; family rivalry and conflict, struggle with governments and foreign powers, internal wrestling with conscience and sin, friendship and hostility, war and peace. Canonical reading orders this familiarity. Once the basic elements of human existence, as depicted in the Old Testament, are drawn up into God's providential order through scriptural accordance, the experiences of Old Testament Israel are seen in a new light. Christ's light, which shines on them, shows them to be far more than historical curiosities, the aimless struggles of a small confederation of ancient tribes. Christ infuses the scriptural account of these struggles with moral authority, making them a "divine commentary" on the contemporary experience. Otherwise put, the Old Testament is crucial to Christian piety because it does not describe providence in impersonal and abstract terms, but rather draws specific contemporary Christian experiences into the scriptural order that governs the world.[112]

Jones believes that good Christians find there is no greater joy than being able to reflect upon the course of their lives "and celebrate the mercies they have received."[113] And, indeed, this was the experience of the Israelites themselves: they

> Discoursed together on the miracles God had wrought in Egypt, with the perils of the wilderness, their various encampments, the victories they had obtained, and the cities they had destroyed; and repeated the wondrous narrative to their children, listening around them.[114]

We can well expect, says Jones, that Israel's experience will one day become that of all the saints; the ability to reinterpret human experience

---

111. Jones, "Providence," 215.

112. It must be emphasized, however, that in Jones's hermeneutic the Old Testament is not found to be necessary only to the extent it connects with contemporary experience. Jones's hermeneutic finds a place for the Old Testament even in instances that the New Testament appears to be far more relevant. The interpreter who draws a comparison between his own experience and that of the early Christian believers is still required to interpret the experience of the believers in canonical context before he applies it to himself.

113. Jones, "Providence," 224.

114. Jones, "Providence," 226.

providentially will be part of the blessedness of heavenly existence. In heaven the saints will

> Look back upon the vicissitudes of this mortal life; and ... will delight for endless ages, in comparing the trials they underwent, the dangers they escaped, and the mercies they received in this their pilgrimage; adding thereto the greater wonders of their walk through the valley of the shadow of death, their resurrection, ascension, and glorifica- tion, which are yet to come; all of which will furnish matter for such songs, and be celebrated with such sounds, as no ear hath yet heard, nor can it enter into the heart of man to conceive.[115]

One of the songs, Jones observes, that the saints in heaven will sing is "the song of Moses the servant of God."[116] Hutchinson's defense of Moses as pro- genitor of God's very own natural philosophy is extravagant. But Jones's defense of Moses may well be more extravagant still. For Jones, the Christian that picks up the book of Exodus and sings the Song of Moses as her own has a foretaste of glory.[117]

CONCLUSION

For Jones, the canonicity of the Old Testament relies upon the demon- stration that it is the voice of providence. This demonstration regards Old Testament words, as well as their New Testament counterparts, as figures which unveil the providential import of historical and natural-philosphical objects. Jones's notion of the figurative language of Holy Scripture replaces Hutchinson's hieroglyphic view of the Hebrew tongue. This enables Jones to extend Hutchinson's emblematic interpretation of cosmological realities to the full range of scriptural objects, and by means of these objects, every created thing. Jones's thoroughgoing emblematicism integrates the sensualist and biblicist aspects of Hutchinsonianism and brings consistency to them. Whatever the object in question, its providential interpretation requires both

---

115. Jones, "Providence," 227.

116. Jones, "Providence," 227.

117. The Song of Moses found in Exodus 15 begins as follows: "I will sing unto the LORD, for he hath triumphed gloriously: the horse and his rider hath he thrown into the sea. The LORD is my strength and song, and he is become my salvation."

that it be studied in its created particularity, and that it be interpreted in light of Christian Scripture. Objects found within Scripture, such as divine names and attributes, must be interpreted canonically before they can be utilized in constructive theology. Similarly, objects found in the contemporary world are drawn into the world of Scripture by this same process.

While Hutchinson's apologetic depended upon the unparalleled divinity of Old Testament words, Jones's hermeneutic presupposes that Old Testament and New Testament words are equally divine. The Old and New Testaments each have a discrete witness, and the location of them both within the larger context of the Christian canon strengthens their ability to make themselves necessary for providential discernment. This being said, the Old and New Testaments do not, for Jones, passively relay providential import. As light is refracted through a prism, so too Scripture alters the character of the providence that is discerned. As Jones studies the particulars he encounters in Scripture, they become the basis of a providential vision that shuns abstraction. As Jones puts it, "the logicians teach us, that they always dwell upon *generals*, who wish to deceive us about *particulars*."[118] Inasmuch as the Enlightenment was, as Peter Gay suggests, "a voyage into abstraction," Jones can be interpreted as a Counter-Enlightenment thinker.[119] But since Jones's rejection of abstraction is his appropriation of the sensualism that accompanied the rise of the new empirical science, his work confirms that the clash between Newtonian abstraction and Hutchinsonian particularity was an "in-house" debate between competing Enlightenment perspectives.[120]

Jones's refusal to embrace abstraction is most evident in his rejection of the Newtonian devolutionary philosophy of history. Jones can be sometimes heard complaining of the increased infidelity in English society, but he does not make this assessment the basis of a philosophy of history.[121] Jones does

---

118. Jones, "Providence," 12.

119. Peter Gay, *The Enlightenment: An Interpretation; The Science of Freedom* (New York: W. W. Norton & Company, 1969), 128.

120. Taylor argues that the idea that the victory of the *philosophes* was inevitable is often fueled by the problematic assumptions that "under certain conditions, human beings will just come to see that scientific thinking is valid, that instrumental rationality pays off, that religious beliefs involve unwarranted leaps, that facts and values are separate" (Charles Taylor, "Two Theories of Modernity," *Hastings Center Report* 25, no. 2 [1995]: 25).

121. The one place I have found where Jones adopts primitivist rhetoric is in his *Letter to the Church of England*, where he mentions the hope of restoring the church "as nearly as might be, to the primitive pattern." Jones bemoans the fact that "revolution hath succeeded Revolution;

not uphold the Anglican establishment because he claims to know its eschatological significance. He endorses it because he is convinced that God's providence always works through the established order. For Jones, providence does not function as it does for deists, in generalized and abstract terms. Providence is not restricted to God's establishment of a natural and moral framework within which creatures have the freedom to explore and create their own providential meaning.[122] To the contrary, God's providence operates on the microcosmic as well as the macrocosmic level. Every object has a unique providential location, and humans are invited, through Scripture words, to explore and uncover it to the extent that Scripture itself explores and uncovers it.

Providential discernment is therefore a matter of relating the part to the whole rather than the whole to the part, and in this Jones's approach betrays the influence of the new experimental science. For Jones, providential discernment is a science of induction. First, particulars are studied empirically in their particularity. They are then related, as scriptural figures, to other scriptural particulars. This accordance is itself the process by which the part is related to the whole—God's providential order of the world. Thus, if a child were to ask Jones about the providential meaning of a flower, he would tell her that it is an emblem of the glory of man, which fades away.[123] And if a fellow theologian were to ask him the same question, he would offer the same answer. He might well divulge several interesting and profound reflections upon this relation that he would withhold from the child, but his reflection would always remain a reflection about flowers and mortals as scriptural figures.[124]

---

every one worse than the former" (Jones, *A Letter to the Church*, 1). Jones's rhetorical emphasis is markedly different than his friend and ally, the last non-juroring bishop, Thomas Cartwright. Cartwright continually elevates the primitive standard, and he looks back longingly to the perfect unity of the primitive church as an ideal that appears to have been hopelessly obscured and impossible to achieve. Cartwright's rhetoric is far closer to that of the Tractarians than that of his contemporary allies. See Thomas Cartwright, *A letter to Jonas Boucher*, April 1794, Non-juror Add. MS D. 30, Bodleian Library, Oxford, UK.

122. Taylor speaks of an anthropocentric shift at the cusp of modernity, which granted credibility to the idea that we only owe God "the achievement of our own good" (Charles Taylor, *A Secular Age* [Cambridge, MA: Belknap, 2007], 222).

123. Jones, *The Book*, 14–15.

124. Jones calls the flower "An Emblem of Mortal Man" (Jones, *The Theological*, 11:197). See also Jones, *Four Discourses*, 6–10, 29–33.

Providential discernment for Jones is not a matter of speculating concerning the great movements of history, but of coming to appreciate the form of creaturely existence. Providential discernment is embodied, protracted, and always limited. This is why Jones takes such great interest in the catechesis of children. Providential discernment begins at birth as the infant begins to respond to the environment into which he has been placed. As his intellect expands, the child will encounter the temptation to become a "freethinker" and be swept up in the intellectual pride that leads to abstract and ideological reasoning. But even as the child reaches adulthood and comes to the height of his intellectual powers, he will not, if he is wise, move beyond his divinely instituted ability to reflect upon the objects he encounters and the revelation he has been given in order to do so.

CONCLUSION

—

"I do not concern myself with great matters
or things too wonderful for me."
—Psalm 131:1b (NIV)

"Providence," says Katherine Sonderegger, "is a doctrine about God: God's way with us creatures; God's act towards and in the cosmos; God's mastering and directing; God's breaking down and healing, his killing and making alive."[1] Providential discernment is the science of describing particular human experiences as acts of God. The writers commonly known as "Hutchinsonians" examined in this study, George Watson, George Horne, and William Jones, all follow John Hutchinson in emphasizing that humans are dependent upon God's initiative because human creatures do not have native access to such divine counsel. Hutchinson had originally written his natural-philosophical works because he worried that Isaac Newton, Samuel Clarke, and their associates had claimed for themselves what only Scripture could provide: the ability to uncover the mysteries of God's engagement with his world.[2]

Hutchinson's emblematic hermeneutic reclaimed the Old Testament as Christian Scripture by making the Old Testament the basis of providential discernment. But because his apologetic is consumed with the task of divulging natural-philosophical order, his work implies that nature is subject to God's beneficent government and history is not. As Watson, Horne, and Jones applied Hutchinson's emblematic interpretive method to the entire scope of Scripture, however, they found themselves interpreting both natural and historical objects as emblems of divine light. This application

---

1. Katherine Sonderegger, "The Doctrine of Providence," in *The Providence of God*, ed. Francesca Aran Murphy and Philip Ziegler (London: T & T Clark, 2009), 145. John Webster similarly emphasizes that providence is a doctrine about God. "Providence," says Webster, "is that work of divine love for temporal creatures whereby God ordains and executes their fulfillment in fellowship with himself" (John Webster, "On the Theology of Providence," in *The Providence of God*, ed. Francesca Aran Murphy and Philip Ziegler [London: T & T Clark, 2009], 158).

2. John Hutchinson, *The Religion of Satan, Or Antichrist, Delineated* (London: 1736), 2; George Watson, *A Letter from the Author of a Late Discourse on the XVIIIth Chapter of Genesis, to the Monthly Reviewers* (London: 1758), 8–9; Horne, *An Apology for Certain Gentlemen in the University of Oxford* (Oxford: 1756), 12–14; William Jones, *The Catholic Doctrine of the Trinity* (London: 1756), xii.

elevated the epistemological status of historical and historically conditioned knowledge and led to the flowering of Hutchinsonian tropological exegesis.[3] The Hutchinsonians were able to present a compelling defense of the Old Testament by demonstrating that, as an equal partner in the Christian canon, it played an indispensable role in helping Christians find their place within God's world.

SCRIPTURE AND PROVIDENCE

The story of the wrestlings of the Newtonians and Hutchinsonians with the Old Testament confirms that it fell from grace at the cusp of modernity because of a shift within the culture concerning the identity of history. Given that the eighteenth-century Old Testament was already a historicized text, a change in the status of the Old Testament accompanied this shift. While the antiquarian scholars of the Renaissance had taken for granted that history was the forum of God's providential oversight of his creation, this providential vision was compromised by the conviction that nature, rather than history, is the forum of God's providential care. Given the historic importance of the Old Testament for establishing that history is a work of God, it comes as no surprise that the rise of the this devolutionary view of history precipitated the fall of the Old Testament.

The wrestlings of Newton, Clarke, Hutchinson, Watson, Horne, and Jones with the Old Testament are equally wrestlings with history. As they struggled to find ways to reckon with an unruly Old Testament text, their presuppositions about history actively propelled them, both in terms of the methods they employed and the conclusions they reached. Newton hoped to confirm the divine authorship of the Old Testament by means of making it the source of mathematical certainties because he took for granted that history had a corrosive effect upon divine truth. This negative valuation of history causes him to engage Old Testament exegesis as the art of extracting mathematical certitude from the text. It was obvious to his protégé Samuel Clarke, however, that the Old Testament was not, as Newton believed, a catalogue

---

3. George Watson, *A Seasonable Admonition to the Church of England: A Sermon Preached before the University of Oxford at St. Mary's* (Oxford: 1755), 3; George Horne, *A Commentary on the Book of Psalms* (Oxford: 1776), 1:ii; William Jones, *A Discourse on the Use and Intention of some Remarkable Passages of the Scripture* (London: 1798), 13.

of immovable numbers. This compelled Clarke—who can be regarded as a harbinger of modern Marcionism—to demote the Old Testament to a sub-scriptural status.

Hutchinson hoped to save the Old Testament, but as he shared Newton's assumption about the devolutionary character of history, he needed a mechanism that would allow him to simultaneously de-historicize and celebrate the Old Testament text. This he found in the antiquarian commonplace of the hieroglyph. For Hutchinson, select Hebrew words could be refashioned as ancient word-pictures which unveil the divine meaning of the objects of the natural world. Once Hutchinson's disciples let go of his Newtonian understanding of historical devolution, however, they no longer felt it necessary to privilege select Hebrew words as hieroglyphs. Given their providential understanding of history, they were confident that God's Word was authoritative for Christian life and conduct, whether it was given in Hebrew to Moses or in Greek to Paul. For Watson, this providential understanding of history was the basis of a canonical hermeneutic—it compelled him to search for the meaning of particular texts by interpreting Scripture with Scripture. Horne's providentialist understanding of history generated a providential understanding of Scripture, nature, and church, but it also led to the decentering of Scripture within his thought. With Jones, however, this understanding of history fueled a robust figural scriptural hermeneutic which regarded Scripture as the basis of history. The textual labors of each author in this study confirms that historical frameworks determine exegetical outcomes.

We might describe this reality by appealing to Charles Taylor's notion of "embodied background understanding." By this Taylor means the "unformulated (and perhaps even unformulable) understandings ... that *could* be formulated as beliefs, but aren't functioning as such in our world." These include my "understanding of myself as an agent with certain powers, of myself as an agent among other agents," and, Taylor adds, my understanding of myself as "an agent moving in certain kinds of social spaces, with a sense of how both I and these spaces inhabit time, a sense of how both I and they relate to the cosmos and to God."[4] Thus, while the researcher might,

---

4. In his article "Two Theories of Modernity," Taylor complains that theorists have often been content to describe transitions taking place at the cusp of modernity in terms of shifts in explicit doctrine. Taylor argues that this favors the prejudice that "modernity arises through the

with luck, find explicit statements people have made about providence, the researcher who finds such statements elusive would be foolish to conclude that the doctrine of providence was unimportant, since it expresses itself at the level of embodied background understanding. As such, it is formed by and expressed indirectly within "modes of ritual, by the kinds of prayer we have been taught, by what we pick up from the attitudes of pious and impious people, and the like."[5]

The current study is consistent with Taylor's groundbreaking research inasmuch as it affirms that the importance of the doctrine of providence becomes evident when research extends beyond formulated beliefs to include cultural frameworks and practices. Yet it also confronts the surprising lack of attention Taylor gives to the Bible in his construction of modernity. If modes of ritual and prayers and attitudes are all the purveyors of the doctrine of providence, then surely too scriptural discourse. Historically, views about providence are expressed exegetically in Christian contexts. This is because the Bible is part of the world and because the Bible talks about God. Those who comment upon the Bible can manage to avoid making statements about providence only with difficulty. And even when they intentionally avoid such statements, their commentary easily betrays their own opinions about God's involvement with his world. This suggests that Taylor may be right to overlook the Bible in his discussion of background understandings, since discourse about the Bible functions, directly, as formulated belief.

The story of the Hutchinsonian quest to save the Old Testament suggests that the Bible is not merely the passive recipient of providential views. Engagement with the scriptural text drove the developing Hutchinsonian understanding of God's ways with his world. In particular, the devoted study of Old Testament words pressed the Hutchinsonians toward a robust understanding of God's providential oversight of nature and history both. The Hutchinsonian answer to the question "What is God doing in the world?" is "the Bible." The Hutchinsonians therefore do not treat the Bible merely

---

dissipation of certain unsupported religious and metaphysical beliefs" (Charles Taylor, "Two Theories of Modernity," *Hastings Center Report* 25, no. 2 [1995]: 28). Taylor insists that there are two deeper levels of understanding that theorists must acknowledge. The first is the symbolic, which expresses itself in rituals, symbols, and works of art. The second is "embodied background understanding" (Taylor, "Two Theories," 29).

5. Taylor, "Two Theories," 29.

as a source which they can consult in their quest to find the hand of God. With Jones in particular we note that—to borrow a phrase from Ephraim Radner—"'Divine providence' is an abstracted synonym for 'the scriptural canon of Old and New Testaments.'"[6]

The impetus behind Hutchinsonianism, as a movement, was the fear that Christian scholars were asking Newton to carry the burden which the Bible had traditionally held. These scholars were historicists in the sense that they interpreted the Bible as a product of history; but they were also providential historicists since they believed that historical scholarship doubled as a mechanism of providential discernment. When they placed the weight of providence upon history, they realized that it was a burden too heavy for history to bear. The disappointment the Newtonians felt with the historical record and which gave rise to their devolutionary view of history was not the skepticism of the chastened historicist, but the despair of the earnest Christian searching for the hand of God in the world.

Newtonian devolutionary history was the by-product of a historical moment which was soon to pass. And with its passing, Newtonian devolutionary history too went "the way of all the earth" (1 Kgs 2:2). But the basic assumptions inherent in their devolutionary philosophy of history were passed on to scholars across Europe and bore fruit not merely in specific intellectual endeavors such as logical positivism, but in the construction of modernity itself. We can note, in particular, how devolutionary history was an important antecedent of the quintessential Enlightenment discipline: philosophy of history. Philosophy of history can be regarded as an eighteenth-century invention, but by the end of the eighteenth century, it had already taken Europe by storm. The very idea of Enlightenment itself depended upon the rise of philosophy of history. The savants of the Enlightenment were those who declared that they alone had the ability to overcome the devolution of history and welcome a new age of reform and progress. But they were only able to do so because they assumed, like their Newtonian forebears, that the artifacts of providence, like seashells scattered on the sands, were accessible to the wandering yet discerning eye. This lends credence to Reventlow's bold claim that the eclipse of the Old Testament as Christian Scripture at the

---

6. Ephraim Radner, *Time and the Word: Figural Reading of the Christian Scriptures* (Grand Rapids: Eerdmans, 2016), 235.

turn of the eighteenth century marks the dawn of modernity. For it was only with the rejection of the traditional Christian understanding of Scripture as the providential order of the world that an Enlightenment project could get off the ground.

The refrain of the Hutchinsonians well into the nineteenth century was a message of warning to all who put God to the test by offering to others a yoke that neither they nor their ancestors had been able to bear (Acts 15:10). Like Newton, the Hutchinsonians took the epistemological consequences of the fall very seriously. While this led Newton to dismiss the work of others, he remained supremely confident of his own ability, as a priest of nature, to unveil the divine and mathematical form of the world. Hutchinson, like Newton, boasted that he had, by his natural-philosophical acuity, found the very hand of God. But as Hutchinson's disciples followed his directive and returned to the Old Testament, they came to believe that Scripture words alone had this revelatory capacity. This has inclined many commentators to regard them as anti-intellectuals and even fideists. Yet for the Hutchinsonians, the elevation of Scripture words was emphatically not an appeal to Christians to "just believe."

The Hutchinsonians demanded that Christians apply themselves with utmost seriousness and devotion to the difficult task of "rightly dividing the word of truth" (2 Tim 2:15 KJV). They equally affirmed that Christians should study secular learning with diligence. Horne, as we saw, celebrated the "widely different nature and genius of each science" and was thus able to endorse Newtonian physico-mathematics and Hutchinsonian scriptural-philosophy as mutually-informing enterprises. Horne's concern was to ensure that each mode of learning was assigned its proper place, and, in Horne's configuration, to regard Newtonian physico-mathematics as the successor of the textually-based natural philosophy of the Renaissance is to commit a category mistake. While Renaissance natural philosophy is a mechanism of providential discernment, physico-mathematics, as the science of measurement and proportion, is not; for providential discernment is not a matter of cold, hard description, but of peering into the mystery of the incarnate Word.

For Horne and Jones, Newtonian physico-mathematics occupies the same methodological space in empirical science that the historical-grammatical method occupies in hermeneutics. Jones, for his part, affirms that as a human artifact—a product of history which testifies to history—every Bible shares an alphabet with the language in which it is written and is accordingly "the subject of critical industry; and much useful labor hath been employed by learned and pious men in learning the letter of scripture from the ambiguities to which all language is subject."[7] Jones equally insists that this learning be put in its proper place. Studying the language of Scripture as human language and studying it as divine language are different pursuits. They must be kept conceptually distinct, however integrated in practice. Studying the language of Scripture as human language teaches about the world behind the text and the place of the text within it. But at most this approach can only serve as preparatory work for the science of providential discernment. Critical scholarship depends upon the further acknowledgement that the human words of the Bible are also divine and therefore figuratively ordered, set within the larger theophanic frame of creation. As Jones puts it, "the language of revelation goes a step farther, and uses some things as the signs of other things; in consequence of which, the world which we now see becomes a sort of commentary on the mind of God."[8] Some have been inclined to see the Hutchinsonian emblematic interpretation of Scripture and the historical-grammatical approaches of modernity as competing exegetical methods. Indeed, the *Monthly Review* summarily dismissed Jones's published *A Course of Lectures on the Figurative Language of the Holy Scripture* as "unable to bear the test of sound criticism or sober reasoning."[9] This assessment seems to be unable to acknowledge the distinction between critical and figural exegesis. But treating historical-grammatical approaches as mechanisms of providential discernment is a category mistake, just as evaluating figural approaches according to modern exegetical criteria misses the mark.[10]

---

7. William Jones, *A Course of Lectures on the Figurative Language of the Holy Scripture* (London: 1787), 6.

8. Jones, *A Course*, 9–10.

9. Anonymous, "Art. IX. A Course of Lectures on the figurative Language of the Holy Scriptures," *The Monthly Review, From January to June, inclusive, 1789*, vol. 80 (London: 1789): 403.

10. In this, Jones's approach harkens back to that of the great Cappadocian, Gregory of Nyssa, who insisted, in his exposition of *The Life of Moses*, that historical exposition and Christian meditation remain conceptually distinct. For Nyssa, *historia*, the exposition of the historical account of Moses's life, was not a secular account since it presumed God's involvement. (How could it be, since it depended upon the words of the Bible!) Yet such an exposition, however satisfying, could never be more than merely the preparatory work required for *theoria*, the divine contemplation

For the modern critic, it is enough to study and expound the history in question, for such an exposition is itself providentially disclosive because history is the grounds of providence. The one who understands the history thus, in this act of understanding, identifies the hand of God. The Newtonians can be regarded as a source of this conceit, for they had no doubt that the natural philosopher that gave a true account of the mechanical workings of nature simultaneously mastered the science of providential discernment. Conversely, within the emblematic frame of the Hutchinsonians, understanding Scripture is itself the goal of providential discernment, since providence is not an attribute of history or nature but is rather an abstracted synonym for "the scriptural canon of Old and New Testaments." The success of the Hutchinsonian project to revive the fortunes of the Old Testament was that it insisted that Scripture is the grounds of providence, and in this it refused to allow the Old Testament to inhabit a framework which ultimately regarded it as dispensable.

SCRIPTURAL EMBLEMATICISM AND CREATURELY EXISTENCE

In drawing upon the well-established tradition of emblematicism, the Hutchinsonians creatively exploited the potential of Scripture words to reframe the objects of the world as emblems of an overarching moral order. The Hutchinsonians applied this tradition anew within an Enlightenment context captivated by empirical science.[11] If empirical knowledge is fundamental to the acquisition of authentic natural-philosophical knowledge, they reasoned, so too it must be necessary to discern God's hand within the world.[12] The challenge, for the Hutchinsonians, was to convince their empirically minded contemporaries—and particularly those who had embraced the Newtonian conceit that the providential order of nature was unveiled by physico-mathematics—that the mediation of texts was necessary for providential discernment. But emblematicism was also intuitive to

---

of the history in question for purposes of Christian edification. See Gregory of Nyssa, *The Life of Moses*, trans. Abraham J. Malherbe and Everett Ferguson (New York: Paulist, 1978).

11. John Manning, *The Emblem* (London: Reaktion, 2002), 38.

12. John Hutchinson, *Moses's Principia, Part II* (London: 1749), xxxvi; George Watson, *Christ the Light of the World: A Sermon Preached before the University of Oxford at St. Peter's* (Oxford: 1750), 7; Horne, *A Commentary*, 1:81; Jones, *A Course of Lectures*, 435–36.

eighteenth-century sensibilities given that it was coherent with the sensualist epistemology of the day. Hutchinsonian scriptural emblematicism presented the objects found in the Book of Nature and the Book of Scripture to
the Christian public as juxtaposed empirical artifacts which invite mutual
interpretation.

While for the Hutchinsonians Scripture words are emblematic mottos
which reveal the workings of God, these words depend upon the world to generate this knowledge: for within the emblematic frame, mottos only generate
providential knowledge when they are set in apposition to images—images
which depict the world. Hutchinson intended to give an account of the basic
elements which underlie human experience—the sun which warms, the light
which gives sight, and the air which grants life. Once Hutchinson identified
these presently experienced realities within the pages of the Old Testament,
the stage was set for the emblematic enactments of the later Hutchinsonians.
Having overcome his suspicion of human words as historically embedded,
they were able to identify Scripture words as created artifacts which serve as
interpretive keys for providential discernment. As scriptural emblematicists,
the Hutchinsonians received Scripture words anew as objects of sense, and
they received other objects of sense, conversely, as words which are somehow revelatory. Jones gives voice to this blurred distinction between words
and things when he claims that "God hath made larks to teach us what we
ought to be."[13]

By their consistent application of a sensualist epistemology to natural-philosophical specimens and Scripture words, the Hutchinsonians
oppose rationalists such as Clarke who suppose providential discernment
can be achieved through deductive reasoning from first principles. Although
commentators have described the Hutchinsonian sensualist epistemology
as Lockean, I have de-emphasized this connection.[14] For Locke, knowledge
must be acquired by means of engagement with sensual objects because

---

13. William Jones, *The Book of Nature* (London: 1788), 6.

14. Albert Kuhn, "Glory or Gravity: Hutchinson vs. Newton," *Journal of the History of Ideas*
22 (1961): 318; X. William Carroll, "Hutchinsonisme: Une vue de la nature come Théophanie au
cours du dix-huitième siècle" (PhD diss., University of Strasbourg, 1968), 245–46; C. B. Wilde,
"Hutchinsonianism, Natural Philosophy and Religious Controversy in Eighteenth Century
Britain," *History of Science* 18 (1980): 3; C. D. A. Leighton, "'Knowledge of Divine Things': A Study
of Hutchinsonianism," *History of European Ideas* 26 (2000): 161.

there is no such thing as innate ideas.[15] This leads Locke to believe that individuals must generate their own knowledge through personal reflection. The Hutchinsonians agree with Locke that there is no such thing as innate ideas.[16] But for the Hutchinsonians, this makes humans dependent upon the ideas of others and, most importantly, upon Scripture.

While Locke's sensualism entails the rejection of tradition, Hutchinsonian sensualism establishes the need for it. For the Hutchinsonains, the things humans encounter from birth—families, various public institutions, and creation itself—have been providentially ordered by God, and they exercise their providential vocation prior to and independently of our encounters with them; they exert a powerful influence upon us before we can hope to influence them, for God has ordained that they would serve as our teachers and our guides.[17] Thus, Jones complains that while the revolutionary descendants of Locke wax eloquent about "the *natural rights of man*," these exist "in a *state of nature only:* that is, of man considered as an *unsociable independent savage.*"[18] Jones insists that this condition exists only in abstraction, for "as soon as man becomes a member of society ... he is bound as a *moral agent.*"[19] The established order seems, to the secular eye, to be calling out for revolution. It must be upended, for the form of the Lord within it is nowhere to be seen. For the scriptural emblematicist, however, the world which receives us before we receive it is to be upheld since it is "a commentary on the mind of God."[20]

---

15. For an introduction to Locke's epistemology, see I. C. Tipton, ed., *Locke on Human Understanding: Selected Essays* (Oxford: Oxford University Press, 1977).

16. William Jones, *An Essay on the First Principles of Natural Philosophy* (London: 1762), 8.

17. See, for example, William Jones, *The Book of Nature* (London: 1788). For an account of how belief in tradition can form the basis of an approach to ethics, see Alisdair MacIntyre, *Three Rival Versions of Moral Inquiry: Encyclopaedia, Genealogy, and Tradition* (Notre Dame, IN: University of Notre Dame Press, 1990).

18. Jones, *The Theological,* 12:458. Natural rights are, Jones continues, "the rights of eating, drinking, sleeping, hunting, fishing, propagating his species, whipping his children, and defending himself against wild men and wild beasts."

19. Jones, *The Theological,* 12:458. See also Jones, *A Letter to John,* 11, 14. Charles Taylor is only echoing Jones when he derides the representational epistemology of Descartes and Locke in the following terms: "The very idea of an individual who might become aware of himself, and then only subsequently, or at least independently, determine what importance others have for him and what he will accept as good, belongs to post-Cartesian, foundationalist fantasy" (Taylor, "Two Theories," 32).

20. Jones, *A Course,* 9–10.

The scriptural emblematicist recognizes, however, that gaining access
to the mind of God is no easy thing. Its achievement requires something
more than simply proof-texting a scriptural text. This is precisely Jones's
assessment of Thomas Paine's (1737–1809) Lockean defense of the French
Revolution.[21] First Samuel 8:7 recounts that God told the prophet Samuel
that the Israelites desired to have a king because they had rejected God as
their king, and Paine seized upon this verse to argue that human kingship is
inconsistent with divine kingship.[22] Jones insists, however, that "to make our
case in England parallel to this; and to show from the case of the Hebrews,
that we ought not to have George the Third for our king ... some monstrous
suppositions must be made."[23] The providential significance of all objects,
even Scripture words, is obscure and can only be grasped as they are subjected to what the church fathers called "the mind of Scripture." Though the
Hutchinsonians were not immune from proof-texting, their hermeneutical approach suggests that it is only as knowledge of particulars is filtered
through Scripture that their location within the providential order is distilled.

For the Hutchinsonians, the Book of Nature and the Book of Scripture
can be described as overlapping realities. Indeed, the set of the objects within
the Book of Nature is also the set of the objects found within the Book of
Scripture. This does not mean that human interpreters can always note a
one-to-one correspondence between the things they see and the words of
Scripture. But it does mean that the providential significance of every object
of sense can be at least partially understood when Scripture is interpreted
with Scripture and nature with nature. Because Newtonianism rejected the
emblematic conviction that words are necessary for providential discernment, it generated an anemic natural-philosophical apologetic, which was
given new life by William Paley at the end of the eighteenth century in his
so-called "Watchmaker Argument." Within the Newtonian frame, each object
of the natural world testifies to its Creator in the same way: each object
confirms the original act of divine creation. No object is indispensable, for
what one object teaches, so does another. Within the Hutchinsonian figural
frame, however, each object testifies to its Creator with a distinct voice which

---

21. Thomas Paine, *Common Sense: Addressed to the Inhabitants of America* (London: 1792), 16.

22. William Jones, *A Letter to John Bull, Esq. From His Second Cousin Thomas Bull* (London: 1793), 26–27.

23. Jones, *A Letter*, 27.

is rendered through Scripture words. The distinctiveness of this voice is given both in the particular features of the object itself and the particular Scripture words which are used to interpret it. Thus, while Newtonianism presses toward philosophical monism, Hutchinsonianism upholds created distinction. And while Newtonianism draws the eye away from creation to ruminate upon a distant Watchmaker God, Hutchinsonianism beckons the eye back to creation in the hope of getting a glimpse of the immanent Word.

Given that Hutchinsonianism treats all Scripture words as figures of providential discernment, it elevates the Old Testament to the status of equal partner in the Christian canon. This equilibrium however, does not obliterate the distinction between Old and New. There are at least two ways in which Hutchinsonian scriptural emblematicism creates a unique profile for the Old Testament. The first is a direct consequence of the size of the Old Testament. The Old Testament occupies a central position within an emblematic framework given that it has three times as many words as the New Testament. But the importance of the Old Testament for providential discernment isn't just a function of its size. Its importance stems from the fact that the New Testament is sparse in its depiction of human life. And we might note that even in the detail it gives, it must be seen primarily as a divine commentary upon the life which is rendered in the Old Testament rather than life as it was lived within the Roman Empire. The Old Testament gives an expansive account of human life as it is received, under God, in all of its textured nuance and contradiction. Were it not for the Old Testament, we could only say with difficulty that the Bible speaks about our world. And it is our world, as depicted in the Old Testament, which Christ redeems.

The second reason the Old Testament has a unique profile for emblematic providential discernment has to do with the body of Christ. It is true that the New Testament is, as Radner has put it, forced to come to terms with "the disappearing body of Jesus."[24] But the documents of the New Testament, as apostolic witness, testify to the transformative presence of this body within human life. While Christian tradition has historically affirmed that this body is equally present within the Old Testament, the history of biblical interpretation confirms that finding it there has been a matter of struggle and wonder

---

24. Ephraim Radner, "The Exegesis of the One God," in *The Identity of Israel's God in Christian Scripture*, ed. Don Collett et al. (Atlanta: SBL, 2020), 34.

both. The Christian that labors after Christ's disappearing body finds in the Old Testament the order of this particular experience. The task of finding the figure of Christ within the pages of the Old Testament thus becomes, for Christians, the probationary yet redemptive hardship of searching for his fleeting presence in their own lives.

Figural readers of the Old Testament acknowledge that providential significance is not readily apparent. To interpret an object as an emblem or figure is to acknowledge that its significance is not contained exclusively within it, but rather depends upon another. The interpreter who treats either a biblical or a contemporary object as an emblem or figure equally acknowledges that her interpretation is "provisional and incomplete."[25] As Jones puts it, "As there are many wonders in Nature, into which no eye can penetrate, so can we discern but in part of the manifold wisdom of God in the inexhaustible treasures of his word."[26] Once people come to believe they can achieve providential discernment without Scripture, they will happily do so: in a world in which scholars boldly claim direct access to providence, the voices of figural readers are easily drowned out. And when individual interpreters, such as Horne, sometimes claim direct access to providence and sometimes admit only mediated access, their pursuit of mediated access tends to contract. The preference for philosophies of history over figural views of history that marks the modern era is not unrelated to the contracting of scriptural authority witnessed since the eighteenth century.

Figural reading is characterized by an intellectual humility that makes upholding scriptural authority possible. Figural readers turn to Scripture because they acknowledge that they cannot hope to discern the providential order of either history or nature. Hutchinson may have been off base in the way he sought to resuscitate the Old Testament as a source book for natural-philosophical knowledge. He was, however, right to discern that the intellectual project of the Newtonians was corrosive to scriptural authority. That

---

25. As Auerbach puts it, "figural interpretation implies the interpretation of one worldly event through another; the first signifies the second, the second fulfills the first. Both remain historical events; yet both, looked at in this way, have something provisional and incomplete about them" (Erich Auerbach, "Figura," in *Scenes from the Drama of European Literature*, Theory and History of Literature 9, ed. Wlad Godzich and Jochen Schulte-Sasse [Minneapolis: University of Minnesota Press, 1984], 58).

26. Jones, *A Discourse*, 32.

Newton was willing to claim for himself the ability to conceptually order the entire scope of chronological history (not to mention the fact that he believed he had found the epoch of the Olympiad!) betrays an intellectual hubris that is allergic to scriptural authority. Newton's valuation of history as subject to corruption led him to believe that his role, as scholar and reformer both, was to impose a mathematical and conceptual analysis upon the historical record to reintroduce providence to history. Newton's legacy therefore isn't merely to be found among speculative ideologues such as Clarke. It is to be found among all well-meaning religious reformers who look with horror upon the devolution of history and claim to have identified the means of overcoming it.

Figural readers refuse to concede to secularism that the providential order of the historical realm is inaccessible. Indeed, they insist that wonderful and surprising knowledge of God's providential ordering of history can be achieved through engagement with Scripture words. Nevertheless, because they refuse to impose conceptual frameworks onto the historical record, they can still say, "I do not concern myself with great matters or things too wonderful for me" (Ps 131:1b NIV). This is more than appropriate given that we live in an age in which philosophers concede that the basic questions surrounding the philosophy of history remain fundamentally unanswered.[27] Perhaps the basic question concerning providential discernment, given this state of affairs, however, is not the question of the extent of human cognitive capabilities.[28] Perhaps the basic question is where to begin. If the Hutchinsonians were still with us, they would ask that we begin the quest for providential discernment with the Old Testament. For these Scriptures leave no doubt as to where we are: O Lord, "my times are in your hands" (Ps 31:15 NIV).

---

27. According to Little, these include "the nature of the reality of historical structures and entities," "the nature of causal influence among historical events or structures," the role of "the interpretation of the 'lived experience' of past actors" in historical understanding, and a valuation of "the overall confidence we can have about statements about the past" (Daniel Little, "Philosophy of History," *Stanford Encyclopedia of Philosophy*, accessed July 20, 2015, http://plato. stanford.edu/entries/history/).

28. The assumption that the virtue of intellectual humility is a matter of identifying the extent of human cognitive limitations continues to be widespread. Dow, for instance, endorses intellectual humility as "an uncompromising honest appraisal of the capacities and limitations of our minds" (Philip E. Dow, *Virtuous Minds: Intellectual Character Development* [Downers Grove, IL: InterVarsity, 2013], 70–71). One of the difficulties with this approach is that the idea that humans have the ability to discern exactly how far they can proceed before they pass the pale of human reason may well contradict the very notion of intellectual humility.

EPILOGUE

—

THE END OF HUTCHINSONIAN SCRIPTURAL EMBLEMATICISM

The early nineteenth century proved to be the high watermark of Hutchinsonian influence.[1] In 1800 there were several bishops with strong ties to the movement, and in the first decades of the century Hutchinsonian influence continued to grow, building upon the scholarly contributions of Horne and especially Jones.[2] Jones told his student William Kirby (1759–1850) that he was surprised to find that his anti-revolutionary pamphlet *Letters to John Bull from His Brother Thomas* had been read "from the king to the cobbler."[3] In 1792 Jones founded, with William Stevens, the Society for the Reformation of Principles, which Peter Nockles attributes with granting High churchmen "their own organization and agenda,"[4] and in 1793 Jones and Stevens again combined to create the *British Critic*.[5] The quiet Nayland parsonage became

---

1. Hutchinsonianism arguably had an even greater influence in Scotland than it had in England. Hutchinsonian Alexander Nicoll from Aberdeen was elected Regius Professor of Hebrew at Oxford in 1822 (John Henry, introduction to *Newtonianism in Eighteenth-Century Britain: Moses's Principia* [Asheville, NC: Thoemmes Continuum, 2004], xxx). Katz remarks that in 1820 there was hardly a single non-Hutchinsonian minister in the diocese of Aberdeen (David S. Katz, "The Occult Bible: Hebraic Millenarianism in Eighteenth-Century England," in *The Millenarianism and Messianism in Early Modern European Culture, Vol. 3: The Millenarian Turn; Millenarian Contexts of Science, Politics and Everyday Anglo-American Life in the Seventeenth and Eighteenth Centuries*, ed. James E. Force and Richard H. Popkin [Dordrecht: Kluwer Academic, 2001], 124).

2. Churton comments that Jones "retained to his last years the lively spirit of a boy with more than a common share of manly wisdom," and his most lasting contributions to the movement were made in old age (Edward Churton, *Memoir of Joshua Watson*, 2nd ed. [Oxford: 1861], 15–16).

3. Jones also told Kirby that the king and queen had read it and that 30,000 copies "went off at a single order" (John Freeman, *The Life of Rev. William Kirby, M.A.* [London: 1852], 37).

4. Peter Nockles, *The Oxford Movement in Context: Anglican High Churchmanship, 1760–1857* (Cambridge: Cambridge University Press, 1994), 271.

5. The story of how the Tractarians came to take control of the *British Critic* is an interesting one. Nockles draws attention to the way Pusey used Watson's good name in order to gain control of the magazine before breaking off from old High-Church principles (Nockles, *The Oxford*, 277–82). Churton believed that the Tractarian takeover of the *British Critic* was its death. "It was

the center of activity both for aging Hutchinsonians, including Stevens, Wetherell, John Parkhurst (1728-1797), and Samuel Glasse (1735-1812), and young students, including Kirby and Joshua Watson (1771-1855).[6] The self-effacing Stevens, who referred to himself simply as "Nobody," went on to found the Club of Nobody's Friends with Joshua Watson. The club mutated into the Hackney Phalanx under the leadership of Watson and the "bishop-maker," Henry Handley Norris (1771-1850). The Phalanx came to exert an enormous influence on ecclesiastical appointments, and its philanthropic initiatives rivaled those of the more famous evangelical Clapham Sect.[7]

The first decades of the nineteenth century also witnessed the erosion of the scriptural basis of the movement and, with this, its distinctiveness. What remained was Hutchinsonian establishmentarianism, and under Watson and Norris the movement morphed to become a wing of what can justly be called the High-Church Party. This is not to say that the influence of Hutchinsonian scriptural study immediately ceased. The Rivington publishing house, the house that had helped found the *British Critic*, published Jones's collected works in twelve volumes in 1801, 1810, and 1826. Jones's scriptural studies were also diffused to a wider readership through the publication of individual works. His *Lectures* were published at least eight times in London, as well as in Philadelphia and Oxford.[8] Horne's collected works were published on four occasions in London and three in New York,[9] and the demand for his commentary on the Psalms was remarkable: it was printed in full or in part on at least forty occasions in London, nine in New York, six in Edinburgh, three in Philadelphia, two in York, and one in Dublin, Oxford, Glasgow, and Warsaw.[10]

---

abandoned," Churton says, "after it had ceased to represent the principles which gave it birth, on the shoals of a later and more unhappy controversy" (*Memoir*, 1:29-30).

6. See William Jones, *A Letter from a Tutor to His Pupils* (London: 1780). See also Freeman, *The Life*, 34-40; Churton, *Memoir*, 27-29.

7. During Liverpool's long premiership, Norris gained the title of "Bishop-maker": "It was said that every see was offered to him, with the request that if he could not take it himself, he would be so good as to recommend someone else" ("Review of T. Mozley's Reminiscences," *The Literary Churchman and Church Fortnightly* 28 [1882]: 249). See Robert Andrews, *Lay Activism and the High Church Movement of the Late Eighteenth Century* (Leiden, Brill, 2015).

8. London (Hamilton, 1808, 1811, 1821, 1849; SPCK, 1850, 1854, 1863-1864, 1890); Philadelphia (Harrison, 1818), Oxford (Parker, 1848).

9. London (Johnson, 1809; Rivington, 1818, 1830; Longman, 1831); New York (Standord and Sworts, 1846, 1853; Onderdonk, 1848).

10. London (Robinson, 1802; Lackingham, 1804; Baynes, 1806; Johnson, 1808; Rivington, 1811, 1816, 1819, 1820, 1822, 1823, 1826, 1830; Lindley and Murray, 1812; Rivington/SPCK, 1812; Suttaby,

Through widespread publication, Hutchinsonian scriptural study became part of the religious fabric not just of High churchmanship but of the nation.[11] A few editions of Horne's commentary, notably Edward Irving's 1845 edition, included new scholarly introductions, but most publishers came to treat the work as strictly devotional.[12] Jones's work on figuration equally came to be endorsed and applied instrumentally. For example, leading evangelical Edward Bickersteth (1786–1850) found Jones useful as a theologian because of his powerful defense of orthodox Trinitarian doctrine, and helpful as a biblical interpreter because of his work on figures and types.[13] In Bickersteth's work there is, however, no indication that Jones's emblematic hermeneutic might serve as the basis of a providential vision. Jones's disciple Kirby, one of the founders of the modern discipline of entomology, continued to promote Jones's thoroughgoing scriptural emblematicism.[14] But it is within the movement itself that the contraction of Hutchinsonian figuration is most apparent.

Hutchinsonian William Van Mildert (1765–1836), one of the original members of the Club of Nobody's Friends, rose to become one of the most important churchmen of the first half of the nineteenth century. He is chiefly known as the champion of the *ancien régime* in the tumultuous years leading up to the parliamentary reforms of 1829–1832, and as founder of the University of

---

1815; Sharpe, 1820; Richardson, 1821; Tegg, 1824, 1836, 1839, 1840, 1842; Whittaker, 1825; Longman, 1831, 1835, 1843, 1856; Webster, 1835; Hatchard, 1836; Rickerby, 1836; SPCK, 1843, 1848; Robinson, 1845; Richardson, 1849; Nelson, 1851; Bohn, 1852; Nelson, 1860, 1871; Ward, 1900); New York (Ward, 1824; Irving, 1845; Carter, 1845, 1849, 1854, 1856, 1859, 1869; Onderdonk, 1846); Edinburgh (Lindley and Murray, 1812; Smith, 1813; Gilles, 1829; Blair and Bruce, 1829; Nelson and Brown, 1831, 1835); Philadelphia (Bradford and Inskeep, 1812; Towar, 1822, 1833); York (Wilson, 1812, 1829); Dublin (Napper, 1800); Oxford (Crowther, 1802); Glasgow (Chalmers, 1825); Warsaw (1839). Horne's commentary continues to be in print.

11. The ability of Horne's work to make itself useful to Christians who did not share the Hutchinsonian perspective is perhaps what allowed it to eventually outstrip Jones's.

12. A characteristic example of this devotional approach is W. W. Robinson's edition entitled *A Pocket Classic: Commentary on the Penitential Psalms, Psalms for Pardon of Sin, and Intercessory Prayer* (London: 1845). Christians wanting to engage the Psalms academically turned instead to Thomas Hartwell Horne's *Introduction to the Critical Study and Knowledge of the Holy Scriptures* (London: 1818), which by the 1830s had become mandatory reading for Oxonian undergraduates.

13. Edward Bickersteth, *The Works of Rev. E. Bickersteth, Rector of Manton, Hertfordshire* (New York: 1832), 643, 649. For Bickersteth's approach to figural reading, see Bickersteth, *The Works*, 41.

14. Kirby is widely regarded to be one of the fathers of the modern discipline of entomology. Kirby's fascination with the tropological significance of insects has its roots in Jones's comprehensive tropological vision. See J. F. M. Clarke, "History from the Ground Up: Bugs, Political Economy, and God in Kirby and Spence's Introduction to Entomology (1815–1856)," *Isis* 97 (2006): 25–58. See also Freeman, *The Life*.

Durham (1832). Van Mildert's sermons "stood squarely in the Hutchinsonian tradition" of Horne and Jones.[15] Van Mildert sets out to defend figural reading in his *Bampton Lectures*. He articulates several rules for determining when such reading is appropriate, and he insists that the "most flagrant abuse" of figural reading is "the violation of the literal sense itself."[16] He observes that

> The best writers agree that before figurative or mystical interpreta-
> tion be admitted, some urgent reason, even something like necessity,
> should be produced, either for receding from the literal meaning of
> the words, or for engrafting upon the words themselves.[17]

Horne only employs figural reading when he finds that the literal sense is unable to render devotional import, but he nevertheless views figural and literal interpretation as consistent since both can be fruitfully employed devotionally. Van Mildert, however, insists that the literal sense must explicitly call for figural reading, and this leads him to define the relationship between figural and literal interpretation negatively: figural reading must be studied not because of its explanatory power or its ability to render tropological or devotional readings, but because it is an unruly beast that must be tamed and subdued. Van Mildert's great fear was that revolutionaries and enthusiasts were threatening the religious establishment, and this fear dictated his response to Hutchinsonian figural reading. As he rose to become the great defender of the establishment, the scriptural basis of this defense, which he had inherited from Horne and Jones, was all but forgotten.

It was with the High-Church descendants of the Hutchinsonians, the Tractarians, that Hutchinsonian scriptural emblematicism had the most lasting effect.[18] Edward Pusey and John Keble had a high regard for Horne

15. E. A. Varley, *Last of the Prince Bishops: William Van Mildert and the High Church Movement in the Early Nineteenth Century* (Cambridge: Cambridge University Press, 1992), 42.

16. William Van Mildert, *An Inquiry into the General Principles of Scripture-Interpretation, in Eight Sermons Preached [...] at the Lecture Founded by the Late Rev. John Bampton, M. A.*, 2nd ed. (Oxford: 1815), 241.

17. Van Mildert, *An Inquiry*, 239.

18. Horne deserves recognition as the fountainhead of Tractarian piety. Horne's eucharistic piety was consistent with that of nineteenth-century High churchmen. Nevertheless, this piety seems to have been regarded as extremely idiosyncratic in Horne's day, and it can therefore hardly be used to substantiate his leadership of a distinct party. Magdalen College archivist Darwall-Smith observes that "Magdalen became the stage on which the new President developed his distinctive devotions. He observed fasting; in the 1780s he placed lighted candles on the

and Jones as theologians and as biblical interpreters. Keble's figural reading of Scripture, as expressed in Tract 89, *On the Mysticism attributed to the
Early Fathers of the Church*, and that of Pusey, as expressed in his "Lectures
on Types and Prophecies of the Old Testament," both bear strong marks of
Hutchinsonian influence.[19] Pusey's predecessor as Regius Professor of Hebrew

---

altar during celebration of the Eucharist; and he occasionally practiced private confession—all
very unusual things at this date" (Robin Darwall-Smith, "The Monks of Magdalen, 1688-1854,"
in *Magdalen College, Oxford: A History*, ed. L. W. B. Brockliss [Oxford: Magdalen College, 2008],
339). Darwall-Smith also relates that the young demy Henry Best was surprised by Horne's
religious formality: "The President," says Best, "even bowed to the altar on leaving the chapel,
without any dread lest the picture of Christ bearing the Cross, by Ludovico Caracci [sic], should
convict him of idolatry. Here we all turned towards the altar during the recital of the Creed"
(Henry Best, *Four Years in France* [London: 1826], 8-9). Horne's espousal of "Catholic" devotion
to Christ is seen in his sermon *Christ the Object of Religious Adoration: And Therefore, Very God: A
Sermon Preached before the University of Oxford, at St. Mary's* (Oxford: 1775). Horne was "one of
the few Georgian theologians to win approval from Tractarians in the 1830s" (Darwall-Smith,
"The Monks," 266). Darwall-Smith is convinced that the formal worship practices of the Oxford
movement had their rise at Magdalen through the influence of Horne and Horne's successor
Martin Routh. The relationship between Hutchinsonianism and Tractarianism is highlighted
in Nockles, *The Oxford*, 13, 16, 23, 45-47, 54-58, 65, 194, 270.

19.   Edward Bouverie Pusey, Lectures on Types and Prophecies of the Old Testament: written
mainly in July—August, 1836, LBV-151, Pusey House, Oxford, UK. John Keble, *On the Mysticism
Attributed to the Early Fathers of the Church* (London: 1841). The most complete treatment of the
relationship between Hutchinsonian and Tractarian figural exegesis is George Derrick Westhaver,
"The Living Body of the Lord: E. B. Pusey's 'Types and Prophecies of the Old Testament' " (PhD diss.,
University of Durham, 2012). Westhaver pays tribute to Jones as Pusey's most direct antecedent.
His fundamental complaint is that Jones is restrained in his application of figural exegesis. He
criticizes Jones for only using figural readings authorized by the New Testament (Westhaver, "The
Living," 276). Because Jones consistently employs the principle of canonical mediation, there is a
sense in which all his interpretations are "authorized" by Scripture. Nevertheless, although Jones
may well stick to conventional figural readings in his lectures, his discourses and sermons are
filled with creative and sometimes curious figural readings of scriptural texts. See, for example,
Wiliam Jones, *Zoologia Ethica: A Disquisition Concerning the Mosaic Distinction of Animals into Clean
and Unclean* (London: 1773). Westhaver claims that one could read Jones's lectures alongside Van
Mildert's lectures without "the clear sense that they were advocating a radically different kind of
approach" ("The Living," 279). Even my brief treatment of Van Mildert makes it plain, however,
that Van Mildert's extremely truncated figural reading looks nothing like Jones's thoroughgoing scriptural emblematicism, as articulated in chapter 6 of this work. Westhaver concludes his
treatment of Jones's relation to Pusey by observing that Pusey's claim that "Cain's first sin was
not murder, but the refusal to read the history of his parents typically, would seem out of place in
Jones' *Lectures*" ("The Living," 279). In actual fact, Pusey may well have taken this idea from Jones.
Jones claims that the end of patriarchal emblematic interpretation came not with Cain's sin, but
with Adam's (Jones, *A Course*, 264, 265). Jones himself borrows this idea from Hutchinson (John
Hutchinson, *A Treatise of Power Essential and Mechanical* [London: 1732], 43). Nockles observes that
one of Jones's sermons "strikingly prefigures" the argument Pusey makes in his lectures (Nockles,
The Oxford, 207). Westhaver has refined his arguments about Pusey's relationship to Jones in
Continuity and Development: Looking for Typological Treasure with William Jones of Nayland
and E. B. Pusey," *Bulletin of the John Rylands Library, Religion in Britain, 1660-1900: Essays in Honour
of Peter B. Nockles*, 97, no. 1 (2021): 161-78.

at Oxford, Alexander Nicoll (1793–1828), was a Scottish Hutchinsonian who sought to defend scriptural figuration according to the principles of sound criticism. The Old Testament, Nicoll argued, could not be jettisoned given the New Testament's prominent "admixture of Hebraeisms."[20] Pusey, for his part, followed Hutchinson both in praising the Hebrew tongue as the "picture-language of the East" and in treating Hebrew words as emblems of light. The figural reading of the Old Testament that Pusey endorses in his lectures, like that of Jones, is thoroughgoing. Pusey refuses to be constrained by the figural readings of the New Testament authors, and he is willing to apply his figural method to every created object he encounters.[21]

What distinguishes Pusey and Keble's hermeneutic from that of Jones and Horne is Pusey and Keble's extensive appeal to the church fathers.[22] The extent of his appeal points to the fundamental difference between the Hutchinsonian and Tractarian approaches. Following eighteenth-century deist Thomas Woolston (1668–1733), Pusey and Keble insist that figural reading is a key component of pristine Christianity.[23] Pusey boasted, "Whatever I have received, I received on the authority of the Ancient Church."[24] The figural hermeneutic he received he received from the early church, and this compels him to endorse it.

---

20. Alexander Nicoll, *Sermons* (Oxford: 1830), 106; see also 141–98. Pusey completed and published Nicoll's Bodleian catalogue in 1835 (R. S. Simpson, "Alexander Nicoll," *Oxford Dictionary of National Biography*, July 20, 2015, http://www.oxforddnb.com.myaccess.library.utoronto.ca/view/article/20171?docPos=2).

21. Westhaver, "The Living," 214–56. Pusey's claim that "everything is a type" echoes Jones (Jones, *Four*, 4; *A Course*, 43).

22. Westhaver observes that, unlike Pusey, Jones seldom quotes patristic sources (Westhaver, "The Living," 278n77).

23. Woolston reasoned that if his contemporaries were truly committed to the reinstitution of the primitive ideal, they needed to embrace the primitive biblical hermeneutic. See Thomas Woolston, *Origenis Adamantii Espitola ad doctores Whitbeium, Waterlandium, Whistonium* (London: 1720). See also *The Life of Thomas Woolston, with an Account of His Writings* (London: 1733); David Ney, "Reconciling the Old and New Testaments in the Eighteenth-Century Debate over Prophecy," in *Change and Transformation: Essays in Anglican History*, ed. Thomas P. Power (Eugene, OR: Pickwick, 2013), 89–91.

24. Edward Bouverie Pusey, "A Letter to the Bishop-Elect of Oxford, 27 November 1845," in Henry Parry Liddon, *Life of Edward Bouverie Pusey* (London: 1894), 3:44. The extent to which Pusey endorses Jones, therefore, is the extent to which he finds that Jones is at one with the church fathers. "Jones," says Pusey's biographer, is one of those found "in communion of thought and sympathy with the ancient church" (quoted in Westhaver, "The Living," 270). The mysticism that Keble sought to reintroduce to his context through the figural reading of Scripture is likewise that of the church fathers.

The extent to which the application of this hermeneutic is itself necessary to assist in his grand project, however, is unclear. If Pusey's extant
sermons are any indication, the answer seems to be that it is not that necessary at all.[25] When Keble, on the other hand, left Oxford and disappeared
into the obscurity of Hursley, he brought his patristic figural hermeneutic
with him and deployed it as the basis of his homiletic.[26] The figural reading
of the Old Testament passed silently from Pusey and Keble to a few Anglo-
Catholic Victorian poets such as Christina Rossetti (1830–1894), and it found
robust expression in the twentieth century through the scriptural figura-
tions of the great Anglo-Catholic theologian Lionel Thornton (1884–1960).[27]
Pusey and Keble's figural hermeneutic, however, was widely ignored. It was
ignored not because it was regarded as peculiar—though it was—but because
it was deemed unnecessary for the reinstitution of apostolic Christianity.[28]

The Tractarians were zealous in their quest to obtain historical knowledge. Following the universal historians of old, they sought historical knowledge because they wanted to understand God's providential engagement with
history. But above all they sought historical knowledge because they wanted

---

25. I have not been able to access all of Pusey's extant sermons, but a preliminary survey
suggests he preached from the Old Testament even less than Clarke did. Indeed, he had little
reason to, since his primary object was to introduce New Testament Christianity into his own
context. Pusey's *A Course of Sermons on Solemn Subjects* has seventeen sermons on New Testament
texts and two on Old Testament texts. The third volume of his *Parochial Sermons* includes nine-
teen sermons on New Testament texts and only one on an Old Testament text. A mere 6 percent
of the sermons included in these two volumes are on Old Testament texts (Edward Bouverie
Pusey, *A Course of Sermons on Solemn Subjects* [Oxford: 1845]; *Parochial Sermons*, vol. 3, rev. ed.
[Oxford: 1873]).

26. See Maria Poggi Johnson, "'The Feeling of Infinity' and Parochial Life: John Keble and
Figural Reading," in *All Thy Lights Combine: Figural Reading in the Anglican Tradition*, ed. Ephraim
Radner and David Ney (Bellingham, WA: Lexham Press, 2021), 237–54.

27. See Elizabeth Ludlow, "Let Us Kneel with Mary Maid: Christina Rossetti and Figural
Reading," in *All Thy Lights Combine: Figural Reading in the Anglican Tradition*, ed. Ephraim Radner
and David Ney (Bellingham, WA: Lexham Press, 2021), 307–24; Jeff W. Boldt, "The Whole Bible:
Lionel Thornton and Figural Reading," in *All Thy Lights Combine: Figural Reading in the Anglican
Tradition*, ed. Ephraim Radner and David Ney (Bellingham, WA: Lexham Press, 2021), 341–58.

28. Nockles observes that the work of the Tractarians sometimes appeared as if it were
designed to offend (*The Oxford*, 281). Within such a mindset, the peculiarity of Pusey's lectures
was regarded as a strength, and Pusey appears to have capitalized on this fact. He flaunts curious figural readings of passages because they highlight the extent to which his countrymen
have veered off the ancient path. Westhaver acknowledges that Pusey's lectures were almost
completely ignored by his ecclesial allies and descendants ("The Living," 280–81). Westhaver
also points out that other Tractarian efforts to revive patristic figural reading were regarded as
"out of place" and became "potent weapons against Tractarianism" ("The Living," 282).

to overcome history's obfuscation of pristine truth.[29] Like the Newtonians, they pursued historical knowledge of the primitive church as the basis of their restitutionist project. John Henry Newman (1801–1890), like Newton, was confident he could conceptually order the confusing morass he encountered in the pages of history. As he sifted through complex webs of historical testimony as Newton had done before him, he identified, on one hand, the vast hordes of heretics who threatened to overwhelm Christian truth, and the faithful remnant on the other.[30] Yet his researches were hardly satisfying because he sought to identify not merely the trajectory of history but his place within it. Newman needed to be able to identify the winners, and, above all, he needed to know he was on the winning side.

> My stronghold was Antiquity; now where, in the middle of the fifth century, I found, as it seemed to me, Christendom of the sixteenth and the nineteenth centuries reflected. I saw my face in that mirror, and I was a Monophysite. The Church of the *Via Media* was in the position of the Oriental communion, Rome was, where she now is; and the Protestants were the Eutychians.[31]

Newman looked to history to order his thoughts about his place in history. To make sense of the madness, he adopted a conceptual framework which he then imposed on historical particulars.

What mattered to Newman in his comparison between the Church of England and the Monophysites was the conceptual analogy that could be drawn using the overarching categories of heresy and orthodoxy.[32] It mattered very little that Church of England theology could hardly be compared with Monophysitism. As figures of history, the Monophysites and Anglicans were easily fashioned into one-dimensional figures of heresy. Furthermore, it is because they were reinterpreted as figures of history that they were so easily dismissed as the "losers" in the historical drama. As figures of history,

---

29. Nockles, "Survivals or New Arrivals? The Oxford Movement and the Nineteenth-Century Historical Construction of Anglicanism," in *Anglicanism and the Western Christian Tradition: Continuity, Change, and the Search for Communion*, ed. Stephen Platten (Norwich: Canterbury Press, 2003), 145.

30. Even Newman's own sister, however, complained that he tended to "proof text" history by appealing only to those authorities that supported his views (Nockles, "Survivals," 173).

31. Newman, *Apologia, Pro Vita Sua & Six Sermons*, ed. Frank M. Turner (New Haven: Yale University Press, 2008), 226. See also Frank M. Turner, *John Henry Newman: The Challenge to Evangelical Religion* (New Haven: Yale University Press, 2002), 335–36.

32. Frank Turner, *John Henry Newman* (New Haven: Yale University Press, 2002), 335

Monophysites and Anglicans stand trapped and exposed within a devolutionary historical scheme. Their purpose, like Samuel Clarke's Jews and Papists, is to highlight the excellence of the true religion of the true church.

It might be asked whether anything would have changed had Newman taken history to be a figure of Scripture rather than history. It is impossible to know—not merely because the question is speculative, but because Scripture could have drawn Newman to numerous different conclusions. It is safe to say, however, that the belief that history is a figure of Scripture would have complexified Newman's analysis of his own historical and ecclesial identity. Newman might well, for example, have concluded that the Church of England was harlot Israel, the idolatrous house of Jeroboam that had been cut off from the righteous branch of Jesse. On this account, however, Newman would have been pressed to integrate into his analysis the troubling reality that "faithless Israel is more righteous than unfaithful Judah" (Jer 3:11 NIV).

In 1860 journalist and historian John Mathew Gutch (1776–1861) published *Watson Redivivus: Four Discourses, Written between the Years 1749 and 1756, by the Rev. George Watson, M.A.* In the introduction to the work, Gutch gives an account of how he came to "rescue" the discourses "from obscurity." Gutch relates that he had been reading Jones's *Lectures Upon the Figurative Language of Scripture* when he stumbled upon his tribute to Watson and Watson's *Christ the Light of the World.*[33] Gutch recounts how he managed, through considerable effort, to obtain copies of four Watson discourses. Gutch believes that, although he had been prevented by his "advanced age" in rendering assistance to the clergy in the administration of their schools and in "aiding them in visiting and reading to their poor and afflicted," he hopes that he has "found another method" of conferring some good upon the Christian community: "the republication of these Discourses."[34]

Gutch describes the Christian community he hopes to bless as having been beset by "angry discussions and divisions." He adds, nevertheless, that he rejoices to see that

---

33. The query Gutch sent to *Notes and Queries* begins as follows: "When men of such high reputation as the Rev. William Jones, of Nayland, speak in terms of commendation of any publication, we are naturally anxious to become acquainted with its contents" (John Mathew Gutch, preface to *Watson Redivivus: Four Discourses Written Between the Years 1749 and 1756 by the Rev. George Watson, M.A.* [Oxford: 1760], ix).

34. Gutch, "Preface," viii.

there are many of its ministers inculcating and inviting a closer union between themselves and the laity, as a means of mitigating such unbecoming controversies, and expressing their deep regret at the introduction of those innovations which are so nearly allied to Romish practices, and causing so much schism among Christians.[35]

Gutch's complaint against those who instigate "angry discussions and divisions" against extreme forms of clericalism and against the institution of "Romish practices" is undoubtedly directed to Newman and the Tractarians.[36] Gutch does not specify how he believes Watson's discourses will provide an antidote to these perceived problems.[37] He simply suggests that they are representative of a more moderate churchmanship that is able to bring the clergy and the laity together rather than drive them apart.[38] The strong emphasis that historic High churchmanship had placed upon the providential basis of the church establishment stands in stark contrast to the Tractarian promotion of disestablishment, and Gutch may well have endorsed Watson's sermons as a call to Anglicans of all stripes to unite and reclaim England for an established church.[39] Gutch may well have also seen Watson as a moderate because he was able to integrate doctrines that were being used by Anglicans to levy party politics.[40] For Gutch, Watson's scriptural emblematicism has the capacity to bring Christians together because it asks Christians of all ages and intellectual capacities to begin at the same place. It asks them to begin with the concrete objects that form the basis of creaturely experience and

---

35. Gutch, "Preface," vii–viii.

36. Gutch was almost certainly personally acquainted with Newman. Newman had been the curate of his father, John Gutch (1746–1831), at St. Clement's.

37. He concludes his introduction by affirming that he does not hesitate "to commit these discourses to the judgment and criticism of a discerning public" (Gutch, "Preface," xxiv).

38. Nockles remarks that the Scottish Hutchinsonians and non-jurors "protested their independence from the Tractarians" in vain (The Oxford, 308). In England some of the most important criticisms of Tractarianism came from theologians with strong ties to Hutchinsonianism, including Churton and Palmer (Nockles, The Oxford, 277–310).

39. Gibson finds that the Tractarians joined with radical reformers and evangelicals in portraying the eighteenth-century Church of England as the figure of ecclesial devolution (William Gibson, The Church of England, 1688–1832: Unity and Accord [London: Routledge, 2001], 5).

40. On the sacramental vision of the Tractarians, see Owen Chadwick, The Mind of the Oxford Movement (Stanford, CA: Stanford University Press, 1960), 191–99. On evangelical biblicism, see D. W. Bebbington, Evangelicalism in Modern Britain: A History from the 1730s to the 1980s (London: Unwin Hyman 1994), 12–14.

then interpret these concrete objects, as they are able, through a common lens. Scriptural emblematicism is the basis of a conservatism that asked people to begin not with the past, as they believed it was, or the future, as they hoped it would be, but with the present. And because it asked Christians to begin not with what was, or what might be, but with what is, it provided a nonideological alternative to the restitutionist ideologies that were doing battle for the soul of the Church of England.[41]

---

41. Nockles, "Survivals," 145. Since Marx, the term "ideology" has been largely used to describe the way in which power structures control the thinking of individuals. This, however, was not the original meaning of the term. The term can be traced back to Destutt de Tracy. For de Tracy, ideology was "positive and progressive." De Tracy hoped that if humans could liberate their ideas from religious and metaphysical prejudices, they would create an ideology that would be the basis of a utopic society. My usage of the term "ideology" corresponds to that of de Tracy inasmuch as I am using it to describe the tendency to establish conceptual frameworks that are then imposed on particulars. David McLellan, "Ideology," in *Encyclopedia of Philosophy and the Social Sciences*, ed. Byron Kaldis (Los Angeles: Sage, 2013), 458.

AFTERWORD

—

The "Quest to Save the Old Testament," in David Ney's felicitous description of a sometimes quixotic struggle, has been an ongoing Christian struggle since the beginning of the church. Only in modernity have the main opponents to the Old Testament been mostly assembled in the church. Ney's discussion of one of the key arenas of this modern moment of internal Christian debate, in eighteenth-century Britain, is fascinating, subtle, ground-breaking, and brilliant. It is also theologically challenging, exposing some of the essential issues in contemporary Christian biblical interpretation in a way that illuminates their complexity and inescapable importance.

At the heart of Ney's study are the key topics of history and providence as they pressed themselves upon the minds of early modern European thinkers. By the eighteenth century, these topics had gripped the concerns of natural and religious philosophers in Britain in an almost obsessive way, with an insistence that remains at work in our own culture, if described with new terms: How are the heavens moved? Why do nations fall upon others with violence? Where shall we find a place in our hearts for the trees and grasses, the cliffs, thunders, and earthquakes that surround us or sometimes engulf us? How do the small decisions of our lives end up shaping our destinies in ways we never expected or often hoped? If any of this "fits" together, how then shall we live? And if not ... ?

The Old Testament, it turns out, addresses the topics of history and providence in a uniquely comprehensive fashion in the way it details the creation of God and the events of God's people and other peoples as it traces the shape of human decision and response. Within the Christian context of the eighteenth century, the struggle with the great questions of the world's shape was, by definition, a struggle with the Old Testament. But the Old Testament, it also turns out, does not yield clear and resolving responses to the era's theodical questions. Diverse and alternative answers were proposed or given, and the Old Testament's established role as the lens of providence was quickly destabilized in favor of more clear-cut and streamlined frameworks of understanding, some naturalistic, some ethical, some political, none proffering the richness and complexity of the Old Testament's expression of God's life. We live today in the wake of this great reduction, as well as in the sometimes destructive conflict of its vying simplicities.

Ney lays all this out with a marvelous detail and synthetic breadth. But more instructively, he illumines early modernity's battle over history and providence by bringing into light the remarkable work of a group of Christian thinkers who understood the theological and moral stakes at play, took them seriously, and worked out a way through the thickets of dispute along a path faithful to the tradition of the church. Their work was one of compassion, aimed at the worries of the time. The Hutchinsonians are today viewed as an eccentric fringe within eighteenth-century British Christianity, studied sparsely as foils to putatively more important scientific and political thinkers. But Ney not only recovers something of their actual influence, which was significant, but demonstrates the sophistication and still compelling character of their work, at the heart of which was their revaluation of the Old Testament's divine meaning as providentially ordered history.

The great Hutchinsonians, like George Watson, George Horne, and William Jones (who received their common moniker as supposed disciples of an earlier and perhaps truly eccentric writer, John Hutchinson), were thinkers attuned to the values and habits of their intellectual culture. Empiricists of a sort (Ney calls them "sensualists"), they shared a contemporary concern with the world and its shape, with people, creatures, things, events. Like many of their fellow scientists and political moralists, they were committed to treating these worldly or sensual realities with utmost seriousness, including those of moral challenge. In this respect, they remain contemporary in their outlook even for our day. Yet their Christian faith, as well as their subtle realism, encouraged a deeper engagement with Christian Scripture that enabled them to escape some of the easy logical dichotomies of their peers. They instead appreciated what the Old Testament provided: a vision of divine complexity and beauty. When brought into an informing relationship with the world and its difficulties, the Old Testament, it seemed to the Hutchinsonians, was far more truthful, accurate, and honest in its descriptive claims than were the alternative simplifying theories of history emerging in their time. And if so, the God of the Scriptures was far more interesting and attractive than the emerging deities of vague benevolence and abstract order they were now being offered.

Much of the Hutchinsonian task, which Ney carefully traces, involved the commendation and application of what today we call a "figural" reading of Scripture, what they tended to label "emblematicism." The interpretive frameworks and theories that this approach involves have resurfaced in recent days. For the Hutchinsonians, these ways of reading Scripture were not only traditional and authoritative but also subtle, respectful, and intellectually humble in contrast to the developing conceptually reductive alternatives of the early modern period. Figural reading was also, they felt, morally compelling in its fruit, yielding a vision of the world as God's that seemed better to reflect God's own infinitely profound nature and power. Ney is a masterful guide to this whole tradition and the arguments and interests it encapsulates, a rich content that remains poorly mined to the present. Following this story, its characters, and their writings is an exciting demonstration of the communion of saints and scholars that continue to surround us even now, however bereft we may sometimes feel.

The "Quest to Save the Old Testament" exposes, of course, its own limitations even in its phrasing: neither the Old Testament itself needs "saving," nor are human beings the ones to do it in any case. But this irony was hardly lost on the Hutchinsonians, who understood well that the providential power of the word asks less that we reconstitute it for others than that we simply articulate and display it. History is God's, and it is God's way of sharing his life with his creatures. But this divine way is divinely spoken of in scriptural terms, not philosophical conceptions. Whatever the Old Testament is, it also is God's, and this double divine possession—history and Scripture—leaves human beings, and especially faithful human beings, ever dependent for their understanding of reality upon the gifts of God himself. The Scriptures of the Old Testament are "old" not in their obsoleteness but in their venerable power to enlighten on their own terms—that is, God's terms.

Along with all its other historical virtues, Ney's volume has a good deal to tell us about the great Age of Enlightenment in which the Hutchinsonians flourished, not only tempering crude characterizations of the period's thinking but also indicating how the search for "light" can end in divine luminescence as readily as it may in the withered fields of human autonomy and imperious rationalism.

To that degree, there is nothing wrong with the quest in itself. The Hutchinsonians were indeed philosophers and profoundly skilled scholars. They took seriously the things of the world to the extent that they insisted that God be accountable for them: if God is the most intimate cause and shaper of the world—the world's artist—then the human vocation to understand it on the terms of God's gifts, with Scripture at the center, must fuel the infinite care of our scrutiny. Just here the Hutchinsonians serve as models for the intellectual life in a manner that weds Athens with Jerusalem, the way of wisdom with God's manna offered from his hand in the wilderness. Ney's book is historical theology at its best, for it puts in a clear light the God who, in sharing his history with our own, gives the gracious gift that stands at the heart of the gospel.

Ephraim Radner
Toronto, Ontario
The Third Sunday in Easter 2022

BIBLIOGRAPHY

—

PRIMARY SOURCES

UNPUBLISHED MANUSCRIPTS

A letter reacting to Newton's death from *Mist's Weekly Journal*. Keynes MS
129.13, King's College, Cambridge, UK.

Allen, Mr. A letter to John Woodward, 15 December 1725. Add. MS 7647, no.
24. Cambridge University Library, Cambridge, UK.

Cartwright, Thomas. A letter to Jonas Boucher, April 1794, Non-juror Add.
MS D. 30, Bodleian Library. Oxford UK.

Chillingworth, William. A letter from Chillingworth to an unknown
recipient, Add. MS 7113, no. 3, Cambridge University Library,
Cambridge, UK

Clarke, Samuel. The letters of Samuel Clarke. Add. MS 7113. Cambridge,
Cambridge University Library, UK.

Craig, John. A letter to an unidentified recipient, dated 7 April, 1727.
Keynes MS 132, King's College, Cambridge, UK.

Horne, George. Journal entry, 28 April, 1786. Add. MS 8134, A3, p. 52.
Cambridge University Library, Cambridge, UK.

——. Papers of George Horne. MC: PR29 MS 2/1, fols. 66–136. Magdalen
College Archives, University of Oxford, UK.

Hutchinson, John. Early natural philosophical experiments. Add. MS B 2
6063. Catcott Collection. Bristol Central Library, Bristol, UK.

——. Letters from Hutchinson to Woodward, MSS Gough Wales 8,
Bodleian Library, Oxford, UK."

Jackson, John. A letter to Samuel Clarke, 26 February, 1715. Add. MS 7113, no.
12. Cambridge University Library, Cambridge, UK.

Jones, William. A letter to George Berkeley Jr., 29 January, 1762. Add MS
39311, p. 109. The British Library, London, UK.

————. MS Sermons by the Rev. W. Jones of Nayland. 2 vols. Pusey House, Oxford, UK.

Maclaurin, Colin. The Letters of Colin Maclaurin. MS 206. University of Aberdeen, Aberdeen, UK.

Newton, Isaac. A short Schem of the true religion. Keynes MS 7. King's College, Cambridge, UK.

————. Draft chapters of a treatise on the origin of religion and its corruption. Yahuda MS 41. National Library of Israel, Jerusalem, Israel.

————. Draft chapters of The Chronology of Ancient Kingdoms Amended. Yahuda MS 26. National Library of Israel, Jerusalem, Israel.

————. Drafts concerning Solomon's temple and the sacred cubit. Yahuda MS 2.4. National Library of Israel, Jerusalem, Israel.

————. Drafts of the 'Short Chronicle' and 'Original of Monarchies.' MS 361 (1). New College Library, Oxford, UK.

————. Draft passages on chronology and biblical history. Yahuda MS 25. National Library of Israel, Jerusalem, Israel.

————. Exposition of 2 Kings 17:15–16. MS 130, Harry Ransom Humanities Research Center, University of Texas, Austin, USA.

————. Exposition of 2 Kings 17:15–16. Yahuda MS 21. National Library of Israel, Jerusalem, Israel.

————. Fragment on the history of apostasy. Yahuda MS 18. National Library of Israel, Jerusalem, Israel.

————. Irenicum, or Ecclesiastical Polyty tending to Peace. Keynes MS 3. King's College, Cambridge, UK.

————. Of the temple & synagogues of the Jews. Yahuda MS 26.3. National Library of Israel, Jerusalem, Israel.

————. Original letter from Isaac Newton to Richard Bentley, 10 December 1692. 189.R.4.47, ff. 7–8. Trinity College Library, Cambridge, UK.

————. Papers relating to chronology and 'Theologiæ Gentilis Origines Philosophicæ.' MS 361 (3). New College Library, Oxford, UK.

————. Part of an exposition of 2 Kings 17:15–17. MS 437. The Babson College Grace K. Babson Collection of the Works of Sir Isaac Newton. Huntington Library, San Marino, CA.

————. Rough draft portions of and notes for 'Theologiæ Gentilis Origines Philosophicæ' and 'The Original of Monarchies.' Yahuda MS 16. National Library of Israel, Jerusalem, Israel.

——. Seven drafts of Newton's defence of *The Chronology of Ancient Kingdoms Amended*. Yahuda MS 27. National Library of Israel, Jerusalem, Israel.

——. Three bundles of notes for a work on the ancients' physico-theology. Yahuda MS 17. National Library of Israel, Jerusalem, Israel.

——. Two incomplete treatises on prophecy. Keynes MS 5. King's College, Cambridge, UK.

——. Two Notable Corruptions of Scripture. MS 361 (4). New College Library, Oxford, UK.

——. Isaac Newton, Untitled Treatise on Revelation. Yahuda MS 1.1. National Library of Israel, Jerusalem, Israel.

Pusey, Edward Bouverie. Lectures on Types and Prophecies of the Old Testament: written mainly in July—August, 1836. LBV–151. Pusey House, Oxford, UK.

PUBLISHED BOOKS AND TRACTS

Aboab, David. *Remarks on Dr. Sharp's Two Dissertations*. London: 1751.

"Art. IX. A Course of Lectures on the figurative Language of the Holy Scriptures." *The Monthly Review, From January to June, inclusive, 1789*, vol. 80 (London: 1789): 402–407.

Bacon, Francis. *Novum Organum: Or True Directions Concerning the Interpretation of Nature*. London: 1620.

Bate, Julius. *A Defence of Mr. Hutchinson's Tenets in Philosophy and Divinity: In Answer to the Objections of Mr. Simon Berington*. London: 1751.

——. *The Examiner Examined*. London: 1739.

——. *The Scripture Meaning of Aleim and Berith*. London: 1751.

Bedford, Arthur. *A Defence of the Doctrine of the Holy Trinity, and the Incarnation of the Son of God, from the Testimony of the Most Ancient Jews: In Eight Sermons, Preached at the Lady Moyer's Lecture*. London: 1741.

——. *An Examination of Mr. Hutchinson's Remarks, and Mr. Catcott's Answer by the Author of the Observations*. London: 1738.

——. *The Examination of the Remarks upon, and Mr. Catcot's Answer to the Observations upon His Sermon*. London: 1737.

——. *Observations on a Sermon Preach'd before the Corporation of Bristol*. London: 1736.

Bentley, Richard. *Eight Sermons Preach'd at the Honourable Robert Boyle's Lecture.* Cambridge: 1724.

Berington, Simon. *Dissertations on the Mosaical Creation [...].* London: 1750.

Best, Henry. *Four Years in France.* London: 1826.

Bickersteth, Edward. *The Works of Rev. E. Bickersteth, Rector of Manton, Hertfordshire.* New York: 1832.

Boas, George, ed. and trans. *The Hieroglyphics of Horapollo.* Princeton: Princeton University Press, 1993.

Boyle, Robert. *The Works of the Honourable Robert Boyle.* 6 vols. London: 1772.

Burke, Edmund. *Reflections on the Revolution in France.* Edited by Frank M. Turner. New Haven: Yale University Press, 2003.

———. "Edmund Burke to George Horne, 9 December, 1791." In *The Correspondence of Edmund Burke*, 6:455–56. Edited by Alfred Cobban and Robert Smith. Cambridge: Cambridge University Press, 1967.

Butler, Joseph. *The Analogy of Religion, Natural and Revealed.* 3rd ed. London: 1740.

Chandler, Thomas Bradbury. *The Life of Samuel Johnson, D.D.* New York: 1824.

Catcott, Alexander, Jr. *A Treatise on the Deluge.* London: 1761.

Catcott, Alexander, Sr. *Answer to the Observations.* London: 1737.

———. *The State of the Case between Mr. Bedford and Mr. Catcott, in Answer to Mr. Bedford's Examination.* London: 1738.

———. *The Supreme and Inferior Elahim.* 2nd ed. London: 1742.

Caesar, Julius. *C. Julii Caesaris quae extant.* Edited by Samuel Clarke. London: 1712.

Cappel, Louis. *Arcanum punctuationis revelatum.* Leiden: 1624.

Carroll, William. *Remarks upon Mr. Clarke's Sermons, Preached at St. Paul's against Hobbs, Spinoza, and other Atheists.* London: 1705.

Cherbury, Herbert of. *De Veritate.* Translated by Meyrick H. Carré. Bristol: University of Bristol, 1937.

Cheyne, George. *A New Theory of Acute and Slow Continu'd Fevers.* 2nd ed. London: 1702.

Churton, Edward. *Memoir of Joshua Watson.* 2 vols. 2nd ed. Oxford: 1861.

Clarke, Samuel. *A Collection of Papers, which Passed Between the Late Learned Mr. Leibnitz, and Dr. Clarke.* London: 1717.

———. *A Demonstration of the Being and Attributes of God: More Particularly in Answer to Hobbs, Spinoza, and their Followers.* London: 1705.

——. *A Discourse Concerning the Unchangeable Obligations of Natural Religion, and the Truth and Certainty of the Christian Revelation.* London: 1706.

——. *A Letter to Mr. Dodwell.* 5th ed. London: 1718.

——. *A Paraphrase on the Four Evangelists.* 4th ed. London: 1722.

——. *A Paraphrase upon Our Saviour's Sermon on the Mount.* London: 1732.

——. *A Sermon Preach'd before the Honourable House of Commons, Church of St. Margaret Westminster.* London: 1709.

——. *An Exposition of the Church-Catechism.* Edited by John Clarke. London: 1729.

——. *One Hundred and Seventy Three Sermons on Several Subjects and Occasions.* 2 vols. Dublin: 1734.

——. *The Book of Common Prayer Reformed According to the Plan of the Late Dr. Samuel Clarke.* London: 1774.

——. *The Great Duty of Universal Love and Charity: A Sermon Preached before the Queen.* London: 1708

——. *The Scripture-Doctrine of the Trinity.* London: 1712.

——. *The Whole Duty of a Christian, Plainly Represented in Three Practical Essays, on Baptism, Confirmation, and Repentance.* 2nd ed. London: 1704.

Clarke, Samuel. *A Letter to the Reverend Dr. Wells.* London: 1714.

Clarke, Samuel, and Gotthold Ephraim Leibniz. *Correspondence.* Edited by Roger Ariew. Indianapolis: Hackett, 2000.

Coleridge, Samuel Taylor. *Aids to Reflection and the Confessions of an Inquiring Spirit.* Edited by James Mursh. London: G. Bell, 1901.

Comings, Fowler. *The Printed Hebrew Text of the Old Testament Vindicated.* Oxford: 1753.

Davidson, Samuel. *Lectures of Biblical Criticism, Exhibiting a Systematic View of That Science.* Edinburgh: 1839.

Forbes, Duncan. *Some Thoughts concerning Religion, Natural and Revealed.* Edinburgh: 1750.

Freeman, John. *The Life of Rev. William Kirby, M.A.* London: 1752.

Gill, John. *The Moral Nature and Fitness of Things Considered.* London: 1738.

Gillies, John, ed. *The Psalms of David, with Notes Devotional and Practical [...] extracted [...] from Dr. Horne's Commentary on the Book of Psalms.* Edinburgh: 1796.

Gittins, Daniel. *An Answer to a Pamphlet Entitled, An Examination of Mr. Hutchincon's Remarks, and Mr. Catcott's Answer.* London: 1739.

——. Observations on some Sermons Preach'd at the Lady Moyer's
      Lectures. London: 1741

Gutch, John Matthew. *Watson Redivivus: Four Discourses Written between the
      Years 1749 and 1756 by the Rev. George Watson, M.A.* Oxford: 1760.

Halley, Edmund. "Ode to Newton." In Isaac Newton, *The Principia:
      Mathematical Principles of Natural Philosophy*, translated by I.
      Bernard Cohen and Anne Whitman, 380. Berkeley, CA: University
      of California Press, 1999.

Hare, Francis. *The Difficulties and Discouragements which Attend the Study of
      the Scriptures in the Way of Private Judgment.* London: 1714.

Hight, Marc, ed. *The Correspondence of George Berkeley.* Cambridge:
      Cambridge University Press, 2013.

Hoadly, Benjamin. *The Nature of the Kingdom or Church of Christ: A Sermon
      Preach'd before the King at the Royal Chapel at St. James's, on Sunday
      March 31, 1717.* London: 1717.

Hoadly, Benjamin, ed. *The Works of Samuel Clarke.* 4 vols. London: 1738.

Hodges, Walter. *Elihu: Or an Enquiry into the Principle Scope and Design of the
      Book of Job.* London: 1750.

Holloway, Benjamin. *Originals Physical and Theological, Sacred and Profane.*
      Oxford: 1751.

——. *Remarks on Dr. Sharp's Pieces on the Words Elohim and Berith.* Oxford:
      1751.

Homer. *Homeri Illias Graece et Latine.* Edited by Samuel Clarke. London:
      1729–1732.

Horne, George. *A Charge Intended to Have Been Delivered to the Clergy of
      Norwich.* Norwich: 1791.

——. *A Commentary on the Book of Psalms.* 2 vols. Oxford: 1776.

——. *A Fair, Candid and Impartial State of the Case between Sir Isaac Newton
      and Mr. Hutchinson.* London: 1753.

——. *A View of Mr. Kennicott's Method of Correcting the Hebrew Text.* London:
      1765.

——. *An Apology for Certain Gentlemen in the University of Oxford.* Oxford:
      1756.

——. *Christ the Object of Religious Adoration: And Therefore, very God: A
      Sermon Preached before the University of Oxford, at St. Mary's.* Oxford:
      1775.

——. *Considerations on the Life and Death of St. John the Baptist.* Oxford: 1769.

——. *Discourses on Several Subjects and Occasions.* 3rd ed. Oxford: 1787.

——. Letters on Infidelity, 2nd ed. Oxford: 1786.

——. *The Character of True Wisdom, and the Means of Attaining It: A Sermon Preached in the Cathedral Church of Christ [...].* Oxford: 1784.

——. *The Theology and Philosophy in Cicero's Somnium Scipionis Explained.* Oxford: 1751.

Horne, Thomas Hartwell. *Introduction to the Critical Study and Knowledge of the Holy Scriptures.* London: 1818.

Horsley, Samuel, ed. *Isaaci Newtoni Opera Quae Estant Omnia.* 4 vols. London: 1782.

——. The Charge of Samuel, Lord Bishop of St. David's, to the Clergy of His Diocese. Gloucester: 1791.

Hutchinson, John. *A New Account of the Confusion of Tongues [and] The Names and Attributes of the Trinity of the Gentiles.* London: 1731.

——. *An Essay toward a Natural History of the Bible, especially of some Parts which relate to the Occasion of revealing Moses's Principia.* London: 1725.

——. *A Treatise of Power Essential and Mechanical.* London: 1732.

——. *Glory or Gravity, Essential and Mechanical.* London: 1749.

——. *Glory or Gravity, the Mechanical or Second Part.* London: 1733.

——. *Moses's Principia.* London: 1724.

——. *Moses's Principia, Part II.* London: 1727.

——. *Moses's—Sine Principio: Represented by Names, By Types, By Words, By Emblems.* London: 1729.

——. *Observations Made by J. H. Mostly in the Year 1706.* London: [1710?].

——. *Reasons for the Bill, Entituled, a Bill for Securing to Mr. John Hutchinson the Property of a Movement Invented by Him [...].* London: [1712?].

——. *Remarks upon the Observations on a Sermon Preach'd before the Corporation of Bristol, and the Lord-Chief-Justice Hardwick.* London: 1737.

——. *The Covenant in the Cherubim: So the Hebrew Writings Perfect.* London: 1734.

——. *The Religion of Satan, Or Antichrist, Delineated.* London: 1736.

——. *The Use of Reason Recovered, by the Data in Christianity.* London: 1736.

J. J. "Anecdotes Relative to the Great Dr. Samuel Clarke." *The Gentleman's Magazine: And Historical Chronicle* 53 (1783): 227–29.

Jones, William. *A Course of Lectures on the Figurative Language of the Holy Scripture.* London: 1787.

———. *A Discourse on the Use and Intention of some Remarkable Passages of the Scripture.* London: 1798.

———. *A Free Enquiry into the Sense and Signification of the Spring.* London: 1772.

———. *A Full Answer to an Essay on Spirit.* London: 1753.

———. *A Letter from a Tutor to His Pupils.* London: 1780.

———. *A Letter to John Bull, Esq. from His Second Cousin Thomas Bull.* London: 1793.

———. *A Letter to the Common People.* London: 1767.

———. *A Letter to the Church of England, Pointing Out Some Popular Errors of Bad Consequence.* London: 1798.

———. *A New Preface to the Second Edition of Memoirs of the Life, Studies, Writings, & c. of The Right Rev. George Horne, D.D.* London: 1799.

———. *A Short Way to Truth: Or the Christian Doctrine of a Trinity in Unity, Illustrated and Confirmed from Analogy in the Natural Creation.* London: 1793.

———. *A Small Whole-Length of Dr. Priestley, from His Printed Works.* London: 1797.

———. *An Essay on the First Principles of Natural Philosophy.* London: 1762.

———. *Four Discourses: (1) The Religious Use of Botanical Philosophy; (2) Considerations on the Nature and Oeconomy of Beasts and Cattle; (3) On the Natural History of the Earth and Its Minerals; (4) On the Natural Evidences of Christianity. A New Edition.* London: 1799.

———. *Memoirs of the Life, Studies, and Writings of the Right Reverend George Horne, D. D.* London: 1795.

———. Preface to *Sermons on Moral and Religious Subjects.* Vol. 1. London: 1790.

———. "Trust in Providence, the Comfort of Man's Life." In *Sermons on Moral and Religious Subjects*, 1:207–228. London: 1790.

———. *The Book of Nature.* London: 1788.

———. *The Catholic Doctrine of the Trinity.* Oxford: 1756.

———. *The Nature, Uses, Dangers, Sufferings, and Preservatives of the Human Imagination.* London: 1796.

———. *The Theological, Philosophical, and Miscellaneous Works of the Rev. William Jones.* Edited by William Stevens. 12 vols. London: 1801.

———. *Zoologia Ethica: A Disquisition Concerning the Mosaic Distinction of*

Animals into Clean and Unclean. London: 1773.

———, ed. *The Works of the Right Reverend George Horne.* 4 vols. London: 1818.

Keble, John. *On the Mysticism Attributed to the Early Fathers of the Church.* London: 1841.

Kennicott, Benjamin. *A Word to the Hutchinsonians.* London: 1756.

———. *Remarks on Select Passages in the Old Testament.* Oxford: 1787.

———. *The Sabbath: A Sermon Preached in His Majesty's Chapel, Whitehall.* London: 1781.

Kirby, William. *The Bridgewater Treatises: The Power, Wisdom, and Goodness of God as Manifested in the Creation.* 2nd ed. London: 1835.

Knight, James. *The True Scripture Doctrine of the Most Holy and Undivided Trinity.* London: 1715.

Lessing, Gotthold Ephraim. "The Proof of the Spirit and of Power." In *Lessing's Theological Writings,* edited and translated by Henry Chadwick, 51–56. Stanford, CA: Stanford University Press, 1956.

Lindsey, Theophilus. *An Historical View of the State of the Unitarian Doctrine and Worship from the Reformation to Our Own Times.* London: 1783.

———. *The Apology of Theophilus Lindsey.* London: 1782.

———. *Vindici? Preistleian: An Address to the Students of Oxford and Cambridge.* London: 1788.

Locke, John. *An Essay Concerning Human Understanding.* 5th ed. London: 1706.

———. *The Reasonableness of Christianity: As Delivered in the Scriptures.* Edited by John Higgins-Biddle. Oxford: Clarendon, 1999.

Maclaurin, Colin. *An Account of Sir Isaac Newton's Philosophical Discoveries.* London: 1748.

MacCulloch, Robert. *Lectures on the Prophecies of Isaiah.* London: 1791.

Mead, Richard. Preface to *The Medical Works of Richard Mead, M. D.* London: 1762.

Moody, James. *The Evidence for Christianity Contained in the Hebrew Words Aleim and Berit.* London 1752.

Morgan, Thomas. *The Moral Philosopher, in a dialogue between Philalethes a Christian Deist, and Theophanes a Christian Jew.* London: 1737.

Murray, Lindsey. "Review of A Selection from Bishop Horne's Commentary on the Psalms." *European Magazine and London Review* 61 (1812): 39–40.

Newman, John Henry. *Apologia Pro Vita Sua & Six Sermons.* Edited by Frank M. Turner. New Haven: Yale University Press, 2008.

——. "An Unpublished Paper by Cardinal Newman on the Development of Doctrine." *The Journal of Theological Studies* 9, no. 2 (1958): 324–35.

Newton, Isaac. *The Mathematical Principles of Natural Philosophy*. 2 vols. Translated by Andrew Motte. London: 1729.

——. "Dissertation upon the Sacred Cubit of the Jews and the Cubits of the Several Nations." In John Greaves, *Miscellaneous Works of Mr. John Greaves*, 405–33. London: 1737.

——. *Optice: Sive de Reflexionibus, Refractionibus, Inflexionibus & Coloribus Lucis Libri Tres*. Edited by Samuel Clarke. London: 1706.

——. *Opticks: Or, a Treatise of the Reflections, Refractions, Inflections and Colours of Light*. 2nd ed. London: 1718.

——. *The Chronology of Ancient Kingdoms Amended*. Edited by John Conduitt. London: 1728.

Nicoll, Alexander. *Sermons*. Oxford: 1830.

"Obituary, Anecdotes, of Remarkable Persons." *Gentleman's Magazine and Historical Chronicle* 70 (1800): 183–84.

"Obituary: Benjamin Harenc, Esq." *Gentleman's Magazine and Historical Chronicle*, New Series 18, no. 2 (1825): 566–69.

Paine, Thomas. *Common Sense: Addressed to the Inhabitants of America*. A New Edition. London: 1792.

Parkhurst, John. *A Greek and English Lexicon to the New Testament*. London: 1769.

——. *An Hebrew and English Lexicon without Points*. London: 1762.

Anonymous. *A Brief Account of the New Sect of Latitude-Men*. Cambridge: 1662.

Pike, Samuel. *Philosophia Sacra: Or, the Principles of Natural Philosophy; Extracted from Divine Revelation*. London: 1753.

Priestly, Joseph. *Institutes of Natural and Revealed Religion*. 2nd ed. 2 vols. Birmingham: 1782.

——. *A Course of Sermons on Solemn Subjects*. Oxford: 1845.

——. *Parochial Sermons*, vol. 3, rev. ed. Oxford: 1873.

Pusey, Edward Bouverie. *A Course of Sermons on Solemn Subjects*. Oxford 1845. and Parochial Sermons, vol. 3, rev. ed. Oxford: 1873.

——. "A Letter to the Bishop-Elect of Oxford, 27 November 1845." In Henry Parry Liddon, *Life of Edward Bouverie Pusey*, 3:43–45. London: 1894.

Ray, John, and Francis Willughby. *The Ornithology of Francis Willughby*. London: 1678.

Reeves, William. *The Apologies of Justin Martyr, Tertullian, and Minutius.* London: 1709.

"Review of T. Mozley's Reminiscences." *The Literary Churchman and Church Fortnightly* 28 (1882): 248–51.

Robinson, W. W. *A Pocket Classic: Commentary on the Penitential Psalms, Psalms for Pardon of Sin, and Intercessory Prayer.* London: 1845.

Sarum, Benjamin. *Preface to Sermons on the Following Subjects* [...] *By Samuel Clarke, D. D.* London: 1743.

Seward, William. "Samuel Clarke." In *Anecdotes of Some Distinguished Persons, Chiefly of the Present and Two Preceding Centuries,* 2:335–38. London: 1796.

Sharp, Thomas. *Mr. Hutchinson's Exposition of Cherubim.* London: 1755.

———. *Two Dissertations Concerning the Etymology and Scripture-Meaning of the Hebrew Words Elohim and Birth.* London: 1751.

Shedd, W. G. T., ed. *The Complete Works of Samuel Taylor Coleridge.* Vol. 2. New York: 1871.

Simpson, David. *Strictures on Religious Opinions.* Macclesfield: 1792.

Spearman, Robert. *A Supplement to the Works of John Hutchinson.* London: 1765.

Spearman, Robert, and Julius Bate, eds. *Abstract from the Works of John Hutchinson.* London: 1753.

———. *The Philosophical and Theological Works of the Late and Truly Learned John Hutchinson.* 12 vols. London: 1748–49.

———. *Proposals for Printing by Subscription the Philosophical and Theological Works of the Late Truly Learned Mr. Hutchinson* [...]. London: 1748.

Swift, Jonathan. *A Tale of a Tub.* London: 1704.

Sykes, Ashley Arthur. "The Elogium of the Late Truly Learned, Reverend and Pious Samuel Clarke." In *Historical Memoirs of the Life and Writings of Dr. Samuel Clarke,* Appendix. 3rd ed. London: 1748.

Taylor, Jeremy. *The Whole Works of the Right Rev. Jeremy Taylor.* Vol. 3. London: 1835.

Teale, William Henry. "The Life of William Jones, M. A., Perpetual Curate of Nayland." In *Biography of English Divines: The Life of Launcelot Andrewes, D. D., Bishop of Winchester,* 345–419. London: Joseph Masters, 1849.

The Life of Thomas Woolston, with an Account of His Writings. London: 1733.

Tindal, Matthew. *Christianity as Old as the Creation*. London: 1730.

Toland, John. *Amyntor: Or, a Defence of Milton's Life*. London: 1699.

——. *Letters to Serena*. London: 1704.

Turnbull, H. W., ed. *Correspondence of Isaac Newton*. Vol. 1. Cambridge: Cambridge University Press, 1959.

Valeriano, Piero. *Hieroglyphica*. Basil: 1556.

Van Mildert, William. *An Inquiry into the General Principles of Scripture-Interpretation, in Eight Sermons Preached [...] at the Lecture Founded by the Late Rev. John Bampton, M. A*. 2nd ed. Oxford: 1815.

Voltaire, "Lettre de Voltaire à L'académie Française." In *Oeuvres complètes de Voltaire*, vol. 2. Paris: 1870.

——. "Lettre VII." In *Oeuvres complètes de Voltaire*, 22:100–2. Paris: 1879.

——. "Platon." In *Oeuvres complètes de Voltaire*, 20:224–30. Paris: 1879.

Walpole, Horace. *Correspondence*. Vol. 35. Edited by W. S. Lewis et al. New Haven: Yale University Press, 1973.

Warburton, William. *Divine Legation of Moses Demonstrated on the Principles of a Religious Deist*. 3rd ed. London: 1755.

——. Letters from a Late Eminent Prelate {W.W.} to one of His Friends. London: 1809.

Waterland, Daniel. "Supplement to the Treatise, Entitled, The Nature, Obligation and Efficacy of the Christian Sacraments Considered." In *The Works of Rev. Daniel Waterland*, 5:499–549. Edited by William van Mildert. Oxford: Clarendon, 1823.

Watson, George. *A Letter from the Author of a Late Discourse on the XVIIIth Chapter of Genesis, to the Monthly Reviewers*. London: 1758.

——. *A Seasonable Admonition to the Church of England: A Sermon Preached before the University of Oxford at St. Mary's*. Oxford: 1755.

——. *Aaron's Intercession, and Korah's Rebellion Considered: A Sermon Preached before the University of Oxford*. Oxford: 1756.

——. *Christ the Light of the World: A Sermon Preached before the University of Oxford at St. Peter's*. Oxford: 1750.

——. *The Doctrine of the Ever-Blessed Trinity Proved in a Discourse on the Eighteenth Chapter of Genesis*. London: 1756.

Watts, Isaac. "On Instruction by Catechism." In *The Works of the Rev. Isaac Watts*, 5:203–36. London: 1813.

Wells, Edward. *A Letter to the Reverend Dr. Clarke*. Oxford: 1713.

Wesley, John. *An Extract of the Rev. Mr. John Wesley's Journal, from Sept. 4, 1782, to June 28, 1786.* London: 1789.

———. *The Works of the Rev. John Wesley.* Vol. 4. 3rd ed. London: 1829.

Whiston, William. *A Collection of Authentick Records Belonging to the Old and New Testaments.* London: 1728.

———. *An Essay Towards Restoring the True Text of the Old Testament: And for Vindicating the Citations Made Thence in the New Testament.* London: 1722.

———. *Memoirs of the Life and Writings of Mr. William Whiston.* London: 1749.

———. *The Accomplishment of Scripture Prophecy: Eight Sermons Preached at Boyle's Lecture in 1707.* Cambridge: 1708.

Wilkins, John. *An Essay Toward a Real Character, and a Philosophical Language.* London: 1668.

Woodward, John. *An Essay Towards a Natural History of the Earth.* 3rd ed. London: 1723.

Woodward, Josiah. *An Account of the Rise and Progress of the Religious Societies in the City of London: &c.* London: 1744.

Woolston, Thomas. *Origenis Adamantii Espitola ad doctores Whitbeium, Waterlandium, Whistonium.* London: 1720.

SECONDARY SOURCES

Aarsleff, Hans. *From Locke to Saussure: Essays on the Study of Language and Intellectual History.* Minneapolis: University of Minnesota Press, 1982.

Abbey, C. J. *The English Church and Its Bishops, 1700–1800.* Vol. 2. London: 1887.

Alexander, H. G., ed. *The Leibniz-Clarke Correspondence.* Manchester: Manchester University Press, 1998.

Anderson, Janice Capel, and Stephen D. Moore. "Introduction: The Lives of Mark." In *Mark & Method: New Approaches in Biblical Studies*, ed. Janice Capel Anderson and Stephen D. Moore, 1–22. Minneapolis: Fortress, 1993.

Andrews, Robert. *Lay Activism and the High Church Movement of the Late Eighteenth Century.* Leiden: Brill, 2015.

Aston, Nigel. "Bate, Julius (1710–1771)." *Oxford Dictionary of National Biography.* http://www.oxforddnb.com.myaccess.library.utoronto.ca/view/article/1664.

————."From Personality to Party: The Creation and Transmission of
    Hutchinsonianism, c. 1725-1750." *Studies in History and Philosophy of
    Science* 35 (2004): 625-44.

————. "Horne and Heterodoxy: The Defence of Anglican Beliefs in the Late
    Enlightenment." *The English Historical Review* 429 (1993): 895-919.

————. "Infidelity Ancient and Modern: George Horne Reads Edward
    Gibbon." *Albion: A Quarterly Journal Concerned with British Studies* 27,
    no. 4 (1995): 561-82.

Auerbach, Erich. "Figura." In *Scenes from the Drama of European Literature*,
    11-76. Theory and History of Literature 9. Minneapolis: University
    of Minnesota Press, 1984.

————. *Mimesis: The Representation of Reality in Western Thought.* Introduced
    by Edward Said. Princeton: Princeton University Press, 2003.

Barbour, Ian. "Ways of Relating Science and Theology." In *Physics,
    Philosophy, and Theology: A Common Quest for Understanding*, edited
    by Robert Russell, William Stoeger, S. J., and George Coyne, S. J.,
    21-45. Vatican City State: Vatican Observatory, 1995.

Barnett, S. J. *The Enlightenment and Religion: The Myths of Modernity.*
    Manchester: Manchester University Press, 2003.

Bebbington, D. W. *Evangelicalism in Modern Britain: A History from the 1730s
    to the 1980s.* London: Unwin Hyman, 1994.

Bertoloni Meli, Domenico. "Caroline, Leibniz, and Clarke." *Journal of the
    History of Ideas* 66 (1999): 469-86.

Blair, Ann. "Mosaic Physics and the Search for a Pious Natural Philosophy
    in the Late Renaissance." *Isis* 91 (2000): 32-58.

Blakney, Raymond, ed. and trans. *Meister Eckhart: A Modern Translation.*
    New York: Harper & Row, 1941.

Boldt, Jeff W. "The Whole Bible: Lionel Thornton and Figural Reading."
    In *All Thy Lights Combine: Figural Reading in the Anglican Tradition*,
    edited by Ephraim Radner and David Ney, 341-58. Bellingham, WA:
    Lexham Press, 2021.

Bozeman, Theodore Dwight. *To Live Ancient Lives: The Primitivist Dimension in
    Puritanism.* Chapel Hill, NC: University of North Carolina Press, 1988.

Bright, John. *The Authority of the Old Testament.* London: SCM, 1967.

Brown, Stuart. "The Regularization of Providence in Post-Cartesian
    Philosophy." In *Religion, Reason and Nature in Early Modern Europe*,

edited by Robert Crocker, 1–16. Dordrecht: Kluwer Academic, 2001.

Buchwald, Jed, and Mordecai Feingold. *Newton and the Origin of Civilization.* Princeton: Princeton University Press, 2012.

Buckley, Michael. *The Origins of Modern Atheism.* New Haven: Yale University Press, 1987.

Burnett, Stephen. "Later Christian Hebraists." In *Hebrew Bible / Old Testament, Vol. 2: From the Renaissance to the Enlightenment,* edited by Magne Sæbø, 785–801. Göttingen: Vandenhoeck & Ruprecht, 2008.

Burtt, Edwin. *The Metaphysical Foundations of Modern Science.* London: Routledge, 1924.

Butterfield, Herbert. *The Whig Interpretation of History.* London: G. Bell and Sons, 1931.

Cantor, G. N. "Anti-Newton." In *Let Newton Be! A New Perspective on His Life and Works,* edited by John Fauvel et al. Oxford: Oxford University Press, 1988.

———. *Optics after Newton: Theories of Light in Britain and Ireland, 1704–1840.* Manchester: Manchester University Press, 1983.

———. "Revelation and the Cyclical Cosmos of John Hutchinson." In *Images of the Earth: Essays in the History of the Environmental Sciences,* edited by. L. J. Jordanova and R. S. Porter. Chalfont St. Giles, UK: British Society for the History of Science, 1979.

Carroll, X. William. "Hutchinsonisme: Une vue de la nature comme théophanie au cours du dis-huitième siècle." PhD diss., Université de Strasbourg, 1968.

Cary, Philip. *Outward Signs: The Powerlessness of External Things in Augustine's Thought.* Oxford: Oxford University Press, 2008.

Casini, Paolo. "Newton: The Classical Scholia." *History of Science* 22 (1984): 1–58.

Chadwick, Owen. *The Mind of the Oxford Movement.* Stanford, CA: Stanford University Press, 1960.

Champion, J. A. I. *The Pillars of Priestcraft Shaken: The Church of England and Its Enemies, 1660–1730.* Cambridge: Cambridge University Press, 2014.

Childs, Brevard. *Introduction to the Old Testament as Scripture.* Philadelphia: Fortress, 1979.

Clark, J. C. D. *English Society, 1688–1832: Ideology, Social Structure, and Political Practice.* Cambridge: Cambridge University Press, 1985.

Clarke, J. F. M. "History from the Ground Up: Bugs, Political Economy, and God in Kirby and Spence's Introduction to Entomology (1815–1856)." *Isis* 97 (2006): 25–58.

Claydon, Tony. "Latitudinarianism and Apocalyptic History in the Worldview of Gilbert Burnet, 1643–1715." *The Historical Journal* 51, no. 3 (2008): 577–97.

Cohen, I. Bernard. *The Newtonian Revolution.* Cambridge: Cambridge University Press, 1980.

Collett, Don C. *Figural Reading and the Old Testament: Theology and Practice.* Grand Rapids: Baker Academic, 2020.

Collingwood, R. J. *The Idea of Nature.* Oxford: Clarendon Press, 1945.

Coudert, Allison. "Christian Kabbalah." In *Jewish Mysticism and Kabbalah: New Insights and Scholarship*, edited by Frederick E. Greenspahn, 159–74. New York: New York University Press, 2011.

———. "Eavesdropper in the Garden of Eden: The Search for the Ursprache and the Genesis of the Modern World." Pages 7–24 in *The Language of Adam/ Die Sprache Adams.* Edited by Allison Coudert. Wiesbaden: Harrassowitz Verlag, 1999.

———. "Forgotten Ways of Knowing: The Kabbalah, Language, and Science in the Seventeenth Century." In *The Shapes of Knowledge from the Renaissance to the Enlightenment*, edited by D. R. Kelley and R. H. Popkin, 83–99. Dordrecht: Kluwer Academic, 1991.

———. *The Impact of the Kabbalah in the Seventeenth Century: The Life and Thought of Francis Mercury van Helmont (1614–1698).* Leiden: Brill, 1999.

———. "Newton and the Rosicrucian Enlightenment." In *Newton and Religion: Context, Nature, and Influence.*, edited by James E. Force and Richard H. Popkin, 17–43. Dordrecht: Kluwer Academic, 1999.

Cowper, Joseph Meadows. *The Lives of the Deans of Canterbury, 1541–1900.* Canterbury: 1900.

Cragg, Gerald. *Reason and Authority in the Eighteenth Century.* Cambridge: Cambridge University Press, 1964.

Dahm, John J. "Science and Apologetics in the Early Boyle Lectures." *Church History* 39, no. 2 (1970): 172–86.

Daly, Peter, and Mary Silcox. *The English Emblem: Bibliography of Secondary Literature.* London: K. G. Saur, 1990.

Darwall-Smith, Robin. *A History of University College, Oxford*. Oxford: Oxford University Press, 2008.

———. "The Monks of Magdalen, 1688-1854." In *Magdalen College, Oxford: A History*, edited by L. W. B. Brockliss, 253-386. Oxford: Magdalen College, 2008.

Davis, Edward. "Newton's Rejection of the 'Newtonian World View': The Role of Divine Will in Newton's Natural Philosophy." *Fides et Historia* 22, no. 2 (1990): 6-20.

Davis, Ellen F. *Opening Israel's Scriptures*. Oxford: Oxford University Press, 2019.

de Lubac, Henri. *History and Spirit: The Understanding of Scripture according to Origen*. Translated by Anne Englund Nash and Juvenal Merriell. San Francisco: Ignatius, 2007.

———. *Medieval Exegesis, Vol 2: The Four Senses of Scripture*. Translated by E. M. Macierowski. Grand Rapids: Eerdmans, 2000.

———. *Scripture in the Tradition*. Translated by Luke O'Neill. New York: Herder & Herder, 2000.

de Quehen, Hugh. "Bentley, Richard (1662-1742)." *Oxford Dictionary of National Biography*. http://www.oxforddnb.com.myaccess.library. utoronto.ca/view/article/2169.

Dear, Peter. *Discipline and Experience: The Mathematical Way in the Scientific Revolution*. Chicago: University of Chicago Press, 1995.

Dixon, Philip. *Nice and Hot Disputes: The Doctrine of the Trinity in the Seventeenth Century*. London: T & T Clark, 2003.

Dobbs, B. J. T. *The Janus Faces of Genius: The Role of Alchemy in Newton's Thought*. Cambridge: Cambridge University Press, 1991.

Dow, Philip E. *Virtuous Minds: Intellectual Character Development*. Downers Grove, IL: InterVarsity, 2013.

Dry, Sarah. *The Newton Papers: The Strange and True Odyssey of Isaac Newton's Manuscripts*. Oxford: Oxford University Press, 2014.

Ducheyne, Steffen. "Mathematical Models in Newton's Principia: A New View of the 'Newtonian Style.'" *International Studies in the Philosophy of Science* 19, no. 1 (2005): 1-19.

Duffy, Eamon. "Review of 'An Eighteenth Century Heretic: Dr. Samuel Clarke.' By J. P. Ferguson." *The Journal of Ecclesiastical History* 31, no. 3 (1980): 369.

Dunn, James David. *Window of the Soul: The Kabbalah of Rabbi Isaac Luria*. San Francisco: Red Wheel, 2008.

Eire, Carlos. "True Piety Begets True Confession: Calvin's Attack on Idolatry." In *John Calvin & the Church: A Prism of Reform*, edited by Timothy George, 247–76. Louisville: Westminster John Knox, 1990.

———. *War Against the Idols: The Reformation of Worship from Erasmus to Calvin*. Cambridge: Cambridge University Press, 1986.

Elliott, Ralph W. V. "Isaac Newton as Phonetician." *The Modern Language Review* 49, no. 1 (1954): 5–12.

———. "Isaac Newton's 'Of an Universall Language.'" *The Modern Language Review* 52, no. 1 (1957): 1–12.

English, John. "John Hutchinson's Critique of Newtonian Heterodoxy." *Church History: Studies in Christianity and Culture* 58, no. 3 (1999): 581–97.

———. "The Duration of the Primitive Church: An Issue for Seventeenth and Eighteenth Century Anglicans." *Anglican and Episcopal History* 73, no. 1 (2004): 35–52.

Fara, Patricia. "Isaac Newton and the Left Eye of History." *Metascience* 22 (2013): 323–27.

———. "Marginalized Practices." In *Eighteenth-Century Science*, edited by Roy Porter, 485–508. *The Cambridge History of Science* 4. Cambridge: Cambridge University Press, 2003.

Faur, José. "Newton, Maimonidean." *Review of Rabbinic Judaism* 6 (2003): 215–49.

Feingold, Mordecai. "Honor Thy Newton." *Early Science and Medicine* 12 (2007): 223–29.

Ferguson, James. *An Eighteenth Century Heretic: Dr. Samuel Clarke*. Kineton, UK: Roundwood, 1976.

———. *The Philosophy of Dr. Samuel Clarke and Its Critics*. New York: Vantage Press, 1974.

Fomenko, A. T. *Empirco-Statistical Analysis of Narrative Material and Its Application to Historical Dating*. Translated by O. Efimov. Dordrecht: Kluwer Academic, 1994.

Force, James E. "Newton, the 'Ancients,' and the 'Moderns.'" In *Newton and Religion: Context, Nature, and Influence*, edited by James E. Force and Richard H. Popkin, 237–57. Dordrecht: Kluwer Academic, 1999.

———. "Providence and Newton's *Pantokrator*: Natural Law, Miracles, and Newtonian Science." In *Newton and Newtonianism: New Studies*, edited by James E. Force and Sarah Hutton, 65–92. Dordrecht: Kluwer Academic, 2004.

———. *William Whiston: Honest Newtonian*. New York: Oxford University Press, 2002.

Foster, Joseph, ed. *Alumni Oxoniones: The Members of the University of Oxford, 1715–1886*. Vol. 4. Oxford: 1891.

Fowl, Stephen. *Engaging Christian Scripture: A Model for Theological Interpretation*. Eugene, OR: Wipf and Stock, 2008.

Friedman, Jerome. "The Myth of Jewish Antiquity: New Christians and Christian-Hebraica in Early Modern Europe." Page 35–56 in *Jewish Christians and Christian Jews*. Edited by Richard H. Popkin and Gordon M. Weiner. Dordrecht: Kluwer Academic, 1994.

Gadamer, Hans-Georg. "The Nature of Things and the Language of Things." In *Philosophical Hermeneutics*, edited and translated by David E. Linge, 69–81. Berkeley, CA: University of California Press, 2008.

Galuzzi, Massimo. "Newton's Attempt to Construct a Unitary View of Mathematics." *Historia Mathematica* 37 (2010): 535–62.

Gascoigne, John. *Cambridge in the Age of Enlightenment: Science, Religion and Politics from the Restoration to the French Revolution*. Cambridge: Cambridge University Press, 2002.

———. "Ideas of Nature: Natural Philosophy." In *Eighteenth-Century Science*, edited by Roy Porter, 285–304. The Cambridge History of Science 4. Cambridge: Cambridge University Press, 2003.

Gaukroger, Stephen. *The Collapse of Mechanism and the Rise of Sensibility*. Oxford: Clarendon Press, 2010.

Gay, J. H. "Matter and Freedom in the Thought of Samuel Clarke." *Journal of the History of Ideas* 24 (1963): 85–105.

Gay, Peter. *The Enlightenment: An Interpretation*. 2 vols. New York: Knopf, 1969.

Gibson, William. "Dissenters, Anglicans, and the Glorious Revolution: *The Collection of Cases*." *The Seventeenth Century* 22, no. 1 (2007): 168–84.

———. *The Church of England, 1688–1832: Unity and Accord*. London: Routledge, 2001.

Glover, Willis. *The Biblical Origins of Modern Secular Culture: An Essay in the*

Interpretation of Western Thought. Macon, GA: Mercer University Press, 1984.

Goldish, Matt. *Judaism in the Theology of Sir Isaac Newton*. Dordrecht: Kluwer Academic, 1998.

———. "Newton's 'Of the Church.'" In *Newton and Religion: Context, Nature, and Influence*, edited by James E. Force and Richard H. Popkin, 145–64. Dordrecht: Kluwer Academic, 1999.

Gorst, Martin. *Measuring Eternity: The Search for the Beginning of Time*. New York: Broadway Books, 2002.

Grafton, Anthony. "Dating History: The Renaissance & the Reformation of Chronology." *Daedalus* 132, no. 2 (2003): 74–85.

———. *Joseph Scaliger*. 2 vols. Oxford: Clarendon Press, 1983.

———. "Joseph Scaliger and Historical Chronology: The Rise and Fall of a Discipline." *History and Theory* 14, no. 2 (1975): 156–85.

———. "Some Uses of Eclipses in Early Modern Chronology." *The Journal of the History of Ideas* 64, no. 2 (2003): 213–29.

Graham, Gordon. "Philosophy of History." In *Concise Routledge Encyclopaedia of Philosophy*, edited by Edward Craig and Edward Craig. New York: Routledge, 2013.

Grant, Edward. *Much Ado About Nothing: Theories of Space and Vacuum from the Middle Ages to the Scientific Revolution*. Cambridge: Cambridge University Press, 1981.

Green, V. H. H. "Religion in the Colleges, 1715–1800." In *The Eighteenth Century*, edited by L. S. Sutherland and L. G. Mitchell, 425–67. A History of the University of Oxford 5. Oxford: Oxford University Press, 1986.

Greene-McReight, Kathryn. "'We are the companions of the Patriarchs' or Scripture Absorbs Calvin's World." *Modern Theology* 14, no. 2 (1998): 213–24.

Greenham, Paul. "Clarifying Divine Discourse in Early Modern Science: Divinity, Physico-Theology, and Divine Metaphysics in Isaac Newton's Chemistry." *The Seventeenth Century* 32, no. 2 (2017): 191–215.

Gürses Tarbuck, Derya. "Academic Hutchinsonians and Their Quest for Relevance, 1734–1790." *History of European Ideas* 31 (2005): 408–27.

———. *Enlightenment Reformation: Hutchinsonianism and Religion in*

Eighteenth-Century Britain. London: Routledge, 2016.

———. "John Wesley's Critical Engagement with Hutchinsonianism 1730–1780." *History of European Ideas* 27 (2011): 35–42.

———. "Paradigm Regained: The Hutchinsonian Reconstruction of Trinitarian Protestant Christianity (1724-1806)." PhD diss., Bilkent University, 2003.

———. "The Hutchinsonian Defence of an Old Testament Trinitarian Christianity: The Controversy over Elahim, 1735-1773." *History of European Ideas* 29 (2003): 393-409.

Hall, Alfred Rupert. *Philosophers at War: The Quarrel Between Newton and Leibniz*. Cambridge: Cambridge University Press, 1980.

Hanegraaff, Wouter J. *Dictionary of Gnosis & Western Esotericism*. Leiden: Brill, 2006.

Hanson, R. P. C. *Allegory and Event: A Study of the Sources and Significance of Origen's Interpretation of Scripture*. London: SCM Press, 1959.

———. *The Search for the Christian Doctrine of God, The Arian Controversy, 318-381*. London: T & T Clarke, 2005.

Harrison, John. *The Library of Isaac Newton*. Cambridge: Cambridge University Press, 1978.

Harrison, Peter. "Philosophy and the Crisis in Religion." In *The Cambridge Companion to Renaissance Philosophy*, edited by James Hankins, 234-49. Cambridge: Cambridge University Press, 2007.

———. *"Religion" and the Religions in the English Enlightenment*. Cambridge: Cambridge University Press, 1990.

———. *The Bible, Protestantism and the Rise of Natural Science*. Cambridge: Cambridge University Press, 1998.

———. *The Fall of Man and the Foundations of Science*. Cambridge: Cambridge University Press, 2007.

———. "Thomas Morgan." *The Oxford Dictionary of National Biography*. http://www.oxforddnb.com.myaccess.library.utoronto.ca/view/article/19239?docPos=6.

Haugen, Kristine. *Richard Bentley: Poetry and Enlightenment*. Cambridge: Harvard University Press, 2011.

Haycock, David. "'The Long-Lost Truth': Sir Isaac Newton and the Newtonian Pursuit of Ancient Knowledge." *Studies in History and Philosophy of Science* 23 (2004): 605-23.

Hazard, Paul. *La Crise de la conscience européenne*. Paris: Boivin, 1935.

———. *The European Mind: The Critical Years, 1680-1715*. Translated by J. Lewis May. New Haven: Yale University Press, 1953.

Hedley, Douglas, and Sarah Hutton. *Platonism at the Origins of Modernity: Studies on Platonism and Early Modern Philosophy*. Dordrecht: Springer, 2008.

Heine, Ronald E. *Homilies on Genesis and Exodus*. Washington, DC: The Catholic University of America Press, 2002.

Henry, John, ed. *Newtonianism in Eighteenth-Century Britain: Moses's Principia*. Asheville, NC: Thoemmes Continuum, 2004.

Hill, Christopher. *The English Bible and the Seventeenth-Century Revolution*. London: Allen Lane, 1993.

Holifield, Brooks. *Theology in America: Christian Thought from the Age of the Puritans to the Civil War*. New Haven: Yale University Press, 2003.

Holt, Ted. "Blake's 'Elohim' and the Hutchinsonian Fire: Anti-Newtonianism and Christian Hebraism in the Work of William Blake." *Romanticism: The Journal of Romantic Culture and Criticism* 9 (2003): 20-36.

Höltgen, Karl. "Francis Quarles's Emblemes and Hieroglyphickes: Historical and Critical Perspectives." In *The Telling Image: Explorations in the Emblem*, edited by Ayers Bagley, Edward Griffin, and Austin McLean, 1-28. New York: AMS, 1996.

Hudson, Wayne. *Enlightenment and Modernity: The English Deists and Reform*. London: Pickering & Chatto, 2009.

Hunt, Lynn, Margaret Jacob, and Wijnand Mijnhardt. *The Book that Changed Europe: Picart & Bernard's Religious Ceremonies of the World*. Cambridge, MA: Belknap, 2010.

Huppert, George. "The Renaissance Background of Historicism." *History and Theory* 5 (1966): 49-60.

Iliffe, Rob. *Early Biographies of Isaac Newton, 1660-1865*. London: Pickering & Chatto, 2006.

———. "Philosophy of Science." In *Eighteenth-Century Science*, edited by Roy Porter, 267-84. The Cambridge History of Science 4. Cambridge: Cambridge University Press, 2003.

———. *Priest of Nature: The Religious Worlds of Isaac Newton*. Oxford: Oxford University Press, 2017.

———. "Those 'Whose Business It Is To Cavill': Newton's Anti-Catholicism."
In *Newton and Religion: Context, Nature, and Influence*, edited by
James E. Force and Richard H. Popkin, 97–119. Dordrecht: Kluwer
Academic, 1999.

Israel, Jonathan. *Radical Enlightenment: Philosophy and the Making of
Modernity, 1650-1750*. Oxford: Oxford University Press, 2001

Jacob, Margaret. "Introduction." In *Newton and Newtonianism: New Studies*,
edited by James E. Force and Sarah Hutton, ix–xvii. Dordrecht:
Kluwer Academic, 2004.

———. *The Newtonians and the English Revolution, 1689-1720*. Ithaca, NY:
Cornell University Press, 1976.

Jalobeanu, Dana. "Constructing Natural Historical Facts: Baconian Natural
History in Newton's First Paper on Light and Colors." In *Newton and
Empiricism*, edited by Zvi Biener and Eric Schliesser, 39–65. Oxford:
Oxford University Press, 2014.

Kalmar, George. *A Short Reply to Mr. Holloway's Remarks on dr. Sharp's Two
Dissertations*. London: 1751.

———. *Censurer Censured: Or a Defence of Dr. Sharp's Two Dissertations &c.
Being a Reply to Mr. Aboab's Remarks. as well as ____. Mr. Bate's Answer
to Sharp's Two Dissertations Answered*. London: 1751.

Katz, David S. "Christian and Jew in Early Modern English Perspective."
Jewish History 8 (1994): 55–72.

———. *God's Last Words: Reading the English Bible from the Reformation to
Fundamentalism*. New Haven: Yale University Press, 2004.

———. "Moses's Principia: Hutchinsonianism and Newton's Critics." In *The
Books of Nature and Scripture: Recent Essays on Natural Philosophy,
Theology, and Biblical Criticism in the Netherlands of Spinoza's Time
and the British Isles of Newton's Time*, edited by James E. Force and
Richard H. Popkin, 201–12. Dordrecht: Kluwer Academic, 1994.

———. *Philo-Semitism and the Readmission of the Jews to England, 1603–1655*.
Oxford: Clarendon Press, 1982.

———. "The Occult Bible: Hebraic Millenarianism in Eighteenth-Century
England." In *The Millenarianism and Messianism in Early Modern
European Culture, Vol. 3: The Millenarian Turn; Millenarian Contexts of
Science, Politics and Everyday Anglo-American Life in the Seventeenth
and Eighteenth Centuries*, edited by James E. Force and Richard H.

Popkin, 119–32. Dordrecht: Kluwer Academic, 2001.

Khamara, Edward J. *Space, Time, and Theology in the Leibniz-Newton Controversy.* Frankfurt: Ontos, 2006.

Kirkpatrick, A. F. "The Old Testament in the Christian Church." *The Old and New Testament Student* 13, no. 1 (1891): 8–15.

Kochavi, Matania Z. "One Prophet Interprets Another: Sir Isaac Newton and Daniel." In *The Books of Nature and Scripture: Recent Essays on Natural Philosophy, Theology, and Biblical Criticism in the Netherlands of Spinoza's Time and the British Isles of Newton's Time,* edited by James E. Force and Richard H. Popkin, 105–122. Dordrecht: Kluwer Academic, 1994.

Knoespel, Kenneth. "Interpretive Strategies in Newton's *Theologiae Gentilis Origines Philosophicae.*" In *Newton and Religion: Context, Nature, and Influence,* edited by James E. Force and Richard H. Popkin, 179–202. Dordrecht: Kluwer Academic, 1999.

Kuhn, Albert. "Glory or Gravity: Hutchinson vs. Newton." *Journal of the History of Ideas* 22, no. 3 (1961): 303–322

Leighton, C. D. A. "Hutchinsonianism: A Counter-Enlightenment Reform Movement." *The Journal of Religious History* 23 (1999): 159–75.

———. "'Knowledge of Divine Things': A Study of Hutchinsonianism." *History of European Ideas* 26 (2000): 168–84.

Le Rossignol, James. *The Ethical Philosophy of Samuel Clarke.* Leipzig: 1892.

Levine, Joseph. "Ancients and Moderns Reconsidered." *Eighteenth-Century Studies* 15, no. 1 (1981): 72–89.

———. *Dr. Woodward's Shield: History, Science, and Satire in Augustan England.* Berkeley, CA: University of California Press, 1980.

———. *The Battle of the Books: History and Literature in the Augustan Age.* Ithaca, NY: Cornell University Press, 1991.

Levitin, Dmitri. "From Sacred History to the History of Religion: Paganism, Judaism, and Christianity in European Historiography from Reformation to 'Enlightenment.'" *The Historical Journal* 55, no. 4 (2012): 1117–60.

———. "John Spencer's 'De Legibus Hebraeorum' 1683–85 and 'Enlightened' Sacred History: A New Interpretation." *Journal of the Warburg and Courtauld Institutes* 76 (2013): 49–92.

Lewalski, Barbara Kiefer. *Protestant Poetics and the Seventeenth-Century*

Religious Lyric. Princeton: Princeton University Press, 1979.

Lincoln, Bruce. "Isaac Newton and Oriental Jones on Myth, Ancient History, and the Relative Prestige of Peoples." *History of Religions* 42, no. 1 (2002): 1–18.

Lindbeck, George. "Postcritical Canonical Interpretation: Three Modes of Retrieval." In *Theological Exegesis: Essays in Honor of Brevard S. Childs*, edited by Christopher Seitz and Kathryn Greene-McCreight, 26–51. Grand Rapids: Eerdmans, 1998.

———. *The Nature of Doctrine: Religion and Theology in a Postliberal Age*. Philadelphia: Westminster, 1984.

Little, Daniel. "Philosophy of History." In *Stanford Encyclopedia of Philosophy*. Article published February 18, 2007; last modified November 24, 2020. http://plato.stanford.edu/entries/history/.

Lloyd, Genevieve. *Providence Lost*. Cambridge, MA: Harvard University Press, 2008.

Lock, F. P. *The Rhetoric of Numbers in Gibbon's History*. Newark, NJ: University of Delaware Press, 2012.

Lonergan, Bernard. *A Second Collection*. Toronto: University of Toronto Press, 1996.

Lovejoy, A. O., and George Boas. *Primitivism and Related Ideas in Antiquity*. Baltimore, MD: Johns Hopkins, 1935.

Lucci, Diego. *Scripture and Deism: The Biblical Criticism of the Eighteenth-Century British Deists*. Bern: Peter Lang, 2008.

Ludlow, Elizabeth. "Let Us Kneel with Mary Maid: Christina Rossetti and Figural Reading." In *All Thy Lights Combine: Figural Reading in the Anglican Tradition*, edited by Ephraim Radner and David Ney, 307–24. Bellingham, WA: Lexham Press, 2021.

MacIntyre, Alisdair. *Three Rival Versions of Moral Inquiry: Encyclopaedia, Genealogy, and Tradition*. Notre Dame, IN: University of Notre Dame Press, 1990.

Magid, Shaul. *From Metaphysics to Midrash: Myth, History, and the Interpretation of Scripture in Lurianic Kabbala*. Bloomington, IN: Indiana University Press, 2008.

Mamiani, Maurizio. "Newton on Prophecy and the Apocalypse." In *The Cambridge Companion to Newton*, edited by I. Bernard Cohen and George Smith, 387–408. Cambridge: Cambridge University Press, 2002.

Mandelbrote, Scott. "Eighteenth-Century Reactions to Newton's Anti-Trinitarianism." In *Newton and Newtonianism: New Studies*, edited by James E. Force and Sarah Hutton, 93–111. Dordrecht: Kluwer Academic, 2004.

———. "Isaac Newton and Thomas Burnet: Biblical Criticism and the Crisis of Late Seventeenth-Century England." In *The Books of Nature and Scripture*, edited by James E. Force and Richard H. Popkin, 149–78. Dordrecht: Kluwer Academic, 1994.

Manning, John. *The Emblem*. London: Reaktion, 2002.

Manuel, Frank. *Isaac Newton: Historian*. Cambridge: Cambridge University Press, 1963.

———. *Shapes of Philosophical History*. Stanford, CA: Stanford University Press, 1965.

———. *The Broken Staff: Judaism through Christian Eyes*. Cambridge, MA: Harvard University Press, 1992.

———. *The Religion of Isaac Newton*. Oxford: Clarendon Press, 1974.

Markley, Robert. *Fallen Languages: Crises of Representation in Newtonian England, 1660–1740*. Ithaca, NY: Cornell University Press, 1993.

———. "Newton, Corruption, and the Tradition of Universal History." In *Newton and Religion: Context, Nature, and Influence*, edited by James E. Force and Richard H. Popkin, 121–43. Dordrecht: Kluwer Academic, 1999.

Marshall, John. *John Locke, Toleration, and Early Enlightenment Culture*. Cambridge: Cambridge University Press, 2006.

Mather, F. C. *High Church Prophet: Bishop Samuel Horsley (1733–1806) and the Caroline Tradition in the Later Georgian Church*. Oxford: Clarendon Press, 1992.

McGrath, Alistair. *The Intellectual Origins of the European Reformation*. Hoboken: John Wiley & Sons, 2008.

McKane, William. "Benjamin Kennicott: An Eighteenth-Century Researcher." *Journal of Theological Studies* 28 (1977): 445–64.

McLellan, David. "Ideology." In *Encyclopedia of Philosophy and the Social Sciences*, ed. Byron Kaldis. Los Angeles: Sage, 2013.

Michalson, Gordon E. *Lessing's "Ugly Ditch": A Study of Theology and History*. University Park: Pennsylvania State University Press, 1985.

Mills Daniel, Dafydd. *Ethical Rationalism and Secularisation in the British*

Enlightenment: Conscience and the Age of Reason. Cham, Switzerland: Springer, 2020.

Moberly, R. W. L. *The Bible, Theology, and Faith: A Study of Abraham and Jesus*. Cambridge: Cambridge University Press, 2000.

Momigliano, Arnaldo. *The Classical Foundations of Modern Historiography*. Berkeley: University of California Press, 1990.

Morgan, Robert and John Barton. *Biblical Interpretation*. Oxford: Oxford University Press, 1988

Morrison, Tessa. *Isaac Newton's Temple of Solomon and His Reconstruction of Sacred Architecture*. Basel: Springer Basel, 2011.

Ney, David. "Allegory and Empiricism: Interpreting God's Two Books in Newtonian England." *Journal of Theological Interpretation* 7, no. 1 (2016): 37–52.

———. "Reconciling the Old and New Testaments in the Eighteenth-Century Debate over Prophecy." In *Change and Transformation: Essays in Anglican History*, edited by Thomas Power, 85–112. Eugene, OR: Pickwick, 2013.

———. "The Multiplicity of Scripture Words: William Jones of Nayland and Figural Reading." In *All Thy Lights Combine: Figural Reading in the Anglican Tradition*, edited by David Ney and Ephraim Radner, 156–71. Bellingham, WA: Lexham Press, 2021.

———. "The *Sensus Literalis* and the Trinity in the English Enlightenment." *Pro Ecclesia* 29, no. 3 (2020): 293–307.

Nichols, Stephen R. C. *Jonathan Edwards' Bible: The Relationship of the Old and New Testaments*. Eugene, OR: Pickwick, 2013.

Nockles, Peter. "Survivals or New Arrivals? The Oxford Movement and the Nineteenth-Century Historical Construction of Anglicanism." In *Anglicanism and the Western Christian Tradition: Continuity, Change, and the Search for Communion*, edited by Stephen Platten, 144–91. Norwich: Canterbury Press, 2003.

———. *The Oxford Movement in Context: Anglican High Churchmanship, 1760–1857*. Cambridge: Cambridge University Press, 1994.

Norford, Don Parry. "Microcosm and Macrocosm in Seventeenth-Century Literature." *Journal of the History of Ideas* 38 (1977): 409–28.

Numbers, Ronald L. "'The Most Important Biblical Discovery of Our Time': William Henry Green and the Demise of Ussher's Chronology."

Church History 69, no. 2 (2000): 257–76.

Nyssa, Gregory of. *The Life of Moses*, translated by Abraham J. Malherbe and Everett Ferguson. New York: Paulist, 1978

O'Hare, Padraic. *The Enduring Covenant: The Education of Christians and the End of Antisemitism*. Valley Forge, PA: Trinity, 1997.

Oakley, Francis. "Christian Theology and the Newtonian Science: The Rise of the Concept of the Laws of Nature." In *Creation: The Impact of an Idea*, edited by Daniel O'Connor and Francis Oakley, 449–52. New York: Scribner, 1969.

Ogilvie, Brian. "Natural History, Ethics, and Physico-theology." In *Historia: Empiricism and Erudition in Early Modern Europe*, edited by Gianna Pomata and Nancy Siraisi, 75–104. Cambridge, MA: MIT Press, 2005.

O'Keefe, John J., and Russell R. Reno. *Sanctified Vision: An Introduction to Early Christian Interpretation of the Bible*. Baltimore, MD: The Johns Hopkins University Press, 2005.

Osler, Margaret J. "The New Newtonian Scholarship and the Fate of the Scientific Revolution." In *Newton and Newtonianism: New Studies*, edited by James E. Force and Sarah Hutton, 1–13. Dordrecht: Kluwer Academic, 2004.

Overton, John Henry. *A History of the English Church: The English Church from the Accession of George I to the End of the Eighteenth Century (1714–1800)*. London: Macmillan, 1906.

Pfizenmaier, Thomas. *The Trinitarian Theology of Dr. Samuel Clarke (1675–1729): Context, Sources, and Controversy*. Leiden: Brill, 1997.

Placher, William. *The Domestication of Transcendence: How Modern Thinking about God Went Wrong*. Louisville: John Knox, 1996.

Poggi Johnson, Maria. "'The Feeling of Infinity' and Parochial Life: John Keble and Figural Reading." In *All Thy Lights Combine: Figural Reading in the Anglican Tradition*, edited by Ephraim Radner and David Ney, 237–54. Bellingham, WA: Lexham Press, 2021.

Popkin, Richard H. "Introduction." In *Newton and Religion: Context, Nature, and Influence*, edited by James E. Force and Richard H. Popkin, ix–xvii. Dordrecht: Kluwer Academic, 1999.

———. "Newton as a Bible Scholar." In *Essays on the Context, Nature, and Influence of Isaac Newton's Theology*, edited by James E. Force and Richard H. Popkin, 103–118. Dordrecht: Kluwer Academic, 1990.

———. "Spinoza and Samuel Fisher." *Philosophia* 15, no 3 (1985): 219–36

———. *The History of Scepticism: From Savonarola to Bayle*. Oxford: Oxford University Press, 2003.

Popper, Nicolas. "Abraham, Planter of Mathematics": Histories of Mathematics and Astrology in Early Modern Europe." *The Journal of the History of Ideas* 67, no. 1 (2006): 87–106.

Proudfoot, Michael, and A. R. Lacey. *The Routledge Dictionary of Philosophy*. 4th ed. New York: Routledge, 2010.

Provan, Iain. *Seriously Dangerous Religion: What the Old Testament Really Says and Why It Matters*. Waco, TX: Baylor University Press, 2014.

Quantin, Jean-Louis. *The Church of England and Christian Antiquity: The Construction of a Confessional Identity in the 17th Century*. Oxford: Oxford University Press, 2009.

Radner, Ephraim, and David Ney, eds., *All Thy Lights Combine: Figural Reading in the Anglican Tradition*. Bellingham, WA: Lexham Press, 2021.

Radner, Ephraim. *A Brutal Unity: The Spiritual Politics of the Christian Church*. Waco, TX: Baylor University Press, 2012.

———. "The Exegesis of the One God." In *The Identity of Israel's God in Christian Scripture*, edited by Don Collett et al., 31–46. Atlanta: SBL, 2020.

———. *Time and the Word: Figural Reading of the Christian Scriptures*. Grand Rapids: Eerdmans, 2016.

Randles, W. G. L. *The Unmaking of the Medieval Christian Cosmos, 1500–1760: From Solid Heavens to Boundless Aether*. Aldershot, UK: Ashgate, 1999.

Rattansi, Piyo, and J. E. McGuire. "Newton and the 'Pipes of Pan.'" *Notes and Records of the Royal Society* 21 (1966): 108–143.

Reedy, Gerard. *The Bible and Reason: Anglicans and Scripture in Late Seventeenth-Century England*. Philadelphia: University of Pennsylvania Press, 1985.

Reno, Rusty. "The Theological Roots of Modern Conservatism." In *The Identity of Israel's God in Christian Scripture*, edited by Don Collett et al., 381–96. Atlanta: SBL Press, 2020.

Reventlow, Henning Graf. *The Authority of the Bible and the Rise of the Modern World*. Philadelphia: Fortress, 1985.

Rowe, W. R. "Clarke and Leibniz on Divine Perfection and Freedom." *Enlightenment and Dissent* 16 (1997): 60–82.

Rudavsky, T. M. *Maimonides*. Chichester, UK: Wiley-Blackwell, 2010.

Ruderman, David. *Jewish Enlightenment in an English Key*. Princeton: Princeton University Press, 2000.

Sack, James J. *From Jacobite to Conservative: Reaction and Orthodoxy*. Cambridge: Cambridge University Press, 1993.

Sandys-Wunsch, John. *A History of Modern Biblical Interpretation*. Collegeville, MN: Liturgical Press, 2005.

Sanna, Gugileimo. "The Eighteenth Century Church of England in Historical Writing." *Cromohs Virtual Seminars: Recent Historiographical Trends of the British Studies (17th–18th Centuries)*, edited by M. Caricchio and G. Tarantino. http://www.cromohs .unifi.it/seminari/sanna_church.html.

Schnorrenberg, Barbara Brandon. "Sarah Trimmer." *Oxford Dictionary of National Biography*. http://www.oxforddnb.com.myaccess.library. utoronto.ca/view/article/27740o.

Seitz, Christopher. "Scripture Becomes Religion(s): The Theological Crisis of Serious Biblical Interpretation in the Twentieth Century," in *Renewing Biblical Interpretation*, edited by Craig Bartholomew, Colin Greene, and Karl Möller, 40–66. Grand Rapids: Zondervan, 2000.

———. *Word Without End: The Old Testament as Abiding Theological Witness*. Waco, TX: Baylor University Press, 2004.

Sharp, Richard. "Watson, George (1723–1773)." *Oxford Dictionary of National Biography*. http://www.oxforddnb.com.myaccess.library.utoronto. ca/view/article/28835?docPos=2.

Sheehan, Jonathan. *The Enlightenment Bible: Translation, Scholarship, Culture*. Princeton: Princeton University Press, 2005.

Shuger, Debora. *The Renaissance Bible: Scholarship, Sacrifice, and Subjectivity*. Waco, TX: Baylor University Press, 2010.

Siegel, Jonathan. "Law and Longitude." *Tulane Law Review* 84 (2009): 1–66.

Simpson, R. S. "Alexander Nicoll." *Oxford Dictionary of National Biography*. http://www.oxforddnb.com.myaccess.library.utoronto.ca/view/ article/20171?docPos=2.

Slaughter, M. M. *Universal Language and Scientific Taxonomy in the Seventeenth Century*. Cambridge: Cambridge University Press, 1982.

Sloane, Mary Cole. *The Visual in Metaphysical Poetry*. Atlantic Highlands, NJ: Humanities, 1981.

Slowik, Edward. "Newton's Neo-Platonic Ontology of Space." *Foundations of Science* 3 (2013): 419–48.

Snobelen, Stephen. "'God of Gods, and Lord of Lords': The Theology of Isaac Newton's General Scholium to the Principia." *Osiris*, 2nd Series, 16 (2001): 169–208.

———. "Isaac Newton, Heretic: The Strategies of a Nicodemite." *The British Journal for the History of Science* 32, no. 4 (1999): 381–419.

———. "On Reading Isaac Newton's *Principia* in the 18th Century." *Endeavour* 22, no. 4 (1998): 159–63.

———. "The Theology of Isaac Newton's Principia Mathematica: A Preliminary Survey." *Neue Zeitschrift für Systematische Theologie und Religionsphilosophie* 52, no. 4 (2010): 377–412.

———. "To Discourse of God: Isaac Newton's Heterodox Theology and his Natural Philosophy." In *Science and Dissent in England, 1688–1945*, edited by Paul Wood, 39–66. Aldershot, Hampshire: Ashgate, 2004.

Sonderegger, Katherine. "The Doctrine of Providence." In *The Providence of God*, edited by Francesca Aran Murphy and Philip Ziegler, 144–57. London: T & T Clark, 2009.

Spurr, John. "'Latitudinarianism' and the Restoration Church." *The Historical Journal* 31 (1988): 61–82.

Steiger, Johann Anselm. "The Development of the Reformation Legacy: Hermeneutics and Interpretation of the Sacred Scripture in the Age of Orthodoxy." In *Hebrew Bible / Old Testament, Vol. 2: From the Renaissance to the Enlightenment*, edited by Magne Sæbø, 691–757. Gottingen: Vandenhoeck & Ruprecht, 2008.

Stephen, Leslie. *History of English Thought in the Eighteenth Century*. 2 vols. London: Smith, Elder, & Co., 1876.

Stewart, Larry. "Seeing Through the Scholium: Religion and Reading Newton in the Eighteenth Century." *History of Science* 34, no. 2 (1996): 123–65.

Strawn, Brent A. *The Old Testament Is Dying: Diagnosis and Recommended Treatment*. Grand Rapids: Baker Academic, 2017.

Stroumsa, Guy. *A New Science: The Discovery of Religion in the Age of Reason*. Cambridge, MA: Harvard University Press, 2010.

———. "John Spencer and the Roots of Idolatry." *History of Religions* 41, no. 1 (2001): 1–23.

Sutcliffe, Adam. *Judaism and Enlightenment.* Cambridge: Cambridge University Press, 2003.

——. "Judaism and the Politics of Enlightenment." *The American Behavioral Scientist* 49, no. 5 (2006): 702–715.

Taubes, Jacob. *Occidental Eschatology.* Stanford, CA: Stanford University Press, 2009.

Taylor, Charles. *A Secular Age.* Cambridge, MA: Belknap, 2007.

——. "Two Theories of Modernity." *Hastings Center Report* 25, no. 2 (1995): 24–33.

Thackray, Arnold. *Atoms and Powers: An Essay on Newtonian Matter-Theory and the Development of Chemistry.* Cambridge, MA: Harvard University Press, 1970.

Thomas, Emily. *Absolute Time: Rifts in Early Modern British Metaphysics.* Oxford: Oxford University Press, 2018.

Tipton, I. C., ed. *Locke on Human Understanding: Selected Essays.* Oxford: Oxford University Press, 1977.

Toomer, G. J. *John Selden: A Life in Scholarship.* 2 vols. Oxford: Clarendon Press, 2009.

Treier, Daniel. *Introducing Theological Interpretation of Scripture: Recovering a Christian Practice.* Grand Rapids: Baker, 2008.

——. "Typology." In *Dictionary for Theological Interpretation of the Bible,* edited by Kevin Vanhoozer et al., 823–27. Grand Rapids: Baker Academic, 2005.

Trevor-Roper, Hugh. *History and Enlightenment.* New Haven: Yale University Press, 2010.

Trompf, Gary. "On Newtonian History." In *The Uses of Antiquity: The Uses of Antiquity: The Scientific Revolution and the Classical Tradition,* edited by Stephen Gaukroger, 213–50. Dordrecht: Kluwer Academic, 1991.

Turner, Frank M. In Introduction to *Reflections on the Revolution in France,* by Edmund Burke, xi–xliii. New Haven: Yale University Press, 2003.

——. *John Henry Newman: The Challenge to Evangelical Religion.* New Haven: Yale University Press, 2002.

Vailati, Ezio. *Leibniz & Clarke: A Study of Their Correspondence.* New York: Oxford University Press, 1997.

Varley, E. A. *The Last of the Prince Bishops: William Van Mildert and the High Church Movement of the Early Nineteenth Century.* Cambridge:

Cambridge University Press, 1992.

Webster, John. "On the Theology of Providence." In *The Providence of God*, edited by Francesca Aran Murphy and Philip Ziegler, 158–75. London: T & T Clark, 2009.

Weir, Heather E. "Spiritual Transformation in Sarah Trimmer's *Essay on Christian Education*." In *Change and Transformation: Essays in Anglican History*, edited by Thomas P. Power, 113–39. Eugene, OR: Pickwick, 2013.

Westfall, Robert. *Never At Rest: A Biography of Isaac Newton*. Cambridge: Cambridge University Press, 1983.

Westhaver, George Derrick. "Continuity and Development: Looking for Typological Treasure with William Jones of Nayland and E. B. Pusey." *Bulletin of the John Rylands Library, Religion in Britain, 1660–1900: Essays in Honour of Peter B. Nockles* 97, no. 1 (2021): 161–78.

———. "The Living Body of the Lord: E. B. Pusey's 'Types and Prophecies of the Old Testament.'" PhD diss., University of Durham, 2012.

Wickenden, Nicholas. *G. J. Vossius and the Humanist Concept of History*. Assen, Netherlands: Van Gorcum, 1993.

Wilde, C. B. "Hutchinsonianism, Natural Philosophy and Religious Controversy in Eighteenth Century Britain." *History of Science* 18 (1980): 1–24.

Wiles, Maurice. *Archetypal Heresy: Arianism through the Centuries*. Oxford: Clarendon Press, 1996.

Williamson, Karina. "Smart's Principia: Science and Anti-Science in Jubilate Agno." *Review of English Studies* 30, no. 120 (1979): 409–22.

Womersley, David. "Against the Teleology of Technique." *Huntington Library Quarterly: Studies in English and American History and Literature* 68 (2005): 95–108.

Yardeni, Myriam. *Le refuge protestant*. Paris: Presses Universitaires de France, 1985.

SUBJECT & AUTHOR INDEX
—

Daly, Peter, 112n44
Darwall-Smith, Robin, 21n41, 267n18
David (Israelite King), 167, 203, 203n91, 204
Davidson, Samuel, 143n9
Davis, Edward, 51n116
Davis, Ellen F., 1n2
Dear, Peter, 50n110, 51–52, 54
deism, 6, 15n34, 62–64, 89n115
de Lubac, Henri, 21n38, 133n118, 209n109, 209n110, 244
de Quehen, Hugh, 25n16
deluge. See flood
Derham, William, 71
Descartes, René, 27n21, 50–51, 65n17, 150, 259n19
devolutionary history, 3–10, 33–38, 81–95, 124–29. See also primitivism
dissent, 64, 86n101, 168, 170–71, 176n6, 185
Dixon, Philip, 85n98
Dobbs, Debbie Jo Teeter, 23–24, 110n37, 125n94
Dodwell, Henry, 148
Dow, Philip E., 263n28
Dry, Sarah, 22n1
Ducheyne, Steffen, 53n126
Duffy, Eamon, 69n35
Dunn, James David, 130n113

E

Edwards, Jonathan, 226n56
Eire, Carlos, 82n87
elahim controversy, 141–44
Elliott, Ralph, 42n84, 43n86, 45
emblematicism
  Renaissance, 18–19, 111–20
  scriptural, 129–33, 152–53, 158–61, 199–207, 226–31, 264–74
empiricism, 29n31, 51n114, 53–55, 157–59. See also Bible; sensualism
England, 6–7, 15n34, 61–65, 93
English, John, 84n98, 122
Enlightenment

and the Bible, 7–10, 15n34, 253
  definition of, 3–4, 6, 247
  Counter-Enlightenment, 8, 17, 148–50, 247
  Moderate Enlightenment, 8, 11–12
  Radical Enlightenment, 6–9, 11, 187n37
entomology, 266
esotericism. See western esotericism.
establishmentarianism
  eighteenth-century, 187–94, 265–67
  Hutchinsonian, 185–86, 197, 265–67
ethereal theory, 109–10, 125, 178–79, 227
Eucharist, 80, 193n53, 267n18
Eusebius of Caesarea, 9
Eve, 78, 125–26

F

fall of man, 49–55, 77–78. See also original sin
Fara, Patricia, 55n133, 57n141, 107n27
Faur, José, 24
Feingold, Mordecai, 24, 39n64, 41–42, 48–49, 53, 57
Ferguson, James, 66n22, 67n24, 74, 76n64, 77
Ficino, Marsilio, 119
figural reading
  Anglican, 5n10, 270
  definition of, 5n10, 133–34, 262–63
  Hutchinsonian, 5, 20, 141, 147n20, 170–71, 255–56
  See also allegory; canonical reading; literal (interpretation); typology; tropology
flood, 32, 40, 104, 152n49, 232n76
Fomenko, A. T., 41n72
Forbes, Duncan, 144n13
Force, James E., 23n4, 28n25, 29n33, 30n35
fossils (geological specimens), 104n11, 104n13, 105n18, 154, 237n92
Foster, Joseph, 154n54
Fowl, Stephen, 5n12
Freeman, John, 211n1, 264n3, 265n6
Friedman, Jerome, 121n82

Friend, John, 70

G

Gadamer, Hans-Georg, 221n38
Galuzzi, Massimo, 35n53
Gascoigne, John, 51n116
Gaukroger, Stephen, 50n109
Gay, J. H., 77n70
Gay, Peter, 57n140, 247,
Gentleman's Magazine, 68n31, 211n1,
    219n29
geology, 104–5, 152n49, 154
George I (English Monarch), 16
Gibbon, Edward, 57n140
Gibson, William, 86n101, 189n41, 193n57,
    273n39
Gill, John, 75
Gillies, John, 201n83
Gittins, Daniel, 142n7
Glass, Samuel, 265
Glover, Willis, 5n11
God's two books, 237–42, 257–58
Goldish, Matt, 3n6, 32n43, 44n90,
    118n70, 135
Gorst, Martin, 40n71
Grafton, Anthony, 9n21, 40n71
Graham, Gordon, 4n8
Grant, Edward, 108n31
Green, V. H. H., 2n4
Greene-McReight, Kathryn, 170n104,
    232n75
Greenham, Paul, 55n132
Gregory, David, 33
Gregory of Nyssa, 256n10
Grotius, Hugo, 9
Gürses Tarbuck, Derya, 142–44, 151–53
Gutch, John Mathew, 272–73

H

Hackney Phalanx, 265
Hales, Matthew, 90
Hall, Alfred Rupert 71n43
Halley, Edmund, 108n29
Hanegraaff, Wouter, 18n36
Hanson, R. P. C., 86n100

Hare, Francis, 216n20
Harrison, John, 44n89
Harrison, Peter, 18n37, 46, 49–54, 60,
    64n12, 82n85, 121n82
Haugen, Kristine, 25n15, 26n17
Haycock, David, 44n88
Hazard, Paul, 6–7, 9
Hebrew
    as Prima Lingua, 44–45, 113, 120–21,
        140–41, 219n31
    civilization, 40–42
    language, 44–45, 1n3, 120–22, 127–29,
        154–57, 219–22
    lexicons, 120–21, 130–31, 138–39, 153n52,
        156n62,
    etymologies, 120–21, 141–45, 176n6
    manuscripts, 13–14, 171n107, 195–99
    vocalizations, 143
    See also hieroglyphics; Israel; Judaism;
        scholarship
Hedley, Douglas, 118n70
Heine, Ronald, 134n120
Henry, John, 70n39, 71n43
hermeneutics, 5–6, 142n75
hieroglyphics, 18–19, 43–44, 119–35,
    141–45
High churchmanship
    eighteenth-century, 174–75, 185,
        187–94, 264–65
    Hutchinsonian, 147, 184–85, 193–94,
        264–67
    See also Oxford Movement
Hight, Marc, 107n26
Hill, Christopher, 15n34, 61–63
historiography
    eighteenth-century, 6–7, 187n37
    Whig, 2–3, 20–21, 22–23,
    Renaissance, 3n6, 9–10, 27–28
    universal, 33–34, 136n125
    See also scholarship
Hoadly, Benjamin 16–17, 62n7, 67, 69,
    89n114
Hodges, Walter, 144n13, 145, 146
Holifield, Brooks, 68n30
Holloway, Benjamin, 144–45, 146

ᵀ

SCRIPTURE INDEX

—

Old Testament

New Testament

Printed in the United States
by Baker & Taylor Publisher Services